MAN'S FREEDOM

Paul Weiss

Professor of Philosophy

Fellow of Jonathan Edwards College, Yale University

NEW HAVEN

Yale University Press

LONDON · GEOFFREY CUMBERLEGE · OXFORD UNIVERSITY PRESS

1950

128
W43

19706

To

Ervin and Arthur

PREFACE

THE PRESENT work was preceded by *Nature and Man*. That work acknowledged nature to be at once vibrant and structured, variegated and ordered, a matrix of continuities and discontinuities, of the free and the necessary, of the unpredictable and the steady, of the good and the bad, a home for man no less than for thing and beast. It focused primarily on the main modes in which an all-pervasive freedom was expressed in divergent, independent ways by the different types of things that make up nature. Freedom was there shown to be ingredient in every causal transaction, to have an inexpugnable place in the fall of a stone, the spring of a cat, the reasoning of man, in history as well as in language, logic, and art. Each was seen to have its own mode of freedom, proof both of its own distinctiveness and of the comprehensive unity of nature. Man stood out as a crucial event in the history of evolution and the history of freedom, the apogee of nature, with traits, powers, promises, a career, and opportunities different from those of other beings.

Man's Freedom, though building on the foundations of *Nature and Man,* is self-contained, capable of being read without reference to the other. Its primary objective is to make evident how man through a series of free efforts can become more complete and thereby more human. Together with *Nature and Man* it formulates a "naturalism," or better an "epochalism," emphasizing the observation that all events and beings have crises points at which, in unexpected ways, they change in pace, direction, and sometimes in nature. Together the books attempt to provide a single study of a world which has room both for the simplest of meaningless acts and for the radical transformative decisions of a creative will, for the rights of things and animals as well as of man, private, political, and social.

The ideals of this book are for me best exemplified by Dr. Richard Sewall and Dr. Wallace Fowlie. I am grateful for their friendship. I wish to thank Mr. Harry Berger, Dr. Robert Calhoun, Mr. Eugene Davidson, and Miss Denise Hoesli for many

helpful comments. Most important, this work—as all my others
—has had the benefit of my wife's brilliant, incisive, fundamental criticism of its substance and form, its ideas, and style.
She has made me rethink crucial ideas, rewrite central passages,
recast my thoughts. My debt to her is immeasurable.

New Haven,
August, 1949

CONTENTS

Part III

The Creative Will

PART I

Society and the Freedom of Preference

I

BEHAVIOR AND VALUE

1. The Limits of Prediction

THE acts and ways of men are to some extent predictable. It could not be otherwise. A man beyond the reach of all prediction would have to break every pattern, including the pattern of breaking patterns. Again and again he would act without excuse, freshly, irrationally, and irresponsibly, and then, just as irresponsibly and unpredictably, would break way to engage in a different activity. Tending in this direction at one moment, he would tend in that at another, without regard for what he was, what was happening, and what others needed and could do. He would intersperse a series of novel moves with a series of conventional ones, but in no determinable order. His acts would be atomic, isolated, unrelated, having no necessary bearing on what had been done, what was alongside, and what was to be. He would have no insistent needs or appetites, imperiously demanding attention or satisfaction. He would be indifferent to everything or would have an infinite flexibility sustained by an inexhaustibly fertile imagination and a boundless supply of energy. There is, there can be no such man.

All of us can be counted on to some extent. We favor some things more than others and tend to act accordingly. Mad or sane, creative or commonplace, foolish or wise, in knowledge and in ignorance, we are confined within ascertainable limits and routines, making it possible for others to tell in advance the kind of things we will most likely do.

It can be predicted when and how even the most unusual man will try to vary his activities. There are ascertainable times when iconoclasts are shocking, and when it is that they collapse into the roles of ordinary men doing ordinary things in ordinary ways. They usually eat, drink, sleep, breathe, and digest as the rest do; they shock and try to shock only at certain times, for example, when things become too routine, too tiresome. Throughout their careers the tendencies of so-called "originals" come to expression in well-definable ways and on set occasions, making it possible for others to tell what they are about to do.

Human "originals" act in unusual ways at anticipatable times.

Their lives are no less surely delimited, ordered, rhythmic than are our own. Unreliable, they nevertheless are never outside the reach of reasonable expectation and control. They behave in regular ways in a recognizable area which happens to be wider than that in which the rest live.

The lives of iconoclasts and rebels, of eccentrics and of some men of genius seem to be unordered from the standpoint of the groups to which they normally belong. Their lives, though, are no less ordered than those of ordinary men. Even from the standpoint of their own societies, they can be understood as men who are stable in ways different from the usual—as men whose unconventionalities are only the usual conventionalities modified, defied, or unappreciated—and that predictably.

No one is beyond the reach of all possible prediction. But no one, too, is completely predictable. For at least five different reasons no one of us can be counted on to the last syllable without qualification of any kind.

Firstly, there is as yet no science devoted to the study of man in his full concreteness. Modern science deals with only some facets of man. It does not now tell us what a man in the concrete is, will be, or will do.

No matter how comprehensive and detailed science may be, it will never enable us to know fully the nature and acts of men. For men, secondly, are flexible and creative. They are not merely beyond the reach of the sciences we now have; they are beyond the reach of an absolutely perfect, an ideal science. An omniscient, scientific intellect might know in advance the answers at which nature and man will arrive, even before they had worked them out in fact. But that intellect's very success would point up a serious defect; it would have no place for the working out of the answer by nature and man. The working out of answers lies forever outside the science and minds which know the answers. That is why there is something to know, why the term "truth" has a meaning, and why there is a difference between the unmoved time expressed in formulae and that living duration, that becoming which is, only so far as it is perpetually and freely made and unmade. The work of nature and society is what science comes to know; their working is what it must always presuppose.

Predictions refer to generalized, classified, abstract situations. It might with justice be said that this man or that will meet each situation with courage, that he will come out of every encounter stronger, nobler, wiser, or fresher than he had been before. There might be little risk involved in counting on him to resist, to feel, and to react within narrow limits determined in advance. But it cannot be predicted precisely how he will act, in society or out of it; actions have definite, specific, detailed natures only when and as they occur.

Predictions refer to what is abstract, general, possible, whereas what happens is specific, concrete, the product of unduplicable, definite, temporal activities, creatively realizing, freshly filling out, making concrete what before was only possible. All attempts to say exactly what will be are blocked by the fact that what will happen is more concrete and detailed than any prediction could possibly say. What will be, even when it repeats what has been, is outside the conditions from which it took its rise. It adds something to those conditions. It is new; its nature could not be deduced from what had been unless account is taken of the concrete process by which it is produced.

Today, for many, this will seem a fairly evident truth. But it was not always so. In the eighteenth century men thought that one plus one, everywhere, in nature and in mind, always equaled two, neither more nor less. Their romantic successors supposed, instead, that the addition of one to one could equal any number whatsoever, even a number infinitely small or infinitely large. Their followers, such rationalizing romantics as Hegel, Marx, Darwin, and Bergson, asserted instead that one plus one, at least in the organic kingdom, always yielded two and a slight fraction, a small surplus value, a tiny variation, a synthesis, making possible a continuous progress upward and onward. Our present knowledge of history and science stands in the way of all three positions.

One and one may at times equal two exactly, but they may and sometimes do sum to a slightly larger or a slightly smaller number. The world is not entirely closed nor completely open. It allows for progress; it also allows for retrogression. It demands neither. We can predict more than the original romantics and less than the traditional rationalists or the romantic rationalists believed. There is a genuine unpredictable becoming in the universe, allowing for but not requiring genuine novelty in outcome.

The processes of nature, the activities of men are confined. We can state the kind of things they will produce, the direction in which they will go. We cannot tell in advance just what concrete results will be produced, not because our minds are too weak but because those results have no concrete natures to be known in advance of their occurrence. The results exist only as terminating actual acts of becoming.

One and one, in the concrete world of things and men, fluctuates around two. Only rarely does it hit two exactly, though it comes close enough to it to make us, for practical purposes, particularly in connection with the monotonous, routinized occurrences of inanimate nature, suppose that one and one were exactly two. This is a world in which there is always some unpredictable concreteness in existence, though it may be very slight and may, for the predictive intellect, be hidden by forms duplicating what was formerly there.

Thirdly, living beings act as individuals, as singular realities with private motivations. And men, in contrast with other living beings, act as persons, with some awareness of the rights of others and of obligations toward them. No matter how pressed a man may be from without he always forges his acts freshly and freely from within, outside the reach of expectations of even the most pertinent kind. A man can be relied upon to do only a kind of thing, in a kind of way, in a kind of circumstance. To forget this is to turn him into a species, an essence which happens to be located here or there but which has no existence of its own, no unique and individual power sustaining an individual concern.

He who wishes to predict what a man will do or be in full detail denies both himself and the other. He forgets that he himself is no bare locus for an abstract formula but a man trying to peer into the future, with hopes, with stresses, with desires all his own. And he forgets that the other also is carving out his own career then and there in the privacy of his substance, alone and somewhat unaware.

Men are unpredictable not because they are mysteries, secret beyond all probing, but because they are richer, more dynamic, more private and individual than any prediction allows. To know a man as he is in fact, we must leave not knowledge but prediction behind. Predictions stop short and must stop short with the general, the static, the stable, the fixed, with being, essence, meaning. There is no place in them for actual creativity, for becoming, for duration, for existence. To get to these we must act when we know, reach beyond abstract formulae and propositions to the being of a world which makes those formulae and propositions true.

Fourthly, we predict for the most part in the light of what we have come to know of the past. Not only do we then fail to take account of what will be in its full concreteness but we tend to overlook the new possibilities which the present has made possible. Today we face possibilities which never were before. Planes to Mars, a cure for cancer, a third world war are new possibilities; they were not fixed in the firmament from all time. Each has come to be quite recently. Before there were jet-propelled rockets, before there were cancer research institutes, before there was a second world war, these were not possibilities, real objective universal frames to be made specific and actual in the course of time, but at best private fancies, imaginings, concepts in human minds. But now they are genuine objective possibilities. Relevant to, conditioned by, and inseparable from what now is, they can be known only by those who take account of what occurs in the present.

Were we quick to grasp the natures of present things and to note how they terminate in relevant possibilities, we would be able to say what the things might in general be and do. But for the most part we build not on what is but on what has been and are quite unprepared for the novel possibilities which the present makes available. Anxious to possess at once the future goods we do not yet have, we tend to ignore not only the novelties of existence but the abstract novelties, the new possibilities as well. There is little harm in this so long as the novelties are few or of little import. The mesh of our theoretical as well as of our practical nets is quite broad. We have too little time, too much pressing work to do to be able to provide for the minnows of existence. But they are there and sometimes make quite a multitude, great in bulk, crushing in weight. If we are not alert to the novelties of possible future history, we can do no more than predict what might be in terms of the past. Since no one of us is ever sufficiently alert, our predictions must express abstractly and for tomorrow in part what is and can be actual only today.

Finally, our activities are structured and sustained by our bodies and the world about. Yet these cannot be entirely depended on. They are not altogether within our control and sometimes they fluctuate radically in nature and function. But no one can fully depend on us if we cannot fully depend upon them. Should our bodies, our neighbors, and our world defy our expectations, we are bound to falsify the trust others have in us. Because our lives, fortunes, and stations are in perpetual jeopardy, our actions can never be perfectly predicted—even if it were the case, which it is not, that we knew just what possibilities we faced and how we were going to attempt to realize them.

Predictable in general, to be counted on to do certain kinds of things and not others, the full, detailed nature of our actions cannot, for at least the above reasons, be known in advance. Reliable, predictable on the whole, we are free in detail, both as biological beings with well-known stable anatomies and appetites and as socially trained men with acquired interests and habits.

No one, unless perhaps for the pleasure of trying out some posture in the perpetual ballet of the schools, has ever seriously doubted such elementary truths as the foregoing, particularly as referring to man, a being with a body and mind, existing together with other substantial beings and subject to nonphysical forces exerted by fellow man and self. The critical intellect rightly demands, however, that all-important positions be not only occupied but won. It demands that we begin in the most modest possible way and that we move on only under the pressure of dire intellectual need. Only thus can we manage both to know with surety and to understand with clarity something of ourselves and the world about. Only so shall we be able to note precious truths now hidden by the roughhewn boulders of common sense. Only in this way shall we be able to separate the solid facts of existence from the prejudice, the desiccated science and the verbalities commonly alloyed with it by those who call themselves the leaders of the young.

Let us for the moment and for caution's sake deal with one another and the world coolly, detachedly, granting ourselves no powers, no existence or truth but those we intellectually must.

2. BEHAVIOR AND BEYOND

What little we know of our fellow man has been gathered mainly by noting his behavior. Only recently, though, has an attempt been made to pursue such observations in a genuine scientific spirit, without prejudgment and without quarter. Inquiries have lately been made into human behavior in relation to literature, religion, economics, and society. None of them, to be sure, has succeeded in giving us more than a grain or two of fact, in part because the approach has never been taken seriously enough, even by those who most ardently subscribe to it. A behavioral inquiry into these domains could be carried much further than it ever has.

A scientific treatment of literature should not only occupy itself with the prose responses of readers but have room for the fact that readers also eat, sleep, and yawn in response to what they read. Such acts do have literature as cause and focus and deserve to be dealt with in a genuine objective behaviorism concerned with literature. Economics has shied away from the study of gambling, sports, prostitution, bribery, and similar profitable and unprofitable undertakings, though these are as objective and as economic as banking and butchering. Anthropology has tended to ignore nearby primitive behavior for that which is far away, and as a consequence we know much less about mobs, clubs, secret societies, fraternities, vacations, social conversation, and home life than we can and should. A scientific approach to religion requires that every phase of it be dealt with openly and objectively. It should be interested in making an accurate record of the length of time men spend in prayer; it should take note of their postures, the degree of success they have met, the pay of their ministers, and the relation this has to the background, education, income, and attendance of the parishioners. A scientific study of religion should encompass the architecture and the heating of the churches, the service, the language of the creeds, the treatment by different races of one another inside and outside the same parish or church, and the thousand other appurtenances of religious activity.

There should be hundreds of institutes filled with scientifically minded men probing relentlessly into every phase of human activity if we are to learn all there is to know. Every type of action should be examined with the same passion and detachment that chemists exhibit when they investigate the properties of earths and metals, rare or common, useful or useless.

A scientific study of man, if carried out to the suggested extent, or even if stopped at some arbitrary point, will have to deal with a heterogeneity of human activities. And it will a) accept all of them as ultimate and equal in every sense; b) treat some as superior to others; or c) presuppose some nonbehavioral facts to enable it to explain what men do and why.

a) A purely behavioral account of man views all his acts as equally valuable, important, ultimate, good, interesting. It may note, but then without comment, that some take longer, that some are more familiar, that some have a wider scope, but it has no reason for selecting any one as being superior to the others. It is therefore unable to distinguish insane from sane men, the more perceptive or appreciative from the less, the perverted from the confused, except as men who, in different ways, behave as the rest do not and are rewarded accordingly. It has no right to say that one man had a better character than others; it cannot rightly condemn any act as wrong or mistaken. Criticism, reform, punishment, remorse, rewards, and education are for it arbitrary ways of making men change their behavior from one mode to another no less legitimate. The account is unavoidably inadequate. A purely scientific theory which accepts all human activity without prejudgment or evaluation cannot cover all the facts. It has no place in its scheme for truth or right. Yet it claims to be true and requires other views to be false. Evidently it demands a dispensation for itself which it cavalierly refuses to any other view.

b) The preceding alternative represents the stage of inquiry where data are collected without prejudice. It has no way of deciding what is good behavior and what bad, what is adequate behavior and what mistaken. These decisions require more than the admission that an act has occurred and that it possesses such and such traits. A norm must be invoked to make such decisions possible.

In practice we often select as norm some repeated established pattern of behavior characteristic of our group or some favored portion of it. All other behavior is then judged by us to be good or bad to the extent to which it conforms to or deviates from the norm. Good table manners are the manners characteristic of the "better," i.e., privileged people ; good laws are the laws most men uphold or say they do. Again and again we take as our norm the constant, the established, the familiar, the average, the privileged, or the majority. So far as we do, criminals and reformers, idiots and geniuses are for us on a footing, falling as they often do equally short of the norm, though in different ways. A tyranny and a democracy, if of equal size and duration and equally close in design to what most or the supposedly best men approve, would be on a par. They would be equally ultimate, beyond criticism.

A society which exemplified a norm would help us test every subordinate part and member as good or bad, depending on how close to its demands they clung. It would be a court of last resort. There would be no legitimate claims of minority against majority once it had decided otherwise ; different groups within it would have no rights against the whole, even when this whole was democratically constituted. In America we cannot sue the post office without getting government permission ; there is nothing in the nature of democracy which precludes the same conditions being extended over every form of activity. When democracy is king, men have room only to achieve the status of subjects. The king may be benevolent but he can also be as despotic, arbitrary, and ruthless as a tyrant once his sovereignty is questioned.

Any system which picks out some type of behavior—be it the behavior of most or the best or the average men—and uses it as the norm for all others is arbitrary and fails to cover the facts. It is a theory which does not pretend to offer only an average or majority or similarly arbitrary view ; it presents itself as being true, as a theory which men ought to accept no matter what the rest say or do. It too is a theory which demands privileges for itself for which it has no justifiable claim.

Some of these embarrassments can be avoided by following utilitarianism and taking that mode of behavior to serve as the norm which is most effective as a means for bringing about some end, such as the welfare of mankind. But then one takes unacknowledged recourse to a nonempirical concept of an end that is supposed to be better than all others, warranting the use of whatever may promote it. The acceptance of some such end as better than others involves the admission that utilitarianism, like every other theory, either begins arbitrarily or presupposes norms which are more firmly grounded than the theory allows a norm to be. Views which grant the existence of only arbitrary norms are inadequate and insufficiently critical, as their very insistence betrays.

c) A purely behavioristic theory contents itself with describing or interrelating activities in a systematic way. It cannot discriminate between the good and the bad, the innocent and the perverse; it has no room for its own truth and its own merits. It cannot rightly go beyond description; to explain, it must ground what it describes in what is not described. Bankrupt, it finally reveals itself to be but a subordinate branch of a wider view which states and justifies the use of such norms as truth and goodness in terms of which it, and derivatively all occurrences, is to be evaluated.

A behaviorism which provides only a scientific descriptive account of man is a pure phenomenalism. It accepts things as they appear. Nothing is evaluated by it, nothing is explained. It does not make provision for a man who can act or for objects with respect to which he can act; it does not predict; it has nothing to say about the rights of things. A much more flexible theory is needed. This is possible, once it is granted that there actually are men, things, properties, and values to be evidenced and interrelated by means of human behavior.

3. HUMAN NATURE

If we are to have a predictive, explanatory science of man we shall have to make a number of presuppositions. First and foremost, we will have to acknowledge something human which behaves. There must be a human nature which underlies and grounds what is done. Without men, every human movement would be but a Humean movement, performed by no one; there would be events, never acts. But then we would leave unexplained why the same beginnings sometimes have different outcomes. The forces to which men are subject are diversely transformed by them, revealing that men have natures which help determine what ensues.

A science of man to be as concrete, flexible, and explanatory as geology or chemistry must at least take account of the parts of man and of him as a whole. It must note the diverse natures of his arms and legs, blood and cells, eyes and ears, and the fact that they are interrelated parts of a single organic being. Only then will it be able to distinguish between him as sick and as well, by taking account of the degrees of disorder, the extent to which different acts, while expressing something of the nature of his different subordinate parts, go counter to one another and thereby obscure his nature. His every act is oriented in something more substantial, or there is nothing which behaves.

Our acts express something of the nature of the parts through which they are expressed and something of the unitary human nature which encompasses and possesses those parts. That human nature, though in its full concreteness unique and unduplicable, has aspects shared by all other men. As a consequence, biology and medicine are possible. And because that human nature is subject to common but transient specifications characteristic of limited groups of men, it is possible to distinguish between modern and ancient, primitive and civilized men.

Different groups of men, when subject to similar conditions, bring about observable results, sometimes differing radically from those produced by others. What they do can be evaluated as better or worse only if there be an objective norm of good human behavior. This alone will enable one to carry out the behavioral theory in a way it has not been carried out before, since it will enable one both to study without prejudice all forms of human activity and to distinguish the foolish from the wise, the good from the bad, the civilized from the primitive, the appreciative from the dull.

Were there no human nature there would be no difference between unmotivated and motivated, intended and unintended, deliberate and undeliberate acts; were the human nature not normative there would be no difference between good and bad acts, the things men ought and the things men ought not to do. Human nature is manifested in acts, but the acts do not necessarily express it fully. Normative human nature is realized in various degrees by actual men, justifying a classification of them as objectively better and worse.

Human nature is no collection of acts; rather it is a locus, a source of them. A tissue of potentialities which the acts actualize in different ways, it can never be exhausted by any series of acts. That is why the death of a man is always tragic, why every death, even when desired, comes too soon. Without doubt, since what is not expressed in act is not observable, we risk reading into man much that is not there. But we can be sure that there is a distinctive human nature which we can misread. It stands to specific acts somewhat as color stands to red and blue or a circle to the infinitude of its possible diameters. Man's common human nature (and derivatively the more complex limited human natures which overlay it) can be discerned in man's specific acts as the generic feature of them all. A constant, it is specified by and expressed in whatever a man does. Something outside them all, it serves to transform common conditions into diverse outcomes.

Human nature is a nonbehavioral fact which human behavior requires for its explanation. It is referred to rather than known; it is an indeterminate presupposed, not a determinate supposed. It need not be attended to so long as we seek to have only a communicable, precisely formulated knowledge of what men do; it must be considered if we are to know why or how they do it.

4. Common and Public Worlds

We behave, you and I, both in common and in divergent ways. Our common behavior records a common world. An adequate behaviorism must presuppose not only a human nature but a common world as well. Our common world may be only a common aspect of our different individual natures, an abstract, constructed scheme having no existence or meaning apart from the individuals from which it is abstracted. Or it may be entirely constituted by our behavior, having no character but that of a single thread uniting different acts and having no existence apart from the acts which it relates. Or it may have an existence apart from us, be a true world for multiple men. Nothing in human behavior will tell us which of these is true. A study of behavior can give no more meaning to "common world" than that it is the correlate—whether this be imaginary, substantial, otherwise knowable, or not—of common modes of action; but a theory of behavior must presuppose a common world in some form or other, for that is where our common behavior occurs and what it records.

All that is recorded in common ways by humans and subhumans, the animate and the inanimate, is correlate to the largest possible common world. That world consists only of things possessing position, number, mass, shape, size, for only these are recordable by everything, machines and animals, strong men and weak. There are smaller common worlds. Orthodox Hebrews share one world; orthodox Sikhs another; midwestern American farmers have one of their own; stockbrokers another. Such smaller worlds answer to the common behaviors of limited groups of beings; they contain much that the largest leave out. In the common world of mankind things are intelligible, sensible, valuable, as well as locatable, measurable, and movable. In the smaller worlds they possess cultural meanings as well. These, though acknowledged by comparatively few, are no less obtrusive and steady than are other traits recorded by a multitude.

Were all men to shout with joy on seeing a sunset, the common joyousness of the sunset would be no less real than its sun and horizon, its location, distance, and color. If a number of men were to withdraw from the flesh of sheep in disgust, the repulsiveness of the meat would be common to them and as real a fact as its texture, color, weight, and shape. Tabooed or abhorred mutton would be a part of a smaller common world than that in which the rest of mankind dwelt. It would be part of a minority's scheme of things, yet for all that real and objective. The objects which exist only for a minority exist as certainly as do the objects which exist for the majority or for all. What only few men take account of is not necessarily a fantasy.

Not only what every machine or every man can report is real. If it were, what could we do with the fact that such reports are finally acknowledged and accepted by very few men? The view that what all men acknowledge alone is real is the view of a minority which thinks it to be true nevertheless. We must make arbitrary and embarrassing assertions to ground the belief that the real possesses only physical traits, that it is bare of all qualities, values, promise, and meaning.

What is commonly acknowledged is a common world; it is no less real for being acknowledged by a few. That there are mass aberrations and widespread illusions it would be unwise to deny. They are known to be aberrations and illusions because they can be accounted for as the outcome of common human powers exercised under special social and psychological conditions. But so far as they are expressed in common behaviors they are as real as anything else we could acknowledge. To try to dismiss the objects of an illusion into the recesses of a human mind would be foolish in practice and foolish in theory. The objects will continue to be recorded by the objectors as well; they will be rejected only by those who take as real merely what can be recorded by machines or by men in other privileged states or who think that whatever men are responsible for is, by that fact, shown to be unreal. That the sun is round and over the horizon is as correct a comment to make about the sun as that it is so many miles distant or weighs so many millions of tons.

There are singular behaviors as well as common behaviors, behaviors which are neither duplicated nor duplicable. Machines as well as men make records which fail to accord with those made by others. So far as this is true, there is no common reality for them. Their records can nevertheless be interrelated to constitute a single record of a *public* world—a world common to none but embracing all. It is one of the main tasks of the natural sciences to provide such a single record. The laws of physics, optics, physiology, and psychology are so many different ways of transforming one singular report into another, thereby permitting one to treat their correlates as variants of one another. By taking account of the differences in our locations, the nature of our eyes, our alertness, sobriety, afterimages, and so on, it is possible in theory, knowing one of these reports, to anticipate the others.

There are large public worlds and small ones, loose ones and tight ones. The world of a cosmic physicist is both large and tight; the world of daily conversation, where we habitually allow for a difference in tones, gestures, and words, is both small and loose. Most of us, most of the time, live in a world in between. We understand the singular behavior of our fellow man (and in some cases of animals and inanimate beings) by taking a rough note of singularities in their history and opportunities and then trying to interrelate them according to patterns sanctioned by tradition and encouraged by experience. Men run to a fire in singular ways, in part because they have different builds and backgrounds, in part because they are at different distances from the fire. We make allowance for these and recognize them to be members of a single public world with fire as a focus.

Tighter worlds are no more public or substantial than looser ones. Their principles of transformation are merely more amenable to cold reason. Larger worlds are no more public or substantial than smaller ones. Their translations are merely more comprehensive; they take in more items. Dogs sniff in quite different ways. Smells are public facts for them, facts which are apparently not also as readily available to the rest of us. Their public world is a limited one, and both for us and for them is but loosely tied together. But it is as stable, as recognizable, as real as any we know, larger or smaller, more tightly or more loosely connected though it be.

Values are just as common and public as are shape and smell. They exist to the very same extent and in the same place. And they can be known in similar ways. Because we see men deal with a table as more than an obstacle, because we see them cover it with lace, keep the children far from it, take it out when the house begins to burn, become angry when it is scratched, removed, or changed, we assert with justice that it has a high value for them. They behave toward it in ways not appropriate to physical features; to say that it has a value is but another way of saying that there is a nonphysical public or common world which answers to their behavior. The value of the table has no more but also no less reality than the table's wood and sheen, its weight, age, size, and durability. Like them it is the correlate of common and public activities—activities more complex and variegated, however, than are needed in order to give an adequate account of the physical aspects of the table.

The value which the table has for men is learned not by looking at the table but by remarking the difference which its presence seems to make to them. The procedure here is not different from the procedure followed when we seek to learn the nature of a being's catalytic or magnetic power, the force it exerts, the mass it has, the inertia it possesses. Even the determination of a thing's position or shape is reached in a similar way, for to know these we must look not at the thing but at the limitations it imposes on what environs it. By studying what effect other beings have on a thing, we learn what meaning and what value these beings have for it.

What is common or public for only some beings has properties only for them; it can be found only in worlds where they are. There are no coal or silver mines for animals, or perhaps even for primitive man; there is only matter underground. For mines to be, one must have begun at least in theory to dig a shaft. There is no sacrament for atheists, no true cross, no genuinely miraculous cures; for church-goers they exist as hard and root as anything, though of course available only for those who act in the very special ways characteristic of various groups in Christendom.

The widest common world, leaving out as it does every quality correlative to man alone, loses at least as much in depth, in content, and richness as it gains in breadth, in application, and in range of confirmation. It ends in the monotone, a world of machines for machines. Narrower common worlds, and finally the narrowest world of the individual, leave out what is certified and certifiable by others. They lose in breadth at least as much as they gain in depth, and end in the aberrant, the capricious world, the world of the idiosyncratic. We can retain the merits of both and avoid their limitations by forging the idea of a basic common world, a world certi*fiable* by any man. What is not part of that basic common world is either a hallucination or an intensive aspect of what is common. The hallucination may be shared by many, the quality may be noticeable by only a few, but because not common to mankind must be denied status in a common human world. The hallucination and the quality can however be interrelated by transformative rules to constitute a public world. In that world it is possible to pass to and from, and to understand what is not common by means of laws which take account of singular conditions and agents.

The only world though which deserves to be thought of as ultimately real is at once basically common and universally public. It is made up of multiple qualitied wholes encompassing a great number of submicroscopic entities. No one knows just what in detail that world is like. We converge on it through science and art, each of which is today fragmentary in its scope and distortive in its report. Not until the basic common qualitied world of mankind is recognized to be the locus of the entities with which science comes to rest, and not until the universally public world of science is recognized to be one in which perceptive men are possible, will we come close to the reality we all seek to know.

5. TELEOLOGY

If a reference is had to nothing more than the human natures and the common and public worlds which subtend behavior, we can find a place for values. But not for everything. Not all that occurs could be explained. Men without any change apparently in conditions or natures often vary the direction of their actions, begin a new series of acts, alter their pace, turn to something else. No study of their activity, no knowledge of the natures they individually and commonly have can cover such facts. Such facts demand a reference not only to recorded traits or values or meanings but to causes or conditions for the occurrence of those traits, values, and meanings. And at least one of those causes is an end, something future, not yet present. An adequate behaviorism, in addition to a human nature and a world, presupposes a teleology.

No nature is exhaustively in the present. Part is also in the future. Each of us, while here and now, terminates in a relevant possibility which defines what we can become and do. It is possible for us to breathe, feel, eat, hope, and think; it is not possible for us to flow like water, to stand as steady as a mountain, or to grow as a tree does. The former, not the latter, are specifications of a future that is open to us as men. They express in limited ways the nature of a quite general, highly indeterminate possibility that is part of the essence of every man. It is to such specific yet still general and indeterminate forms of future possibility that we refer when we predict; it is to these that we look when we hope and fear, think and act. Whatever we are, whatever we do is the unpredictable outcome of an effort to make them present, concrete, and determinate.

To understand what is, it is necessary to refer to what can be. Distinctive natures require distinctive possibilities. This is an old and familiar truth. Throughout the history of thought men have insisted on teleological interpretations of nature and of man, which is to say on interpretations of them in the light of a future to which they point and which they endeavor to realize. But the traditional teleologies have never ultimately satisfied, for they exaggerated the value and power of the future. They tended to reify the possible, to speak of it as though it were nobler, purer, more powerful, more precious than anything that could exist in the present. In the last resort they turned the world upside down, making what is into a creature of what can be, supposing what is not yet, the future, to be more determinate and better than anything that is in the present.

The teleological approach cannot be entirely avoided; nor should it be. The future is relevant to the present, controlling and conditioning it within firm limits. This is the truth which attracted the teleologist, and which he urged and formulated in an exaggerated way. The future conditions the present, but it is not better, more complete, more real than it. We are guided, directed, restrained by it. Otherwise we could conceivably act in ways which had nothing to do with what was to be, and thus could self-contradictorily bring about what was impossible. Whatever we do realizes in some determinate form a relevant possibility that now lies before us; our being and our acts cannot be divorced from that possibility unless we could conceivably become and bring about what cannot be. We can imagine a world with all its content vanishing without a trace. But this it could not do unless there were for it a future possibility of vanishing, unless whatever replaced it was first a possibility which awaited that vanishing before it became realizable.

All actions are conditioned by what is possible. It could not be otherwise. A world of entities cut off from the possible is a world cut off from the future, a world wholly and exhaustively in the present. No time, no temporal succession of events would be possible in it. To be in the future, it must be possible to be in the future and this requires a possibility now future, to be realized in the course of time. If there were no such possibility there would be no goad forcing present things out of their present positions, driving them on to act and thus to create in time.

Things have natures so far as they allow for some occurrences and preclude others. Because the future is inseparable from and conditions the present, beings can have definite natures, are able to do certain things and not others, can be transformed in this way and not that, substantiating our predictions and justifying our hopes and fears. A future external to but relevant to the present is necessary if a present being is to be definite, distinctive, promising to be and do only a few of the things that are logically possible.

Because what is requires what may be, there must be possibilities. These possibilities are external to the things in the present; they provide them with an objective indeterminate future to be made present and concrete in the course of time. But though objective, those possibilities constrain what is now; they are directive of the things in the present, effective on them now, enabling those things to act so as to bring about what is possible. All beings are richer in meaning than they are in fact, referring as they do to the external future as an objective restraint.

Future possibilities are effective in the present. In the case of men they not only limit from without but also condition from within, turning them thereby into purposed beings. This idea of internal conditioning after a long period of unjustified neglect has been revived by contemporary existentialism. Rightly insisting that the future is ingredient in the present in the form of meanings suffered and enjoyed, it tends, though, to exaggerate, and seems to say that there is nothing more to the future than its meaning in the present. Usually implicitly, but occasionally explicitly, it denies that there is a real future outside and beyond present men. As a consequence, existentialists are forced to deny that beings have steady, definite natures, essences, identities.

Existentialist philosophers are idealists. They repeat with new accents the supposition of Descartes that men are trapped inside the narrow confines of their separate egos and that they cannot escape except by miracle. In the effort to know themselves, existentialists have lost the world, and themselves as members of it. For what could a present existent be on which nothing really follows? What is a future which is only a stress in the present? To have a nature is to be related to future external possibilities; by denying that there are such possibilities, these philosophers deprive themselves of the opportunity to make sense either of the present or the future and thus of existence in time.

6. Privacy and the Independent Object

It is necessary to acknowledge not only human natures, singular, common, and normative, but common and public worlds as well and the forceful possibilities which are of their essence. But if the full range of human promise, activity, and achievement is to be understood, it is necessary to go further and acknowledge the privacy of man.

Men internally subject themselves to possibilities future to themselves—as is evident from their preparations—thereby determining what they are to do and revealing the values they set on things. This activity is outside the reach of any publicly oriented science. Yet we must take account of it in order to explain why men change their roles and pace, and when. It makes possible a scientific account of the sequences of action characteristic of men in different societies at different times and, most evidently, when subject to threat and blame.

Each one of us is a unique being confronting the rest of the world in a unique fashion. Other beings show us but sides of themselves. No one of us knows or experiences the side it shows others, since we each can see only what it shows to us. Each of us lives privately. No one else has my eyes, muscles, mind, interests, individuality; no one else can see the very things I do in the way I do. My things are seen by me in a rich and ineradicably personal setting of past, present, and prospective experiences. They cannot be made to stand by themselves unless paradoxically one could destroy the experience in which they alone occur. I cannot see what you do unless somehow the two of us could become one.

You encounter others in privacy just as I do; your experience is not mine. The quality, the flavor I sense, I sense alone, secretly. But then how can I know that you do not duplicate my experience? How can I know that the object which I experience does not show you the very face it shows me? If your experience is really private to you, I have no right to say your experience is not identical with mine.

I cannot live out your privacy, enjoy you from within, unless I can get within you and thereby become you and thus cease to be myself. I cannot know your experience as undergone by you as you. Your experience of green and mine are two distinct experiences. But they may, for all that, be in every detail the same. I do not, I cannot possibly know, precisely because your experience and mine are private and distinct, whether what you see is identical with what I do or not. Our private experiences are incomparable. Yet we can distinguish them by the manner in which we act while all else remains the same. Men, though their natures are similar and all else appears unchanged, act in varying ways. To account for this, acknowledgment must be made of the differences in their private experiences.

The acknowledgment of privacy is the acknowledgment of a value-drenched phenomenon, marked as it is with the total meaning of a human life. It encompasses everything from the thinnest of feelings to the richest of values that exist by being lived through. We are able to distinguish subtle from gross, expressive from unexpressive behavior only so far as we have antecedently admitted that there was a rich content which activity was to express.

Private encounters occur because men have unitary cores which hold the encounters together. Without such unifying cores there would be only a plurality of private encounters; there would be no one to act. Answering to that core is an independent object. Were there no such object there would be encounters but nothing which was encountered. That object stands outside the encounter in the same way that the core does, making it possible. A behaviorism to be satisfactory must then make still another assumption: it must assume that there are independent objects as well as a human nature, a common world, teleology, and private experiences.

Because there are objects which are independent of me, I can encounter them. Were there no objects independent of me, my privacy would exhaust the world, and by that very token my privacy could not be cut off from anything else and thus be truly private. I have a privacy over against an object not yet encompassed, an object which limits the private encounter, which allows it to terminate in but not to engulf the being of what is encountered. The encountered object, while internally related to the experiencing of it, is external to myself who experience it.

The content of experience provides knowledge because there is something not knowledge, given with the knowledge, of which it is the knowledge. Did we not have an acquaintance, dim, unarticulated, unfocused though it may be, of a substantial, independent world when and as we have knowledge, we could not rightly say that there is meaning to such terms as "knowledge," "truth," or "error." These depend for meaning on independent objects which are other than the knowledge we have of them. We can never know that knowledge, truth, error have application if we do not grasp that something and use it as a test of the viability of what we claim to know.

There never would be a problem of truth were it not that the solution is already in our possession. He who does not know something beyond his conceptions never has occasion to ask whether what he knows is true. A world exhausted by my experience would be a world in which there was nothing still to know, in which there was no action or causation, no past to be remembered, no future to anticipate, no present to be known.

Solipsism, the view that only I exist, is absurd. To whom can I be reporting the view? Were there only myself, solipsism would not state a position but define a universe of which I and my objects were parts, precluding either of us from claiming to be stark alone. The most that a solipsist can maintain is that he is the owner of all content, that everything is adjectival to his substantial ego. But then evidently he can speak only to fantasies. And since his ego is outside all the content of which he has any knowledge, he has no justification for saying that the ego exists. Whatever reason he has for affirming that it exists is reason enough for affirming that other beings do too. If he knows he is, he knows much more than privately enjoyed content warrants; if he knows that he alone is, he knows much more than the knowledge of himself would warrant. The solipsist knows much too much to know so little.

You may encounter what I do. If so, you will have a private experience of which I can have no direct knowledge. But should you act, on encountering this thing, in ways which are different from those you exhibit on encountering something else, you will provide evidence of what the encountered object means to you. You will then enable me to know not what you privately experience or even what you dimly apprehend in the background and which stands over against you as an independent object, but the difference that object makes to you in a situation where both you and it continue unchanged. I cannot know the qualitative feel you have of the force which some body exerts on you. I do not know whether or not you experience the force and whether or not you are aware of the source of it. But I can know, by studying your actions, the degree, direction, and thus the existence and nature of the force as making a difference to you in a common or public world. Caught though all traits are in an internal relation to you, experienced though they are in privacy, you, by means of the behavior you exhibit, tell me something of the meaning other realities have for you.

If no provision is made for the existence of real substantial beings, limiting the experience which terminates at them, no place is allowed for knowledge, truth, and error, for rights and claims, for interplay between men and a world beyond. Those real independent substantial beings are objective, adumbrated loci for what we privately encounter. They provide nonbehavioral, nonobservable explanations of why men's acts are more than expressions of natures, experiences, or possibilities; why human effort makes a difference to what is to be.

The tree over there *is* green *for* me because the tree is at once different in nature from the things I then see as red or blue, round or large, and because I look at it in an individual way. The green is but one of many features of the tree; the tree's bulk and attractiveness, its age and its size are also experienced by me in privacy as traits subtended and sustained by the tree itself.

Those who through their actions make evident that they see the tree and see it as attractive are sensitive or appreciative; those who make evident that they see it as decorated with qualities have operative senses; while those who treat it only as an obstacle, a thing to be pushed, pulled, or avoided are themselves so far material beings. Because men act in all three ways they must be said to be at once sensitive, perceptive, and active, with correlates which are at once valuable, sensible, and material.

The material aspect of the tree is an abstraction from the total tree, as surely as is its color or its value. Because its material aspect is always in evidence, the fact that it alone is recordable by impersonal and steady instruments does not make it more independent or objective, more genuinely common or public than other aspects, or make it constitute the substance of the objects experienced. It means only that flesh answers to flesh, matter to matter.

7. Man's Creativity

Just as men need the possibilities that lie beyond them, so they need the actualities which coexist with themselves. Just as they, by internally possessing the future in the form of a compulsive objective, try to anticipate the full realization of it, so they anticipatorily and freely lay hold of contemporary existents in the effort to govern themselves from within as they are in fact determined by them from without. Men creatively act on valuable, sensible, material beings as a consequence of their creative use of the possibilities that concern them. Their creativity with respect to the possibilities and to the beings about them is presupposed by an adequate behaviorism.

A man is a being in double disequilibrium, with an essence partly in the future and an existence partly at a distance. He recovers the one in part in the form of a guiding meaning, the other in the form of a limiting status. The more of the meaning and the higher the status he achieves the more mature he is, for he thereby makes himself from within one with what he is from without.

Each of us is finite, denied, defied by all others. Because others exist no one of us is perfect, possessing all reality in himself. Our finite natures are in part a function of the rest; the others help determine what powers we can exert and what effect we can have. This truth was effectively underscored by that benign genius, A. N. Whitehead. He made an entire generation see that there is no thing in this world which is "simply located," here and not also somehow there. He saw too that what is here and what is there must somehow be one. He thought that this result is to be achieved by somehow transporting what was distant into what is here and now and making it part of the latter's being—a speculation warranted by what we know of the nature of eating and of knowledge. A more important and in a sense a more obvious point was, however, overlooked. We become one with others more often and surely by endowing them with the status of boundaries for us. We do this automatically in a minor way when we deal with them as beings who resist us, as the termini of our vision, and as fellow creatures. We do it in a major way and sometimes deliberately when we act on things as part of the same social world with ourselves. It is this point which Dewey perhaps has seen better than anyone else. Since he refused to deal with man from within, though, he had no being for which others could act as boundaries. A teleologist in space instead of time, he exaggerated the role of that which lies beyond and limits men.

Whitehead was inclined to internalize the world in consonance with a reluctantly adopted idealism; Dewey instead was inclined to externalize man in consonance with a belatedly adopted empiricism. But everyone has his inside and his outside. Each can improve his status by accepting the demands of the future and adopting as his own the claims embodied in what is distant.

Every one of us is not only helped but blocked by others. They derange our efforts; they spoil our aim. We end with what we do not need and without that which we badly want. To meet such frustrations we try to concern ourselves with more comprehensive possibilities than we did before. If we succeed we will be able to act from within in ways which take more adequate account of what frustrates us from without. We will change our concerns, "evolve."

Higher types arise from lower when, to meet the frustrations of existence, they concern themselves with and thereby act in terms of more comprehensive possibilities than the lower acknowledge. Man offers no exception to this process. He arose as a result of a strategy on the part of frustrated lower beings. He owes his existence to the effort of an ape-like being which in the face of hindrances once made itself subject to a possibility more comprehensive than those which it had ever faced.

The possibility which confronts man is the most indeterminate, the most comprehensive, the most general of possibilities, as is evident from the sweep of his mind, the range of his curiosity, and his ability to attach himself to any kind of thing. This general possibility every thing and every act illustrates somehow. Unknowingly, unconsciously, privately, and steadily, from birth to death, a man has it in steady focus. Because he is conditioned by it he is able to match on the inside, though only in a very general, indeterminate way, the limitations which had been imposed and thus had frustrated him from the outside. He stands more and more erect in nature and the more he lives in the light of the possibility which is his true concern. He is of course also occupied with more specific possibilities. There is no opposition, however, between them. The all-comprehensive possibility occupies him as a being contrasting with all others, as one possessed of a self; the specific possibilities occupy him as a being who both possesses and quickens this one body. Since an actual man is a man with a self and a body, he is one who at once faces an all-comprehensive possibility and limited possibilities, the latter providing delimited, determinate specifications of the former.

The all-comprehensive possibility is equally relevant to all things and occasions. It guarantees that the self will remain identical no matter how the world changes in content, for the self clings to it as a defining essence. But it does not help a man to act appropriately in this situation or that. Adequate action requires the use of limited possibilities which are pertinent to the situation in which a man now is. Environing things condition men in ways for which their all-comprehensive, highly indeterminate possibility does not prepare them. They limit men in unexpected ways; hem them in, frustrate them, conditioning them externally in ways for which they are not internally prepared. Such frustrations cannot be met by having recourse to a broader possibility. Only the acknowledgment of more and more specific forms of the initial possibility will ever enable a man to prepare from within to meet the specific challenges of specific things now existing without.

Only if a man internalizes limited specific possibilities can he guide himself by what he should, if his inward acts are to accord with his outward adventures. Unlike subhuman beings which to make their insides accord with their outsides blindly struggle to deal with broader and broader, more and more indeterminate possibilities, thereby changing in nature, man remains a man and yet progresses. He responsibly determines his acts by more and more specific yet comprehensive forms of that single all-comprehensive possibility which is the concern of his self, and comes to the end of all advance only when he freely makes the all-comprehensive possibility privately and publicly as determinate as it can be. He becomes more and more complete the more he makes himself and his acts appropriate to the external conditions to which he is subject.

A man's inside, at the start, is quite indeterminate but privately conditioned; his outside in contrast is determinate and externally conditioned. To harmonize them and thus to be no longer divided against himself he must creatively replace the highly general control of other beings, which the all-inclusive possibility permits him, by more and more limited controls, answering to the determinations to which the other beings subject him. The more radically he remakes himself the more certainly will he have entirely new material with which to work the next moment. Evidence of his creativity is to be found then whenever his acts show that something has acquired a new rank, that he did not merely interact with other beings but creatively acted on them, that he produced, that he made something.

When men produce they make not only other things but themselves in a way. They reconstitute themselves, thereby expressing themselves more or less adequately in the form of measurable, observable behavior. But the behavior will not answer entirely to the nature of the creativity. They are creative before they produce. Productivity presupposes, it does not therefore explain, creativity. But the creativity does change the import of what one confronts; even before something is bodily done to things they are re-evaluated, and this fact is expressed in tensions, preparations, attitudes, justifying, after they have been so expressed, a later inference to man's previous creativity but not allowing one to know just what it was when it was taking place.

Creativity produces values which may not be noted. It makes it possible for values to exist and to be acknowledged without the fact becoming manifest in overt action. To deny that a man privately acknowledges values or makes decisions would be to deny that there were values and decisions until they had been verified or made available for verification—foolish suppositions since value and decision are precisely what are *to be* verified, and in terms of which all other checks are to be evaluated.

Even when the decisions and values men acknowledge are made evident in their behavior, it still remains true that the behavior is not to be identified with the decisions or the values. The explanation, the origin, and focus of human activity do not necessarily exhaust the value which they have as their explanation, origin, or focus. The beauty of a picture perhaps explains why it is hung in a museum and why men speak of it in admiring tones; but the beauty does not consist in its being hung on the wall or in its being spoken about. Museum directors would be happier men than they are if hanging a picture on a wall and having it spoken of favorably were to make it beautiful. They are unhappy because it is their task to buy and hang up what is beautiful before it is bought, hung, and praised. Those museum directors who are interested in predicting which works the majority, the noisiest critics, the patrons, or whomsoever they respect or fear will make the object of their laudatory ejaculations are men who can keep abreast of current habits and will probably maintain their jobs for longer periods than most, but they will be unable to explain why certain pictures are approved and not others, why beauty is important, why men ought to appreciate it, and thus why museums in the first place are desirable. Beauty makes a difference to men, a difference which they record in the way they thereafter act toward the beautiful object, and thereafter toward other objects for which the experience of beauty has sensitized them. The experience of beauty is a crucial creative experience altering the course of one's activities in relation to other things.

Beauty experienced is ingredient in things; it is a value which remains in them whether appreciated or not—unless it be true also that the color and the design, the shape and the weight of the things, and we the experiencers as well also disappear when unrecorded. Each thing has values which without loss to their objectivity and independence can be given a public status and meaning by men. If men produced these values out of a nonvaluable world or mind, they would be amazingly powerful beings, complete creators of something which holds them in fief. This romantic theory masks itself today as steely eyed and rigorous, scientific and cautious. But it is no less capricious than one which supposed that there were transcendent values to which men might point but which they could never help determine. Man creates but he has material to work on; he faces objective possibilities but he also creatively determines and expresses them.

8. Summary

A careful inquiry presupposes nothing beyond what is required to explain fully what is observed. Justice to human activity requires every supposed adequate theory of man to meet at least six conditions. The unity and variety of human acts demand the recognition of a normative human nature; the existence of common and interconnected modes of action compels the acknowledgment of common and interconnected realities; the directed persistence of men over time is inseparable from relevant and compulsive possibilities; an adequate grasp of the fact of experiencing requires the admission that men have private adventures; rights, truth, and action presuppose the existence of adumbrated, independent objects; man's purposed productivity and control demand the admission of a human power of free creativity. Neither science nor art alone takes full account of the qualitied, valuable, substantial objects which exist over against men, the evidences which action provides of man's own substance, or the creative power by which he reconstitutes himself and others. The most significant of the omissions is the last, for man is primarily a reconstituting, a creating being.

In different ways and at different times men transform things into components of institutions, cultures, societies, civilizations. They make them thereby richer, give them new careers and meanings, infuse them with mind, and endow them with larger purposes. They do this because they can do this, and they can do this because they are free to do this, because they have natures which they can express in a world which allows a place for the expression. Men are free without and within to act so as to remake themselves and things about. The way they act provides a clue to what they are, but only because they already are beings able to and therefore free to act.

II

STATIC FREEDOM

1. Native Freedom

PHYSICISTS say that a body is free to move if it is capable of moving or turning in some direction. Theologians speak of their Gods as infinitely free because capable of doing an infinite number of things. Though often opposed in spirit, temper, objective, and even terminology, they are here in close accord. In their different ways they stress a meaning of freedom we in our ethics and politics have too often been inclined to overlook. Freedom is not for them a negative concept stating that some exterior limitation has been removed. It is a positive idea referring to a power, to the capacity of their objects to act and express themselves in their characteristic ways. It is a freedom which may or may not be exercised; it is a static freedom, a freedom which is one with ability. To be statically free is to be able; to be able is to be statically free.

Ability—and therefore static freedom—has many meanings. The most fundamental is *native*. This comprises all those capacities which belong to a being because of the nature and structure it has. It covers all that a being could possibly do or become. Everyone has his own kind of native freedom which he did nothing to achieve; he has it because he has one nature rather than another. Fish have a native ability to live in water, birds a native ability to fly; we, who are not able to do these things, are able to inquire and to think, to master an art, to learn a science, and to make use of tools. Each is able to do certain things because of the essence, structure, nature it has and which precludes its doing other things. He who has a native freedom in one respect is without it in another. It is this freedom which is presupposed by creativity and which grounds private encounters, public acts, and the changes to which men subject common conditions.

Not even God has unlimited capacities. Even He has a limited native freedom, unable as He is to swim or to fly, to eat or to walk, to learn or to write. He cannot know the future before it is in existence, undo the finished past. It may be better not to be in a position where these are necessary or desirable. But that is not the question. The point is that He, just like every other being, has only a limited native freedom. Yet though theologians have constantly remarked that God can do only the good, cannot contradict Himself, cannot annihilate Himself, and cannot make a twin of Himself, they have almost at once denied themselves and tried to affirm that He is completely free, possessed of unlimited capacities. This blurs His countless limitations, limitations which He needs to keep Him in contrast with other beings. By terming God infinite we do not remove but accentuate the difference between the infinite and the finite and make evident that what the finite is natively free to do the infinite cannot unless it thereby becomes finite in the process.

The conclusion has a somewhat paradoxical ring; it seems wrong to say that freedom exists only so far as a being is limited, for to be limited is to be confined, restrained, blocked, and therefore not free. Limitation and freedom are opposed, but it is only because there is restraint in one respect that there can be freedom in another. To have a capacity to do certain things it is necessary first to exist and to exist as distinct from other things. It is to be limited, set over against, opposing, resisting, and reacting to others. If we could rid a being of all limitations we would make it so indefinite that it would be distinguishable from nothing. But, self-contradictorily, it would also be distinguishable from things which had limited capacities. The completely indefinite is definite enough to be self-contradictorily the indefinite thing it is.

The native freedom characteristic of one kind of being differs from that of another. Cats are free in ways dogs are not, and conversely. Because both of them are highly developed mammals they share certain modes of freedom not open to others. Both of them are free to eat, feel, move, reproduce, a freedom which they specialize in different ways. Though both are free to reproduce, the dogs are free only to reproduce dogs, the cats only cats. In addition, each has its own range of freedom which the other does not share. The cat is not free to bark, the dog is not free to mew.

Within each kind there are further differences. Dogs do not merely differ from cats; they differ from one another. They form distinct varieties, some of which cannot even be interbred. There are some dogs which can be trained to hunt but not to fish; others which can be trained to guard but not to stop barking. The great Dane has a range of freedom which the dachshund does not share; the dachshund is able to do things the great Dane cannot. And inside a given variety there are individuals which differ considerably from one another. Some of them have an ability to learn what others cannot. The freedom of one dog is different not only from the freedom characteristic of cats but from that of other dogs, similiar or different in shape and parentage. And what is true of dogs is true of cats, of plants, and of man.

Each being has a degree and mode of static freedom; to destroy this freedom is to destroy the being. An animal which is not able to do the things that dogs are wont to do, which has no ability to bark or swim, to eat meat, to be domesticated, or to interbreed with other dogs, is a dog only by courtesy, even though its ancestry may have been unimpeachable. It is not necessary that any one dog have all these abilities or that the abilities all dogs now share remain the same forever. Native freedom is not a fixed and unalterable quantity, whether it be the freedom of dogs or the freedom of men. It can vary in range and character from individual to individual within a common kind and can have a different cut for all of them at some distant time.

In addition to a *common* native freedom without which a being would cease to be of a certain kind, there is in each a *variable* native freedom which differs from individual to individual and from time to time. Both common and variable freedom exist by grace of nature. Grounded in the very substance of beings, they are the preconditions for the acts of which those beings are capable. At once individual and a member of a kind, charged with promise for the future, each being has a common and variable native freedom which it can creatively exercise.

Each being, animate or inanimate, has some value, some degree of excellence. Unified to some extent, it is not sheer chaos; possessing some internal harmony, it is not pure evil. To destroy it is to do some wrong. But to do wrong is to breach a right. It is because each being has a natural right to be the kind of thing it is and not some other that it is wrong to destroy it—and conversely. Because it exists it has a right to insist and resist, to endure and to change. If in addition it is alive, it also has the right to live and to grow, to feel and to reproduce. If it is human as well, it has the further right to inquire and to reason, to engage in an art, and to adopt a religion. These rights all ought to respect, or risk the guilt of destroying an irreplaceable value.

If we refuse to acknowledge that other beings have rights, we will have to deny them to ourselves for the same reason or we will have to separate ourselves off from the rest of nature as beings who are made of radically different stuff. If the rights of others do not endanger ours, the destruction or modification of theirs will be unwarranted; and if ours are not superior to theirs, the destruction or modification of theirs, though perhaps excusable, will be wrong. No matter how desirable the destruction, mutilation, or modification of others may be, the loss of value which they involve is always wrong. Those who hunt for need have an accounting to make, just as those who hunt for pleasure. The latter merely have more to answer for.

Just as common capacities ground common rights, variable capacities ground variable rights. There are different types of men and unique individuals within the different types; each type and each individual has its own set of capacities not shared by others, entailing a separate set of rights. Faced with the question as to whether a man is to be educated or is to be permitted to be a citizen, we need ask only whether or not he has the power to exercise that common native freedom which is his because he is a man. Only those ought to be excluded from these activities who have no control over their minds. The question how much education ought to be given or what position in the state a man should occupy is to be settled by taking account of his special capacities which, even if constant for him, are variable over the range of human kind. Variable rights are special rights commensurate with special capacities. To ignore them is to ignore important differences between men; to allow their acknowledgment to obscure the common rights is to forget that individual human beings are after all only men.

2. Conditional Freedom

Native freedom is presupposed by all other kinds of freedom. It is not inexplicable, uncaused. There is a history behind each kind of being, accounting in part for the capacities it has. Or, even more narrowly, no being now exists but has had an origin and thus depended on the exercise of freedom by some other being, involving the use of its common and variable capacities. My native freedom owes its being to the exercise of freedom by my parents, and the stuff out of which my body was formed was free to combine and interplay to shape me as I am today. Taking each being by itself, its native freedom is part of its very substance; taking it from the standpoint of its origin, its native freedom is something which came to be through the exercise of freedom on the part of others. Substantially, native freedom is first; temporally, it is consequent on a freedom exercised by others.

Because all beings have a native freedom, all have natural rights, and conversely. Their natural rights limit man's right to use them. Man has no *absolute* right to vivisect or eat animals, to destroy natural beauties, to waste material or even to make excellent use of it. His obligation to preserve and improve extends far beyond mankind. Success and tragedy are always closely linked; there is much wrong brought about even in the best of acts. Though mankind in practice and in conscience has repeatedly recognized the rights of nonhuman beings, its theories of ethics, politics, and morals have been all too human, denying in principle what was acknowledged in fact. How inhumanly human it is to say that a man has no rights at all. But how humanly human it is to say that man has an unrestricted right against all the rest of nature—and how wrong.

Besides a native freedom, all beings have a *conditional* freedom, making possible the exercise of some portion of their native freedom. A being may have lungs in fine shape but there may be no oxygen available. It may be able to eat but have no food. Possessing a native freedom it may lack the complementary conditional freedom which enables it not merely to be free but to act freely.

Without the native freedom given by healthy lungs and stomach, oxygen and food would be but gas and organic matter. Without the conditional freedom given by available oxygen and food, lungs and stomach would be but passageways for pain. Only a being free in both senses would be free to be itself and exhibit what it was. It alone would have not only abilities to exercise but abilities which could be exercised.

Conditional freedom is native freedom viewed from the outside, the native freedom of others as making possible the exercise of one's own. It varies considerably from time to time and from place to place. In the winter a man has less conditional freedom of movement than he has in the summer, impeded as he is by the wind and the snow and the clothes he wears. A man's conditional freedom varies considerably when he leaves the street and gets into an airplane.

If past practices offer any guide, these illustrations may prove misleading. Philosophers have used similar ones before and have come to the conclusion that what is here termed conditional freedom is only a negative freedom, a freedom which ensues when obstacles are removed. The cage, they remark, deprives the bird of its freedom to fly where it likes. Open the door, they say, and it will acquire a negative freedom, a freedom to do what it could not do before. But the bird did not first have to be caged in order to be free to fly. It was natively free to fly before it was caged; opening the door makes a difference to its conditional freedom. It is thereby enabled to exercise, not to acquire, its native freedom to fly.

3. THE VARIETIES OF CONDITIONAL FREEDOM

There are five basic varieties of conditional freedom: a) primary, b) epochal, c) transitory, d) local, and e) social. The primary is presupposed by the others; all presuppose a native freedom.

a) *Primary conditional freedom* is a freedom to interact with other beings. Guaranteed by the structure of the universe, it is a freedom no one can abridge, for to keep something from interacting it is necessary to make it interact with the bounds imposed. All that can be done is to control the special forms that primary conditional freedom will assume, the way in which it will be exhibited in the other succeeding four modes.

Primary freedom enables one to exercise those minimum abilities of resistance and insistence, change and movement characteristic of any thing. It is another's native freedom as making possible the exercise of one's own. The foundations of cosmology are contained here. Whatever happens results from the interplay of beings whose common abilities have the double function of defining their own native freedom and the conditional freedom which they provide for others. The basic structure of the occurrence is determined by the manner in which they interplay; the details of the occurrence depend on the manner in which the freedom is displayed.

In this universe each being possesses a minimal native freedom and provides a primary conditional freedom making possible the exercise of the native freedom of the rest. If things were treated as though they possessed only a native freedom, the correct philosophy would be that of Leibniz' monadology, with its isolated beings, each of which had capacities that it exercised privately, alone, and unsupported. Interaction, togetherness, public time would then be meaningless concepts. Were things treated instead as possessing only a conditional freedom, the correct philosophy would be an occasionalism, defining a situation in which no thing would act but all would be acted on. Once again, interaction, togetherness, and public time would be meaningless concepts. Each being is at once subject and object, natively free within and offering a conditional freedom to the beings which lie outside it.

b) By existing, a being provides a minimum condition for the exercise of freedom by others. No being, however, merely exists. Each exists as a certain kind of being, sharing some native abilities with others. These shared abilities define a specialized conditional freedom that prevails only so long as that kind of being exists. When men first came on the scene there was a loss of the conditional freedom possible to other beings in one direction and a gain in another. They attained a freedom to be remolded by men in ways they could not be molded before, at the same time that they lost the freedom to remain unmolested, untouched by human concerns. Whenever any new kinds of beings come to be, they make possible regions of freedom not possible before and close up regions which could have been explored.

The content of the universe is constantly changing, usually at a sluggish pace. Taken by and large, the same kind of things exist today that existed thousands of years ago. This persistence of kinds of beings defines the total conditional freedom which characterizes an epoch. Within the frame of such *epochal* conditional *freedom* the scientific story of the universe is told. It is not a story which grows much by the accumulation of details. It must be revised, sometimes quite radically, again and again to make provision for new bodies with new abilities which have for the first time come into existence. New kinds of rays, new kinds of planets, and even new kinds of substance make their appearance for the first time and change the promise of all the rest. It is now becoming more and more evident that the universe does not offer an unalterable range of possible action to things; it is becoming more and more evident that it is no longer possible to hold to a doctrine of God-given laws or to deny real novelty and fundamental change. Laws of nature are habits in things, their abilities rigidified. The arrival of living organisms changed the economy of the world, affecting its laws and giving a new range to the conditional freedom open to others.

Epochal freedom is not necessarily a freedom utilized. There was land before there were beings who made use of their native abilities to crawl and glide. But until they made use of them, their actual behavior was substantially what it had been before there was land. To be sure, the manner of crawling and gliding was shaped by the land over which they had to go, but without a native ability to start crawling and gliding there would be nothing to do but to continue to swim.

Epochal freedom is a cosmic concept having a limited though usually long-range temporal span. Within that span changes in ability occur which, though they do not affect the basic temper of the epoch, make a difference to the promise of the beings within it. Beings with new abilities may appear for just a moment; they may pass away before they have an opportunity to make possible the expression of abilities on the part of others. At almost every moment there are new varieties of freedom which pass away before use can be made of them. The openings which an epoch allows may be neglected and as a consequence the opportunity to be free in a special way may be irretrievably lost.

c) There is nothing to be done with respect to that primary conditional freedom which mere existence defines, except so far as we decide just what is to exist and where. And there is very little that can be done with respect to that epochal freedom which kinds define, except so far as we can eliminate, produce, or alter the existing kinds. The world on which we act, however, is but a small part of the universe; the difference we make to the fixed and epochal freedoms of others makes little difference to the whole.

Transitory freedom is much more within the reach of our control than are primary and epochal freedom. Native, variable freedom viewed from the outside, it enables us to mold ourselves and acquire new abilities outlasting the conditions which made them possible. The natural placidity of the cow made its domestication possible and led men to develop an ability to care for animal kind. The cow gives man a transitory freedom he otherwise would not have. Should the cow disappear, he obviously would no longer be free to domesticate it.

There was a time when men did not know how to care for animals. Until they learned, there was only a limited opportunity for animals to breed to the best effect and no possibility of their developing loyalty toward human kind. Our ability to care for animals provides them with a particular kind of transitory conditional freedom; their domesticated natures, in turn, provide a transitory conditional freedom for us, enabling us to do those things which require companionship, beasts of burden, or protection.

d) It is rarely that we become interested in any of these preceding modes of freedom. The static conditional freedom that interests man is primarily *local*, a *freedom* available to him here and now. It is because this freedom has such a short span and range and yet must be commensurate with man's inalienable rights that the doctrine of natural rights must exhibit an internal flexibility or give itself up as inadequate. We have natural rights to health, food, and shelter, to reason and to friends. But we live in different regions, under differing conditions. A man in the arctic cannot do what a man in the tropics can, and conversely. Those in the mountains are not as free to walk or breathe as those in the valleys, though their legs, lungs, and inclinations may be just as strong as those of the others. Their laws, habits, and manners, their diets, legislation, and occupations should be quite diverse.

We are locally free to do certain things here and now; we are temporally free to do what the conditions of the time allow. We are epochally free to do what the universe permits and have a primary freedom to do what sheer existence makes possible. The first is a specialization of the second, this of the third, and the third of the fourth. We are locally free only within the frame of freedom provided by the others. Severally and together they define what could be done. They do not reveal what will be, what should be, or what is permitted to be done. These are matters which require us to take account of *dynamic* freedom, of creativity, the act of making the indeterminate determinate, the future present, the abstract concrete. This is a disoriented power if it is not brought to bear on that union of transitory and local freedoms which constitutes *social freedom*, the freedom to act without fear or jeopardy in society.

e) We are social beings, all of us, exercising a social freedom creatively, a transitory freedom pertinent to what is now at the focus of our interests. It is a neat and difficult question whether we have this freedom from the very beginning of our careers or whether we acquire it over the years. That question we must now try to answer. Whatever the answer be, though, it cannot affect the fact that social freedom overlays and specializes the more permanent and wider-reaching native, common freedom which marks us off as men.

III

THE SOCIALIZATION OF MAN

1. THE CONVENTIONAL WORLD

WE are social beings. This much seems evident. What is not immediately clear is whether we are social by nature or social through training. Can a man be a man without being social? If not, how is it that some can be hermits and enemies of society; how is it that the embryo or infant, not social to begin with, can become social eventually?

A man has a nature before he attains the status of a social being. He is not essentially, inescapably, through and through social; he becomes social under conditions which might be otherwise. The process of socialization is not merely a process of training him to assume social relations to various objects, to exchange an early social allegiance to certain things for a more publicly satisfactory allegiance to other things. It is possible for men to live apart from society, miserable, truncated, and even conditioned by society to some extent though they be. Everyone retreats from society many times during the day, and all of us partly fall out of it when we act as merely physical or biological beings. We might remain outside it indefinitely; it is conceivable that we might never enter it at all. Were that the case, we would undoubtedly suffer grievously and lose whole ranges of freedom and right. But this is quite another thing from saying that we would so far cease to be human. Were men through and through social, the human embryo would be much more complex and subtle than we ever suspected, and all criticisms of society as opposed to the individual, would be foolish and inane.

Though Aristotle seemed quite clear at times that man was a social animal, he did apparently feel there was something amiss. In any case he offered different accounts of man in different places. There is a rather wide chasm dividing his biological, psychological views from those expressed in his ethics and politics. In the Aristotelian biology and psychology a man is defined to be a rational animal, possessing a power of reason in and by himself without which he would cease to be human, and which no other being in nature could possess. In the ethics and politics man is defined to be a political or social animal, dependent on outside conditions which vary from place to place and time to time. The two were not and cannot be brought together, for each defines as essential to a single, undivided man what the other finds unnecessary. The first definition moreover is unsatisfactory even when made to refer to man as outside society; the second is unsatisfactory even when restricted to man as part of society. The first makes no provision for any difference between males and females, leaders and followers, adults and children, and has application therefore only to abstract and not to concrete human beings. The second definition takes no account of that common human nature which precludes the use of others as slaves.

No theory of man is adequate if it does not allow that a man can be human and still can exist apart from any society. None can be adequate which does not go on to show how even those engaged in menial tasks are as human, as natively free, and can be as full-bodied members of society as the others. Men are born unsocialized; differently conditioned men are equally human.

It is the virtue of the social-contract theory of Hobbes, Locke, and Rousseau, that it makes a bold attempt to meet the challenge of these considerations. These thinkers in different ways affirm that it is possible for men to exist outside society. They explain men's entrance into society as being the result of a decision to give up individual liberty to gain a mutually guaranteed security. The theory, however, begs its own question as surely as does the Aristotelian, though in a more subtle form. It supposes that individuals are not only fully human apart from society but that they are already fully social. It supposes that they are capable of making social contracts. Yet social contracts can be forged only by full-grown, civilized men. Only these are capable of recognizing their proper interests in the face of socially significant opposing interests, only these can make agreements and pledge themselves deliberately. The men with whom a satisfactory theory of the origin of society must begin are less formed, much less mature than those which a social-contract theory needs.

Society is no cork floating on the ocean of physics or biology but a power for enriching and utilizing whatever physics and biology might encompass. When men act as gross physical and biological beings, they are outside their societies—but only because they are at the same time inside. Their acts are bounded in ways which are due to their societies, even when those acts violate the intent or demands of the societies. He who hits another spends physical energy and gets a physical result. But society relates that result to a host of others in ways not within the province of physics. It endows the act with social values, gives it a limit in space and time it otherwise would not have, retains a hold on the men even though they may themselves have put aside all social claims.

A society is part of a universe. He who lives in it lives inside confines much narrower than he need have, because he thereby obtains a completion, a satisfaction not possible to him outside it. The variety, the security, the intelligence, the art, sciences, philosophy, and religion, the language and history which society makes possible grace what otherwise would be a life lost in the senses, a series of what would at best be but inconsequential, transient pleasures.

Society is a universe in which even the world of physics, even the stars in the heavens are contained as parts, with values, connections, force they otherwise would not possess. Understanding how it can come to be is one of the hardest and singularly neglected tasks we have to face today. Without a clue, or perhaps more justly we should say, overwhelmed with clues, we ought to be quite happy if we can offer even only the vaguest of hints and suggestions.

He who was incapable of experience would be unable to function in society. Society might occupy itself with him, as it does with hurricanes and garbage, trees and dogs, but he would not have any interest in it. He would not be one it could teach to restrain or modify dispositions and appetites, or to put aside what was attractive to his senses or insistent on its presence for the sake of what was less appealing or less obtrusive.

Animals herd together, fish swim in schools, but only men form societies. Animals support one another; they cooperate, they are often intelligent and considerate. They act purposively to realize possibilities benefiting others, sometimes at a sacrifice to themselves. But at one and the same time they are too closely and too loosely bound together to be able to be socialized. They are so thoroughly in the grip of the possibilities which lie outside them that they are little more than interlocked items in a group, without the power to retreat from the rest and thus to accept or deny on their own what they are given from without. Yet they are much more loosely united with other animals than men are with other men, even on shipboard or across a gaming table. Animals, unlike men, have no capacity to judge one another in terms appropriate to all other situations. They are linked with one another firmly but from without; humans are loosely associated with one another on the outside but firmly from within, as able to take account of one another all the time.

A man might conceivably experience as an animal does, thoughtlessly, without judgment or understanding. He might have no appropriate form prepared for the reception of what he experiences.

Though he then would have experiences, he would not experience, enjoy, judge. These activities require the use of a possibility to order the content; they turn possibilities into general forms or categories. Only he who makes such use of possibility can be socialized, for only he accepts from within what limits him from without, and therefore can be a person at once apart from and united with others.

Geography and climate, the possible kinds of habitation and degrees of intensity of population, the kind and quantity of food, shelter, and tools that are available and the manner in which they are to be obtained—in short, differences in material and opportunity—force men into different situations. They lead a number of men to occupy themselves with distinct possibilities and thus be ready to respond in corresponding ways toward similar things. Only in a universe where all had the same opportunities and materials, where everyone could achieve exactly the same results with exactly the same means and effort, could men form a single group, all having the same attitudes toward the same things. It would be hard to conceive a world more monotonous. Fortunately it would be very difficult to make it real. Men always have formed and must continue to form multiple limited groups. Only a restricted number of them assume the same attitudes toward the same things, since only a few are faced with the same limited possibility and with the same kinds of things. Poetry, science, and philosophy may enable men to recognize their kinship with others, but all the while they will remain members of their own groups. Those groups are not societies but gatherings of beings who have come to respond concordantly. Within these they pass most of their lives. The group classifications, the divisions and distinctions characteristic of their group languages, habits, practices, and work serve to triangulate the facts they confront. They define a *conventional* world. In terms of these men live; it is by these they swear; it is for these they are often quite willing to die; it is out of this that society and social man most likely arose; it is to this they usually return and come to rest.

The objects that are correlative to men as members of a conventional world are at a distance from the men and have their own careers. As the termini of the men's responsive attitudes, these objects have features they otherwise would not have. The attitudes endow a bird with the status of an omen, a spirit, a fellow creature, an enemy. These are genuine features of the bird, though of course only of the bird as an object in a conventional world, only of the bird as over against conventional men and not of the bird as of interest to the biologist. The two birds, the biologist's and the conventional man's, are of course one, since it is a distant, independently flying living being toward which the conventional man takes his group attitude, and it is an experience-able bird in this conventional world that the biologist describes as having an existence outside the confines of convention. The two are hopelessly asunder only for those who suppose that a convention is subjective, private, not actually impinging on something external, or for those for whom only conventional men and conventionalized objects exist.

It is possible neither to get completely outside one's group and grasp the nature of things as wholly beyond the reach and taint of every attitude nor to remain wholly inside one's group and grasp them as mere objects of convention. Men get outside their groups only in conventional ways and with respect to conventionally defined objects. Negations cling to subsequent affirmations, making evident the pertinence of what goes on here and now; the existence and limitations of conventions are not canceled when denied. Reciprocally, to remain inside a group it is necessary to attend to real beings with independent natures. To insist on nothing but conventions is to abstract groups and objects from objective nature and thereby make the conventional man an abstracted caricature of what he actually is.

Wisdom is the outcome of a triple lesson well learned to the effect that there are conventions, that all men are conventionalized beings living in groups, and that there is a truth which transcends and allows one to compare and judge different conventions. We have all, to some extent, learned the first lesson and know that there are conventions. We are aware of some men, even in our own groups, whose attitudes are not like ours and who thus accept some things as possessed of traits and importance we ourselves not only do not see but often vehemently deny. Indeed today apparently all but plain men, children, and a few philosophers—who are on one side the two in one—seem to suppose that everything we see and say is compacted of conventions. A truth which no one was very likely to overlook, the truth that there are conventions and that most of the objects men acknowledge are at least in part conventionally shaped by them, is thus exaggerated and made to hide that greater truth beyond, which wisdom masters as its third and final lesson. But before that point is reached, the second lesson, that all men are conventionalized beings, has to be well conned in its full import.

Just so far as men are conventionalized, they form groups which differ from one another, groups which, in the absence of a standard beyond all conventions, are valuationally on a level. One group of men —usually our own—is sometimes said to be more liberal, more closely knit, healthier, braver, more efficient than any other. But it is questionable whether such comparisons are meaningful, except so far as one is able to escape from the confines of his conventions to some degree and look down on all groups detachedly in terms which are neutral to all. Comparisons of groups as better or worse require an appeal to an external criterion in terms of which they can be objectively and impartially compared.

The recognition of the equality or incomparability of different conventions is a barrier against the common temptation to want others to accept one's own conventions solely because they are one's own. He who claims that his conventional world is superior to that of others, for no other reason but that it is his, is provincial. If he contents himself with remarking that others should live in terms of his conventions, he will usually be less annoying and less dangerous than he would be had he tried to force the acceptance of his conventions on others—but he would still be provincial. Inaction, social laissez-faire, indifference, and even tolerance provide no sure warrant of the existence of a liberated spirit.

A sophisticated man is not less provincial than an innocent missionary; he is just less intrusive. Each views his own set of conventions as absolute and as alone respectable; each implicitly or explicitly commits the blunder of supposing that others should adopt what is in fact not suited to their abilities, histories, practices, and needs, and therefore what would be bad from the vantage point of those others. Each takes what is essential to himself as a conventionalized man, absolutizes it, and, at least in imagination, imposes it on others, thereby misunderstanding himself, overlooking the limitations of conventions, and doing a grave injustice to his fellow man.

The sophisticate inclines to be cynical in an easygoing way; he rejects the conventions of others but does nothing to make those others change their ways. The missionary in contrast is a sentimentalist, inclined to urge others to imitate him. He tries to alter them, though for the best of reasons. Each usually forgets that from the perspective of others he is just as unenlightened and just as foolish. When we cajole, bribe, threaten, or force others to wear our kind of clothes, to follow our dietary rules and rituals, to adopt our method of governing, our church, our pedagogy, our grammar or economy, we are rarely engaged in the noble act of making them better than they were. Ours is most likely the questionable act of making them misbehave, of making them do violence to their own attitudes, or of making them into imitations of ourselves.

The attempt to force one's conventions on others is, fortunately, usually doomed to disappointment. Conventions are deep rooted, to be altered or displaced only by changing radically the kinds of situations in which men find themselves, and thus the kinds of possibilities they will be able to internalize. Definitions of incest vary from group to group but seem as close to each as very flesh. And in a way they are. The conventions of a group are of its substance; the men are what they are in part because of the weight they assign to various things. They are not merely in space or in an environment, happening to assume some position toward other beings; they cut themselves off from most of the world to become conventional men bounded by conventional objects.

Different men need different things; they act on different objects, they act in different ways. If they are to live at all well, they must live at different rates, engage in quite different enterprises, stress different capacities, bind themselves with different conventions. It takes a wide variety of diets to keep all men well nourished. Each group of men has a right to forge its own conventions, unless and so far as they conflict with the demands of a sound standard outside all conventions, justly measuring the worth of each.

A convention is both an article of faith and a guiding groove. It is lived through and is lived for. Its existence depends on the readiness of men to protect it against actual threat and even against the idea that it is not final and absolute. Without such protection its vigor is sapped and its adherents confounded by the strident claims of antagonistic groups. It is one thing, however, to accept a convention defensively and another to accept it offensively. A defensive acceptance demands that the convention be treated as absolute and final for the members of the group whose order it defines; an offensive acceptance demands that it be insisted on as correct for other groups. The former allows others to cherish their own conventions; it is satisfied to stress the truth that conventions prescribe the limit of a conventional man's universe, that within its confines they find the goods they need in order to be men in that group. It expresses a partiality similar to that which men show for their mothers, language, children, and bodies, a partiality which, though it may conflict with, still allows for the partiality others may exhibit toward their own mothers, language, children, and bodies. Offensive acceptance of a conventional world goes much beyond this, since it demands that no defensive acceptance of other worlds be allowed by other men, that others be forced to do what is wrong in the perspective of their own conventions, that they change themselves into us for no reason but that we are we and they are not.

Offensive conventionalism takes the admission that one conventional world is not inferior to other conventional worlds to mean that one of the conventional worlds is superior to the rest. It is a consistent doctrine because it argues in a circle, asserting that a given convention is better for no other reason than that the convention requires its adherents to say this. But that very argument justifies other circles, equally insistent, equally perfect, which just as consistently and illegitimately insist on the superiority of their own conventions.

Offensive conventionalism compares conventions by belittling the conventions the thinker does not follow. Defensive conventionalism allows for greater fairness, but only because it does not venture a comparison and evaluation. Where the one supposes that "not inferior to others" means "superior to others," the other supposes that it means "incomparable with others." Both ignore the alternative that it may mean "comparably superior or equal to others," that there may be standards beyond all conventional schemes in terms of which they can be significantly and legitimately judged.

Defensive conventionalists tend to be skeptics. Tolerant of other conventions, they abjure all comparison. But in that way they tend to prejudge the evidence, unreflectingly putting aside the supposition that there are objective grounds for good comparisons. The tolerance of mature anthropology, a tolerance characteristic of all science, is quite other than this. It is an objective tolerance, expressing a willingness to examine all the evidence and to allow to each thing the merits it has. It would be as fatal to confuse it with the tolerance of the skeptic as it would be to confuse action with passivity, impartiality with prejudice, consideration with indifference, science with supposition, catholicity of affirmation with hesitance, doubt, and denial. It is of the essence of anthropology to affirm that all conventions deserve consideration, that they are all to be viewed sympathetically from within, that no one of them is to be prejudged as being less ultimate, respectable, or important than any other. Nothing in it requires the denial that truths outside the limits of a conventional world can be glimpsed and used by the members of that conventional world. Indeed, since anthropology is a science offering steady truths and having an interest in every conventional scheme, it must be the case that some anthropologists at least must be able to exist both inside and outside the boundaries which they, like the rest of us, inevitably adopt.

2. Culture

Conventions have quite long spans. They change but slowly, for they are the products of fairly stable possibilities expressed in fairly steady attitudes. They owe their existence to transitory and local freedoms exercised in common ways. Only after a whole group of men has changed the character of its acts or directed them toward a new area of things do we find an appreciable change in the nature of a conventional world. But changes there are. We are constantly being faced with new situations and must therefore take account of new possibilities, internalizing them and expressing them in the form of fresh attitudes toward the things about.

In a world of flux like ours, sluggish though it be, it is more the constancy than the changes of a convention which require explanation. Constancy is a product. To have something steady in such a world it is necessary to reachieve it at successive moments. Constant conventions are those which have been constantly re-established. Perpetually on the verge of slipping away into that environing jungle of natural things which is on the other side of our conventional boundaries, our conventions must be reinstituted all the time, carved out of material which has its own nature and career independent of us. A man may grow up to be respected as wise and perceptive and yet never question the supposed right to make other slaves, or the ultimacy and unimpeachability of the view that women and children are chattels. Forced again and again to take some account of their intrusive humanity, he must, if he is to continue to maintain the convention, reaffirm what he accepted before. He must change his attitudes constantly, make them flexible enough to make provision for the incursion of new data. We conventionalize independent beings, not conventionalized ones. What we conventionalize always to some degree defies our conventions and must be overcome at every moment.

So far as beings act independently of men, men must, to maintain a hold on them as true bounding parts of themselves, respond to them creatively. So far as they do this, through the agency of acquired, concurrent habits, they turn themselves into cultural beings. The *cultural* world is that portion of the environment which is approached in habitual yet flexible ways, enabling men to outride the rise and fall, the radical alteration, and even the structure of the conventions which they have so far shared. It has a characteristic future with which its members are concerned, giving it a character and enabling it to have a career through time.

Because it lacks a controlling future a convention can only persist or pass away; because it possesses one, a culture has a career in which the self-same possibility is realized often in dissimilar but related guises. The culture comes to an end when the realization of the possibility makes some new possibility more relevant or when a change in the temper of the men and their objects makes for a new cultural character with a new corresponding future. But while it lasts that future is the ideal of the culture, the limits of most men's horizon, the face of their living God, what James Feibleman has termed the "implicit dominant ontology" of their group.

By honoring tyrannicides men sometimes create tyrants; by giving way to their appetites they sometimes discover much worth in what they once threw away. They can so realize the good of their cultures or can be so changed in nature or circumstance that they will be concerned with quite new possibilities. For better or for worse we today have a cultural future which differs considerably from the future our ancestors once faced, and from the future our descendants undoubtedly will face.

The cultural world of a man is that portion of the experiential environment which commonly habituated men make essential to their different beings. No man however can concentrate on all the objects of his culture. In the course of his life he is subjected to innumerable noted and unnoted institutional pressures, and concentrates on but few of the objects which constitute the culture within which he lives. He and his fellows are given and live out different roles. They occupy limited places, have limited functions, deal with but a limited number of cultural objects, and thereby get ready to become more fully socialized.

3. Social Training

Did all men approach the same things with the same attitudes, their culture would have both a distributive and a collective meaning. Each man would be the bearer of his culture, epitomizing the whole. No one would have a distinctive task to perform; each would mirror the others and the culture as a whole. There would be no possibility of a society arising, for this depends on men filling distinct but interlocking limited roles.

Each of us spends much of his life realizing fewer goods than his culture allows. We are primarily carpenters, teachers, machinists, mothers, and fathers, all to be sure inside one culture but partially unconcerned with what others do and how we and they are in cultural accord. We are men occupied with a fragment of our culture but in an intensive way; in short, we are cultural, not cultured men, social units, members of families and clans.

We become socialized first under the pressure exerted by our immediate relatives. The first and most effective agency for socializing man is the family. It turns the newborn, socially dependent but not socialized infant, a being biased and disposed in nonsocial ways with perhaps a faint memory of past goods enjoyed in quiet isolation in the womb, into one which will spend most of its time keeping within the rutted tracks of socially endorsed roles. It converts the infant from a being who tries to use external things to obtain private satisfactions which its memory tells it to expect into one who, for equally private but socially warranted satisfactions, acts responsively to, takes account of the needs and natures of, what is socially endorsed.

The newly born infant enters a family—a subordinate, ordered subdivision of society, an institution—not altogether prepared for it. The infant, just as surely as the other members, is a substantial, independent being with its own rhythms and impulses, no matter how much like the others it may first seem to be in appearance and mentality and no matter how much it needs the others in order to live and prosper. The father, mother, sisters, and brothers in different ways acknowledge it to have a distinct familial position and even familial rights and privileges. But since, unlike them, it is as yet without familial functions, without tasks or obligations, and thus is a being which does not take deliberate or habitual account of the needs and rights of others, it must be molded until it does. The family trains it to become a constituent of it, to live as part of as well as in it, to sustain it as well as to be sustained by it.

An infant is a member of a family who cannot engage in familial tasks. It becomes a child when it can engage in some of them. A child or, for similar reasons, one who is sick, abnormal, or senile is not capable of carrying out completely his familial task of filling one of a number of interlocked roles. The child becomes a normal adult member of the family only when he assumes the role of one who works to continue and enhance the good of all the members of the family.

The tightness of family bonds, the very success of the family as an institution, endangers the society. The family in one way is the enemy of society; it is a universe to itself, with its own planets and sun, resisting with all its might the pull of other planetary systems to make it part of a single whole. Families dilute political courage, they quiet public zeal, they make selfishness apparently noble by extending its benefits to a limited few who will most likely reciprocate. It is necessary that there be institutions, besides the family, demanding of their members that they act with others to realize objectives, desirable to all, outside the interest of members of a family. These other institutions train their members—as the family rarely does—to be members of wider groups than themselves and of the society which encompasses them all.

The health of society requires that the members of families be forced into other institutions as well; there will then be some assurance that public virtues are well ingrained. Without the training provided by playground, school, religion, army, and market, men would remain familial beings, without a common meeting ground with others except that which necessity demands and expediency provides. There would be no society but only a mosaic of independent families momentarily and tentatively held together by the accident of history and the pressure of circumstance, like allies in a war, nations in an international peace conference, or participants in interracial discussions.

A society is a group of interrelated conventional, cultural, institutional men, a tissue of interlocked roles, some of which were acquired by birth, some by accident, and some deliberately. In each there are males and females, young and old, those with greater and those with lesser prestige, the disinherited, the producers, and the consumers, all of whom are counted on to engage in distinctive activities while exercising a common transitory freedom.

In a society all rely on each to fill his role. Because others are usually reliable, each one of us can stay within his own narrow scheme, confident and content. Were our reliance entirely misplaced, we would not know what to expect and thus what we ourselves were to do. Society has no other way of punishing a man but by changing his role. Whoever fails to live up to his role risks a compelled social change in role, permanently or temporarily. Some expression of annoyance, made manifest usually by assigning the offender a role having less prestige than the one he occupied before, is the normal accompaniment of such a compelled change.

If an offense is mortal, if it is felt to jeopardize the very existence of society, society severs itself from the offender by alienating or by destroying him. Even then it relies on him to behave as one filling a role in that society. Let a man fail in the most extreme way and he will continue to be relied upon, though for different things from those he did before. He will never be entirely abandoned even by those who resolutely put him aside. Society expects him to live up to its traditions of honor and courage, even while undergoing its most severe chastisements and deprivations, for it recognizes no human right or status outside its own confines. A man is relied upon, even when his crime is radical, to respond appropriately to the limiting conditions his society imposes on him.

During infancy and much beyond, parents, teachers, playmates, and friends mold the child's nature. They reward him with their good opinion, thereby supporting his opinion of himself and strengthening that inconstant courage with which he usually faces the unknown. Sometimes they reward him with good opinion and good things, with extra benefits he needs and wants. Remembering these goods, he thereafter views the things others urge on him as though they were sources of value greater than that which the things of themselves promised.

In these ways a man learns how to measure up to his role. He becomes *trained*, disciplined. If his training is to be constant, uniform, and socially useful, in accord with the training of others, he must be habituated to respond in similar ways to similar objects. We can be trained to refuse the most palatable foods, even when starving, to die for a piece of cloth, torn and bespattered, to deny our reason, to abandon everything that we would normally cherish and that other societies endorse, and to take instead what we and others might otherwise neglect or despise. Our responses in society are dictated, not by an appreciation of what the food or flag itself promises but by what the society adds to the actual promise, what rewards it will in fact assure us if we do what it demands. Our training is a process by which our inclinations are redirected so that we come to accept unpromising things as the source of great goods. We need this training to make us substitute what we natively want for what may be almost valueless. We need only little training to make us promote the good of some men, animals, or things, for we remember what benefits accrued to us from them in the course of nature; we need a great deal of training to promote the good of all those in our own society, not to speak of mankind, and with more insistence and effect than we exhibited when we promoted the good of the few.

Training men for itself, as the family primarily does, or for a world beyond, as many other institutions do, is long, uphill work. Objects in which men are or might be interested must be replaced by others which the institution promises will bring greater rewards. The new objects may even be physically or perceptually the same as those toward which the men had interestedly turned, but so far as they are objects of responses which are dynamic and flexible they are actually possessed of a meaning and an import they did not have before. In addition to their size, number, shape, and weight, their color, texture, smell, and taste, they have an attractiveness, importance, social value, helping constitute permissible or even commanded material with which the trained man deals responsively.

We never live entirely outside our societies and some institutions which those societies include; we always speak and think in rhythms and terms provided by them. But the accent is always our own; we always look beyond our society even when we make no use of what we see or even deny that we looked at all. Were men, as is sometimes said, only social creatures, mere products of the routinized influences of others, they would be like characters in a novel, mere fictions without genuine existence of their own. They could not then ever attain the stage where they could help form their societies, not to speak of leaving them, defying them, or transforming them.

The claim that man is but a social animal is urged with a vigor and individuality that belies what it purports to say. Only he who has looked outside the borders of his society can rightly claim that these provide the only universes there can be for men—but *he* already has shown that at least he can get outside it, if only to gaze into the vast abyss of nothingness and report to the rest of us the vacancy he saw there. He differs from the rest of us not in his ability, his freedom to get beyond the limits imposed by his society but in the paucity of the results he obtains when his ability is exercised. Forever social, always a member of some institution, a man is not yet and never will be completely socialized. But he can be much more socialized than he is. And the more reliable he is the more reliable we will find others to be. This is a most promising and dangerous truth. It points the way to peace and harmony but also to slavery and mechanization. History is the record of the pathetic struggle of man to reach the one and yet avoid the other. So far it has proved to be primarily a story only of minor successes and major failures.

Because a socialized man is a trained man he is relied upon and held *accountable*, whether or not he can and will act willingly or unwillingly. The question as to whether men can will freely is irrelevant to society and its institutions, for they expect nothing of men but that they deal with what has been socially endorsed in socially approved ways. Unfortunately for society the world is constantly changing. What was once obtained and now expected in the society is not always forthcoming. The expectant memory of what is socially urged is often doomed to disappointment; society does not make good the promise men were trained to read into socialized things. No matter how well trained its members may be, they are confronted, again and again, with new situations which no mere training could prepare them for.

There are many things society requires for its own health and continuance for which it can make no provision, since these are beyond its prevision. The very good of a society demands that men be ready to act not only as they have been taught to do but in other ways as well. Men must be helped to meet and match unknown new demands. Training adapts men to a future which is like the past; for the society's own welfare society must be limited in power, so that men can still take proper account of a future which may be different from the past and thus act appropriately now.

4. The Presuppositions of Society

Each institution, no less than the society as a whole, has its characteristic future, determined by and controlling what is here and now. The future of the institution is its *objective*. More abstract and general than the institution, that objective assures the institution identity and meaning even when the institution changes in membership and content. Generalized, the objective of one institution becomes the common objective of a number, enabling them all to be diverse and comparable illustrations of a single good. No matter how dissimilar and unrelated institutions are, there is an objective more or less remote which they can be said to realize in diverse ways. But taken as it is, an organization with its own limited objective, each institution has its own requirements to which all subordinate groups are subject in the same way that it is subject to the objective it shares with other institutions.

Each institution is directed toward its appropriate objective for a stretch of time and realizes it more or less in concrete, somewhat unpredictable ways, to constitute the course of its history. The different objectives of different institutions diversely express a common *social good*. This in turn specifies a still more abstract indeterminate possibility appropriate to all the societies with which one's own interplays. This abstract possibility, overarching a number of societies, is an ideal of *civilization* to be realized in different societies at different rates and in different shapes, somewhat as institutions realize in diverse ways the common objective of all the institutions in a society and as groups within an institution realize in different ways the common objective of all the institutionalized groups.

Social goods are possibilities, the future as distant, harmonious, and pertinent to socialized men. They, like all possibilities, limit the kinds of things we can possibly do. They also prompt theories of destiny and fate which lull us into the belief that we are mere pawns in history, being moved relentlessly to some far-off goal. We should be such pawns were it not that we can and do lay hold of objectives and ideals and use them to dictate from within just what action is to take place. History is not only lived; it is also made. Men are governed by possibilities but they can govern themselves by them too, and in any one of an endless number of possible ways, beyond the´reach of knowledge though not necessarily of all shrewd, predictive surmise.

He who clings to and uses the good of his society to dictate to himself what he is to do makes himself one with his society in spirit and in act, inwardly as well as outwardly. He is a *socially moral* being, a loyal man rejecting all other ideals. Every society needs such men; everyone makes some effort to elicit men's loyalties. Even totalitarians who seem interested only in making men act in dictated ways and who succeed in large part in doing this need men who are more than well trained. They too need men who determine themselves by means of the ideal which is pointed at by, and extends beyond, the society as it now is, for they too need some men with initiative, some men who are creative, some men who are free. Totalitarian states make up but a fragment of all there is and can be, and must paradoxically therefore allow for ideals outside themselves and for men who act in terms of these, even if only to promote the totalitarian good.

Each situation, each institution, each society is over against others, smaller, larger, and alongside it. Each has to meet the competition of the gnawing appetites and the warming pleasures of the body as well as the glories which a more distant, more universally applicable ideal holds open to men. The existence of every society is in real danger so long as men can be tempted to pledge themselves to reach such quite different ideals. Were a man not to make his purpose one with society's, only those of his acts which had been routinized would have specific bearing on what is socially available. Inwardly he would not be truly social. Behind society's surface he would live as an alien who could, by turning another way, escape, deny, and perhaps destroy the society. Men must either be trained so that they are ready to meet every possible turn and curve in the course of society's history or they must acquire the art of so preparing themselves from within that they can meet adequately the varying challenges with which they will be presented from without.

Men will always dream of nobler worlds, believe in better Gods. Their childhood memories, their random fancies, their religions, and occasionally their glimpses into the dim future beyond make them uneasily aware that their present social good is too narrow and specifies a broader ideal in an arbitrary and perhaps unsatisfactory way.

We are constantly on the verge of dealing with things not sanctioned by our society or of dealing with them in nonsanctioned ways. And were this not so, if man could be kept from realizing anything but the characteristic objective of his own society, if he could be so well trained that he lived only to promote it, society would have to try to make him consider other goods as well. For its own sake a society must refuse to socialize men to the limit of their capacities, for it needs men who are faithful, not merely constant; who have spirit, not merely enthusiasm; who are loyal, not merely conscientious; who have decided for and not merely sided with it. Only such men will be able to help it maintain itself and possibly prosper in an indifferent and often antagonistic world. If men did not know there were competing goods society would have to teach them that there were, for only if they have the opportunity to put other goods aside can society stand over against all possible as well as all actual determinants of human action. Only then could it become a true leviathan in whose belly all men live. Anything less than this would leave the most stable and powerful of societies in constant jeopardy to the vagrant thoughts, the sudden impulses, the vague surmises of men, and the unpredictable turns of daily and cosmic history. Man wonders; he gives himself problems; he asks himself questions. He does not wait for the machinery of existence to break down, as pragmatism supposes, before he tries to think a little. He thinks in order to get to the future ahead of time, to complete himself in principle before he has a chance to complete himself in fact. No matter where he is, how threatened and confined, how rewarded and well pleased, he will always entertain prospects sometimes not accepted and perhaps not acceptable by his society. The dictator can reach his goal only by killing curiosity—but this unfortunately requires the destruction of the men he needs in order to have a society at all.

A society *of* men contrasts with a society *for* men. The latter can get along with humans functioning as socialized *animals;* the former needs social *men*, beings who voluntarily make themselves the source of the acts which society needs but cannot entirely, through training or threat, assure. It needs men who fulfill themselves in the society by acting responsively on the socially valuable to realize that transsocial good, that ideal of civilization, which the society now inadequately exhibits.

No society is endorsed by everyone in it. Not all are faithful to it constantly or to a high degree. And the society can get along for a while even when endorsed by no one, particularly when nature and men continue to move in familiar grooves. Ultimately, though, unless there be some on whom society can rely for loyalty, there will be no one on whom it can rely in crises. Only he who is loyal to his society can be looked to for leadership, for heroic acts, for vision, for guidance. He alone can meet the frustrating facts of existence with the freshness, the adroitness, the responsiveness which will bring about the good that the society must realize if its promise is to be fulfilled.

Society relies on men to do what it endorses. The reliance is supported by force and persuasion, by the promise of injury or reward. It also trusts men to be loyal to it—and this cannot be demanded or forced. A part of all oppressive force serves to destroy the desire to endorse the oppressor. Tyranny is self-defeating, suicidal. Every tyranny dispatches itself, later than most men usually want but often sooner than they expected. The one thing tyranny cannot generate is loyalty; it lacks flexible men alert and ready to promote it all the time. Loyalty requires free men, self-compelling beings, men who see something good in what they adopt. They can be hoodwinked, led to focus on some singular societal good as though it were the highest and most inclusive of all goods. But the acceptance of that good as the internal guide of their acts is something no one can command or even guide from without. It awaits the free, creative action of the man from within in the face of genuine alternatives, sometimes only faintly glimpsed but still present, adoptable, and often attractive.

Loyalty fluctuates; it cannot always be counted on. There is no moment when men may not fall short of what full loyalty requires. This is a desirable state of affairs, even for society. Only he who can vary in his loyalty to the present objectives of society can act for the best interests of that society when those interests require the violation of codes and practices socially approved and long entrenched. Unless what society should have is always what it wants, it is desirable that some men at least aim beyond the objective which characterizes the society then and there.

Justice to the requirements of society requires that a man guide himself by an ideal of a civilization where the arts and sciences flourish and all men prosper. He must see this as deserving of adoption, regardless of all threat and force, and make it permeate his being. It must appear to him as a true good, though in a limited, human, palatable form, to be brought into the whirlpool of daily existence in whatever way he can. A society so constituted that such an ideal has no appeal to its members exists precariously, on sufferance. When the next sharp crisis in human affairs arrives, when the next new prophet appears in the land, the most rigorous training that such a society can provide will be but a memory, slowing but not preventing men from turning elsewhere.

Only a few men can be safely relied upon to determine their activities by means of a proper use of a civilized ideal. It takes good judgment and neatly adjusted efforts to make that ideal serve as an agency enabling one to continue to live in routine ways in normal times and in unexpected though appropriate ways at unexpected times. Novelty is itself a novelty; unpredictable, undeducible outcomes may or may not duplicate or repeat what had been before. This means that we must be constantly prepared for the recurrence of the familiar no less than for the incursion of the new.

Social wisdom demands that most men should adopt the objectives of their societies and not leave much room for variation in activity; it demands also that there be loyal, creative leaders pointing the way toward a good greater than that now realized. It asks that the risk of bad judgment be reduced without precluding responsible flexible action by a few. The good society is made up both of men who loyally adopt its good in variable ways and of men who devote themselves to realizing that good in constant ways, the two diverging considerably in practice only on inclement days.

5. Society and Civilization

Society needs both routine men and flexible ones. The double need too often divides it, and almost every institution within it, into antagonistic parts. The routine and the flexible men internalize the same ideal differently ; too often they come to act solely in terms of different, limited, and perhaps antagonistic goals pertinent to the limited fields with which they have accustomed themselves to deal.

Routine begets conservatives, men who favor what has a long history and is approved by the more reliable members of the society. In this they are arbitrary, but no more so than are the flexible men who become liberals, occupying themselves primarily with realizing what now is not but may soon be favored by most. Conservatives are partly behind, liberals partly ahead of their times. In different ways they serve a good appropriate only to a part of society. Neither measures up to the whole of society as a changing totality in a changing world, for this requires that, unlike the conservative, they sometimes do what they disapproved of doing yesterday, and unlike the liberal, that they sometimes do tomorrow what they did today.

Those are genuinely young, in fact if not in years, who have short histories and have not yet been chastened by experience ; they generally tend to be liberals. In contrast with them are the genuinely old who, having longer memories and colder blood—and usually some possessions to boot—tend to be conservative. There will always be the two divisions and they will always be in conflict, obvious or hidden, muted or brazen though the division be. Since it seems probable too that there will always be the clumsy and the adroit, the weak and the strong, the timid and the bold, even the rich and the poor, despite all appearance of unanimity and calm, every society will always be in some self-conflict, a place where men and practices meet in opposition.

Taken nakedly as it is, in its concreteness and in its full richness, our society is little more than a number of not entirely coordinate groups, each with its limited objective. Were there no pertinent good for all these groups, there would be nothing that one could rightly say about these groups and their different practices but that they were different, one no better than the others. We could not criticize any one of them, with justice treat it as inferior, even if it were less efficient, weaker, more conservative, more radical, or smaller than the rest. Were there no social good enabling us to evaluate different subordinate groups and thus with warrant to compare them with one another as better or worse, there would be no ground on which we could stand and prefer even our own. And were there no historically stable social morality, no ideal of civilization overarching yet pertinent to all transient social moralities and goods, there would be no basis for evaluating the different societies. Only such an ideal or some greater enables us to avoid the folly of either equating all societies and practices or arbitrarily insisting that one is better than others.

The observation is not profound. One turns expectantly therefore to writers on ethics for some reference to that ideal. The expectation is rarely and but partially realized. Throughout the ages ethics has been a subject insisting on some limited set of principles, some quite obviously limited good, characteristic of the quite limited subgroup of which, because of birth or good fortune, the authors are members and which they claimed alone expressed the ideal which all societies and all men should realize. It is indeed hard to find a work on ethics in which a number of puny principles and ideals are not advanced as absolute, right, fixed. It is evidently difficult to avoid slipping into a discussion of the duties and virtues of men, considerations which stem solely from the established practices of one's group or at best of a transitory society.

The well-born Greek aristocrat casts a permanent shadow over the ethical reflections even of a Plato and an Aristotle. These men, breathtakingly bold in so many fields, have nothing to say in defense of the poor or against the institution of slavery. Bentham and Mill, while laying down principles which they held to be applicable to all men and all times, brought into their accounts the transient views of the liberals of their day. They made much of performance and success but had little to say on behalf of good motives. Kant, anxious to deduce the whole of ethics, thought it not strange to illustrate his principles by invoking the arbitrary judgments of the Calvinistic thinkers of his day. He thought it absolutely, unqualifiedly wrong for a starving man afloat on a raft to eat a rotting can of beans to which he had no commercial claim. Today there are writers in England who stake their all on the thesis that keeping one's word is absolutely right. A decent man, in England, perhaps tends to keep his word in almost every transaction, and in the light of English customs it may be right that he should. But in other places, at diplomatic conference tables, in revolutionary times or in crises, many transactions are conducted on different grounds and sometimes with full justice to all involved. How wrong it would be for a slave or a prisoner of war to keep his word not to run away. Having been deprived of his rights by force, he can be under no compulsion except that of expedience to himself or his fellows to remain enslaved or confined. He even owes it to himself to break his word, if by that means he recovers his rightful status or is enabled to benefit his fellow man. Over and over again private property, free enterprise, and even the pursuit of pleasure or torture have been urged as eternally justifiable, absolutely right, when they did little more than reflect the practices of the ruling class. Today, in the name of democracy, men are told that what the majority decides alone is right. Dreyfus must then certainly have been guilty. We must then believe that numbers sum to some other right beyond that appropriate to numbers.

That society is to be favored most in which men are at their best; failing this, that one which makes it possible for all to attain the state of being at their best. Just what the best possible life is and what specific character a society must have in order to promote or express this is a question as difficult as it is important. Would that we could persuade one another to resist the temptation to insist on some idealized form of our social objective and try together to determine what it is that all men ought to realize. It is very hard for a man to escape his locality and his time, very hard to see his own prejudices in a clear light, particularly when they are endorsed by his friends and approved by the multitude. No one can be certain that he has himself entirely skirted the danger, that he has avoided absolutizing his own prejudices. Whether he has or not, not even the most astute of his contemporaries but only history can finally decide. Yet an effort to avoid such absolutization must be made. This is best done perhaps by keeping alert to the hints contained in passing thoughts, by attending to the views of those often not thought respectable by most, and by remembering the obvious truth that what is endorsed by oneself and friends, the majority, or even all mankind is not necessarily what ought to be. It might then be possible for more men to focus on that ideal of civilization which all societies exhibit in divergent, fragmentary, and often distorted forms.

Acknowledgment of the ideal of civilization permits an escape from the callousness which places all existent societies on a level and from the provincialism which identifies the good with what is one's own. It frees us from the embarrassment of having to say that patriotic fascists are on a par with patriotic democrats, as well as from the possible conceit which declares that only democracies have a right to be. It allows for the affirmation that one's own society is superior to others but then only so far as it is known to be more closely in conformity with the demands of the ideal. Enabling the discovery of the limitations of societies and the direction they must be pointed toward, it makes it possible to see how to improve one's society and others as well. Pertinent to all societies, it offers men an attainable ideal, alone worth their loyalty as sensitive men immersed in practical affairs. It provides a fitting objective for men who get things done and yet know that still better things can and ought to be.

The ideal of civilization can be acknowledged and yet not used. It can be made the object of hopes for men who continue to practice as they had before. Our aspirations can be considerably ennobled while our politics remain as questionable as before. Or the ideal of civilization can be insisted on in some limited version pertinent to some one society alone. The men in that society will then act better than they had but not so well as they might. The ideal of civilization must, while standing apart, serve to interrelate the limited versions of it at which different societies aim, if we are to be able to remain loyal to our own society and yet make it one of a number of different but compatible illustrations of a single good.

Every society has its own nature, its own needs, and its own aims, each exemplifying the ideal of civilization. But only those are civilized whose nature and needs are controlled by that ideal. They differ from ordinary societies somewhat as a deliberate act differs from an inadvertent one, a conscious man from a sleeping one. Both may in fact bring about the same results but only the former internally takes account of what actually hems it in, and thus though just as limited as the other, is never as frustrated.

A social *creature* has a definite station and appropriate tasks which harmonize with those of others only fortuitously or because they have been forced into concordance by some superior power. A social *being*, in contrast, guides himself by the future of his society and thus by the consideration that he is to act in accord with other men. Beyond him stands the civilized man, the man who guides himself by the ideal of a civilization which his society has yet to attain.

The civilized man is needed by society for its own good, since he alone is ready to act on behalf of the good which the society, to be perfect, in harmony with others, must embody. Despite all determinations, despite the bitter truth that society holds each of them accountable for what he does, no matter what he intends or cherishes, some men, at least, are needed by society to stand outside it, when and as they are reliable members of it. Society requires some at least of its members to be free of it and thus to be free to go beyond it and make the ideal of a civilization their own.

For society's sake the ideal of civilization should be internalized, made part of man's being, the guide and motive of his acts on what here and now confronts him. For his own sake, too, this should be done. Men should, while acting out limited roles in limited situations, make provision for what lies outside so as to be able to fill limited roles properly and yet exemplify principles which can be equally but differently exhibited elsewhere. They will then, though localized and restricted in range and effect, be able to act as men who are at home in all societies, in spirit and sometimes also in act. They will have freed themselves from the temptation to suppose only that to be right which pleases them or which makes them well-greased joints of the body politic.

Though the solution is more difficult to attain in life than it is in theory, the leading Romans managed the one and not the other. In the most diverse communities, with their different codes and practices, customs and beliefs, they remained true Romans, occupied with and realizing the selfsame good. For quite a while they kept a fine balance between ideality and practicality, refusing to immerse themselves in limited situations without regard for what might be beyond and refusing to occupy themselves with any ideal broader, more indeterminate, or more remote than that of their civilization. Using them as a guide, it is possible to make a bold, good response to the otherwise vexing question as to how men should behave in lands or in parts of their own country where some are socially and even legally discriminated against, denied common privileges and the exercise of native human rights. In a slave society no upright judge will mete out the same punishment to master and slave; if he did he would tear down the society itself and injure the slave he thought to help. But he will treat the slave as a human being, as a man deserving sympathy and consideration. It is right to fall in with the established practices but never so far as this requires a denial of the humanity of men. A man has a right to free speech, a right to worship as he wishes, provided that he thereby does not prevent other men from being human in their own way. There is a limit to tolerance as there is to every virtue; its object is to subserve the good of man, not to destroy it. And there is a limit to intolerance as there is to every irritation with what seems to be wrong; its object is to remove an ill without destroying the substance which alone makes the removal worth while.

As a rule men tend to adopt socially presented goods in the form of limited objectives characteristic of their roles or institutions. Occasionally they will adopt them as objectives pertinent to every institution but with singular relevance to their own. Ideally, they will accept them as special forms of a greater good and only then will they be able to be, while in society, more than social men.

The politically wise Romans could not possibly outlast the much less practical, unorganized, socially foolish Hebrews, their depaganized followers, and their Christian offspring. It is not possible to live happily in any variant of that most successful Roman world, for despite the beautiful balance it exhibited between tolerance and intolerance it did not note the need for man to deal with goods beyond the province of any society no matter how well civilized.

All of us know that we ought to go counter to the whole temper of our societies at times, since this temper in any but a perfect society makes impossible the realization of what ought to be. We are ill at ease the more socially comfortable we become. Man will never rest until he realizes ideals that are free from the restrictions characteristic of his time. He has a faint awareness that there are customs which are cruel and vicious, though long endured and never questioned, for he sees that he persistently overlays what is constant, general, and generic with variable, limited, and sometimes distorting features. Man is probing, restless. Instead of passively waiting for some ideal to be presented and then more or less accepting it, he darts out again and again to touch possibilities beyond those which his society expresses, and freely makes them his own.

By accepting the ideal of civilization or some subdivision or specialty of it, men turn it into a privately adopted, desirable *goal*. A goal is an external possibility which a man intends to realize by means of some existent. Not an *ultimate end*, not a totality of value justifying what is done, it is still something desired, if only as a means for getting to an ultimate end.

A man adopts a goal so that he can match from within the conditions which limit him exteriorly and thus make himself a unified, more complete being. Things about are the means by which the goal is attained. The goal justifies their selection and use, gives importance to them as means promoting what has been accepted as a good to be attained. It forces some one of these means to the fore, making it a preferred alternative.

A goal is selective, dictating what is to be used to bring itself about. It helps us to answer by decision and effort what limits us; it helps us to take cognizance of what is interplaying with us. It enables us to put aside most of the things we encounter and to concentrate on a few of the most effective means for realizing it. By deciding for ourselves what a goal is to mean to us, we make ourselves into *moral, accountable* men, men who move through the morass of contemporary fact burdened by the vision of what we would like to be and would like to have real.

IV

FREEDOM OF PREFERENCE

1. THE PARADOX OF MORAL RESPONSIBILITY

A MAN is and should be held socially accountable for whatever issues from him but he is not morally responsible unless it also originates with him. He is to be credited only with what he can put himself into, freely carve out of given material, make his very own.

A morally responsible man, like any other, is a limited, conditioned being, hemmed in, compelled. There are good reasons for whatever he does and his course can often be charted well in advance. Still he is free, a being whom nothing can make decide this way or that. Both statements seem absurd. If there is a reason why he does this rather than that, there is a reason why he does not do otherwise. A reason compelling the selection of x is a reason preventing the selection of what is not x, and therefore a reason why the selection of x is not free and he not responsible for it. Whatever reasons there be which compel a decision are reasons which prevent men from assuming the burden of responsibility for what they plan to do. If there be a reason for the decisions men make they are neither free nor responsible for those decisions and thus do not really make the decisions themselves. What compels a decision to go one way rather than another defines a man to be only a place, an occasion in which a decision can be made by a conflux of predetermined elements, not a being who forges a decision, who acts creatively. But on the other hand, if men could be free to select one thing rather than another, regardless of all conditions, causes, appetites, reasons, what is their freedom but caprice? Their decisions, because not the outcome of a prior state of affairs, because not compelled by any force or reason, would be undetermined, arbitrary, having only an adventitious relation to what they in fact are, what they want, and to what is happening in the world about. But then how could they be responsible for their decisions? Decisions which have nothing to do with what a man is, wants, or can obtain, which alight on alternatives having no relevance to what has been or is to be, are decisions over which a man has no control and which cannot be credited to him.

A responsible man is one who freely determines what is to be. He both originates and controls that for which he is responsible. If he originates nothing he is too determined, if he controls nothing he is too amorphous to be responsible. Were he to originate or control everything, on the other hand, he would be responsible, but as a god and not as a man. A responsible man is a limited one, a confined one, who is neither compelled nor capricious. Nothing provides a sufficient reason making him alight on this alternative or that; nothing is so indifferent to him that he can indifferently alight on it without regard for what it is and what he might have done.

We are both conditioned and free. But if conditioned we seem not free enough to be responsible for what we decide; if not conditioned we seem too free to be responsible for what we decide. In either way it seems impossible to say that we are responsible men, men who freely but for good reasons select what we do.

Unquestionably, men favor one thing when here and another when there, one when in this society and another in that, one thing when trained in such and such habits early, another when trained late. We incline one way when ill and another when well, one way when young and another when old. We express ourselves with a rhythm, a strength characteristic of us, as men with just these histories and in just these positions.

Yet no man is an automatic saint or sinner, a mere creature of force or impulse or even of character and mind. Honored for benefits he bestowed, criticized and punished for injuries traceable to him, he knows at times he did wrong in one case and not in the other on his own responsibility. He knows there are times when he acted freely in the face of what he had been taught and trained to do. He knows he is not entirely in the grip of any power, whether this be a government outside or a disposition or character within. His decisions are not forced by what is past or present; they are not functions of, mere creatures of, any existent state of affairs, of possibilities or actualities, private or public. He can defy and deny society and all its works. He can become a malefactor or a conformist, pacifist or warrior, mystic or petty bourgeois, and act as more than a function of time and place, ancestor and past achievements. Did men but unavoidably echo what they had heard, transmuted automatically though it be perhaps by them a little, who is it that can tell us that this is so? Could any but a free man, one who deliberately and responsibly accepts some assertion as his very own, say significantly that all men are in the iron grip of conditions within and without? He who speaks significantly speaks responsibly. If he cavils or if he lies, he does so freely. What he offers as true he offers as something for us to consider on its merits; he does not present it as a compulsive cause to effect whatever it may. Truths can be offered only to men who are free to accept or reject them. Unfree men might be able to say "yes" to them and nod as if they approved, but they would not be able to adopt them, to accept them as their own. The denial of man's freedom is a denial of man's responsibility; it wipes out in its utterance the possibility that it be a truth that men can offer to one another for adoption.

He who insists that men are free acknowledges that men are more than reservoirs of past conditioning. He allows that they can decide which one of a set of alternatives is to be selected; he grants that they are free to utilize dynamically, in an unconditioned way, whatever it is that conditions them. But he risks losing hold of the truth that men are molded by training and are dated in speech, clothing, work, idea, image, aspiration, fear, and hope. This truth is as important as the other. We should not be satisfied with less than both.

We are free to select any alternative, yet there are reasons for our selecting what we do. We can intend otherwise than we now do, but we do intend as men who are, want, and have undergone specific things. We are neither free from all conditioning nor inexorably bound. We have neither too much nor too little freedom. We have just enough to be responsible.

As a rule we follow our inclinations. These have, in the main, been forged under pressure over which we have had little control. He who knows us can often make a shrewd guess as to which one of a given set of alternatives will have the most appeal for us and thus which one we will most likely prefer over all others. But he can never be sure just which one we will in fact prefer, for it is we who determine which alternative will have the greatest appeal; it is we who decide whether what is most likely to be preferred by us will be preferred by us in fact.

2. INGREDIENT AND DERIVED APPEAL

We are quadruply conditioned—twice from without and twice from within. We are hemmed in both by future possibilities and contemporary actualities and we deal with them from the vantage point of established characters and transient dispositions. The possibilities and actualities dictate what is the range of material with which we shall deal; our character and dispositions dictate what items in those ranges we shall find most appealing and therefore what it is with which we shall in fact deal.

At every moment some one of a set of alternative things or acts appeals to us more than the others do. It answers to our natures, native and acquired; we incline toward it, favor it. Perhaps that toward which we now lean should be rejected. Perhaps it is beyond our power to use; perhaps it is bad for us and for others. Whatever the truth about it be, the fact is that we do favor it and not something else; it and not something else appeals to us. Were we of different natures, had we been trained differently, we might have favored something other than what we now do. But favor something we always do.

We favor one thing more than others for a reason. It appeals to us more than any other does. No two objects could possibly appeal to us to exactly the same extent unless they could be on all points interchangeable, duplicating one another in every respect in relation to us—unless we could be in the position of the hungry ass who, as the old poser has it, was placed equidistant from two bales of hay and who, because they had exactly the same appeal to him, could decide in favor of neither and therefore starved to death. But the situation supposed could not possibly occur. An ass inclined no more toward one bale than toward another would have to be perfectly symmetrical in body; wind, sun, and shadows would have to be eliminated; there could be nothing on one side which was not precisely duplicated on the other. And every twofold bodily tendency would have to be repeated in the form of twofold mental tendencies. Such prerequisites reveal that the imagined ass is an imaginary, not a real, ass.

No one knows what an ass thinks about, if anything. But if there ever were two bales of hay which were equal in every respect, and if he did not lean in the slightest toward one more than toward the other, to the right, say, rather than to the left, to the one nearer the tree rather than toward the one farther from the tree, the ass would undoubtedly starve to death. But that would be because he was even more asinine than an ass has a right to be. No man, in any case, could be in such a predicament. No man is perfectly symmetrical in body, in disposition, in orientation. Left and right have a different import for him; background makes a difference; there are thousands of associations which endow one of two quite similar things with a greater appeal for him. He is never faced with alternatives which appeal to him equally; at most he faces alternatives having an equal appeal in this or that respect or alternatives that appear to have an equal appeal though they actually appeal to him unequally. And so far as alternatives are equal, he has the power to make them unequal.

We necessarily select the alternative which appeals most. It is this that we find most desirable. Not to select it would be to turn instead toward what does not beckon to us as much and therefore cannot, except arbitrarily, be taken instead. Only because sitting appeals more than walking do we now rather sit than walk. We may subsequently find that it was a mistake to sit; walking should have appealed to us more perhaps. But here and now it is sitting that appeals, and just so far as it does we can do nothing else but favor it over walking.

The alternative with the greatest appeal is the alternative we always select. This would preclude our being free to select any other alternative were it not possible for us to add freely to the appeal which an alternative initially possesses. An alternative possessing an initial slight or even negative appeal can have its appeal increased until it is greater than the appeal of any other alternative. The increase is due to us and us alone, the outcome of the creative exercise of native freedom. Let us not ask for the moment whether or not we capriciously select the alternative whose appeal is to be increased or whether or not we add appeals without guidance or control. The questions must be asked and must be answered. For the moment let us be content with remarking that though we must take the alternative with the greatest appeal, we are not compelled to select any particular alternative since it is up to us freely to determine just what comparative degree of appeal an alternative is to have.

The alternative actually preferred is an alternative which compels. We have to select it, for it is the alternative which has the greatest appeal. This appeal, though, is a product of two appeals, an *ingredient* and a *derived*. The ingredient appeal is that which the alternative possessed initially; it is one over which we then and there have no control. It answers to the nature we have; it is the correlative of our capacity to select and adopt; it expresses the nature of our conditional local freedom. The derived appeal, in contrast, owes its being to a dynamically free act of ours. It is an appeal derived from a possibility by creatively turning it into an individual goal.

The act of adopting a possibility and thereby turning it into a goal is an act inseparable from that in which the appeal of the goal is added to the appeal of presented alternatives. Because we approach all alternatives as possible means to an adopted goal, we are in a position to add to their ingredient appeal something of the appeal of that goal. By treating them as possible means, we place the alternatives in a new context. We subject them all to a new condition; we allow them to acquire additional appeals to the degree that they accord with the requirements of the goal. Whichever one of them will turn out to have a greater total appeal than all the others will necessarily be selected. Compelled though we are to select it because it has the greatest appeal, we are nevertheless responsible for selecting it, for it is always up to us freely to determine just which alternative is to be made most appealing by the goal. It is we alone who determine just how to subject alternatives to the influence of a possibility in the form of an appealing though not necessarily worthy goal and thus dictate which alternative is to have the status of an accepted means.

We identify ourselves with our goals in various degrees, giving them the status of accepted (but not final) goods, demanding realization. The goals help us determine which of a number of possible means will be preferred. A change in the way we freely adopt a goal will compel us to prefer a different means among the same set of alternatives. It is ourselves alone who determine what degree of appeal a goal is to add to the alternatives. We are pivotal points standing between and relating an ideal possibility and present things. We are agencies by which both the future and the present are made mutually relevant and thereby more determinate than they had been. Without the means the goal would be but a vague fancy; without the goal the means would be but stuff encountered. We bring the two together, enabling the goal to acquire body and a genuine hope of achievement and enabling the means to acquire an instrumental value and the dignity of being preferred over others, and thus to be true goals and true means. We change the future into a privately accepted, determining goal while making the present into a means for realizing that goal. Through our agency the ideal bestows on some alternative a new dignity, a new value, new functions, raising it to the status of a means which we must select because we have adopted as our own the goal which it promotes. Through our agency a thing bestows on a goal the status of something to be realized; the selected alternative supports the goal, allows it a grip on muscular fact.

In the process of enhancing both alternative and goal, we too become enhanced. By identifying ourselves with the possibility which controls us from beyond and by accepting as means the things that now hem us in from without, we become effective beings, men who are in themselves a little more in accord with what they are externally compelled to be. Far from perfect, we sometimes radically distort the possibility when making it into a goal or radically deny ourselves by taking certain objects as means. Far worse off than we were before, far worse off perhaps than we would have been had we been fully determined by exterior forces, we are still men who have in part remade our possibilities, some of our contemporaries, and ourselves. We freely bring the good within ourselves to make it sometimes a lure to folly; we freely increase the appeal an alternative has to make it sometimes a mischievous means; we freely relate the two wrongly to make ourselves sources of avoidable evil. Whether we make for better or for worse, we help determine what our goals will be and help define what alternative will irresistibly appeal.

The more firmly we cling to a goal, the more appeal does it bestow on the alternatives we face; the more fitted an alternative is to promote a goal, the more surely does it achieve that maximum appeal which makes it preferred. If we turn halfheartedly toward a goal, we add little to the ingredient appeal alternatives have, apart from that goal, and will most likely do what we were originally inclined to do. If an alternative is not suited to bring about our goal, no matter how attractive it may otherwise be, it will not appeal to us as men occupied with that goal, and we will unhappily but certainly abandon it for some other. We would have no decision to make, having made our decision already.

A goal defines all the alternatives to be possible means to it. It is a sun shining with different intensity on different places but shining on them all nevertheless. Those that are themselves quite luminous will shine bright though far away; those with little or no light of their own will shine brighter than the rest if only brought close enough to the source of all light. Each alternative has relation to the goal; each can help bring the goal about in a different context and along a different route than that which is essential to the others. By adopting the goal in one way, with one intensity rather than another, some alternative is selected that would not have been selected otherwise as being most fitted to promote that goal. It may be the case that some other alternative would promote the goal much better, but the goal as accepted with such and such a degree of determination denies that it is the alternative to be preferred, that it is the alternative most suited now.

The goal's appeal is offered to all the alternatives as capable of promoting it somehow. But only one alternative is actually *preferred*, accepted as more suited to bring about the goal than the others. Only one is actually *selected*, attended to while the rest are neglected; only one is actually *intended*, responsibly focused on as that which we will endeavor to use—preference, selection, and intention being but three phascs of a single process, expressing the same result from the vantage point of the goal, the individual, and the two together.

A goal is brought to bear on all alternatives freely in an act which endows some one alternative with a maximum appeal and thereby compels its selection. Once we have decided how much weight the goal is to have for us, there is only one alternative we could possibly select. But there is no necessity, before the decision has been made, that just that alternative be selected. We could have adopted the goal with a different emphasis; there is nothing in the goal or our natures which specifies what is to occur when these two come face to face. Because we could have done this, we are men who can freely prefer, freely select, freely intend, even when we do what was expected of us by all. And we know we could have done this, we know that we are free to take any alternative whatsoever, for we know that we are active, creative when we prefer.

Preferences don't happen; we do not sit idle watching possibility and alternatives collide within our minds or with our hopes. We make the one pertinent to the other by treating one as goal and the other as possible means in conformity with principles which govern the acts of all. All activity in time is creative, free, imposing determinations on indeterminate future possibilities. When we turn a possibility into a goal we determine it by giving it something of ourselves. We freely dictate to ourselves, through the agency of the goal, what it is we will prefer, select, intend.

The preferred alternative always has the greatest total, not necessarily the greatest ingredient appeal. An alternative with little or no positive ingredient appeal may therefore be preferred to one with a great ingredient appeal. If it is, we will continue to incline toward, to like, to want, to be tempted by the alternative with the great ingredient appeal. We will accept the other alternative not because we want it, not for its own sake, but for the sake of the goal we have adopted. Free action has inescapable consequences, as those who pull triggers often belatedly discover. When we pull the trigger of acceptance of a goal we set in motion the determination of some alternative as superior to others in appeal. We thereby compel a preference for it as surely as we compel the death of this man rather than that by the manner and time we freely pull the trigger of a gun.

The goal we adopt and the alternative it helps us select are for us, then and there, most desirable. From the vantage point of our own needs, in terms of the rights of others or in the light of an absolute standard, neither goal nor alternative might be worth adopting. A goal is a limited, appealing objective by means of which we determine what alternative is to be preferred. It is not necessarily desirable and it is not ultimate. It is merely the objective we adopt so far as we are socially conditioned beings; what we prefer because of it is not necessarily choiceworthy, objectively right or best; it is only what for us is the best means to that goal.

What is preferred may be preferred with annoyance, repugnance, reluctantly, since it may have little ingredient appeal. It may not be what should be preferred; it may not be what is appropriate for men socially conditioned in this way or that. We are conditioned beings, but what we prefer is not a product of our conditioning, even when we prefer in consonance with that conditioning.

Sometimes we select repugnant alternatives. We take bitter medicine to get well, preferring it to other alternatives because its total appeal is greater than theirs. If we did not adopt the goal of getting well, our bodies would spew out the medicine without ado. For its own good we make the body drink and swallow what it finds repugnant. And we can do this because we are more than bodies, because we can privately, responsibly, and freely adopt the goal of health and thereby dictate that medicine should be selected over much more tempting alternatives.

3. THE ART OF PREFERENCE

Any one of a set of alternatives may be intended whether or not it has little or no ingredient appeal. If we favor fishing over hunting, if we incline toward the prospect of seeing fish struggle on hooks rather than toward the prospect of seeing animals shot while on the run, we can nevertheless envisage hunting in such a way as to make it preferred to fishing. If we could not do this, we could not avoid intending to fish when hunting was the other alternative.

Though hunting may not appeal to us as much as fishing does, there are times when we will prefer hunting to fishing. When animals run wild, endangering the lives of men and fish, even the most ardent fisherman among us is ready to lay down his line and take up his gun. Fishermen prefer to hunt in such a case, not because hunting has more ingredient appeal for them than fishing but because it is more appealing when it is viewed as a means for attaining the adopted goal of eventual peaceful fishing.

Peaceful fishing is a possibility which a man's nature, his environment, and training might make him favor as a goal. But it is up to him to decide how to adopt it as a good, how to identify himself with it.

Inclined though he might be toward fishing, his identification of himself with the goal of eventual peaceful fishing will make him concentrate on hunting as the preferred alternative now. Were the fisherman only a tissue of inclinations, with an inclination toward fishing dominant, he would be able to do nothing but fish. Since he is free to adopt a goal in countless ways, he can, however, assess his various inclinations and end by selecting any. He could use the goal of eventual peaceful fishing so that it involves him now but little and as a consequence he could avoid preferring to hunt at present. The decision is his and his alone. Precisely because he must freely and responsibly decide the question of what effect his goal is to have for him, it is he and he alone who freely and responsibly decides which alternative to take.

In exercising his freedom of preference the fisherman reconstitutes himself. He escapes from the conditioning which makes him incline toward fishing rather than hunting by making himself the bearer of a goal. No longer is he under the necessity of following the bent of his inclinations. He may follow them or conform to them or he may go directly counter to their insistent counsel. Able to dedicate himself to the realization of his goal with different degrees of intensity, he makes himself into a purposive being who endows this or that alternative with a derived appeal in addition to what it has ingrediently. He freely anticipates the future, brings it to realization now—not in act, to be sure, but in intent—as a good to be realized through the agency of this means or that.

While reconstituting himself the fisherman transforms his goal. He changes it from an *acceptable* into an *accepted* determinant of his actions, from what he would like to have real into what he pledges himself to try to make real. The change is neither capricious nor compelled; it is freely produced. Were it not possible for the change to occur, his goal would be as indeterminate at the end as it was in the beginning; it would be a general possibility to which all alternatives would be equally pertinent as possible means. Were the change from acceptable to accepted goal forced on the fisherman, whether by an external power or by his own inherited or acquired temperament, he would have goals given to and taken from him regardless of any determination on his part. His would not be true goals but fixed ideas imposed on him for a while and controlling his activities. The fisherman who hunted would be a compulsive hunter, in the control of the overpowering thought that there should be eventual peaceful fishing; he would not hunt in order to realize the goal of fishing. He would not be a normal fisherman with a family, country, ambition, hopes, who freely changed his activities from time to time but a mad machine made and broken by circumstance.

Living men are men who decide how much influence their goals are to exert and therefore what they are to select; sane men are men who freely reject goals they had accepted when these are found to lead to the selection of intolerable alternatives. Because fishermen no less than the rest of us are both living and sane, they can and do freely determine just how they are to accept as goals whatever possibilities they now confront.

While reconstituting himself and his goal a man reconstitutes the alternatives he faces. In the beginning his alternatives are blindly competitive, unequally appealing objects of inclinations. At the end they are unequal, too, but as means to a freely adopted goal. The inequality at the end may differ considerably from the inequality that existed at the beginning; what was favored initially may not be that which is favored finally. To suppose that a change in the status of the alternatives does not occur is to suppose that a fisherman is a creature of his inclinations, that he cannot avoid hunting even though he changes his relation toward his goal of eventual peaceful fishing.

New prospects change the temper of the fisherman as they do all men; circumstance and opportunity help force new inclinations to the fore. Still, it is the fisherman alone who can say how much effect the new prospects are to have on him and thus how much he must yield to his inclinations. If we ignore the effort which he makes to insist on his goal, we will be bound to say with the determinists that everything but the fisherman makes a difference to what the fisherman does. The fisherman lives in time and carves out a route that never was there before, though the structure of it might well be expressed in laws and the outcome of it might be predicted by and large. Like every other being he creates the future that is to be, imposing determinations on abstract possibilities. He does this not only through action in a public world but privately as well, adopting a possibility in the shape of a goal and thereby turning one of many preferable alternatives into a preferred, a selected, an intended one.

The fisherman freely reconstitutes himself, his goal, and his alternatives. He makes himself into a purposive being, makes his goal into a determinate and determining part of himself, and makes some one alternative into a preferred means. He does this in fresh, creative acts which are not, and thus are not available for knowledge, until they have been gone through. The act is no blind reorganizing process, occurring within the unfathomable depths of his being. Freedom is not beyond the reach of denial or affirmation, a something-we-know-not-what which must be presupposed in order that an ethics be possible. Nor is it contingency, the absence of necessitation. It is not chance or spontaneity, caprice or unchartered routes which are actually honeycombed with undiscovered law. It is an intelligible process by which the indeterminate, the possible, the future, the good, is made determinate, actual, present; it is an activity by which the general is specified, specialized, delimited, given one of a number of possible concrete shapes. Preference is but one of its many modes.

Preference is a creative, readjustive activity in which goals and means are made mutually determinate. Like every other process it takes time and presupposes an agent imposing determinations on and thereby realizing future possibilities. It can no more be reduced to its conditions than reasoning can be reduced to reasons, movement to rest, becoming to being. It has a nature of its own, but of course only when and as it takes place. We can understand well enough where it started, where it goes, and how it exhibits in a special form the freedom characteristic of every temporal being.

Unless we are to say that fish and rainbows, walks and watches, skipping and eating are unintelligible, we have no warrant in principle for supposing that preference is so. Though preference occurs within the recesses of a man and though it involves a possible defiance of long-intrenched expectations, it has a structure which men can know, though only when it actually is available for knowledge. We can know what that structure is, in general, in a speculative inquiry; but to know it in the concrete we must watch an act of preference being exercised by a living man.

Man is an architect, an engineer, an artist, a molder, a maker of himself. What he uses for material is given to him, but the way he uses it is decided by himself alone. There is no predetermined direction in which he must turn, no decision he must make before he in fact decides. But having remolded himself, dictated to himself the place a goal is to have in his economy, he cannot avoid the consequences; he selects this alternative, not that.

Since it is man who decides just how much weight his knowledge is to have for him, he can know the good and yet intend the wrong. But having embraced the good he knows, he cannot avoid intending whatever is for him a means to bring that goal about. He thus both can and cannot do wrong knowingly. An animal, in contrast, has no ability to reconstitute itself, to give itself a goal, to intend something freely, though it acts freely in time, publicly determining relevant possibilities in concretely novel ways. It must pursue that alternative to which it is most inclined; it has no power to decide how much weight to give to a goal, no power to decide for itself just which alternative it is to pursue.

An animal is unable to mold itself. What it does, even when guided by knowledge or insight, even when flexible and adroit, is what it could not possibly avoid. It is never free enough to be responsible; that is why it can be completely trained. We may punish it as a way of training it further, but to judge it as somehow wicked or virtuous is as sensible as judging a stone for having split or a tree for having grown.

Animals can learn to do automatically what men can do only by calling on a fallible power of preference. And what animals learn they usually can apply. Their inward leanings come readily to outward expression. But these very advantages make animals both unprepared for the novelties of existence and unable to live inwardly; they cannot enjoy in imagination what might be impossible for them to have in fact. Having no power to prefer freely, animals cannot, like men, increase their stature by taking thought, ennoble themselves by forging good intentions in the privacy of their being. Better adjusted than men, they have no occasion to hold themselves responsible for what they might never bring about in fact.

Freedom of preference is an exclusively human power. But it is not employed at every stage of a man's career. Embryos, infants, and idiots, adults when asleep or in a stupor do not exercise it. These but vaguely grasp external possibilities; if they internalize the possibilities, they internalize them automatically and to a predesignatable extent. Active adults focus more sharply on the possibilities they confront, but they often fail to internalize those possibilities with sufficient flexibility. All of us somewhat spasmodically vary the manner in which we tentatively adopt our goals, stopping finally at one place rather than another more out of impatience than out of judgment. We examine not all but a few of the alternatives available; we express rather than reconstitute ourselves, forge decisions on insufficient evidence, and thus fall into routines, even when for our own good a radical fresh decision is imperative.

The exercise of a freedom of preference is not difficult. It is indeed but little for a man to do. Precipitate, not judicious; irritable, not considerate; reactive, not responsive; unimaginative, not perceptive —we exercise our freedom at arbitrary times and within arbitrary limits. We are internally but part of what we have been forced to become from without. Taken as we are and not as we ought to be, we are discontinuously free men, and in a double sense. Firstly, we are free to prefer only part of the time, and secondly, only with reference to a broken series of occurrences. Neither discontinuity is essential. A mature man will continuously focus on a goal in a genuinely experimental spirit, tentatively and continuously varying the manner in which he insists on it until he finds that point where, without doing too much violence to himself or his objects, he actually selects what the goal defines to be the best of the available means. The glory of our age is that there are so many men who are mature; the tragedy of humanity, a ground for cynicism and despair, is the apparently inconquerable, bitter truth that only a fraction of mankind is, even for short spans, what all can in principle be continuously.

Preference is an act of the self, not of the mind, though it usually begins and ends with known goals and means. It is possible to a man because he has an ambivalent relationship to the future. From the start he both holds on to it as the distant object of his concern and accepts it as a pertinent good. He is incomplete, in disequilibrium. His effort to complete himself makes him try to internalize and realize the future privately. Should he thus succeed in internalizing the future, he will succeed in completing himself only in part, for he will but prepare himself for the realization of his needed good in actuality.

Preference, because it is a way of seizing, utilizing, and determining a possibility, is a way of getting to the future ahead of time while still actually in the present. It allows us to condition ourselves inwardly as we are being conditioned outwardly; it still leaves us incomplete. To be fully complete we must act as well as prefer, and then in such a way as to realize the good in ourselves and others.

Under the compulsion of a drive to complete himself a man is forced to adopt some goal somehow and to some extent, and thus to determine what alternative to prefer. Freely produced, the act of preference is thus forced on him; it is an act he cannot avoid engaging in. It might have started with a different goal or ended with a different alternative. Whether it does or not, its outcome is necessary since it is the product of the definite adoption of a goal by a definite man in a definite set of circumstances. Freedom is always ringed by necessity. It is necessitated and necessitates. It involves the use of unavoidable material to produce what must be.

Freedom of preference is a freedom seriously confined. The goal it uses as the final determinant of what is to be done and the alternatives among which the preference must be exercised represent but a segment of what there is. Goals are not ultimate ends and preferred means are not always most choiceworthy. Freedom of preference does not take account of all the values involved in a situation. It is also a freedom which does less than freedom might. What we do in public is no bare extroversion of what we intend; our accomplishments depend at least as much on what the world demands as on what our goals prescribe and we intend. Many preferences never come to expression and most actions distort somewhat the preferences they express, thereby revealing the transformative power of a partly alien body and an environing world.

Because it allows itself to be challenged, defied, determined by the body and the world, freedom of preference must be constricted considerably from within to enable it to answer adequately the circumstances conditioning us from every side. Then and then only will it be possible to transform it into broader, richer, more satisfactory forms of freedom, enabling us to come closer to the end of our perpetual struggle to be men.

V

REASONABLE PREFERENCES

1. Wish and Approval

OUR goals bear the marks of place and caste, as the Marxists have made so clear. But they are our own. And as the Freudians insist, the way we cling to our goals reveals something of our most private natures. Yet they are more than extroverted introversions. Because he neglects the personal note, the Marxist cannot account for what he himself would acknowledge as his own high morality and great courage in accepting the Marxist ideal in a non-Marxist world. Reciprocally, Freudianism, because it neglects the external component of preference, makes it impossible to account for the perspicacity and resolute objectivity toward the truth which the Freudian presumably incorporates. Neither allows for both wishes and preferences, the impotent and the powerful, the determined and the free. Neither allows for true decisions, for the free selection of alternatives.

To approve a goal is to desire to make it real, to use it to dictate the preferential selection of some alternative as a proper means to it; it is to adopt it, insist on it, to intend, to prepare to do what it prescribes. When we adopt a goal without reflection we approve of it no less surely than when we adopt it with reflection, for we just as truly subject ourselves to it voluntarily. Quite often though we hide this sort of adoption from ourselves by thinking at the same time on some nobler objective, on one more in consonance perhaps with what someone else endorses. When we do this we adopt one goal but wish for another. The wished goal will serve to draw our attention away from the goal we have adopted. We will then admire high ideals but prepare to bring about something else, perhaps even what these ideals disown.

Reluctant to give up alternatives toward which we are most inclined, we are tempted to adopt those goals which require the selection of those alternatives, and to content ourselves with wishing whatever goals are socially or ethically endorsed. In this way we win for ourselves the questionable joy of admiring what we think we ought to promote and the doubtful joy that comes from an indulgence in our inclinations. We become self-indulgent men who, warmed by the idea of doing good, do what we like.

The self-indulgent man allows his inclinations to dictate to him just how he is to hold to a goal. He not only refuses to adopt whatever goal prevents him from selecting what his inclinations favor but he uses it to hide from himself whatever goal he does adopt. He says to himself that his goal is the laudable one of being friendly and that this requires him to be brutally frank. But he merely wishes, he does not desire, to be friendly; he adopts not friendliness but whatever goal there may be which allows him to speak his mind. The idea of being friendly is his excuse and opportunity for denying to himself that he is a willing creature of his inclinations.

No man is ever entirely free of this fault. None wholeheartedly approves of all the goals he happens to focus on, no matter how widely and thoroughly endorsed they be by the rest. All indulge themselves somewhat. Yet none gives way entirely to his inclinations; all pay some attention to what society wants and try to restrain their inclinations accordingly. What is finally intended is not too dissimilar from that which was initially favored, but it is sufficiently different to make evident that it was prescribed by a goal somewhat like the one which was socially sanctioned. Men's decisions are the outcome of efforts which take some account of the demands of socially approved goals as well as of the demands of the inclinations.

It is rare for men to conform completely to society, rare for them to indulge themselves wholly. Instead they forge and approve goods enabling them to stand somewhere in between. Men are governed partly by society and partly by their inclinations. They are geared to promote the common good and tensed to promote their own. That is why they can be lived with and can live with themselves.

When sages urge us to defy our inclinations, to prefer alternatives with little ingredient appeal, they but tacitly urge us to adopt some goal which makes such defiance imperative. The advice is idle if nothing is done to make that new goal desirable. A man's preferences cannot be changed by telling him that a goal has been endorsed by others, that its adoption would benefit him, or that it will make him a better or a happier man. He must be taught to see in it a worth which warrants his adopting it. The advice of the sages is mischievous if the recommended goal is inferior to the goal that a man tends to adopt. A goal compelling the denial of what everyone wants and enjoys is surely inferior to others, unless, which seems incredible, all inclinations ought always to be suppressed. The sages' advice is good only because it underscores a suspicion, justified by experience, that we are not always inclined as we should be, and that by following our inclinations we usually do not adopt, but only wish, the goods we call ideal.

In changing circumstances a man must change the manner in which he adopts his goal, for to realize the same goal different things must be done in different circumstances, and this requires the goal to compel the adoption of new means. He who opposes his inclinations all the time cannot cling in a steady way to the selfsame goal. His opposition would require him to reject a previously adopted goal again and again in favor of others whose presence he may never acknowledge to himself. He would be forced again and again to wish his originally adopted goal and actually adopt some other, for in this way only can he persistently oppose his inclinations. The more steadily opposed to his inclinations he is, the more irresolute and self-deceived will he be with respect to the goal he wants to reach.

The inclinations do not form a fixed set, unchangeable in number, power, comparable force, and import; they are not always wrongly directed; they do not always operate in the same ways. They ought sometimes to be followed, sometimes to be defied.

2. DELIBERATENESS AND DECISIVENESS

Wish can serve as a cover for self-indulgence; it enables one to attend apparently to some ideal objective and yet actually pursue another goal. It is the wishing, not the nature of the objective wished, that allows inclinations their head. Some other objective could be wished instead, without affecting the fact that when we wish, some unnoted goal is actually approved and used to make us select some object toward which we were antecedently inclined.

When we wish we hold a prospect in suspense because we are adopting some competing goal. When we deliberate we also hold some prospect in suspense, but for a different reason. Having already adopted a goal which demands that we change the alternatives we face, we deliberate because we are in doubt as to which one of these alternatives we should take in order to realize some subordinate goal. We seek something which, apart from the subordinate goal or our inclinations, makes one of the alternatives deserve to be selected.

He who hesitates is not lost. He seeks a way of setting off one alternative from the rest and prepares himself to select it as a means to the subordinate goal now held in suspension. Hesitation, as an integral part of the act of deliberation, is a way of picking out a means for a goal not yet adopted, a way of prescribing to just what degree that goal is to be made one with ourselves.

Desiring to go to town, we must decide at the fork whether to take the right or the left road. The right may be that toward which we are inclined because of its foliage, because we are in the habit of turning to the right, because it is shaded, and for a hundred different reasons which determine us effectively despite our unawareness of them. We will take the right if we merely follow our inclinations or if we guide ourselves by the goal of going to town. But we may have antecedently adopted some such distant goal as being reasonable men or men on the side of good fortune, and have viewed going to town as a subordinate, intermediate goal. The distant goal would require us to take only that road to town which was supported by a reason or was favored by good fortune. It would require us to hold in suspension the subordinate goal of going to town until we have found the reason, tossed a coin, rolled dice, etc., and thereby made one of the roads more appealing than the others.

The road supported by reason or chance may be the left. Supported though it may be by reasons or chance in just the way we wanted it to be, it need not be followed. We do not have to take the left road; we could take the right instead. If we do, we make manifest that we had already preferred the right road, that we sought our reason or tossed our coin not in order to make a decision possible but to confirm or hide a decision already made. We would not be men who were hesitant or undecided but men who had adopted as their distant goal one which demanded that we find excuses in reason or luck for what some already accepted subordinate goal demands.

Unlike periods in which excuses are sought for preferences already made, periods of hesitation and indecision are times when factors are sought and added to given alternatives so as to change their appeal. They are times when, under pressure of the distant goal to make a decision among apparently equal alternatives, we refuse to adopt a goal until we have found some way of sharply remarking some one alternative as a satisfactory means to it. They are times when a distant goal is adopted so as to make preferable a refusal to decide between presented alternatives. Since no one can hesitate or doubt without living, all of us when we hesitate and doubt must have, at least tacitly, adopted a goal of living which makes the search for reasons or for signs of good fortune preferable to an immediate selection of some presented alternative.

Hamlet's question was not "to be or not to be." That question was already decided. A decision to debate the question is a decision to be for a while. Hamlet's question was "Is there a better reason for being than for not being?" Having adopted the goal, "living as a rational being," he was led to seek a reason which would make suicide or continuance the preferable alternative, regardless of his inclinations. He could have decided not to seek a reason, and therefore to live or die depending on which alternative happened to be favored at the moment by his inclinations in the circumstances. But instead he decided to seek a reason and to live while looking for it. He found a reason which made continuance the preferred alternative. That alternative might not have been the one toward which he was most inclined. He might have been most inclined to commit suicide. He decided to continue not because (were this the case) he was inclined to do so but because reason supported this alternative for him, a rational being whose father had been murdered.

Doubt and hesitation are unpleasant and unwanted states we try to bring to a close by decisions. Forced on us because we have already adopted a goal which does not allow us to deal with alternatives in their presented form, they compel us to look outside the presented alternatives for something which would make one of them preferable to the others, regardless of the ingredient appeal it might have. At times of crises and in emergencies it is better not to doubt or hesitate; at those times it is better to decide directly and at once to take whatever alternative some adopted, limited goal requires for its realization.

Men well cushioned against the world make a virtue of deliberation, hesitation, and even skepticism. Those whose backs are against the wall make a virtue, instead, of their ability to reach a quick decision. The deliberate man wants to do what is more intelligible, reasonable, fruitful either by itself or through its connection with something else known, approved, or wanted. The decisive man wants to sharpen and perhaps change the alternatives he faces. He who is deliberate cherishes relevance, objectivity; he who is decisive cherishes rapidity, action. It is desirable to have both and thus to be men who are at once reflective and effective.

In mathematics and in law, in logic and in philosophy, in science and in history, the reason for a decision is usually more important than the decision itself. What is wanted is something that can be used again and again. We there stress principles, rules, universals, explanations, using the decision primarily as an occasion for the reason to be manifest. But in practical affairs, when lives and goods are at stake, it is usually more important to make a decision with respect to presented alternatives on any grounds than it is to find a good reason for making it in one way rather than another. The individual case is of paramount importance here, not the principle in terms of which it is decided.

It would be foolish to decide a metaphysical question by following inclinations or by submitting to the dictate of even such a broad goal as that of the happy life of civilized men. A reason is wanted, some warrant for the alternative we take, beyond the appeal it makes to us and besides its power to promote the actualization of the ideals of our society or the solution of this or that limited problem which, for the moment, happens to be to the fore. On the other hand, it would be foolish to hunt for a reason why one should save one's brother rather than one's sister when a fire has trapped them both. A decision is wanted.

We are deliberate at one time, decisive at another; one or the other we must always be. Even when idle or irresponsible we take one or the other position, deciding for our present activity or using it to promote the next. Even to float with the current, to take what comes, requires of us a constant decision to accept what happens. The decision need not be consciously forged or known when it takes place; it is the outcome of our need to be, not of our capacity to be conscious or to know.

Since we deliberate to find a satisfactory support for some alternative, and since we can never obtain all the data that would be pertinent to the issue, in a sense all our hesitations and doubts are grounded in a decision. We are all decisive men varying only in the amount of time we spend in search for a few more relevant characteristics which will help mark off more conspicuously one of the alternatives from the rest. We are always effective to some extent, for better or worse. We differ from one another largely in the degree of our effectiveness and in the way and the extent our effectiveness is altered by our deliberations.

As a rule men do not try to see how much support they can find for each of their alternatives; men rarely in quiet and with care decide as genuinely rational beings or as clearly on the side of fortune. Decisions are usually made on the run, in incomplete abstraction from the pressure of the inclinations. Man is not wholeheartedly rational but rational only to some extent, willing to settle his score with fortune by taking as sufficient the evidence of a rolling die or a horoscope hastily cast. And this is as it should be, for otherwise he risks putting off decisions endlessly and thereby at every moment in fact deciding to do what he was most inclined to do.

Those who pride themselves on their rationality too often have an excess of leisure and seek an excuse for not deciding issues. While insisting that they want to weigh every case carefully and to examine both sides dispassionately, they eat and sleep, work and play in consonance with what their inclinations demand. Sometimes it would be better were they more debonair, more ready to accept some alternative though the evidence in its favor is not decisively clear. There is little wisdom in the refusal to help a friend in distress because we would like to see what could be said for the alternative of letting him struggle.

Something can be said for letting him struggle. Something can be said even for punishing him. He has vices. A well-placed punishment might benefit him and others. Yet it is man's task to help him and to help him now. This requires us to adopt not the distant goal of being rational but that of being men who are prepared to intend whatever alternatives now will bring about great goods. Goals of rationality and the like, which demand an endless search for extra factors to weigh in a situation, are subordinate goals to be decisively put aside at the point where they force one to ignore the demands of ultimate ends and their consequent reference to objective rights and duties. He who is rational is not always reasonable; he thinks too much. He who is reasonable is always rational; he uses his reason to realize some higher good.

3. Reasonableness and Fanaticism

The degree of intimacy with which a goal is adopted determines what alternative is selected; the goal makes a difference to one's nature, forcing one to support or suppress inclinations in various degrees. The more tightly a goal is held to, the more thoroughly a man is transformed and the more radical may his opposition to dominant inclinations prove to be. Since men change over the years, and since they differ one from the other, there can be no common or steady degree to which some common goal is to be adopted if they are to use it always for the selection of the selfsame alternatives. He who would do as the Romans did must do what they never could. His attitude toward the ideals of Rome cannot be like theirs, one made part of them by training. He must take a much more intimate, resolute grip on that ideal if he is to prefer what the Romans did. He who in ripe age is as much devoted as he once was to the glories of the stage, the hopes of the state, or the ideals of knowledge is in effect more devoted than he ever was, since he is more integrally part of his ideal and thus more prepared to put individual needs and desires aside.

In all cases, here or in Rome, in youth and in age, we are men who can prefer any of the alternatives we confront as means to the goals we cherish. No matter how well indoctrinated, no matter how accustomed we may be to hold some goal at some definite position and thus to dictate to ourselves which alternative to select, we are always able to change the relation which the goal has to us and thereby determine the selection of different alternatives. We can put aside the alternative with the most ingredient appeal and prefer instead another, no matter how little ingredient appeal it may have. With equal freedom we can prefer the alternative which has the greatest ingredient appeal; otherwise we would never be free to intend anything but the repugnant. If alternative x is preferred to y, their roles could have been

interchanged. Regardless of our inclinations, and regardless of the
decision we finally make, x and y are equally open to us. If we incline
toward x we could prefer y ; if we prefer y we could have preferred x.

Any alternative can be preferred over all others. Let us face this
thesis with a very hard case. Consider a man faced with the alternatives of helping his son or killing him. The one appeals, the other does
not. Yet the man is able to prefer the second to the first. He is able to
face the alternative of killing his son as preferable to the alternative
of helping him prosper. Were this not possible the father would be an
automatic instrument which selected its course with no more independence than a stone selects the path through which it falls. He would
intend or not intend to kill his son willy-nilly, and nothing but the
course of the world would be at fault.

A man can freely prefer to kill his son. The idea shocks the imagination. For this there is no better sedative than the Bible. Its story of
Abraham and Isaac makes it somewhat easier to see that the situation
imagined is within the realm of possibility. Abraham loved his son.
He wanted Isaac to prosper. But when Abraham viewed the killing of
Isaac as a sacrifice demanded by his God, this most unpalatable of
alternatives became the preferred alternative. Abraham intended to
realize this alternative because his goal was to be one with God, and
this required him to go against his inclinations and prefer the death
of innocent Isaac. The most repugnant of alternatives was here converted into a preferred one by being freely made into the best means
to the goal of remaining one with God.

If killing a son can be preferred to saving his live, the reverse is also
true. A father can prefer to keep his son from all harm. Abraham intended to kill his son because he took the words of his God in such a
spirit as to require this intention. But he could have given a different
interpretation to the words he thought he heard. He could have treated
them as a code, as the words of a devil, as part of a hallucination, or as
irrelevant to what he was to do. He could have used them to tell him to
accept the goal of a possible unity with God in such a way as to require
the selection of an alternative other than that which was apparently
being divinely recommended. He could, without abandoning his goal
of obeying God, have rejected whatever his God was supposed to ask
him literally to do. And this would have been eminently reasonable,
for true obedience to the divine entails a refusal to make the innocent
suffer. By being more reasonable and yet without ceasing to be religious, Abraham could have avoided terrorizing Isaac. Isaac undoubtedly had nightmares throughout his later life, all because Abraham listened so uncritically and obeyed so unreasonably. Sometimes
the ways of God are beyond all understanding, but is it reasonable to

believe that the only or best way He had to test Abraham's faith required that Abraham scare the wits out of Isaac?

Abraham's problem in principle was not different from what every one of us must face at every moment. It is up to each to decide reasonably or unreasonably. Capable of intending any alternative, we will, if we are reasonable men, intend only that which can bring about an adopted goal. This means that at some times we must vary the point at which we adopt the goal. If we are well adjusted, apace with nature, we will reach the proper position without reflection; if we are intelligent, we will adopt a distant goal of being reasonable in such a way as to compel the selection of whatever alternative to our knowledge promotes a desired subordinate goal, and thus will determine the point at which the subordinate goal is to be adopted through the help of the alternative it is to favor. A reasonable man is at once intelligent and well adjusted; the alternative he selects is an excellent means to both subordinate and distant goals.

It is not easy to be reasonable. Knowledge has but a short reach and adjustments are forged in consonance with the past rather than with what is or is about to be. The most reasonable decisions may at times require an opposition to what knowledge endorses. Only the superstitious would stab the picture of an enemy; it is not intelligent to suppose such an act to be an effective means for realizing the goal of killing him. Yet the stabbing of the picture may so encourage a man, give him so much confidence and courage, that he turns what would have been a questionable venture into a most successful one. It is intelligent to bait the hook before fishing. Yet because of something in the nature of the bait or the fish of which we know nothing, it may be better, if fish are to be caught, not to bait the hook at all.

There is considerable difference between being ignorant of and ignoring nature, between being deceived and deceiving oneself, between being uninformed and being unintelligent. No man knows and no man can know exactly what results will ensue on any act. Still, when he makes his decisions he should make use of whatever knowledge is available regarding the course of events; otherwise he will intend an alternative which most likely cannot serve as a means to the goal he wishes thereby to realize.

The most reasonable decision may sometimes require the breaking through of the limits within which well-adjusted men live. In times of crises it is most desirable to innovate, invent, to select new means in order to attain old goals; but this the well-adjusted man is not usually prepared to do. We ought, then, not be too well adjusted. This does not mean that we should be maladjusted. There is a great difference between one who is not well adjusted and one who is maladjusted, between one who is not well habituated and one who is wrongly habituated, between one who is badly prepared and one who is prepared to do something badly. No man can be perfectly adjusted, so completely one with nature that he keeps abreast of its every turn. But he should be so well trained that his decisions take account of its more steady beats and vibrate with its more constant rhythms.

Those who are most ignorant and least well trained will use wrong agencies to obtain wanted results. In expression and achievement they may be hard to distinguish from fanatics. Yet they are quite different in nature and intent. Fanatics may have considerable knowledge and good habits, but may refuse to put them to good use. As a rule, they hold their goals at some self-satisfying distance, selecting the means those goals require, regardless of how such selection does violence to their knowledge of the world or the training which enabled them to live so long. While those who have dim intelligence and are poorly trained freely vary the use they make of their goals, the fanatic holds on to his in a steady way. The reasonable man differs from both; he makes use of available knowledge and good habits to help him focus on that alternative which will realize the goal in fact.

We can prefer an alternative which we believe will, in the course of known nature, promote the goal or we can prefer an alternative which could promote the goal only if nature, as we know it, was not pertinent. We can imagine hunting or sleeping, praying or eating, standing, or telling stories to be indispensable means for catching fish. There is no evidence that these are relevant, and the man who preferred these alternatives to baiting his hook would be either unintelligent or maladjusted. But he would still be free to prefer it, and for the purpose of promoting successful fishing. Whether it be known that an alternative is the correct one to prefer or not, given this or that as the goal to be reached, it can be freely preferred or rejected.

Normal men are reasonable as a rule. For them there are alternatives they cannot prefer without doing violence to what they know and what they are habituated to do. It is up to them though to decide in the act of preference whether or not they will be reasonable. They could, if they would, be unreasonable and take alternatives which they, as men with such and such habits making use of such and such knowledge, are now forced to reject. Given any two alternatives, they can prefer either, though the price for taking one of them may be that they must then give up an effort to be reasonable.

All men tend to defy what they know of nature; they tend to be unreasonable when such knowledge stands in the way of their preferring the alternative to which they are most inclined. But they can be reasonable. Decisions can always go as they reasonably should. No one can say in advance which way they will go. It is always for each to decide whether to favor the alternative toward which he is antecedently most inclined or the alternative which knowledge reveals to be the best of all the available means or some third alternative in between. We decide when and as we reconstitute ourselves, when and as we make ourselves into men who live in nature while holding on to goals as intimately, as loyally as our intelligence allows or into men who subject themselves to the dictates of a goal adopted regardless of the alternative it demands. The result cannot be known in advance of the act of deciding and thus in advance of our going through the process of remaking ourselves as reasonable or unreasonable men.

Under the influence of language, experience, and custom most men prefer alternatives which are related to goals within the frame of a nature partly known, partly surmised, partly lived in, partly misconstrued. Early and unconsciously, late and consciously, they confine the scope of their preferences. They prefer as reasonable men whose intelligence and habits have been qualified and restructured by a definite society at a definite period of history. They are the "reasonable" men of whom lawyers speak, the men who provide the standard in terms of which negligence and insanity, reliability and accountability are defined. No one, however, is reasonable all the time. All allow their imaginations to run away with them to some degree, and all have a superstition or two. Even the most hardheaded of businessmen have been known to be willing to open an office on the thirteenth story of a building, if only it was numbered 12a. Sometimes such men are sensitive and attempt to veil their superstitions in somewhat the way the astronomer did when he was criticized for hanging a horseshoe over his door: he said he did not believe it made any difference; still, he understood it brought good luck even to those who did not believe it.

All men would like to select the alternative with the greatest ingredient appeal while adopting the most desirable, attainable goal. Unfortunately, each one of us is frequently compelled to abandon one or the other. Our hope is that we can be reasonable men who adopt goals in such a way as to make preferable those alternatives which have considerable ingredient appeal. Only then, without denying ourselves, will we be men who intend to realize what we should.

4. EDUCATION

By paying attention only to those cases where preferences conform to inclinations, the illusion is fostered that freedom is an illusion. One then becomes embarrassed when subsequently faced with men exercising preferences in favor of what they are not inclined to accept. Their preference is unquestionably dictated by something, a goal. But this is not the object of inclinations.

Every preference can be made to conform to some dominant inclination. Because our habits and the world change with time, we must, to follow the inclination, sooner or later change our goals, vary the adjustments we make to the world, or vary the use we make of our knowledge. We will have to alter our intents and acts for no other reason but to give that dominant inclination its way in changing circumstances. If we do this we will deny ourselves the opportunity to be purposive, to adopt in a persistent way within, the possibility which controls us from without.

A purposive man guides himself by a genuinely pertinent future. If intelligent and well adjusted he intends objects he externally faces; he decides privately to be in accord with what externally limits him. Environed only by intendable things, by objects to be used as means, he is tempted to say to himself that the world was created for him to use, that nothing has any rights of its own, that nothing has a value or a meaning except so far as it helps him fulfill his purposes. The temptation is both weakened and strengthened somewhat by education.

All of us have been educated, if only through the medium of literature and conversation to appreciate a few things at least, to recognize them as having a nature and a value all their own. We treat some horses and dogs and sometimes birds, flowers, mountains, and rivers as having an importance independent of their instrumental value. To maintain with Spinoza that we ought to view them and all the rest as though they had no worth, no attractiveness apart from serviceability, is to ask in the most educated tones that we go contrary to our education, that we live outside a world we never should wish to nor can leave.

Our education is fragmentary and distortive. It hides much that innocence sees. It points up objects that should be left in the background. These are faults, and serious ones. But they are not its gravest. What is basically wrong with our education is that it teaches so many to believe that few or no things have value apart from their usefulness for men—an almost inevitable consequence of the fact that education's perspective too often stops with man inside an institutional frame. This explains the common habit of speaking as though nothing besides man had a right, a worth, and a dignity, as though everything but man could rightly be used as a means only. We but reach the common ground of Hebrew and Greek, of St. Francis and Blake, when we remark that there is beauty and tragedy and joy, richness and depth, an infinitude everywhere if we would but look. It is this to which a good education should reintroduce us.

Every society teaches its members that there is some worth in some of the other members in that society. If it be civilized it teaches its members, through the medium of institutional education, to extend their appreciations to all men. Were it perfectly civilized it would employ education to make men appreciate whatever there may be. No such society exists as yet. Until we have it, though, we can do nothing more than be content with knowing that our appreciations should extend further than they do. That knowledge is ours now because we now know that our education is incomplete, because we know that human freedom, though different in scope and quality, is continuous with that of all other beings, because we know that man is a being in nature, coordinate with as well as superior to others. We now know, though too often in the dimmest and vaguest way and in opposition to professional commitments to antagonistic theories, that if we stop our appreciations at man we tear him away from a substantial, many-hued world in which he originated and in which he lives.

Education is recollection, said Plato long ago. He put his insight into the form of a myth, saying that souls once dwelt in a world apart and now need only to be helped to recall what once they knew. The myth gravitates about a truth. Education is an agency for establishing and stabilizing visions previously achieved. But it is also an agency for making new insights possible. It uses the past not merely to illuminate or even to enrich the present and the future but to warrant a steadier and more penetrating perception of them than we had before. It builds on appreciations and extends them.

We come together with others spontaneously in work, in games, in festivals, in simple discourse. We associate with them for a moment or so, act together in harmony, interplay with them in flexible, mutually reactive ways. We then discover to our delight that we thereby obtain a joy which our associates never of themselves offered to provide. That joy we remember and wish to have repeated. Remembering it, we expect, when re-encountering our previous associates, to repossess the joy again. Yet except so far as we re-establish the association we formed with those beings, we cannot obtain that desired joy. Having learned that the pleasures of dancing, of common meals, of common prayer, of walking, talking, and sleeping together, of hunting and exploring, of immersion in the affairs of nature are not ours to recapture unless we dance, eat together, and so on, we come to recognize that we must look at some of the things about as coadjutors, if only to make possible and to realize our private joys. But to see something as a coadjutor is already to glimpse something of its true worth, since it is to recognize its nature, disposition, independence, and strength.

Were there some instrument by which our appreciation of others could be established and promoted, could there be some device by which we could be helped to appreciate all that we do not now appreciate, we would no longer be subject to contingent encounters in order to have something to appreciate. Language and song, dance and prayer are just such instruments. They effectively extend our appreciation to things we have not yet met face to face. Rarely, however, are they used as much more than institutionalized forms we must be trained to master. We can, fortunately, transcend those limitations; we can use these instruments in fresh, individual ways to constitute genuine, concrete bonds uniting us with different beings in the expectation that we will obtain in new situations goods similar to and perhaps even greater than those we once obtained in previous associations.

In the last resort no man can educate another. At most a man can be taught only how to teach himself. Educated men are self-educated. Socially trained, helped perhaps by a host of teachers, they must themselves individually use the available stores of knowledge so as to enter into participative activities by which a more than individual good can be realized and their associates truly appreciated. Teachers provide opportunities; they offer special forms of association serving to make easier new associations. They are examples, models, aides, and critics for those of us who learn. We watch them to see what habituated, disciplined, yet creative living and thinking are like. It is the pupil who learns, and there is nothing the teacher can do for him to make his education assume one shape or follow one course if he decides otherwise. Education is self-education, a free activity by which a man extends the range of his associations and is thereby enabled to bring about goods that never were before, and to appreciate in others what otherwise would be undiscerned.

Education enables a man to form associations more diverse and fruitful than those achieved by accident. It does not require of him that he actually associate with many beings. All it demands is that he work with any being which will help him to realize a common good, and thus that he appreciate the independent worth of anything as a possible coadjutor in the promotion of that good. It does not demand that he actually work with these. Education is life made dramatic, freed from irrelevancies, enabling us to get closer to the good we seek by allowing us to use anything as instrument but not requiring us to use any particular one. Education is a means for anticipating what one would have learned in a somewhat haphazard, impure form had one been content to learn only the lessons of experience. It makes us appreciate what we never did before and readies us to appreciate what we have not yet met.

The educated man is occupied with a good relevant to himself and others. At the same time he unknowingly constitutes and is constituted by a further, a more absolute good which has pertinence to the values things actually have of themselves and not merely to their values as coadjutors or as objects of appreciation. He owes it to himself to learn, to know, to isolate, and to internalize this good, for only in this way can he condition himself adequately by what controls him. The nature of this good is not, however, easy to discern. Nevertheless he must struggle to master it, for only thus can he come to know what a man should know, and thereby learn why it is that no one can rightly hope that education alone will make him a whole man.

PART II

Absolute Morality, Choice, and Law

VI

ABSOLUTE MORALITY AND ULTIMATE ENDS

1. PLEASURE AS THE GOOD

SIMILARLY educated beings face a common appropriate future, a good, a realizable harmony of their different possibilities. Of the many who have come to the length of acknowledging it, most, it seems, have thought its name was pleasure. And there is warrant for the belief. All men seem to want pleasure; all know it is desired and most believe that sometimes it is desirable for others. Even those who subscribe to theories which deny that men ought or can accept pleasure as a good approve of it in act, live in terms of it in fact. It is a good for all, rich, vital, intensive, private, a glow that makes life precious, valuable. It is as close to the substance of what humans truly desire as anything theorists have urged.

"Pleasure," however, is a rather accommodating term. It can be and has been stretched until it covers any and every state of actual or prospective satisfaction, mental or physical, self-profiting or self-injuring. With but little ingenuity it can therefore allow for the contention that the acquisition, possession, or expression of self-denial and self-sacrifice, the bitter knowledge of distressing truths, the suffering undergone at a stake or in a torture chamber are so many different forms of pleasure, desired because desirable, actually enjoyed under the covering of an apparent abhorrence.

Pain is not pleasure. Since it may be good to undergo pain, if only to gain great pleasure, pleasure cannot be the only good. The position that pleasure alone is good must then be abandoned for the position that other things also, e.g., pain and what it brings about, are good but are to be perversely termed pleasures. To maintain that pleasure is the good it is necessary to deny that suffering and indifference are good, or be content with winning only the victory that can be bought with a pun.

Pleasure is a warm and welcome feeling tone, a gratifying glow, a satisfaction lived through. If we could abstract it from its causes and its effects it would represent a finality, an ultimate in being, forever opposed to suffering and indifference as the good from the not good.

But pleasures have careers, causes, and effects. Some disrupt and some corrupt. Some stand in the way of further pleasures. He who takes pleasure, without further ado, to be the good must be ready to take as good what often prevents him from having the good again. Good pleasures should be distinguished from bad. The glow that accompanies an increase in health and strength is a pleasure differing qualitatively from the feeling which accompanies a willful debilitation. The latter may please in a way, but its pleasure is streaked with disagreeableness; we are pained while we are pleased, suffer our enjoyment or enjoy our suffering. We are not entirely pleased. Unless we can cut off the pleasure from what sustains and provides it, our feeling tone here is quite different in quality from that which we have when we are pleased by what is through and through agreeable.

The thesis that pleasure is the good requires an antecedent discrimination of good pleasures from bad. But then it becomes evident that the former are sought and cherished not because they are pleasurable—for what is being rejected is also pleasurable—but because they are good. And if the good which the good pleasures embody can also be found elsewhere, if it qualifies what is not pleasure but something else, other things besides pleasure could be embraced for the same reason that good pleasures are.

Perhaps there is nothing in pleasures which makes them good and which might make other things good as well. May it not be that pleasures alone are good, and are good as a matter of brute fact, beyond which it is impossible to go? If so, everything else would be either bad or indifferent. The expectation, memory, or knowledge of pleasure would either spoil it or add nothing to it. The savoring of pleasures in prospect or retrospect and the knowledge of them for what they are would not be good. Moreover, were all things besides pleasure bad or indifferent, it would always be right to do anything to them in order to obtain pleasure. We would then be justified in ruining any number of beings, human or subhuman, if only pleasure came. But such pleasure, even if ecstatic, is not and cannot be good. A pleasure bought by ruining others is not a good pleasure; and what is not a good pleasure is not a good.

A good pleasure requires acts which improve or at least do not debase us and others. There is an intrinsic connection between the good of a pleasure and what is to be done to obtain that pleasure. He who seeks to have good pleasures must take account of other things and work on them to benefit them and himself. But this is only another way of saying that what is wanted is not pleasure simply but that pleasure which accompanies or ensues on the good acts of good men. Such pleasure is an essential part of happiness.

2. Happiness as the Good

Happiness is a state in which one enjoys only good pleasures, pleasures bought by improving or at least not injuring others and himself. It is a more likely candidate for the office of an absolute good than pleasure is, for unlike pleasure it excludes what is evil, bad, destructive. But it too will not do.

Happiness is to be achieved only by not being sought. Just as we spoil our laughter by becoming conscious of it, so we lose and spoil our happiness by being interested in it. We become happy not by striving to become happy but by seeking and attaining some other end. The man who is constantly looking for ways to be happy can never be happy actually. But a knowledge or search for the good does not diminish it or prevent its attainment. We know that happiness is not the good and thus not our proper end because we know that an interest in happiness is a way of losing it.

Man is genuinely interested in the adventures and welfare of other things and beings, even when that interest jeopardizes his happiness. He sympathizes, pities, grieves; he is concerned with a good wider and richer than happiness is or could be. Happiness is too narrow and private an end to satisfy anyone who is self-aware. No man is so a master of himself that he is content to be himself. His good lies in part in losing himself, in not fulfilling himself in himself, in not being merely happy. A man who was only happy would not be very happy.

No man apparently can reach that degree of callousness where he can remain happy long while others suffer. Every social knife has a double edge and cuts him who wields the knife as well as him who undergoes the cut. We men are symbiotic, clutching at one another. Whatever happiness we could have is one which we privately gain by realizing a common good. A genuine happiness is the happiness of interlocked and mutually dependent humans, infecting and altering one another's private tonalities. The happiness each seeks is a specialized form of a happiness in general which others enjoy concurrently. If others are not happy also, we cannot be happy long. Unquestionably we are indifferent and grow fat while others starve. We look misery in the eye and see nothing that concerns us. Still we are never happy by ourselves; we must at least cushion our happiness by the envy of our fellows. And then, to keep ourselves human, we must see it as that which they somehow through their envy acknowledge to be a good worth having.

Men alone can be happy, but the happiness must be the happiness of man, the happiness which other humans could also have and ought to have in their own way. To say this is to trench on the thesis that happiness is the true good, when this good is understood to be the greatest possible summation of the pleasures of the greatest number of men. The thesis is exciting. As the much-neglected Halévy has made evident, though, it is beset with many difficulties, not the least of which is that it has no place for obligation and thus no way of urging men to adopt it as their end. But perhaps more serious is the fact that happiness, even when conceived of as a good to be attained by men together, is too limited an end to provide the good for all that is. A true absolute good is a good for beings other than men as well as for men. Other beings also have values deserving to be preserved and enhanced.

He who devotes himself exclusively to the attainment of happiness for all men will neglect a host of other values and will therefore reduce the worth of the world, and incidentally what sometimes helps make for the possible happiness of men. At the very least we should say that a man should be concerned with enhancing the values of things in the world in order for human happiness to be achieved. But this advance in position, great though it is, falls far short of what the facts require. The world is not made for man any more than man is made for the world. Each thing has its value, its own kind of excellence, worth, power, and integration, deserving to be preserved and enhanced. We should serve them for their sakes no less than they should serve us for ours. He who would ignore the values ingredient in others reduces the value of himself. It takes a man to appreciate the value of things, of plants and animals, and of men.

Happiness, moreover, is a subjective state, lived within, the form which an objective good acquires when realized in a personal way. The goodness ingredient in it is an objective good specialized by men in one way and by other beings in other ways. An interest in this good is an interest not in the happy form it might assume for men but in it as deserving realization everywhere.

Happiness is the good of socially interlocked men interplaying with things for mutual benefit. It specializes a good which is relevant to men as associated with one another and with other beings. That good which it specializes is an ideal of order, pertinent not only to them but to others as well, a relevant possibility allowing each to be in harmony with the rest and in such a way that the values of each are preserved or enhanced.

3. The Ideal of Order

Where we have order we have harmony, a structure in which each being has its excellence, function, and area in consonance with the rest. But no actual group is perfectly ordered. Everywhere there is some disorder, some conflict, some lack of integration. Each is defective, some less, some more so than others. Since to know the defects of anything is to refer to a good which it does not but should embody, the acknowledgment that an actual group is to be improved is an acknowledgment that it does not provide a standard in terms of which the improvement is to be made. Only an ideal order, or some existent order idealized, can provide the standard in terms of which actual groups can be judged. Were there though no other good than this, there would be no value left for irrationality, turbulence, spontaneity, impulsiveness, the defiance of rules and established ways.

Good men serve not the good of their organizations, their societies, or civilizations, even when these are idealized. They serve some greater good. They cherish order but not order alone. They tear the fabric of rules, rituals, and habits which bind men, and point to and try to realize more than these or what they allow. Some acts, involving an opposition to the order that prevails or is about to be realized, are good.

Order of itself is not necessarily desirable. It may bind men too much. Whatever order we have achieved or have in prospect may reflect our tendency to follow routine paths. It may be the outcome of unimaginative, inflexible moves and give testimony to our failure to do justice to our promise as creative, self-forming beings. If we occupy ourselves with the achievement of order, we shall most likely end by becoming impotent idealists living perforce in a world alien to that whose spirit we reflect. Our every act must be in part a re-formation, a revolution, an overturning of established ways in the creative attempt to realize a good of which order, because harmonizing but not itself perfect, is at most one part. We must act as beings of flexibility and inventiveness, ready to ignore the requirements of order if in this way we can better promote and enjoy a truly social good. Only in a mythical organization are men and their activities excellent and their patterns fixed forever. Every mode of action must be altered with circumstance.

A socially *moral* man resists identification with the prevailing customs, manners, codes, and rituals of the day. He is devoted to the good of his society, sometimes even in defiance of its edicts. He readies himself to share in the new modes now in the offing. He changes his behavior over the years. When young he suppresses some of his longing for the utopias that fill his dreams; when old he conquers his nostalgia for the practices which were satisfactory only for his time. And occasionally he opposes some, perhaps at times even all, of his fellows.

It is unquestionably better to live in harmony with fellow men over the years than it is not to live in harmony with them at all or for only a short time. It is better to be in sympathy with them than in perpetual opposition. Conformity to the practices that prevail makes such harmony rather easy to attain. Yet conformity to the practices that prevail is far from being a final good. A socially moral man has to stand apart from his fellows occasionally and decide for himself, perhaps in opposition to them, just what is to be done. He may understandably be swept away by the excitement of a mob; he is by the very limitations of his knowledge and energy forced to act often in routine ways. But he and we will often regret what he then does and will sometimes come to see, if only belatedly, that there is a higher good than acting as others would or do, or as he had previously.

What we all need, even when by word and deed we most emphatically deny it, is moral courage, the ability to reorder ourselves and others all the time.

4. MORAL LEADERSHIP

He who has moral courage is a moral leader. He may not be conspicuous. The truest leaders are sometimes quite in the background. They are not necessarily socially prominent; they do not always wield considerable power. Leadership is a question of ideals and their attainment, not of force or recognition. It refers to men who forge ahead in some dimension, whether this be approved at the time by others or not. It characterizes those who work to bring about a socially moral world, a world of harmoniously interrelated individuals, organized but flexible, habituated yet creative, living in one of many societies in which fellow men and some social objects are genuinely appreciated and treated accordingly.

Unless there be moral monsters, men who are opposed to the realization of the good of men and the beings with whom they are associated, unless there be men who are morally blind and never lured by that good, and unless there be men who are morally impotent and can never bring that good to realization to any degree, all must be leaders at some times and in some places. They may be treated as malefactors, as fools and failures, because they do not fit neatly inside the world as it for the moment is. They may not have the degree of intelligence, the skill, and power required to bring the morality to realization; yet in intent and in partial accomplishment they may still be leaders, flexibly exercising individual powers to bring about a good pertinent to others as well as to themselves, and in such a way as to help them move further forward than they otherwise could.

We all make tentative stabs at genuine leadership in some dimension of human activity. For a moment perhaps we dart out for a distance and in a direction others never tried, and which could lead other men to positions higher than those they have already attained. But these tentative stabs at leadership are not sustained by circumstance; they are too much out of harmony with what could be understood or readily assimilated, and serve only to relieve for a moment the monotony of regular work. Not many of us become successful leaders. And those who do, do not actively lead all the time. They are partly carried by prestige and by their past achievements; they lead because they have led. Others could have led just as well. The common ideal can be realized by any and for all.

Each man has an opportunity to lead in some direction at every moment, if only as one who moves forward or waits when these are necessary, who makes a witty remark when humor is needed, who smiles when others frown. Each is a unique being whose individuality provides an unduplicable locus in which the good is to be displayed. Each has unique contributions to make. This man or that may not be able to paint or write with any power, or may do so without much distinction. Unless we unnecessarily narrow the idea of what is genuine creative work, though, we cannot claim that he is without artistic ability. There are countless ways of using media and countless arts which have never really been exploited. Despite the long history of painting which has enriched civilization, we have only in recent times come to see how to use solid colors with great effect. Despite our knowledge of Chinese and Egyptian art, we still hold tight to our conventional perspectives, shadows and light, and the use of models. We paint on canvas and only occasionally on paper; we use oils and occasionally water colors; we sculpture in marble and occasionally in granite, onyx, silver, bronze, or wood. Our musicians hold to a special type of musical scale; our dancers dance within the limits of three or four set positions; our actors perform within traditional rules, prescribing how a man should gesture, intone, declaim, and move about. Left over are thousands of natural and artificial materials to be used in innumerable ways to give unexpected beauties and truths. Ignored are the thousands of tentative uses we are constantly making of familiar materials, the hesitant, timid, momentary attempts all of us make to open up new domains. Were each to find that medium most appropriate to his genius, all could drive in tandem beyond the elementary level where we now are in art. And if we can do it in art, we can do it elsewhere. Each, precisely because he is a unique being with his own gifts, past, temper, and opportunities, can win for all new techniques and results. At the very least we can master new arts or so press on with the old ones as to leave earlier ages far behind. We sing today in harmony; the Greeks did not. We can sculpture today in soap and ice; a few centuries ago men never did. We now create in poetry and in philosophy, as teachers and as labor leaders, as machinists and as ballplayers in a way men never did before. And this is but the beginning.

Only some men can excel in the arts as we know them now. For all to be leaders in art, they must be enabled to create in ways and for results appropriate to their natures and abilities. Democracy seeks to do nothing less than make all men artists and in all fields for the benefit of all. Its hope lies in our ability to find for each that individually congenial mode of activity and type of result which will enable him to express his powers to the full, and thereby realize in a unique and desirable form a good for multiple socialized men.

Individual activities, though unique, irreducible, and incomparable, need not conflict. There is no conflict between those who write sonnets and those who write epics, between pianists and violinists, between those who paint landscapes and those who paint seascapes. Yet all of them go their own ways, exhibiting with individual accents common ideals of beauty and workmanship. The demands of moral ideals could similarly be met in individual, desirable, and compatible ways if only we would take creative account of the inequalities which the past and the present impose on equal men.

Unequal because of what they have already achieved, unequal because they must be given quite different opportunities to achieve the equivalent of what others attain, men because equally human are intrinsically on a par. If there be a single kind of result they are expected to bring about, the inequalities, the differences between them, must be ferreted out and stressed. Appropriate opportunities to lead and benefit the rest must be unequal and somewhat diverse.

Inequality in public status offers an occasion for providing unequally placed men with unequal opportunities. Not to seize the occasion is but to perpetuate a difference which fails to correspond to what the men internally are and might become. To give the crippled and the sound the same opportunities is to force the first to extend himself more than the second and thus to become less significant just so far as he responds to his opportunities with the same interest and concentration that others do. The humanity of a crippled man is worth as much as the humanity of the sound. But this means that he must be helped more if he is to make it equally evident.

As it now is, all men are offered about the same kind and degree of opportunity in all fields. And they reply to them with about the same effort and in a rough ratio to their past achievements. Those who are unfortunately placed to begin with consequently remain as a rule behind throughout. If they are to use their powers to the full and thereby realize the good of themselves, of their groups, and of the others with whom they are united appreciatively, they need different, unequal opportunities. Only then could they become more than good social men, only then could they become genuine *socially moral* men, men who work to realize a good which has a place for order and variety, for tradition and change, men who do not merely conform or merely revolt, merely repeat or merely innovate, but who creatively try to give to themselves and other members of their society what they all deserve and need.

Social morality is not a function of society. Yet because dependent on the instrumentalities of education and the opportunities which society provides, as society changes morality often does. There is some justification then for the common habit of supposing that moral and socially endorsed goods are identical or correlative. But socially moral men can put aside the goods endorsed by their own societies and concentrate instead on some other, more appropriate to the natures and needs of their fellow men. Appreciating many things which society may ignore, the socially moral man is able to benefit many whom the society cannot.

Men are molded by, and are never entirely separated from, their societies, times, and crafts. Nevertheless they pursue and realize genuinely moral goods, goods pertinent to themselves and the beings they have learned to appreciate, even when their societies deny that these ought to be. Through the help of education they become socially moral men, men concerned with the moral good, a good for the beings in their society but which the society may ignore or even disown. Some social moralities and their appropriate moral goods are worse than others and of even less worth sometimes than the prevailing conventions and established societies. This however is a truth we can know only because we have some grasp of an absolute morality.

5. Absolute Morality

In many societies the miser is criticized. There is sense to the criticism only if it makes sense to refer to ideals which it is right to pursue. If all we could rightly ask of a man is that he do what his goal demands, it would be absurd to criticize the miser; if all we could rightly ask of a man is that he do what others approve, it would be absurd to ask whether these others approve rightly and thus whether they criticize the miser justly. The miser is criticizable because he violates a social morality pertinent to himself and all with whom he lives. That morality is not an absolute morality; it is a social morality, one of many, in some of which—not too alien in contour and spirit to our own—something like a miser is a man thought wise and good. When thrift and gold are god, a miser is but a pharisee holding a little too close to the letter of the law; his fault is too great, not too little, zeal to conform to the morality that prevails.

Different social moralities have features in common. In diverse ways they specialize an absolute morality, the ideal of the more than civilized, of the more than educated man, of the man who does more than appreciate, who has duties and commitments toward the animate and the inanimate, the large and the small. It alone of all the goods with which we have so far dealt is pertinent to things as they are and not merely as objects used or appreciated. It alone enables us to pass judgment on the societies, civilization, and moralities too often, in opposition to one another, urged as absolutes.

When we try to answer the question as to whether Rousseau and Tolstoy, Thoreau and Gandhi were right in looking askance at their societies, even when idealized, we turn to the good of absolute morality for guidance. When we quarrel with Westermarck or hesitate before some more recent formulation of his relativistic thesis, we turn not to a morality we find most congenial but to an absolute, an ideal morality which it and other moralities independently and sometimes antagonistically exemplify. We are aware of it, if only faintly, much more than we suspect, for it is of this we speak with a confidence born of familiarity when we say to ourselves and one another that we want a peace with vigor, a kind of order shot through with individuality, in which each of us will be at leisure, tasting to the full, with maturity and poise, the goods that grace this globe. But we seem unable to hold that ideal apart from the limited goods of our societies and organizations, and thus almost at once reduce what we faintly glimpse to the status of a good for a transitory group.

Not all find an absolute morality sufficiently clear or desirable to make them put aside temptations and distractions in the way of its realization. Nor will they, until they have been taught to work and concur with many others, to develop their own capacities more fully, and to reassess and perhaps radically reorder what they encounter. Only then could they be in a position to discern and use a steady, objective standard unaffected by historic changes; only then could they have a legitimate criterion of what they ought to do; only then could they have an intelligible ground for judging what is and is to be.

Because most men do not seem to acknowledge such an absolute either in thought or in act, because they pursue much more limited, transitory, and mutually antagonistic goods, the pragmatists are in a sense right when they insist that none of the usual objectives, and thus none of those favored in textbooks of ethics, is an absolute, a genuine, ultimate, final, untestable test of all else. But pragmatism as a rule goes further than this and claims that no absolute is possible.

It is mistaken. Everyone, pragmatists included, faces and makes use of two absolutes in fact. One is an individually preferred, uncriticized principle by which he justifies all he does and all his estimates of others; the other is an ultimate ideal which defines his use of his principle to be right or wrong. The pragmatists constantly speak of the incomparable excellence of a life of adventure or experimentation; they urge the scientific method as the universal solvent of all ethical and incidentally all political, logical, and philosophical difficulties and extol the democratic way of life over all competitors. These constitute the basic principle which they use to justify the lives they lead and would like others to lead. But since this principle is really questionable and has indeed been seriously questioned, the pragmatists really presuppose, too quietly for themselves to notice, that it has been favored over all others because supported by an ideal which, in the nature of the case, has a different rank and strength from what it evaluates. The pragmatist, though an inconoclast with respect to all goals, is a dogmatist with respect to the principle which endorses his iconoclasm and a self-contradictory thinker with respect to that absolute morality which he needs in order to warrant what he dogmatically affirms. That absolute morality, a single, all-encompassing possibility, is pertinent to everything we do. To make it internal to ourselves is to treat it as an *ultimate end*, at once defining our duties and justifying our choices.

Those who are primarily occupied with ultimate ends do not always fit inside established schemes. Though not always oblivious to their worth, we find their presence trying, in part because their presence and behavior offer a constant criticism of our own. As a rule we do not care whether others act for moral reasons or for any reasons but only whether their acts keep within the boundaries of established good order. We do not care much whether a man stops at a red light through the exercise of freedom, by habit, or under a compulsion exerted by his muscles. We normally act, and perhaps merely react, to violation of social requirements, inflicting punishment, not always physical in form, on those who fail to conform. Yet all the time we know that conformity is not the highest good, that there is an ideal in terms of which actual moralities and societies are to be evaluated, making evident that there are times when right is sometimes on the side neither of those who merely conform nor of those who merely revolt against the customary ways.

Socrates is a man in whom the defenders of both society and social morality found, they thought, a perfect justification. He has been thought a man who showed a necessity for defying society and he has been thought a man who showed how one could be a moral man. But actually Socrates did violence to both society and social morality, and largely because he did not insist enough on an absolute moral good which transcended both.

Socrates was a danger to Athens. He made generals and statesmen the butt of the young and the irresponsible, and had as one of his products the vicious Alcibiades. From the viewpoint of the society Socrates deserved punishment; from the viewpoint of social morality the society deserved pity or scorn. But neither perspective is adequate. It is petulant in the face of Socrates' fate, disastrous to him, to thought, and to Greece, for one to claim that a knowledge of social morality is all that the good life requires or that there is nothing else to do but to live immersed in one's times. It was Socrates' duty to live in his society so far as this was in consonance with what an absolute morality demands. It was the duty of his fellows to encourage Socrates so far as this did not require the destruction of the world in which men live and which alone makes it possible to realize high values.

Socrates was too absorbed in the problems of social morality to do justice to men both as they are and as they ought to be. His fellows were too absorbed in their society to know what was appropriate to a sound social morality. They did not see what Milton saw, "Men of most renowned virtue have sometimes by transgressing most truly kept the law."

Socrates underscored what was vital to men who wish to live in a Greek society made excellent. But his criticisms were destructive of his own and perhaps any other possible society. He should have conformed more to his society's ways and taken better account of its needs while pointing beyond it. Reciprocally, the Athenians should have been more than Athenians; they should have noted how defective their society was and tried to serve a good beyond it. Socrates forgot that a socially moral existence could be one in which men are miserable and frustrated and that it could exist and continue only if supported by a world outside. But they were more shortsighted, for they denied and ignored the social morality which they needed to justify their practices and ways. Both fell far short of a recognition of an absolute morality in terms of which men and societies are sometimes and ought always to be judged.

VII

FREEDOM OF CHOICE

1. The Objectivity of Value

VALUE is a natural phenomenon. Excellence of any kind, beauty, power, purity, comprehensiveness, and their negates are facts as hard as smell and shape, number and size. With thinkers of a century or so ago, it could of course be said that there were no values in nature. But since the world we daily confront is permeated with values, we should then have to say that the nature we daily know is an illusion, a man-infected, man-distorted nature. We should have to maintain that man had the fatal and unique gift of endowing what was in fact valueless with the appearance of value, and thus, alone of all beings, of self-deceptively hiding nature from himself.

The denial that nature has a place for values takes many forms. One asserts that value is a category of the human mind, an inescapable frame in terms of which all that could possibly be known inevitably fits. But instead of denying value to nature this view denies reality to it. If the only nature we could possibly know is a nature with values in it, we cannot possibly know a different nature. Whatever features are universal, inescapable, integral to whatever nature we know are obviously essential parts of the only nature of which we have a grasp. Only a theory based on no fact could then urge, as this does, that values are alien, irrelevant, dispensable, illusory, deceptive, man-made factors. If no matter where we looked or turned, no matter what we thought or believed, we always found values of some kind, values would be as ultimate and as natural as anything else we could know. To deny reality to values would then be tantamount to denying reality to the beings of which those values were an essential part. On the hypothesis, though, that nature would be the only nature we could know.

The thesis that nature is devoid of values assumes that we can look upon nature bare, neutral, and wild. But then our separation from nature must take place inside or outside the nature we normally know. If inside, some natural thing will help or hinder us in our attempt to transcend the very world of which it was an integral part; it would be instrumentally good, exercising, for this result, some good capacities.

A purely neutral thing cannot become a *desirable* instrument enabling us to see nature as devoid of value. We would have to turn away from experience to know the facts. And if we could manage this, we would have to say it was neither good nor bad for us to be free of the value category, and that therefore there was no point in our trying to get rid of it.

He who urges us to transcend a reference to values supposes not only that we can exist apart from known nature but that it is neither good nor bad that we do this. When he speaks of value as an illusion he must say that the illusion is no better or worse than the reality. Yet the theory that values are alien additions to a value-free nature is not without some apparent justification. On the one hand the sciences devoted to providing an objective account of nature seem to have no place for them, and on the other hand we do read into things values which reflect more the flavor of our attitudes than the nature of things. Values do change with custom and experience, love and hate, hunger and passion. What pleases the African disgusts the Chinese, what delights the young displeases the old; a friend's smile is pleasing, an enemy's ugly; the odor and look of food change in value rapidly in the course of dinner; in fear and trembling we repel what in rest and at peace we embraced as good and satisfying.

What is admirable in one place and time is not so in others. This fact, the prop and substance of what sometimes passes for enlightenment, is much too flimsy to sustain a theory that there are no values in nature. We would have to back it up with such hazardous suppositions as 1) that the sciences do not and should not deal with values; 2) that what is transitory, what fluctuates with time, place, civilization, is not an objective fact in nature; 3) that knowledge which is emotionally tinged or grounded is necessarily irrelevant or erroneous; 4) that so far as something is relevant to our interests it is not part of nature; 5) that what has meaning in relation to man has no analogous meaning in relation to other beings; 6) that what is relational is not part of nature; 7) that what is private is entirely other in nature and being from what is common.

1) That sciences do not now make value an object of their inquiries seems to be a fact. Yet since all that can be known in some possible experience is an appropriate object of science, values cannot be denied the right to be scientifically studied. Unless they are not matter of fact—the very question at issue—they are not beyond the reach of some science at some time. Such a science—which no more denies legitimacy to nonscientific approaches to value than a geometry or physics does to a philosophic investigation of the nature of space—would take account of realities which every other science presupposes.

Science presupposes that its supporters can distinguish between what is important and what is unimportant. Were this distinction without objective warrant, the sciences would be grounded on a distinction not supported by the nature of things; what the sciences assert would be arbitrary. But if the sciences are arbitrary, the fact that they do not deal with values will not go to show that values are unreal; on the contrary, it would be reasonable to expect that with a shift in assumption the scientist would be able to see the values the rest of us do.

2) The knowledge we most cherish is that which remains unaltered as we shift our places and our times, that is untainted by transitory, avoidable conditions, that tells us what we are, as natively and primarily free. It is doubtful, though, whether there is any truth unaffected by time, free of all historic reference. At any rate no political, sociological, historical truth has concrete content except so far as it refers to some local, changeable circumstance. And science, too, would seem to have some bearing on the temporal aspects of the world. Nature does not exclude the transitory, the changing, the fluctuating, the local; if it did, it would be a domain of self-enclosed, eternal beings and it would be doubtful whether any science but mathematics would be possible. Science takes account of the number, position, momentum, and grouping of beings in nature. If these transient facts are allowed to be real, we have reason sufficient for granting reality to transitory values too.

3) There seem to be, however, transitory objective realities and transitory subjective ones. It seems one thing to say that an eclipse is now occurring and another to say that a rose now seems prettier to me than a daisy does. The one, though only momentary, is part of a scheme of things whose principles pertain to all that is, everywhere. It can be seen from thousands of angles and by any number of men; it can be recorded by instruments. The other is a private matter, not existent or knowable except from this or that perspective and then as beyond the reach of any machine-like recording device we have. The one is an object of a clear-eyed, duplicable reason and a communicative language; the other is the object of a confusing, private emotion. It is dubious, though, whether this kind of opposition occurs anywhere but in textbooks. There never was a rational knowledge unaffected by emotion or a public language which was pure syntax without tonality and stress. There never was an emotional acknowledgment which was devoid of all objectively cognizable content. Each man sees the eclipse in his own way, with his own emphases and private predilections; and each expresses his appreciation of the rose in publicly ascertainable tendencies to act. What we must intend to affirm when we

disparage emotionally toned assertions as not reporting what is there is either the truism that they do not report what a pure reason would—which no more disqualifies the reports of the emotions than of the reason—or that the emotions tell only what things are in relation to what lies outside them, which of course does not disqualify an emotionally toned report at all.

4) The prettiness of the rose, it is tempting to say, depends on the kind of interest taken in the rose. Let us turn away, let us look at it with other eyes. We will then find that, though the rose remains just as it was before, its prettiness is gone. The rose seems to be an objective, adamantine, rugged fact. It blooms whether we like it to bloom or not, whereas a change in our attitude suffices to tear from it even the pretense of being beautiful.

It is extremely doubtful whether we would ever know the rose or any other thing if we had no interest which it terminated. Without some interest we would look neither here nor there, not note this instead of that. Still an interest in the rose seems to differ from an interest in its beauty. The interest in the rose seems to be a steady, common type of interest, the very same kind of interest with which we approach all the other things we know; whereas tastes seem to differ and to generate independent, idiosyncratic interests, each terminating at different things as beautiful or good. The distinction cannot be maintained. We can take the same interest in the beauty of the rose that we can in the rose itself; other men can do the same and with the same effect. Conversely, we can perceive the rose while changing our interest in it and we can keep on liking the rose even though it fades. The value of the rose to us is relevant to the kind of interest we take in it, but this means nothing more than that an interest in its beauty is distinct from and somewhat independent of an interest in its odor, shape, and color. The former is appreciative, the latter cognitive. They are both objective, public, steady, and reliable, both subjective, private, fluctuating, and unreliable.

5) Let it be granted that only man has a sense of value, that he alone judges things to be good or bad, ugly or beautiful, important or unimportant, and that these terms have meaning only with reference to his nature, his wants, or his fears. It does not follow that he is therefore mistaken when he talks of values. Because no other beings can judge, it does not follow that his judgments are in error, that they do not report what is there in fact. Man has a unique gift of appreciating values; he also has a unique gift of making fires, of cooking, of speaking grammatically, of laughing and praying, of writing and reading. He makes errors and he forms prejudicial judgments. Neither the one nor the other is evidence that he is not in nature, act-

ing together with others and exemplifying the same principles the others do, and expressing in his peculiar way the natures things have though perhaps only as perceptible to him.

We are sometimes mistaken in our judgments of the goodness or badness of things, of their beauty or ugliness, just as we are sometimes mistaken as to their color, weight, number, and strength. We do read our private, biased views into what we see, and thereby come to love and hate that for which we can find no reason except our feeling of jubilance or sadness. But whatever we judge, whether correctly or incorrectly, objectively or not, we judge as men who live in a world we understand, who are part of nature, subject to forces and influences, exercising powers and capacities similar to those which others exhibit. Otherwise we would be continuous with nature on one side of our being, the side on which no judgments occur, and would be cut off on the side in which they occur, thereby becoming two beings and incidentally denying the relevance of our judgments to nature.

Beings have value in relation to man. They have this value at least in part and some of the time because they promise to perfect or injure him. For a similar reason they have values in relation to one another. That things promise well or ill for one another is just as objective a truth as that they promise to act on or to resist one another, though to be sure, unlike us who sometimes know, subhuman beings never know the values things have for them. Every trait of this knife, its sharpness and hardness, its shape, size, weight, resistance, and motion, exists as a concrete, observable datum only in relation to something beyond it. Like the value of the knife it has the status of a relational, public trait only so far as there are appropriate objects in terms of which the knife's complex relational nature can be manifest.

6) Values and other traits are equally relational. They are not therefore unreal, intrusions, hiding nature from us instead of presenting it to us. If they were, nature would encompass only what exists apart from relation. It would so far be inexperienceable, unencounterable, an I-know-not-what for whose existence and character there could on the hypothesis obviously be no evidence. We obviously know much, much more than this about nature; a knowledge of it as it is in itself can be obtained only by extrapolating and speculating on what we know of it in relation. Nature is primarily the domain of interplaying things in space and time; it possesses whatever traits may accrue to things in the situations in which they in fact are.

7) Things must have a value not only for one another but in and of themselves, unless either they have no status in and of themselves or such a status is divided off from what they are in relation to others. But without some status of their own they would not be able to enter

into relation. Relations which are internal to their terms, which engulf them without residue, have no terms at which to terminate. There are relations only so far as there are things which can be related. And those things have natures of their own dictating what kind of relations can connect them with others. It is the sharp that cuts, the strong that presses, the weak that breaks; it is ice that is cold, the merciful who are generous, the timid who are frightened.

Values can be introduced into nature so as to distort or hide what is there, giving to a thing in relation a value other than the value it actually has. But it is not necessary that values be introduced so as to distort or hide. They can enhance. Men sometimes endow objects which are value laden, both in themselves and in relation to other beings, with values they otherwise would not have. They thereby do not falsify nature; they enrich her. They introduce something that was not there before. But this is not error, unless it is error, too, to make a ship or a flag, or unless it is error, too, to love and thereby transform what is loved. These man-produced values are not the only values there are; they add something to the values things have of themselves.

Each being in nature has some value, some degree of worth, depending on how it perfects and harmonizes its components and exercises its powers. Were beings without value, they could be changed but never injured or improved; there would be no loss or gain if one or all were destroyed or continued, altered or multiplied. A world without value is one in which there could be nothing amiss, in which there was no good or evil, in which it was indifferent to every being whether it or others persisted or perished, remained as they were or were changed. It would be a world we never knew; indeed, it cannot even be entertained without entrenching on the self-contradiction that it would be good to know a value-free world.

The attempt to get to a value-free world is the outcome of a laudable but confused effort to understand what things are apart from a local morality. It rests on the erroneous supposition that once we free ourselves from the framework of our morality we will be free from all values whatsoever. It falsely supposes that to recognize values as part of nature is to distort or to falsify her. The reverse is closer to the truth. Nature is saturated with values. Each being in it has a value both by itself and in relation to others; each has some degree of excellence; each has some bearing on the preservation or enhancement of the excellence of others. All point to and are inseparable from an all-encompassing possible value, a common abstract good, an ultimate end, the object of an absolute morality, enabling them all to be compared and making it possible for man to be subject to inescapable duties.

2. Duty and Commitment

To be fully in and of himself a man must possess whatever makes him a man; otherwise he is a man only because of and from the vantage grounds of others. A man in himself must possess whatever is essential to his nature. He must, to be himself fully, possess that all-encompassing possibility which includes the value of himself and all other things harmonized and unified. By adopting it he completes himself in part, partially satisfies an ontological need to master what conditions him.

By accepting the possibility as his responsibility a man converts it into an *ultimate end*, a totality of value defining his duties and warranting his choices. If he did not use that possibility as an end, he would be subject to it nevertheless, and would thus be subject to conditions which he did not control.

An ultimate end is quite distinct from a goal. A goal is a limited possibility we desire to realize; an end is an inclusive possibility of value it is our duty to realize. Unlike the goal, which serves only to make one alternative more appealing than others and thereby determines its selection as a means to bring about that goal, an ultimate end determines which of a number of alternatives we *ought* to adopt in order not merely to do what is effective but to do what is right.

Whatever we do involves some loss in value, and we are *committed* to whatever ultimate end promises to make good that loss. We would not be committed were there no values in nature, were no values lost, or were there no conceivable way in which the lost values could be recompensed. Without real values, true evil, and a conceivable warrant for wrongs produced, there would be no commitments.

Duty is what our ultimate end requires us to do. It is the compelled outcome of a free, often unknown commitment to an end, to an absolute moral good. Had things no value in themselves which a man's acts could in some way affect, he would have no duties, since there would then be nothing which the good could require him to do. Because things have values of their own, he can be required to realize an ultimate end in and through them, thereby preserving or enhancing the values they have.

We have duties because our ends are prescriptive, demanding that certain things and not others be done. Our ends in turn are binding on us because we have so acted in the past that we, to be ourselves, must realize those ends and not others. Commitment is the unavoidable outcome of free, public action. We are committed by what we do, and this regardless of what we know or intend, whether we are good or whether we are bad. What we do commits us to some end, and this in turn defines our duty.

Whatever losses we produce we are required to make good. And losses we inevitably do produce, even when we do our best and do the best that can be done. Every act reduces and must reduce the value of something. The most beneficial of acts involves the weakening or annihilation of what might be preserved or enhanced. Something must be leaned upon, utilized, consumed, restructured, subordinated, if something else is to be achieved. To accomplish anything we must make use of material and instruments, expend and dissipate energy. The value of some things is necessarily reduced by us even when we concentrate on increasing the values there are. Our best efforts, no less surely than our worst, inevitably prepare us for the commission of some wrong which, to be made reasonable, to be justified, must have a promised recompense in the form of an ultimate end to which we are committed.

It is impossible to avoid doing some wrong. This does not warrant despair or sanction our doing this or that wrong act. It does not warrant despair, for there are acts which are better than others; we must be on the alert to keep the wrongs we do to a minimum. Nor does it sanction our engaging in any particular wrong act, for though something must suffer, it does not follow that it should be this or that. Were there not enough medicine for all someone would have to die, but it is unjust that it should be you, because you have as much right to live as I. Some wrong will result when the medicine is distributed, but that does not warrant the refusal to distribute any, nor does it warrant the distribution of it in this way or that. Some distribution is better than none; some one distribution is better than others. But none is so perfect that it involves no wrong whatsoever to any thing.

3. JUSTIFICATION

Whatever wrongs are produced must be justified. Even if a wrong were very slight it would still require justification. A slight wrong is still a wrong; unjustified, it is wanton, indefensible. When we do less wrong than we might, we have less to justify, but we still have something to justify. We cannot justify it by making evident that it is an excellent means to some desired result, for that result might be undesirable, bad, requiring a justification of its own, or the act itself might be unnecessary, avoidable, replaceable by one less serviceable but involving less of a loss. In either case, what we did would be unjustified.

We are committed to realize whatever ultimate end makes good the loss in value we bring about. If we were not, we should destroy ourselves. The values we possess are correlative to whatever values there are; as unique, each of us is other than all the others; as valuable, each is coordinate with the infinitude to which they sum; as single, each is the unity of the negations which distinguish it from them. When we reduce the values of any of the things about us, we cancel what defines ourselves to be what we are. To avoid this we must maintain a hold on the very values we are actually destroying. This we do in a way when we regret and also in a way when we remember. But neither regret nor memory reinstates the value as a genuine power correlative to ourselves, dictating not only what is to be done but what ought to be done. We are self-committed beings; we must, to avoid destroying ourselves, hold on, in the shape of an end, to what we in fact destroyed. And we must hold on to that end so long as we have a value which is correlative with and implicated in the valuable things we violated.

We have a duty to do whatever is the best possible thing in the circumstances. But nothing we can do is the best possible in and of itself, for that is the status only of an act which involves no wrong at all. It is possible for us to have a duty only because the ultimate end makes some one alternative the best possible.

If a man fails to do his duty he does not do what is, from the vantage point of the end which he has accepted as of his essence, the best possible. He does not therefore hold on to his ultimate end and therefore does not hold on to the only thing which could justify the wrongs he previously produced. He acts in an unjustified way, a way not sustained by an ultimate end, and thus in a way which goes counter to the commitment to which he inevitably subjects himself in order to be himself.

Because of the losses in value we bring about we are committed toward that ultimate end which sanctions the loss. We must cling to that end and do what it prescribes. Otherwise what was sanctioned by that end would cease to be the best possible act for us to have engaged in. We are bound to the end because it alone provides a sanction for what we did; to give up that end, to follow not its demands but some other's, is to deny to our wrong-dealing act the only warrant it had.

Every act is justifiable. Each is warranted by some ultimate end in which its losses are compensated. Our every act has moral significance because we are committed to ends even when we do not consider them. Committed to an ultimate end, we may yet fail to dictate to ourselves any activity in terms of that end. Then, though our act will be justifiable, it will not be justified. The end justifies what was done only if it dictates what is to be done.

Iago saw the downfall of Othello as eminently desirable. That is why he decided to bring about Othello's ruin. It is not clear whether, according to Shakespeare, this was an alternative which initially ap-

pealed to Iago or whether it was one which Iago preferred because of
some further goal he thereby hoped to realize. But if it was solely
one or the other, Iago would have no ultimate justification for his decision. Yet his choice is justifiable. There is a conceivable universe in
which Othello, who after all was only a man, would not stand above
and apart from others because of his natural strength and gentleness.
He and Iago would be on a level, men with different internal flavors
but with the same intrinsic worth and dignity. In such a universe it
is just and right that Othello's arrogance be humbled, particularly
if this be essential to the existence of a world in which men of wit
and not men of innocence rule, where uncontrolled passion is a vice
deserving whatever punishments it entrains, and where generals act
with reason and not on impulse. Even if Othello were the noblest of
men, deserving only joy and honor, it would be possible to justify his
ruination so long as there is a possible end which makes good that reduction in value. That ultimate end perhaps could never be realized;
but it is one to which a man can be committed as surely as he can to any
other.

Iago, in electing to ruin Othello, committed himself to a future in
which the loss his decision involved was compensated. To keep his decision good it was up to him to make up for the loss it involved. He
should have tried to bring about that excellent world for which
Othello's downfall is a precondition. But Iago was a villain. He did
not, he would not, and he could not sustain the end to which his free
decision committed him. Because he did not live up to the commitment
to which he freely subjected himself when he decided on the ruination
of Othello, he deprived his acts of the warrant they needed from it.
Because he would not live up to the commitment he was a villainous
man, refusing to carry out his voluntary pledge. Because he could not
live up to the commitment he was a foolish man, a man who produced
a wrong which he could justify only in theory, never in fact. Iago may
have had strong motives and multiple excuses, but so long as he was
not willing to live in terms of the ultimate end which alone sanctioned
his decision as the best possible, he turned his acts into unjustified
ones. Because he could not really live in terms of that end he forever
after revealed his acts to be wanton, inexcusable. Because he did not
want to live in terms of that end he forever after defined himself to be
a villain.

The end which alone can justify the ruination of Othello is one
which is correlative to a tremendous loss in value. It is indeed too great
an end for any man to sustain. But it is one thing to ignore it and
another to be unable to live in terms of it. Had Iago, instead of putting
his justifying end aside, tried to realize it, he would not have been the

villain he was. But he would have been a fool, voluntarily dedicated to bring about an impossible end.

A villain and a fool can do the same things and be justified by the same end. The villain though undoes himself, denies what alone made his decision the best possible, whereas the fool is undone by things, since these prevent him from living up to the end he himself accepts as of his essence. The one disengages himself from his justifying end, denies himself, cuts himself in two; the other is disengaged from his end, betrayed by circumstance. The one ignores his duties, the other vainly hopes that what duty requires will somehow be realized. Neither carries out the ultimate end which justifies his acts, the one because he does not wish to, the other because he is unable.

A minor villain could but does not try to hold on to what can compensate for what he did; a minor fool tries but fails to hold on to it. Both the great villain and the great fool commit themselves with respect to an ultimate end beyond the powers of any man to realize, the one deliberately, the other thoughtlessly. Both commit great, irremediable wrongs. But the one cuts himself off from all justification; the other holds on to a possible justification, in a tenuous form and while actually living in opposition to its dictates. The one condemns himself by denying his past; the other condemns himself by clinging to a hopeless future. The one is deliberately inconsistent, deliberately abandoning his sanctioning end; the other is consistent, but only by converting his end into the terminus of a vain desire, acting all the while in opposition to it. The one is beyond redemption; the other is within the reach of miracle.

The great fool and the great villain ruin men. This is quite different from using or even abusing them. Men can and ought to be used as means. And we make them function as means when we talk to them, for we thereby turn them into listeners and companions. We use and ought to use men as merchants, soldiers, and policemen. We then do them some wrong, since we ignore, distort, or obscure their individual natures and what these might need. But we also benefit them, allowing them to be part of that world in which men rely on and help one another. Still the wrong we do must be made good. The bore is ethically as well as socially at fault, for he fails to compensate for his waste of our time. He committed himself in talking to us, but he does not know how to fulfill the duties that were then entrained. Wanting to make good the losses he brings about, he is unable. He should have remained silent.

Kant's admonition that we are never to use men as means only is meaningless, according to his own account, for he speaks of men as possessing a rational core, completely outside the realm where means

are employed. On his own theory of the radical distinction that exists
between the phenomenal and noumenal, the experiential and the rational sides of a man, no full man can be used as a means only. And so
far as his admonition makes sense, and thus has application to a man
who is not divided into a phenomenal and a noumenal being, it is mischievous. A man should be used as a means only, in all sorts of circumstances. The parts of a human chain, firemen running with the hose,
the men in front who serve as barricades for the soldiers behind, are
means, and means only, at the time. What would be wrong would be
a misuse of them as means, the treatment of them so as to reduce their
value unnecessarily while taking advantage of the goods they produce; what would be wrong would be the abuse of them, the employ-
ment of them as means in ways which are not suited to their natures;
what would be wrong would be the ruination of them, the reduction
in their value, whether or not this occurs while they serve as means or
as ends.

4. The Nature of Choice

Choosing is an act in which an alternative and its compensating
end are freely elected. It is an activity possible and necessary if there
are to be duties and responsible action. Were it possible to engage
in action but not possible to elect an end which compensates for the
losses brought about, men would be precluded from justifying what
they do. The value of things or the meaning of duty would in effect
be denied; there would be no necessity to take account of either. Were
men, instead, free to take any one of a number of ultimate ends but
not free to determine which one of several alternative courses to take,
they would inevitably do this or that regardless of what they ought
to do. What a man did would be irrelevant to what he was. By a shift
in perspective a sinner could become a saint, for his selfsame act could
then be sustained by a better end.

If a man is to have a freedom to elect any one of a number of alternatives, there must be available a multiplicity of ends, one of which he
can freely elect at that very time. Each end will have a place for the
beings other ends exclude. One end might allow for more men than
others do. But neither the number nor the kind of things allowed by
an end will affect its value. All ends have the same degree of value, for
all are harmonious totalities of whatever values there are. All ends are
therefore equally good, equally qualified to make good our wrongs.
They differ from one another only in that they prescribe the distribution of the same total value over different ranges of things and thus
serve to justify different alternatives and determine different duties.

Free choice requires that there be a plurality of available alternatives, all equally defensible, all equally capable of attaining the status of being the best possible, of becoming the alternative that is rightly chosen. By itself no one alternative is the best possible; it becomes so only by being supported by an ultimate end in which its losses are reinstated and redistributed to give the selfsame totality of value with which we began.

He who kills a villain destroys the value which the villain has as a man. Not to kill the villain is to allow for the destruction of those things which his villainy entails. With equal justification either alternative can be chosen. We can justifiably choose the first if we also choose an ultimate end which requires the promotion of human welfare even by destroying whatever men stand in the way. We can justifiably choose the second if we also choose an end which demands that no human life be sacrificed or human liberty restrained, even when this is to be attained by having vice rampant. The end for the first is one in which there are no villains and no effects of villainy; the end for the second is one in which villains add piquancy, when moderated so as to combine with all else, to make an excellent end.

Were there no multiplicity of ultimate ends, all equally good, among which we can freely choose at every moment, all good men would have to elect the selfsame end, or a man would be able to choose only among apparent goods. The first supposition overlooks the truth that good men can be committed to quite different ends. Abraham and Lincoln were both good men but committed quite differently. It makes a mystery too of the fact that a man who once was good is now bad, even though nothing attracts a good man but the good. The second supposition denies that any man is ultimately responsible for his choices. For different men different things would seem to be good because of the natures they have, and they, on the hypothesis, would inevitably and more or less erroneously take different objects as their true ends. They would be men who had been forced along paths which ended in taking some apparent, but not actual, good to be good in fact. Accountable to society perhaps for what they decided, they would never be responsible for what they do and could not therefore rightly be praised or blamed. Unless men can freely choose among equally valuable, equally objective ultimate ends, they cannot be responsible for what they choose. And they cannot freely choose if what they choose must be the inevitable outcome of the natures they have, whether those natures be acquired at birth or be gradually achieved with or without the help of some external force.

Nothing inside or out can have human decisions as its inevitable outcome without thereby shearing men from their responsibilities. Men make themselves when and as they decide; what they have been and what they are subject to, help turn them more in one direction than in another, but they never do and never can prescribe what way the men will finally decide to favor. And though different alternatives have different appeals for men, they are all equally justifiable by their respective ends. Each alternative is a justifiable object of choice, but only in terms of its particular end. Each is warranted by an ultimate end different from those warranting others; it becomes an alternative chosen only when and as its correlative committing end is chosen.

When we choose we freely isolate one of a set of alternatives as the best possible; we convert it from a justifiable into an at least momentarily justified alternative. When and as we do this we convert one of a number of equally possible ends into a chosen end, into a determinate component of our being, dictating the nature of our duties. Both of these results are the outcome of the exercise of an internal power by which we recover our equilibrium in part, ready ourselves freely to act on the external realities that now delimit, defy, and define us.

5. Preference and Choice

Freedom of preference falls short of a freedom of choice. Freedom of preference is a privately exercised, dynamic freedom to select and accept any one of a set of envisaged alternatives. It enables us to convert an inclination into an act of intention, a datum encountered into a prospect intended, making it likely that we will act in one way rather than in another. It is not a freedom to act; we can select an alternative freely and yet automatically act in another way; we can be prevented from actually performing what we intend to do.

Whereas preference presupposes a goal with paramount appeal, choice dynamically determines what unity of ultimate end and alternative is most in consonance with our nature. It prepares us for a public exercise of freedom when and as a private exercise occurs. Preference freely selects an alternative; it has no necessary effect on action. Choosing involves the free adoption of an ultimate end as well and stresses one way of acting more than it does others. Preference relates a host of alternatives to some goal, selected under influence from without; choosing relates each alternative to its respective end, freshly adopted then and there from within.

Were our goal the winning of a battle we should perhaps prefer, over all other alternatives, that of shooting at the enemy. But if our ultimate end demands that we never take a life, we will choose some other alternative to that of shooting at the enemy. As a consequence we will oppose the demands made by our goal. The alternative which we will choose will be an alternative we will not freely prefer. Our free choice will prevent our preferring freely, since the alternative we will adopt will be sanctioned by our end but not by our goal.

A goal is inevitably adopted whenever an alternative is actually chosen. That goal makes the chosen alternative an alternative preferred as well. That alternative, since it was already adopted through an act of choice, will obviously not be an alternative which is freely preferred. Adopted because of the end, not because of the goal, it is an alternative we are forced to prefer. Our choice of it precludes our free preference of it, since it denies us the opportunity to make free use of the goal. The means we use will be alternatives which our end then and there sanctions, not what our adopted goal demands.

If we are freely to choose an alternative in such a way as to enable us freely to prefer it as well, we must use our end to endorse the goal as the best possible. Since, in this case, the alternative will also be adopted through the help of the end, the goal will not help us to select the alternative. The goal in such a case will have no other function but that of determining the *manner* in which the chosen alternative will also achieve the status of a preferred alternative.

Our acts of choice are acts in which we inevitably decide to prefer freely or constrainedly, the former if ultimate end and goal are adopted together, the latter if, instead, only the ultimate end is adopted. If end and goal are accepted together we can determine just what role the goal is to play and thus what alternative course we are to prefer; if the end alone is adopted the goal is denied the opportunity of dictating what alternative to take.

Our primary choice is a choice as to whether to compel or to endorse that goal which makes a chosen alternative preferred. If we compel the goal to do this we insist on the alternative regardless of its value as a means. We prefer, but not freely. If we endorse the goal we freely choose and freely prefer the alternative, taking it both as sanctioned by the end and as an effective means to the goal. The latter is the better choice.

6. The Freedom in Choice

Free choice would present an insoluble problem were there no middle ground between a necessitating reason and the absence of all reason. Between a reason which necessitates and no reason there is, though, the act of producing a reason. The reason for choosing an alternative is produced in the act of choice—it is the acceptance of a commitment to a justifying end. The reason for choosing the end is then and there also provided—it is the acceptance of some alternative as the best possible. The two reasons are one, viewed in different ways. The act of choice provides a commitment to an ultimate end and a sanction for an alternative, supporting end by alternative and alternative by end.

There are as many reasons for a choice as there are sets of ultimate ends and alternatives. We may choose our end because it attracts us or because the alternative it favors appeals to us or for some other reason. The alternative may be one which some previously chosen ultimate end supports; its end may be one toward which we were previously committed, though as a rule it is not. When we choose, either the old end or the newly favored alternative must be sacrificed. We cannot tell in advance which it will be. We decide which in the act of choice; it is then and then only that we decide whether to insist on some favored alternative and violate our duty or to conform to our duty and choose some other alternative than that which we most favor.

We favor one choice over others because we tend more toward its end or its alternative. This "because" is exactly what the act of choice turns into a decisive reason. It endows the alternative chosen with a sanction while giving to the correlative end the power to dictate to us thereafter what we are to do.

Determinism describes the nature of alternatives before they are chosen, but only so far as they are relevant to a present state and circumstance. It also describes the nature of alternatives after they have been chosen, but only so far as they are relevant to some chosen end. In both cases the various alternatives are unequal in choice-worthiness. Determinism can tell us therefore that one *must* be chosen. Unfortunately it precludes us from choosing it in fact. It is a theory which requires one to say that a man begins by being compelled to accept an alternative because it appeals and that he ends by being compelled to accept it because it is justified by some adopted end. It has no place for the free act by which a man moves from the state of being compelled by alternatives to the state of being compelled by ends.

Indeterminism describes the nature of the alternatives before they are chosen, but only so far as they are held apart from their justifying ends. It describes the alternatives too after they have been chosen, as no longer objects of inclinations and preferences. It supposes the alternatives, both before and after the choice, to be equally choice-worthy. It correctly informs us that any alternative *can be* chosen. Unfortunately it precludes the choice among them. On this theory one is forced to say that a man begins by being free to accept any alternative because all the alternatives are equally justifiable, and that at the end he is free to accept any alternative because all of them have been freed from the grip of the inclinations and preferences. It has no place for the decisive act by which a man transforms himself from a being free to justify alternatives into a being who has freely justified one alternative.

Determinists ignore the data which reveal that a choice can be free; their opponents ignore the data which reveal that a choice has been made. The one concentrates on the elements of what has already been chosen; the other concentrates on the conditions of a choice still to be made. The one treats the future as though it were already past; the other supposes that the past is entirely future. Both begin and end with alternatives which are untouched by the fact that a choice can be or was made. Neither accurately describes the conditions for or the effect of an act of choice. Both neglect the process of moving from one to the other. Neither is adequate to the act of choice, for this is a process by which a compulsive, because appealing, alternative is made equal to others by transcending the inclinations at the same time that it is distinguished from them by being sanctioned by a chosen end. To choose is to introduce another factor, making a difference to what was there. But this factor neither of the traditional positions allows. They both antecedently define the situation to be one in which no real choice can or does occur. They fail to see that choice is a creative act in which some alternative is altered by being made inseparable from a justifying end.

VIII

CONSCIENTIOUSNESS AND REFORM

1. Thoughtless and Deliberate Choices

MEN choose ultimate ends and alternatives they might have rejected; they reject what they might have accepted. What they accept is, as a rule, what is most in consonance with their inclinations. One who knows them can predict, often with a high degree of accuracy, which alternative and ultimate end they at a given moment will choose. But each man can, and sometimes does, upset the prediction and choose something else; whether he does or not he chooses in a concrete, creative way outside the reach of formulas, predictions, universals, statements, discourse. Choosing usually stops with whatever is favored for extrinsic reasons, though nothing external can determine just what will be chosen.

Most choices are thoughtlessly made. The alternative and ultimate end are taken without adequate consideration of what must thereafter be done. A deliberate act of choosing is one in which the alternative and end have been examined and contrasted with others, and is accompanied by a resolution that the loss of value then and there required will be made good. But deliberation takes time and effort; even the most conscientious and reflective of men chooses thoughtlessly many times during the day. A man is disposed to do what he has always done, without reflection or attention, or to take a rest and let things run their course and so promote the end which those things conspire to make possible. In either case, whether thoughtless or deliberate, he commits himself to act on behalf of the ultimate end which makes his chosen alternative the best possible. In either case he could have chosen to commit himself otherwise.

A thoughtless act of choice is a free choice as surely as is a deliberate one. It need not have gone the way it did. But every act of choice is either thoughtless or deliberate. At every moment some choice is made. When we choose as habit or convention dictates we freely allow other factors to pick out the alternative we will elect and the ultimate end we are committing ourselves to realize, but it is we who have chosen this as one of the possible devices by which an alternative is isolated. We freely choose in such a case between the alternative of following and the alternative of transcending habit, the former precluding the need to choose the course we will pursue, the latter requiring us to engage in another act of choice among possible courses of activity.

Man must choose. He cannot avoid electing one alternative rather than another. What he chooses is freely chosen, but the act of choosing is forced on him. If he is not deliberately for something, he is thoughtlessly for it or for something else. To be indifferent, to be undecided, to allow things to go their own way is to have made a choice in favor of that alternative and ultimate end which, at the moment, are favored for reasons apart from that provided by the act of choice. It is to choose freely what circumstances have chosen already.

2. Conscientiousness

We can choose one way or another, but not until we do choose do we make determinate whether ours is a decision of a man who subscribes to previously adopted ends or abandons them for others. Not until we choose do we decide to live up to our duty or not. The act of choice is the act of deciding what type of man to be. It is the means by which we decide whether to commit ourselves in accordance with our duty or some other way. No preceding decision dictates how the next *will* go, but since it is what we once did that determines what we now have to do, preceding decisions dictate how the next *ought* to go.

By choosing, some ultimate end is made integral to a man's being. The chooser freely commits himself, subjects himself to the necessity of sustaining whatever ultimate end sanctions his elected alternative, for otherwise he would have to deny himself a past. Free to ignore, actually free to put aside whatever ultimate end he may have committed himself to previously, he is not morally free to separate himself from it. It made what was previously chosen the best that was then chosen; if he claims later that he was mistaken in choosing as he did, he maintains that he did wrong to commit himself to that end. But committed he remains. He is forever after a man who chose this alternative or that, who made it then the best possible, and thus who committed himself to realize such or such an end. All that is left for him to do is to decide whether or not to live up to his commitment and thus whether or not to be conscientious thereafter.

Were men without careers, could each of us be broken up into a set of independent moments, we would be outside responsibility. We would have to commit ourselves afresh at each moment without regard to how we had committed ourselves before. Our different acts of choice would be unrelated even where they were consistent. Each commitment would relate to the moment of institution and nothing more and thus be no commitment at all. New decisions would have to be forged regardless of what had been decided in the past. The entire past would as a consequence be irrelevant to what we decided to be. But man is a preserver of the past. We are committed permanently to ultimate ends which contain the values our acts destroy. We must strive to bring about those ends. If we do not, we will be divided against ourselves.

We are committed to ultimate ends from which we cannot free ourselves. They are of our essence. All we can possibly do is to act in defiance of them, thereby committing ourselves to still other ultimate ends. Free to choose new ends at every moment, free to deny our past, free to reject the claim an ultimate end may have on us, free to fulfill or violate our duty, we remain committed today as we were yesterday and by the very same end. It is our deeds which determine whether we are committed to this ultimate end or that, and no wish or hope can free us from the commitment. We can ignore our commitment, we can freely decide not to live up to the commitment we freely assumed, but we cannot decide not to be committed by that to which our deeds committed us. The present is big with the past. Only by recognizing the claim that our past has on us now and by submitting to the dictates of the ultimate end which that past prescribes can we make our existence as unified as is our essence.

Present acts of choice should be forged in the light of past choosings and thus of ends to which we committed ourselves. Otherwise previously chosen alternatives will be deprived of the sanction which made them the best possible alternatives and thus the alternatives which should have been chosen. The conscientious man recommits himself to an ultimate end previously chosen. He is consistent with himself, a man who, by continuing to hold on to the ultimate end which justified previous choices, can continue to affirm that the best possible had been chosen.

Conscience is a mental disturbance experienced when an ultimate end which leaves previous acts of choice unjustified is chosen. It is the felt weight of oneself, as a being with a past, on oneself as freely constituting oneself in the present. It is a tension experienced by the self between what it had once accepted and what it now does. A convert feels a prick of conscience with respect to the life he once led; so does he who has discovered the joys of neglected flesh. The one says that he was once a sinner, the other that he once was bemused. Both say that they were blind and that now they see. Conscience is the eye by which they note that they are not now as once they were.

The mischief produced in the name of conscience offers evidence too strong to make possible the continuance of the common mode of speaking of it as a divinely inspired witness to some abused truth. Conscience does not tell what is right and what is wrong. But it is usually unwanted, a consciousness that something is amiss with us, a witness to our inconsistency. It reports our failure to be conscientious, making us focus on the truth that an act of choice, once acknowledged to be right, is now unsanctioned because not supported by the ultimate end now adopted.

We all have a conscience, for we all have a past insistent on its rights against the free decisions we forge in the present. But we rarely note its presence; its degree of evidence is a function of the extent of the inconsistency it reports. Only if there were a man who acknowledged no ultimate end, or one who never changed his course, would there be a man without a conscience. Instead we have men whose consciences bother them not often and but little, either because they live so much in the present or because they vary in their courses so little over the years.

3. TYPES OF ULTIMATE ENDS

In each decision men freely commit themselves. If they are conscientious they renew a previous commitment, thereby denying conscience cause and voice. If inconstant, they commit themselves in a new way while suffering conscience's nag to do otherwise. In either case they determine how much weight the past is actually to have in the present and thus how moral they are to be. In either case they choose among a number of ultimate ends, each justifying a different alternative.

There are as many ultimate ends as there are exclusive, sanctionable alternatives. Each is a universe distinct from all the others. They are of three types. In one type all that now exists is preserved, enhanced, and harmonized. In the second, part of what now exists is supplanted by new beings. In the third, everything that now exists is supplanted by other beings.

An ultimate end of the first type denies one the right to use anything whatsoever. Since we can never avoid destroying or reducing some things in part or whole, it is not a type of end possible for men. It is possible only for a merciful God, a God who preserves all values despite change, death, and the ravages of time. A man who would commit himself to do nothing but preserve and enhance defines himself therefore to be a God. Since he nevertheless is a man, he compels himself perpetually to choose only what he thinks to be wrong.

An ultimate end of the third type requires one to remove whatever now exists. It is not possible to anyone without infinite power to destroy. He who would choose it would have to be a satanic and creating God in one, destroying a universe and committing himself to make good the loss by creating another. Since men are not gods, good or satanic, they cannot destroy all things and thus cannot commit themselves to an end in which such a destruction is made good.

Only the second type of end, in which some things are preserved, some destroyed, and some enhanced, is an ultimate end possible for a man to hold while still remaining a man. He can wish an end of the first or third type; he can commit himself only to an end of the second type. He cannot commit himself to these others, for whatever he does involves some loss, some gain, and some constancy in values. Only an end of the second type is possible for him; only such an ultimate end can express the nature of a pertinent future relevant to his past and determinative of his duty.

There are many ultimate ends of the second type. Some ought not to be chosen, since they involve a loss beyond human power to make good. He who destroys men may preserve and enhance the rest of the world but he will nevertheless have committed himself to make good a unique, irreplaceable, infinite loss of value. But this he cannot do. It is always wrong to sacrifice a man for any material good, and so far as men are irreplaceable, it is wrong to sacrifice one man for any other.

The killing of one or a million can be justified only if the ultimate end to which such slaughter commits us is one in which the loss can be recompensed. At the very least this requires that the world to be have all the values of that which was given up for it. We cannot avoid destroying much that is precious, but if we are to be justified, we must destroy it for an ultimate end in which what is lost is recovered.

There are two fanaticisms, a hot and a cold, leading men to destroy what never can be made good. The hot is sensitive to values sacrificed, keenly aware of the evil done, but takes for granted that the infinite loss can be made good. It burns with the mistaken belief that man has infinite power and infinite wisdom. Revolutionaries and empire builders, in contrast, are coldly fanatic; they earnestly seek to promote a better world by changing the economy or politics or size of a nation. They may say to themselves that they are willing to make good whatever losses in value their actions involve. But they destroy much more than they could possibly make good. How many inches of ground pushed under a new flag equals a single life? It is questionable indeed whether all the glories of the globe can balance a single moment of human anxiety or the worth of the life that could have been. Nothing less than a world in which a change in politics or geography could yield the value of the millions could possibly warrant what they do. Not deliberately vicious, those who commit themselves to the realization of such an end are as wrong headed though not as bad as are those who deliberately refuse to make good the losses they themselves bring about.

The power of choosing should be exercised within the limits of what is intrinsically realizable; it should be restrained so that we commit ourselves to bring about only what we are able to realize. Otherwise we will be at once perpetually guilty and inconstant, perpetually committed and perpetually committing ourselves to bring about what cannot be. Among the host of ultimate ends that we can choose, and thus among the ultimate ends of the second type, only those ought to be chosen which can be realized. There is a limit on the possible ultimate ends and thus on the alternatives among which a choice should be exercised.

4. Impotence, Maladroitness, and Misfortune

Since we inevitably decrease values, we inevitably commit ourselves. Because of the losses we bring about we are committed to ends we perhaps cannot realize. Yet we are and remain committed whether or not we can realize the end to which we are committed.

Having no funds I cannot pay my debts. But having deprived others of their money by borrowing from them, I must repay them. My failure to pay can be understood and perhaps even excused. But having borrowed I am under a permanent requirement to repay. It is bad logic and bad ethics then to say "ought" necessarily implies "can."

Let us suppose that the money I borrowed was lost by me in an investment which was said by everyone to be the best, the soundest possible, and suppose too that all my money went with it. Will I then be free of my debt? Suppose I cannot find a job, a way of earning money. Am I then freed? Or suppose I used the money in dissipation and am now so incompetent as to make impossible the retention of the job and thus the possibility of earning enough to pay back the money borrowed. If I use borrowed money in such a way as to preclude my paying, I surely am not freed from the requirement to pay it. I ought to pay it but I cannot. We are committed to do what we commit ourselves to do, whether we are able to live up to our commitments or not.

Again and again we find ourselves unable to meet our debts in whole or part. A man may find his brother and sister in a death struggle with a maddened animal and may be unable to save them both. He will be able to do what he should—save one of them—only if he does what he should not—neglect the other. He is *impotent* to do all he must. Or he might be able to save both if only he could shoot the animal; yet he may be so *maladroit* that he might shoot his brother instead. His body may be so poorly organized that it cannot support the alternative which is sanctioned by his ultimate end. Or, finally, he may be too far from the struggle, he may be unable to get close enough to shoot in time to save more than one. The environment might not offer him an opportunity to act appropriately, to save both his brother and his sister. He may be *unfortunate* enough to be unable to do what he should.

The impotent is unable, the maladroit is unprepared, the unfortunate is prevented. None of them can realize his sanctioned alternative. The first plays cards with seasoned gamblers, the second does not know the rules, the third has the run of the cards against him. The first lacks necessary power, the second lacks necessary techniques, the third lacks necessary instruments. None of them can avoid the guilt which flows from a failure to bring about what he ought.

Men should commit themselves so that they are able to do what they ought. They should so act that they are committed to ends whose demands are more moderate. They need not subscribe to the ultimate end of benefiting all mankind or even of helping brother or sister. They owe much to their fellow men, and have used their fellows sufficiently in the past to make it their duty to help them now to some degree. But unless they have done them considerable injury they are not morally required to do more than be of help to some of them some of the time. It might be better if they had different ends, if they concerned themselves with graver problems of interest to more. But on the one hand they are committed no further than they have been committed by their acts and on the other hand there is nothing gained in a commitment to an ultimate end which is essentially beyond their power to realize. Such commitment taints a man with the inextinguishable guilt of having done an uncompensable, unjustifiable wrong.

To avoid committing himself to do what he cannot, a man should try to maximize values on every occasion. No matter how much he enhances values, however, he can never be sure that he will be able to make good the losses he inevitably produces by concentrating here instead of there, by using this in order to benefit that. He may have less to recompense than others have but still he may be without the ability, preparation, or opportunity to do all he should. The best of men is required to make good the minor losses he brings about. But compensation for even a minor loss may at times be beyond him. By maximizing values, he reduces the risk of being committed to an unrealizable end; he does not wipe it out.

Every ultimate end calls for the use of special techniques. Not only ought values to be maximized; men ought to master techniques which enable them to do this most effectively. Not the least of these techniques is that of using the body effectively, of overcoming a natural or acquired maladroitness. Without such a technique a man will find himself committed to do what is, though not beyond human power, unrealizable by him. He can avoid this by preparing himself for the situations in which he will make his choices. The more awkward he is, the more surely will he injure where he should benefit. While failing to do his duty, he will commit himself to bring about other, for him, unrealizable ends.

If his ultimate end requires him to cure, a man owes it to himself as well as to others to master the techniques of medicine; if his ultimate end requires him to kill, he owes it to himself and even to him whom he destroys to act with neatness and dispatch. Since no man can be a perfect master of any one technique, and since no man can master all techniques, each should commit himself with respect only to some of the ultimate ends theoretically open to man. Instead of committing himself to benefit all in all ways, he should commit himself to benefit some to some degree, say by creating works of beauty, by making contributions to knowledge, by improving tools, by encouraging others. Some men are able to do some of these things better than the rest; if they keep within the fields of their special abilities they can avoid unnecessarily compounding wrongs by incapacity.

Some techniques enable men to do more than others. The ability to whistle may come in good stead at times, but it is on the whole less valuable than the ability to cook, to teach, or to make a statue. Each man, unless he never does anything but the most insignificant of things, has a duty to master techniques which enable him to deal with a host of objects under a host of different circumstances. Only thus will he be able to do what he must, again and again.

No one can be certain that his techniques will serve him on every occasion. Techniques are habits, general modes of preparation, and must be creatively used, modeled to fit each case. The most skillful marksman sometimes misses. The mastery of a technique is no guarantee that duties, even of a limited sort, will always be fulfilled; it merely limits the number of times a man will find himself too maladroit to do what he should.

And sometimes, despite a mastery of a technique adequate to a situation, a man may be prevented by bad fortune from doing his duty. Nature is not within his control; space, time, and brute fact stand in the way of the realization of what is within conceivable human power, and for which excellent techniques have been well prepared. To do what he should a man should commit himself to bring about only what occurs within that part of nature over which he has some control.

Instead of committing himself to benefit an indefinite number of men, it would be better for him to commit himself to improve what he can with the instruments at his disposal. The one is a laudable aim but futile; the other is too far this side of heaven but still something within his reach.

No present mastery of nature will protect a man from situations in which he is prevented from realizing ends otherwise within his power. There are no walls in nature. What is now within the realm over which human control is exercised is partly in a realm outside control as well, and often is on the verge of moving further into it. He who is committed to deal only with those things in that part of the world within his control avoids being faced with a host of issues he cannot handle. But he does not avoid all such issues.

The wise moral man cultivates his garden, acts inside that part of nature over which he has control so as to commit himself to make good only minor losses in value in an area within his reach. He reduces to a minimum the number of times he will be proved unfortunate. Should he, in addition, maximize values by means of the best possible techniques, he will have done all a man can do to avoid committing himself to do what he cannot. He will fail to do what he should occasionally, but not as often as others. He may do much less good than others now do, but he will surely always do less harm. He may suffer from the vice of excessive caution, be overtimid, detached, and thus be less than a man should be, but in compensation he will avoid making others suffer for his impotence, incompetence, and ill luck. He will not be the best but he also will not be the worst or most dangerous of men.

5. THE ANTICIPATION OF CRISES

There are times of tragedy, there are special, unanticipatable occasions when what we must do, though within the range of our power, skill, and good fortune, is very difficult to do. Only by grace of an exceptional exercise of determination will we then do what we should. A prior interest in specialized work and limited goals makes it possible to focus on desirable alternatives even while their sanctioning end has become dimmed or forgotten in times of crisis. No one knows in advance whether or not he will act on behalf of some limited goal and therefore choose the alternative it supports; he can know only that if he does so act he may act in line with, though never because of, duty. No one can avoid the task of freshly deciding at each moment which alternative to choose. Prior commitments and habits make likely that one will take this alternative or that. They never guarantee it.

He whose sanctioned alternative has little appeal, either initially or derivatively, has a difficult decision to make. He faces an ultimate test

of character since he must, in the face of a temptation to take a different alternative, try to make himself one who sustains the ultimate end
to which he is committed. He can avoid the test by dealing with the
alternative as something to be preferred and thus as required by a
goal. If his goal happens to be in harmony with his ultimate end, he
will choose what he should, though of course not because he should. He
will elect what a man of good character does, not as a man of good
character.

Most of us do not like to face ultimate issues, and very few indeed
prepare for them. Few try to live *in order to* fulfill their duties; for
the most part we are content if we happen not to violate them. Unprepared for crises, we are sometimes forced to test our characters to the
extreme, and often to our loss. We allow circumstance to dictate when
we are to make an exceptional effort to live up to our commitments.
Had we habituated ourselves to living up to them, we would have
made it easier to choose as duty requires.

There is a nobility in ordinary men that the prudential lack. Unprepared for crises, they subject themselves to radical tests of character which the others have learned to avoid. But then too they are
the men who most often fail to live up to their commitments. The
prudential at least, while avoiding an ultimate test of character, are
more likely not to go against what their ultimate ends demand. They
prepare themselves to adopt sanctioned alternatives by attending to
them as means for the attainment of limited goals. They tend to prefer
what ought to be preferred. Avoiding an ultimate test of character
they deny themselves an opportunity to form their characters to the
extent others do, though, to be sure, in compensation they escape making a radical misstep.

He who faces a crisis head on, as ordinary men often do, subjects
himself to an ultimate test but also risks making a wrong choice. The
prudential have neither great moral successes nor great moral failures
to their credit; others risk great failures but sometimes achieve great
successes, frequently coming out of crises better masters of themselves
than they had been before.

Like the prudential, it is meet to be prepared against crises. Instead
of trying, with the prudential, to make unappealing but sanctioned
alternatives into preferable ones, it is good though, in calm moments,
to forge a good character in a series of correct ultimate decisions. We
need to be prudent, not with respect to alternatives but with respect
to our characters. We should not therefore try to avoid ultimate tests
of character but should seek them out at those moments when success
is most likely. Those who have done this often in the past find that an
occasional incorrect choice has little effect on them. They tend to

decide correctly in crises and to reduce the effect that their occasional wrong decisions will have on themselves. Ready to face ultimate issues, prepared to do what duty demands and because it demands it, they fall short more often than the prudential do but less often than the ordinary. They have richer characters than the one and firmer characters than the other.

6. The Alteration of Alternatives

He who does not do his duty acts so as to commit himself in a new way. He divides himself, subjects himself to two equally insistent demands. His act commits him to an ultimate end he must fulfill even though he was already just as strongly and legitimately committed to a different end. He is a guilty man, a man who does not fulfill his commitment; he is a responsible man, a man who freely commits himself to an end which requires that he abandon his previously accepted end.

Required perhaps to treat all men with kindness, a man may find the task most congenial. He may have the ability, the skill, and the good fortune to be able to complete the task successfully. Nevertheless he may be unable to do it. No one of the alternatives open to a man may be sanctioned by the end he was committed to realize. He might be lost, alone, unable even to choose what his end prescribes. He would be forced then to choose an alternative his end does not prescribe, and would necessarily commit himself to realize a new ultimate end. There are times when a wrong choice is unavoidable.

He who goes counter to his commitment chooses wrongly. The degree of that wrong can be minimized if he alters the alternatives encountered so that one of them at least approximates an alternative which the end could sanction. Unable to be kind to any man, perhaps because there are no men about, he can get things ready for their comfort when they arrive. If only unsanctioned alternatives are available, they must be modified until they approximate as much as possible the nature of an alternative which the ultimate end does sanction; then, though he will still choose what he should not, he will not violate his duty as much as he would otherwise.

The alternative which is to be altered is not one sanctioned by the ultimate end. If it were, no alteration would be necessary. And after the alternative has been altered, what would have sanctioned it before can sanction it no longer. If it could, the alteration would not have altered it. The choice of an altered alternative commits a man to a new ultimate end standing between the one he once chose and the one which would have sanctioned if the alternative had not been altered. It reveals him to be one who does not do all he ought, yet does more than he might. He who alters his alternative so as to make necessary the adoption of an end with the least possible difference from a previously adopted end is as excellent as he could then be, but he is not as good as he should be. No man is wholly good who fails to carry out his commitments.

We commit ourselves by what we do. Were we committed regardless of what we did, it would be willful or callous to say at any time that we are guilty, blameworthy, even though we could not, in the circumstances, fulfill the commitment. Were we committed regardless of what we did, we would be subject to some externally oriented command ordering us to pursue tasks which had nothing necessarily to do with us or how we act. Because it is we alone who commit ourselves by choosing what we could have avoided, incapacity to do what we should provides us with no excuse; we enjoyed in advance the good to which we are now committed and we owe it to ourselves and to it to do what it demands. What we must do may be outside our capacity now. Still, it is relevant to us as beings with values, inextricably united with the values of other beings to constitute a totality of value which must not be reduced unless we are also to reduce the meaning and substance of ourselves.

Should we, when unable to elect any alternative but what a previously adopted ultimate end does not sanction, give up our adopted end entirely and take instead whatever end sanctioned some one of the presented alternatives, we would break away from our past too radically. Ultimate end and alternative should be varied as well as chosen together. We should modify our presented alternatives to whatever extent makes possible the choice of an end having the least possible difference from the end previously chosen, if we are not to fail in our duties more than we need.

Since an end should be sustained to the greatest possible extent, a man ought, when unable to choose what his end requires, take the smallest possible step to a new end. In the light of his past decisions his present decision will be wrong; but in the light of the nature of things his present decision will be the best that could be made. It will be a better decision than that made by men who choose whatever ultimate ends favor the most appealing of the alternatives they happen to encounter, but a worse decision than that made by men who can now do their duty.

It is, however, possible to pay too high a price for consistency. The price is too high if we try to cling to an unrealizable ultimate end and thus are necessarily forced to go counter to that end to a degree circumstance happens to prescribe. The price is also too high if we adopt a realizable ultimate end which is more diverse from the unrealizable end than it need be. It is reasonable only if the alternative chosen is one that has been altered to just that degree which will permit us to realize an ultimate end which is more like the original than any other. Unable to be kind, we can try to help; unable to help, we can try to get ready to be kind; unable to get ready to be kind, we can try to get ready to help; unable to get ready to help, we can prepare ourselves to get ready to be kind. If we are committed to do the first, the rest, though better than other things we might do, are not good enough. They are sometimes desirable because guilt has degrees.

7. Reformation, Re-formation, and Cooperation

It is easiest to meet commitments when they are kept well within the scope of proven power, skill, and opportunity. Evils done should be recompensed, not ignored or multiplied. It is desirable that acts of choice be so forged that the evils produced will not demand on behalf of ultimate ends work that could not be performed. Yet no matter how acts are restricted and guided, men are bound to be committed to ultimate ends whose requirements are occasionally violated. All of us are again and again forced to give up ends to which we are committed, modest though the demands of those ends may be, suited though they are to our capacities and the world in which we live.

To abandon one ultimate end is to embrace another. It is to reform, to adopt a new course, and to make at least a tacit confession that a wrong choice had been made before. Reform is not necessarily for the better, though it always involves the judgment that previous decisions are wrong because no longer supported by the chosen committing end. The alternative previously chosen is, by a reform, deprived of the support which a previously adopted ultimate end provided, and is thereby made into an alternative which should not have been chosen.

Every reform marks a failure to live up to the demands of an end. Since a man is guilty to just the extent that he fails to live up to the demands of an ultimate end, he who constantly reforms is hardly better than he who is self-indulgent. Both lives offer a series of wrong decisions. The perpetual reformer differs from the self-indulgent only in that his decisions are always accompanied by resolves to continue to hold on to the new ends just chosen. He will be approved only so long as men are not too tired to forgive past misdeeds and are hopeful enough to believe there will be no further reform for a while.

Reform contrasts quite sharply with re-form. To reform is to adopt a new ultimate end; to re-form is to reorganize so as to choose an alternative previously sanctioned. At every moment we must do one or the other, reform or re-form. By proper re-formation we can make reform unnecessary, since we can make unnecessary the abandonment of an accepted end. But reform makes re-formation always desirable, since it but points up the need for us to exercise more judgment and power than we had if we are to avoid going counter to our commitments.

The most satisfactory mode of reform is that which makes further reforms unnecessary, which provides an occasion for the adoption of an ultimate end that can be fulfilled at every moment. It presupposes that the support of other men has been or will be won, and in any case that their opposition has been effectively decreased. He who awakens the opposition of the rest increases the likelihood that he will fall short of what his ultimate end commands. He is worse off than one who tries to live as a solitary. The latter in turn is inferior to one who has won the cooperation of others, for what one man cannot do by himself he can often do when helped by others. If we can do our duty only through the help of others, it is part of our duty to try to get them to help.

Both he whose end at this time requires the planting of apple trees for the sake of their shade and he whose end requires them for apples may have to transplant the trees. If the trees are large the men will have to help one another. Each will have to use the other as a means enabling him to do what he should. As a rule, one of them will have to give up, for the moment, an attempt to meet his own commitments and devote himself instead to helping the other fulfill his. He will have to help transplant the trees of the other and neglect, at least for a time, his own. He may do this because he wishes to help the other so as to buy his help subsequently—he may cooperate on a utilitarian basis; or he may help him because help is one of the things his end demands that he give—he may cooperate for a moral reason. He either wants to buy help because he is not yet at the point where he can do what he should or he wants to help because cooperation is required by his end, though not to the same degree as in transplantation. In either way he fails to do something which his end requires, since this demanded that he transplant his apple trees. In either way he tries to prepare for a time when he will fully live up to his commitments. If the other fails to help when his turn comes, utilitarian cooperation, help offered so as to buy cooperation, will represent an error, a mistake, a sheer failure to do what one should; whereas moral cooperation, help given because one's end demands it, will involve a partial fulfillment of a commitment. This latter form of cooperation is evidently superior to the former.

Communities require for their existence the practice of a utilitarian cooperation, and they govern its exercise by rules of law, economics, and social custom. They have no way of asking and no way of insisting on any other form of cooperation. Nor have they any need, since utilitarian cooperation serves all their ends with the most efficacy. Moral cooperation runs the risk of being watered by sentiment and of fluctuating with the energy, disposition, and character of men. Utilitarian cooperation is more stable; it can be given a definite public meaning and be regulated so that there is neither too much given nor too much taken. It makes possible the pursuit of diverse and perhaps equally satisfactory ends on the part of different men, each helping the others to be genuinely moral but in a different way than they themselves are, as we see sometimes in the case of contracts, reciprocal trade agreements, and of arrangements with respect to holy places at the focus of multiple religions.

Plato long ago affirmed that it is not necessary to have all men subscribe to the same ends in order to have a community. This important point has been today reaffirmed by Charner Perry in a quite independent way. Plato recognized at least three cooperating groups in his republic, each with an appropriate end, all serving the greater good of their state. Though best known for those phrases in his philosophy where he remarks on the existence of goods greater and higher than those acknowledgeable in a state, Plato exaggerated the importance of the state and thereby denied himself the opportunity to insist adequately on ends which transcended the state's reach. And because he supposed that there were only three classes, each made up of men with exactly the same commitments, he unnecessarily narrowed the number of possible ends to three. All tradesmen do not have the same ends, nor do all soldiers or all rulers. In each of Plato's three classes there can be multiple men with quite divergent ends who live in harmony, cooperate with one another.

The necessary advance is taken by Charner Perry. Without falling into a hopeless relativity he has insisted on the reality of multiple ends, all equally absolute, ultimate, and valuable. He seems, however, to think that the ends are chosen in independence of all else; his account does not cover the case of ends to which we are already committed because of the losses we brought about. We are bound to certain ends regardless of our desires, whether or not we are conscious of them. Nor are we always committed as we like to be. We choose our ends freely in that we freely reduce the value of alternatives which those ends alone can recompense. We do not choose them in abstraction from all relation to what we in fact do.

Discrepancies and oppositions between men can be overcome if they are willing to abandon an occupation with their own ends at times when these cannot be realized and when cooperation with others will assure that their own ends will subsequently be realized with the help of those others. To cooperate effectively a man must give up the hope of ruling all others all the time, unless it be the case, which seems incredible, that he is superior to all others in all respects and does not have to work on their behalf in order to have them work for him. Men must both rule and serve, for they cannot realize their ends without doing both. None has the right or need to rule or serve permanently or exclusively. Help is needed by all; all need to serve and rule in different degrees and ways and at different times and places, for each is an individual capable of making a unique contribution to the cooperative enterprise of living.

Cooperation may require a man to put aside his own tasks for a moment. It does not require him to abandon them and his chosen end completely. It requires him, for a time, to neglect the alternative his ultimate end sanctions; it requires him to choose an unsanctioned alternative. But it does not require him to choose the alternative because it is unsanctioned or despite a sanction for some other. It requires him to choose it incidentally as part of a sanctioned alternative in somewhat the same way that he might be incidentally required to move arms and legs when he chooses to swim.

Desirable ends sanction goals making cooperation a preferable activity. This means that we should not now act so as to weaken men, for in that way we commit ourselves to an end which, if only because it precludes the purchase of full and effective needed cooperation, we cannot sustain.

Theoretically capable of adopting ultimate ends which others do not tolerate, we cannot do this as a rule except by denying ourselves the opportunity to elicit their cooperation. Men on the whole support or allow for the attainment of only those ultimate ends which do not diverge very much from those they themselves adopt. Such ends alone are therefore actually realizable. For the most part, such ends are within the reach of ordinary decisions and ordinary activities of ordinary men, living together in something like a civilized world. They presuppose acts which require all to cooperate at some points and somehow.

Should a group stand in opposition to others, it will, no matter how strong it is, be bound to defeat itself. After the punitive peace which follows on modern wars comes the belated effort on the part of the victors to help the victims. Viewed as a criminal while being fought, the enemy is soon saluted as a desirable coadjutor. Too late it is learned that the greatest of victors cannot attain his final ends alone. He must support his victims or fail to prepare a satisfactory helper for himself, thereby depriving himself of the aid he will sooner or later sorely need.

IX

THE GOLDEN RULE

1. Presupposed Conditions

FREE to choose among a host of ultimate ends, men ought to choose only among those few which are realizable by them. These presuppose that losses in value have been kept to a minimum—a result to be achieved by taking account of the value which things actually possess and attending to what they need and require. For this purpose there is no more effective aid than what has been justly called the "Golden Rule."

No injunction has met with such universal commendation as this Golden Rule. Hobbes, the materialist, approves of it no less heartily than does the pietistic Kant. Mill, the "enlightened" empiricist, is here not outdistanced by the scholastic theologian, Aquinas. Both Rabbi Hillel and Confucius affirm that it sums up all they have to teach. There are echoes of it in the aristocratic Aristotle and in the slave Epictetus, in Tobias and in Diogenes. It is part of the inheritance of the West as well as of the East. Yet it is affirmed and discovered anew in every generation and by almost every individual, sometimes in a common form, sometimes in a somewhat different dress.

The Golden Rule can be and has been expressed in quite a number of ways. According to Hinduism it says, "Do naught to others which, if done to thee would cause thee pain." The Buddhist believes that "a slansma should minister to his friends and families . . . by treating them as he treats himself." The Confucianist is told, "What you do not want done to yourself, do not do unto others." The Taoist asserts, "To those who are good to me I am good, and to those who are not good to me I am also good. And thus all get to be good." For the Zoroastrian "That nature only is good which shall not do unto another whatever is not good for its own self." Isocrates is reported to have said, "Do not do to others what you would not wish to suffer yourself." To these we should add Hillel's "Whatever thou wouldest that men should not do unto thee, do not do that to them," and the Brahmanic and Christian positive forms, "One should act toward others as one would have them act toward oneself," and "All things whatsoever ye would that men should do unto you, even so do ye also unto them." (The Brahmanic Golden Rule appears in the Mahabharata,

xiii, 113, 9; the others in R. E. Hume, *The World's Living Religions.*
I am indebted to Dr. Wing Tsit Chan for these references.)

The appeal of the Golden Rule is universal, both because it allows
and even tempts as many interpretations as there are modes of self-
regard and systems of ethics and because it has a constant meaning,
epitomizing a basic, inescapable truth. On its face it asks a man to put
himself in the place of another, to see himself as one who is to receive
no special dispensation or preferential treatment. But such an interpretation can readily deprive the Golden Rule of all ethical value.
It can serve to twist the meaning of the rule so that it can be understood to allow or even to urge one to kill, lie, and steal if only he be
willing that another do this to him. Confident that we would like others
to put us out of our misery, we could appeal to the Golden Rule to
justify our killing them in the name of mercy; believing that shrewdness deserves whatever it achieves and that it is the destiny of dupes
to be duped, we might think it good for others to try to lie to and to
steal from us, while we, in the name of the Golden Rule, act in these
ways toward them. An injury which is a consequence of another living
a life as callous, as inconsiderate, as ruthless, as foolish, as brutish as
our own can be justified by the Golden Rule: we need only be willing
to have others treat us as indecently as we treat them, the indecency
being masked by our ignorance or folly. It can be used by those who
believe in fair dealing and by those who do not, by those who think
that all is right and by those who think not all is right that is done in
the name of love, war, or commerce. Any act, good or bad, if approved
when viewed as directed at us can, by the rule, be urged as an act that
ought to be performed. It can be made to justify the inhuman treatment of others if only we are willing to be treated with equal inhu-
manity in return. In the name of the good it can help men embark on
the most mischievous of careers.

These consequences follow because the Golden Rule has been understood to mean that we are to do to others as we would be willing to
have them do to us. Some of the embarrassments would have been
avoided had the Golden Rule been understood with Hobbes to mean
"Whatsoever you require that others should do to you, do that to
them." Instead of an actor being asked, as before, to consider himself
in the role of a patient, a prospective recipient of benefits is here asked
to assume the role of an agent. It is a good rule, for actions are not so
prone to bring about evils when performed in the light of what we
would like to have others do for us. But this new formulation can also
be made to sanction a multiplicity of reprehensible acts. It seems to
urge one who requires flattery to flatter others, one who needs favors
and special privileges to bestow similar ones himself. It can be used

to support an attitude of indifference to all else, proportionate to the degree that its user is self-sufficient. It can prompt the strong to disregard the misery of the weak on the ground that there is nothing which the strong requires from the weak and thus nothing which the strong must therefore do on behalf of the weak. The rich could have no neater warrant for a tolerance which allows the poor to starve without let or hindrance. Since the poor require so much from the rich, the rule, moreover, would put them under the necessity of balancing their great needs with deeds on behalf of the rich, even though these perhaps do not have to be helped beyond that minimal degree required in order to make it possible for men to live together.

The Golden Rule, however, is good in its intent. There are deeds it would exclude; there is no evil it is designed to encourage. It obviously intends something other than the previous statements allow one to assume. It is not a principle of quid pro quo or fair play to be invoked no matter what the game, as the first interpretation would lead us to imply. Nor is it, as the second allows, intended to demand actions adjusted to the actor's capacity to suffer or to need. It assumes that men are in some sense alike, equal, interchangeable, and that what is good for one is good for another. Any interpretation which does not make these assumptions violates the spirit if not the words of the rule.

The Golden Rule rests on the sound psychological observation that an agent who sees himself as recipient as well or a recipient who thinks of himself also as an agent will, more likely than not, do what he should. It helps him discover that what he might approve in one role he does not approve in the other, that what he thought right from one perspective is not right from all and thus not entirely right, not what he ought to do. To follow the rule is to counteract a tendency to ignore what others need and deserve, and thus is to be prepared to do to those others what ought to be done to them.

The rule makes three suppositions. Firstly, it assumes that a man has a sure knowledge of what he wants done to himself, since it is only by such knowledge that he can test what he plans to do to others. If a man did not have this knowledge, he would not be able to apply the Golden Rule, since he would have no basis on which to ground a judgment of what he is to do. Secondly, the rule assumes that what a man wants to have done to him is a good for him; if what he wants done to him is not really good for him, he will use as his guide a bad instead of a good act and do what he should not. Finally, the Golden Rule assumes that what is good for one man is good for another. If what is good for one were not also good for others, a man would be bound to injure others when he did for them what he wanted them to do for him.

The Golden Rule is pyrite and tinsel if men do not know what is good, and if what is good for one man is not also good for the rest. Yet it is notorious that men constantly misunderstand themselves, that they are sometimes dreadfully clear about what they want to have done to themselves, even though this would be disastrous to them and to others, and that they differ from one another, requiring and deserving different things and different modes of treatment. What the Golden Rule seems to require the world only occasionally, if ever, allows. Yet the Golden Rule is used daily by ordinary men; it is a practical rule which works with considerable ease and often most successfully. There must be, therefore, a significant and inescapable sense in which these powerful objections are without force. For the discovery of that sense nothing is perhaps so effective as a support of the objections so far as possible. Universally valid principles do not stand opposed to any truths, no matter how finite, limited, or repugnant. They are instead means for understanding them. Whatever, like the Golden Rule, claims to be firm bedrock invites us to place on it the entire weight of what is other than it; if it can sustain this, it is bedrock indeed. The Golden Rule, to live up to its claim to being a basic moral principle, not only requires that the foregoing three suppositions be true but must help us understand the meaning of the negations of them which we seem to see on every side.

2. Violators of the Rule

Wicked and indolent men apparently misconstrue what they themselves need and thus apparently violate the Golden Rule. And so do others more respected. There are men of unimaginative rectitude who, until they are thrown off the center of their daily acts and thoughts, are unable to discover just what it is they ought to have. Secure, respected, living a life which has scarcely a turn or an eddy, they ask for cold, abstract justice for themselves and others; unknowingly, they keep dormant a desire to be treated by others with understanding, mercy, and kindness. Having confounded what they are with what their environment has given them, they hold faithfully to the Golden Rule and spend their energies piling iniquity on horror. It would be better for mankind if many an upright judge would ignore the Golden Rule and follow instead the *principle of arrogant kindness:* "Do unto others what you would disdain to have done to yourself." That principle is the Golden Rule made appropriate to one who lacks insight, and at the same time, possesses more security, energy, or virtue than others.

The upright judge obscures for himself the nature which is his. As so obscuring what he is and ought to do, he should, if his acts are to be right, follow the principle of arrogant kindness. Then, though still unable to understand what he himself ought to have, he would approximate a little better the kind of acts which are appropriate to men who are, after all, but creatures of limited wisdom and flexible virtue.

Men who are devoted to the pursuit of pleasure, wealth, honor, and even knowledge, doing their best to present these goods to others as well, are often variants on the pattern exhibited by the upright judge. What they seek to do is right; their effort to deal with others as they themselves are dealt with is often salutary. But so far as they allow their passion for their limited objectives to obscure a more fundamental need of other goods as well, their acceptance of the Golden Rule will prove not an occasion for promoting good but a means for multiplying evils.

Others want both pleasure and knowledge, honor and wealth; they would like to weld justice and kindness, courage with tolerance. They have a broader vision than many more upright and secure men. Unfortunately, too often they integrate the different goods into a simple unity, giving wrong or insufficient weight to the different components. They do not grasp the complexity and richness of man, they overstress the value of order, balance, harmony to the disadvantage of spontaneity, drive, and novelty. Not realizing that there is a kind of instability and apparent folly, the product of a keen sensitivity to neglected goods, which is as important as an elementary unification of diverse interests, they neglect an important good in the very act of uniting a number of others, no one of which and no collection of which may be as desirable as that which was neglected. Usually these men do little harm; rarely do they do much good. There is no better illustration of the type than the academic man who almost inevitably finds his level in an educational administrative post. There he devotes himself to the promotion of harmony by ignoring and occasionally destroying creativity. He unifies, integrates, compromises to make an ordered, uninteresting whole.

There is perhaps no device which will enable such men to understand how to act toward those who have deeper springs and stronger passions. But it would help a little if they would supplement their use of the Golden Rule with an occasional reference to the *maxim of dynamic tolerance:* "Do to others that which enables them to do what they can." Then though they may themselves continue in the monotonous task of satisfying most or even all desires inadequately, they may be able to contribute something to the satisfaction of natures richer than their own. The Golden Rule is not a medium for reducing all men to the level of those whose lives are harmonious because they are relatively empty but for lifting them to the highest level men can reach.

The Golden Rule applies to these men just as much as it does to others. Since they occupy themselves excessively with the ordering of things and fail to do justice to the nature of what is ordered, they must use the Golden Rule only after it has been made appropriate to them as appreciative of powers and virtues greater than their own. Were they to make the Golden Rule assume the form of the maxim of dynamic tolerance, they would bring about greater goods than otherwise.

Most men, fortunately, know that significant existence has a rhythm, constantly passing back and forth from the extreme where full satisfaction is obtained for some needs to the extreme where some satisfaction is obtained for all. They are aware of the claims of both freedom and order, of spontaneity and regularity, of creativity and coordination; they know that sometimes one ought to be stressed and sometimes the other. If we had to choose between them we would have to make a tragic choice. It would make no difference which we took; whichever it was would be wrong. But we are never faced with the necessity of deciding sharply between them. There is no genuine freedom without some order, no genuine order without some freedom. A freedom without order would be a freedom without structure or direction, without a base in the past or a terminus in the future; an order without some freedom would be an order without substance, without movement, and without a place in a world of flux. Order without freedom is deadly; freedom without order is chaos. Freedom without order and order without freedom are abstractions from the world in which everything has some degree of structure and stability, some degree of spontaneity and variability. Our problem is never the problem of having only one or the other, but is always the problem of deciding just which possible combination of freedom and order is at the time the most satisfactory and the most fruitful.

Sentimentalists try to combine both sides; they are appreciative of the need to satisfy both an appetite for order and an appetite for freedom. As a rule, though, they confuse a quietus with a satisfaction and fall short of their objective as surely as others do. Most anxious to ease the way for their fellows, to provide them with the objects of their needs, they do not give their fellows the opportunity to obtain these objects for themselves. They use the Golden Rule to deny to men the right to mold themselves and finally, therefore, the right to be themselves. Men require not merely the object of their desires but the satisfaction which ensues when they obtain the object through their own efforts. We are all pelagians, whatever our theology. We know that he who need make no effort may ripen sooner than others. We know even more surely that he rots quicker.

Men do not desire or deserve what others provide, but desire and deserve in ways and with emphases which reflect their individual natures. No man desires or deserves unremitting help. He desires and deserves only as much help and consideration as he is able and willing to use in the best possible way. And what he at once desires and deserves is good for him to have.

The hosannas in heaven may never be as wild and as joyous as they are when men are made the objects of charity. The builders of utopias may be able to construct a state no more glorious than one in which men have identical ends and identical methods for realizing them. No romance is perhaps so thrilling as that in which a diabolic sinner is converted into a saint. But it would be a mistake to disregard the wisdom of the race which teaches that it is better for men to act and strive than to await and receive, that they are individuals whose natures are to be developed, that they can be corrupted by an excess of help, and that they deserve different degrees of aid and attention.

The Golden Rule interpreted according to the spirit of the Gospel of Luke asks us to do to others what we would have them do to ourselves. It allows us to unite freedom and order; it urges us to help others less favorably situated than ourselves. It is one of the best agencies by which men can develop an adequate sense of sympathy for the misery, distress, and human nature of those whom men would otherwise be inclined to despise. There is an enviable nobility in him who, following out the spirit of the passage in Luke, overlooks the stupidities and vices of others, sees them as fellow men, and tries to give them what they need. There is no doubt that such an attitude helps keep men from turning into beasts because others have failed them. But the principle is that of a sentimentalist. It suggests that we not only overlook thievery, hatred, and dishonesty but forget the deserts of the more deserving and dissipate our energies in doing what should be God's work.

The insight of the sentimentalist is deeper than that possessed by him who like the upright judge glories in the way he has obscured his own wants, and is deeper than that possessed by him who like the administrator seeks a ready integration of partial goods. He does not use the Golden Rule for a selfish end; he tries to give others goods he desires for himself. He does a service in suggesting that vindictiveness be restrained and in reminding us that all men are members of a single species, each needing and deserving help and humane treatment. But he fails to make allowance for the need men have to act for themselves. He ignores their unconquerable desire to live a life which must be mastered from within as well as helped from without; he forgets the political and ethical truth that they deserve different degrees of help and consideration. It would indeed be better for the rest of us if the sentimentalist were to delimit the Golden Rule until it became little more than the *doctrine of restricted sympathy:* "Do unto others only part of what you would have them do to you." It would be possible then to preserve a little better the few goods mankind has already attained and obtain a little more readily those which it still ought to acquire.

3. THE VALUE OF THE RULE

The vicious man, the indolent man, the upright judge, the commonplace administrator, and the sentimentalist can all use the Golden Rule so that its ethical value is diminished if not extinguished. Yet there is a sense in which all three suppositions for the effective use of the Golden Rule are fulfilled by them as well as by others. Even these men know themselves to some extent; they too desire as they ought; what they want is also a good for others. This is not to say that they, perhaps even more than the rest, do not constantly misunderstand themselves, misdirect their efforts, and differ from one another in nature, need, and desert. But no one, no matter how blind or perverted, can entirely escape from a knowledge of his own humanity; none can completely corrupt it; and none can erase all that is common to himself and others. Each knows himself to have a mind and a body, sensitive, finite, and active, and that all must eat and drink, that all, to be fully men, must have shelter, friendship, and cooperation, training, beauty, and truth. Even when most perverse, each makes use of and even strengthens his power of expression, his tolerance, or his flexibility. Knowing himself to be one of many instances of man, each knows something of what he ought to have and what is good for others as well.

Man is in retreat from the world in which he lives; each is the negate of everything else. Each is not the others. Each needs from the rest whatever promotes the retreat, whatever can help it stand apart, can make it self-centered and self-contained. Others, however, continue to press in; they insist on themselves. It is never enough to retreat from them; they must be pushed away. And while and as the retreat and repulsion occur, there must be a submission and penetration to the others as part of a process of using and understanding them. The activity of knowledge is a specialized form of this constant, quadruple, essential activity of retreat, repulsion, submission, and penetration; the imprint of all four phases is present in every act of knowledge, though not always equally evident. And because it is, all of us in knowing anything know ourselves and others too.

We retreat and repel, submit and penetrate, all the time. Every effort and motion, every cognitive and noncognitive act, contains all four features. Without retreat there would be no subjects, no focus; without repulsion there would be no privacy, no copresence; without submission there would be no objects, no world acknowledged to be beyond; without penetration there would be no participation, no grasp of anything to balance and terminate us. From the beginning, throughout our careers, in every form of activity, we are men who retreat from, repel, submit to, and penetrate to others existing in the same world with us, some of whom have selves like our own.

Because of our quadruple rhythm we cannot avoid somehow illustrating the Golden Rule all the time. It is because we always exhibit it somehow that we can use it as a guiding rule, underscoring the inescapable fact that while we submit and penetrate to others, we require them to submit and penetrate to us, thereby enabling us to be and find ourselves through repulsion and retreat. However, we constantly emphasize, particularly when we become conscious, some one of these four facets more than we should. As a consequence we do not do all we can and should, and eventually lose both ourselves and others. Since, though, we always act in the fourfold way, doing to them in part as they ought to do to us, neither they nor we can ever be entirely lost.

Each of us has interests in conflict with one another and with the interests of other men. Nevertheless each of our interests genuinely, though partially and perhaps distortedly, expresses something of the common humanity which is in each of us. It may be a man's ambition to use stones as food, but his body will have no part in that endeavor no matter what he does or what he affirms to further his desire. His bodily needs will be inevitably exhibited in his acts, modifying his inclinations to neglect or abuse them, and those bodily needs will be but signal forms of his more comprehensive need to be a full man through the correct exercise of his quadruple power. Though a man may define himself to be a receptacle for bodily pleasures, a natural curiosity, answering to the appetites of his mind and spirit, will soon or late rear its head and sometimes radically change the course of his activities.

The body and mind have appetites of their own incapable of abolition by an emphasis on one of them or by a perversion of their requirements; but the very emphases themselves, even when apparently going the opposite way, are expressions of a single concern for perfection, of a four-headed drive to overcome an incompleteness, a disequilibrium, to be a complete man over against and yet with the others. Our errors arise in large part because we concentrate on specific manifestations and moments of this concern, because we do not stop long enough to discover what these manifestations express and just what would really satisfy them and how. An ambition to make a diet of stones is an expression of a need to eat, and thus to continue to be, through the help of other beings. It demands that we reach outside ourselves to them and retreat with what we then obtain, that we repel that which we do not want, and finally that we submit to the demands of the stones to be handled according to their natures. The right way, though, to deal with stones is not to try to eat but to own, to use, to work with, to know them. The endeavor to deal with them in other ways is but an attempt to misuse them and ourselves, since it is to do violence to their natures and ours.

Beset by some crisis of which pain, confusion, internal conflict, and error are indices, we tend to turn our attention away from the obvious manifestations of our essence and to focus instead on the essence itself. It is then that we grasp effectively in a kind of emotional engulfment that it is always present, always somehow manifest, four-pronged, directed to and from oneself. A crisis offers a challenge to our insensitivity. It shocks our feeling of complacency and security, tears us out of our conventional contexts, frees us from distorting details, forcing us for a moment to see that we are both the focus and the limit of all there is, beings who want to be themselves and can be this only by helping others satisfy a similar hunger.

The Golden Rule offers a means enabling one to determine just what he can do, what he really ought to do, and what he genuinely wants to do; it is a formula expressing the ontological fact that we must balance forward thrust by backward move, giving by receiving. It anticipates the result which a crisis usually promotes, exposing for us the bent of our fundamental concern freed from all irrelevant detail. It points up the truth that even while we seem intent on going elsewhere what we want done to us is whatever makes possible the attainment of perfection, and that this in some way requires of us the perfecting of others.

What is to be done to us is what others ought to have done to them, so far as we are similar. The Golden Rule rightly tells us to guide ourselves by this truth. But that rule can prove mischievous and misleading. Employed in situations where no attempt is made to distinguish between what men desire or say they do and what they need and want, between what appetite and activity actually do and what they ought to promote, it can serve to further, or at least excuse, wrongdoing, narrowness, and stupidity. It articulates our basic concern and can help us satisfy it. Though it is always exhibited in some form or other, there is still no way it or we can guarantee in advance that it will always be used to the best advantage to ourselves or others.

4. The Analytic of the Golden Rule

The Golden Rule has two parts. One contains a command, the other an evaluation. It commands that "we do to others," and evaluates our act in terms of what "we would have them do to us."

In commanding us to "do to others" the Golden Rule urges us to take up an active attitude, to try to penetrate to others, to reach to them, and nothing more; it does not deny that there are things which we ought to do for ourselves. It can have pertinence to us only if we have the power to change our present attitudes, to alter our present control over our minds or bodies, for were this not possible or necessary the Golden Rule would but tell us to do what we always are and must be doing.

The Golden Rule further asks us to put ourselves in the place of others, to do to them "as we would have them do to us." We are told by it to view ourselves as men who are correctly acted on by others, this being the standard in terms of which our acts are to be evaluated. It has meaning for us because we are men who can place ourselves in the position of others, see ourselves from the outside, know these selves to be perpetually retreating, repelling, submitting, and penetrating. If we could not do this, or if this were unnecessary, the Golden Rule would but tell us once again to do what we always are and must be doing. As it is, it tells us now to act from the vantage point of some specialized position and interest in consonance with the spirit of the concern which is of our essence.

The Golden Rule commands that we assume the attitude of an agent; by means of the evaluation it asks us also to view ourselves in the position of a patient. The command also asks us to acknowledge someone else as a possible patient, while the evaluation asks us to look at that patient as a prospective agent. It urges us to be agents having the others as patients and to guide ourselves by what we see when we view others as agents having ourselves as their patients. The union of the command and the evaluation thus involves the consideration of both ourselves and others in the dual roles of agent and patient, as active and passive, as wanting and being satisfied. Its effect is to ask us to act on others as though they were like ourselves, with an active and a passive side, imperfect but capable of being perfected.

There is a difference between ourselves and our imagined duplicates. This stands in the way of our treating them as though they were mere shadows or images of ourselves. By putting ourselves in place of others we do not perform the impossible task of multiplying ourselves, transposing our being to another place while remaining here at the same time. Instead we think of the others as equally individual and unique, determining the same kind of acts we determine—equally substantial, coordinate beings who act on us for the same selfish and non-selfish reasons which make us act on them.

When we take the place of another while remaining where and what we are, we view ourselves as acting on him and he on us and thus view him as an intermediary in an act which begins and ends in ourselves. Since he is understood to engage in a similar act with respect to us, we view ourselves as intermediaries for him as well. The Golden Rule is thus a principle which asks men to see one another as instruments with the same functions, needing and using one another as they are needed and used. Because it is a principle which concerns actions that are self-returning, it not only assures proper treatment to others but assures proper treatment for ourselves. He who truly serves others perfects himself. Were he to do to others something different from what they ought to do to him, his acts would fail by excess or defect. If his acts fail by excess, he wastes his substance, giving others more than they, his equals, require or deserve. If his acts fail by defect, he makes inadequate use of his powers, giving them less than he, their equal, should and can.

All men use one another. We cannot converse without having to assume in turn the role of listener as well as speaker. We cannot give the slightest thing without making someone function as a recipient and thus as an instrument enabling us to be givers. Usually, however, we do too much or too little. The Golden Rule offers a scale enabling us to balance the two. It is a principle of justice designed to make one give neither too much nor too little; it is a guide to mercy, for it helps one to see what others truly deserve.

Both Mill and Kant restated and revitalized parts of the Golden Rule. These parts belong together, for men are at once phenomenal, public beings and noumenal, self-determining ones. And it is the Golden Rule alone that holds them together. It asks us to consider another as an instrument at the same time that we regard him as a self-determining end. The utilitarian principle of fair play or equality follows from it when we think of another as a mere intermediary, without reference to his individual need and nature. Kantian respect follows from it when we think of him as a self-determining being and pay no regard to his functioning with respect to us. To the factor of equal return the Golden Rule adds the element of consideration for the individuality of the other, spicing justice with mercy.

5. VARIATIONS ON THE GOLDEN RULE

When we conceive of others acting on us in a way similar to that in which we propose to act on them we conceive ourselves to be in a symmetrical, dynamic relation with them. This relation usually requires for its establishment a reduction or enhancement of the positions we occupy with respect to one another. When we think of ourselves as having a position superior to theirs, so far as we grant our intrinsic equality with them we grant that our activities are to be disciplined. When we think of our position as inferior to theirs we grant the need for renewed activity by us. The Golden Rule tells us to use others, conceived as our equals, as a standard, dictating in the interest of the good how much we are to move down and how far we are to move up to be publicly on a par with them.

The principle of arrogant kindness, "Do to others more than you would have done for yourself," is to be used by anyone who like the upright judge looks at his fellows from the superior position of wealth, security, happiness, opportunity. By following this principle he is enabled to take account of the greater need of others. The doctrine of restricted sympathy, "Do to others only part of what you would have them do to you," balances the principle. It makes provision for the superior power or smaller needs of others. The combination of the two yields the maxim of dynamic tolerance, "Do to others that which enables them to do what they can." This maxim finds room for the justice of the judge and the mercy of the sentimentalist, limiting each by the other. It stresses the need to see that others have natures other than and as substantial as our own, to be improved from within, not hindered or suffocated from without.

All three variants of the Golden Rule offer useful guides for men who have assumed a wrong attitude toward their fellows; the variants points out a way by which, despite their wrong attitudes, these men can do what they ought. They are the Golden Rule remodeled to fit aberrant, distorted situations. They presuppose the normal form of the Golden Rule and a situation where one looks at his fellow man in the wrong light. They take account of differences in men's power and position but require that the natures and needs of others first be misunderstood. We come to the essence of the Golden Rule only when these limitations are overcome, when we treat it as pertinent to all cases, when we see it as a kind of variable rule having different meanings in different contexts, enabling it to bring about the same results in divergent ways. This requires that it be stated formally as a bare structure and that its different elements be altered, one at a time, thereby changing its import and application to make it relevant to different circumstances. Made perfectly general, universally applicable, the Golden Rule is a matrix of a set of subordinate, more restricted versions, appropriate to special cases.

The Golden Rule asks

a to do to b what b should do to a.

There are seven possible subordinate cases which such a formula allows:

1. a is to do to b what a should do to b.
2. a is to do to a what a should do to a.
3. a is to do to b what a should do to a.
4. a is to do to b what b should do to b.
5. a is to do to a what a should do to b.
6. a is to do to a what b should do to a.
7. a is to do to a what b should do to b.

The first says that a's actions toward b should be right actions, that there is a norm to which he is required to conform; the second says that a's actions toward himself should be right actions. Both together say that there are things we ought to do to others and to ourselves. The first states the result which the Golden Rule should attain; the second provides a reason why it can function. Both, however, leave out any suggestion of a comparison of ourselves with others and are, strictly speaking, specializations, not variants, of the Golden Rule. This condition is met by the remaining five.

The third says that you are to "do to another what you ought to do to yourself." It is a variant derived by denying the other the status of an agent. A guide to helpfulness, it is to be employed when someone is to be advised or encouraged. It presupposes that we know what we should do for ourselves, whether we do it or not. The other, it recognizes, must be helped by us to get what he should. We are asked to act on his behalf in a way which would be good were it directed toward us. His equality is thereby not denied but given an opportunity to be manifest. With this variant as our guide we can see a little better that our children, the young, the impoverished, the ignorant, the unfortunate must be first supported by us before they are in a position to help themselves to the degree that we can now help ourselves and them.

The fourth variant says that you are to "do to another what he should do for himself." It promotes the proper treatment of men who lack the energy, opportunity, or knowledge to act properly for themselves. In contrast with the third variant it helps us to be actively sympathetic, offering us the needs of others as an index of what we should do for them. There is no question here as to our status as patients, nor any question as to whether or not they will look out for themselves. All that we are told is that we are to obtain for them what they ought to obtain for themselves. We transcend the question as to why they do not obtain the desired results for themselves; they may not do what they should because they are lazy, incompetent, prevented. This is here not our concern. All we need to know, to use this fourth variant, is that we have power in excess of theirs, enabling us to get for them what they should have but cannot or will not themselves obtain.

The fifth variant tells you to "do to yourself what you ought to do to another," that you are to treat yourself in the same way you ought to treat the rest. According to it we are to view others as patients only, and are to make ourselves patients to our own acts in the light of what we then discern. In a sense it says that all patients are alike and that we can best know therefore what we as patients ought to have by regarding the rights of other patients. It offers an excellent criterion by which those in authority can learn to govern themselves.

The sixth variant, "do for yourself what another ought to do to you," is to be used by one who is at a disadvantage. It supposes that others should behave toward us in ways which are not opposed to the ways we should behave toward ourselves—indeed, that their correct behavior is to be a model for us. They, it says, are to be viewed only as agents, while we are to be viewed both as patients and agents. Our perfection should be promoted by others as much as possible; by using this ideal as a guide we can act on our own behalf in most desirable ways. Without this rule we would be inclined to do much for ourselves we ought not, or not to help ourselves as much as we could.

The final variant, "Do for yourself what you would have others do for themselves," offers a guide for independent action. It asks each to act on his own behalf in consonance with what would be correct self-regarding behavior by others. Recognizing that all of us tend toward excess or defect when dealing with ourselves, it helps us find a middle ground by referring us, for our standard, to what would be the right action for others to institute on their own behalf. It is to be invoked whenever we are unsure, afraid to be self-regarding.

Each of these variants is the Golden Rule restricted to situations in which an agent or patient fails to assume the position of the other. Unless the Golden Rule is to be appropriate only some of the time, it must be understood to allow for all these variants. And since men have essential traits in common with any divinity there may be (such as mind, will, and value), as well as traits in common with whatever organic and inorganic things may exist (such as power, extension, temporality), it is impossible to restrict the usage of the Golden Rule to men alone without neglecting the value of these other types of being, and the need and right they have to be approached in terms analogous to those appropriate to men.

When we are in a position of subordination, say to some acknowledged God, the only use we can make of the Golden Rule is in the form of the sixth variant, "Do to yourself what you would have that Other do to you." We cannot do anything for Him (and thus cannot use the third, fourth, and fifth variants) ; nor can we guide ourselves (as the seventh requires) by an idea of an obligation which He has to Himself. In referring to Him by means of the sixth variant, we think of what a good God would do, and behave toward ourselves in the spirit of that knowledge.

When, on the other hand, we are in a position of superiority, say to animals and plants, and even inanimate beings, the fourth variant, "Do to others what you would have them do for themselves," becomes relevant. Inferior beings should be helped to the best of our abilities in the light of the special advantages we enjoy ; it is up to us to help them get what they ought to have. We cannot make use of any of the other variants when dealing with them, for these variants either say that we are to act on ourselves (the fifth, sixth, and seventh) or would tell us to use our quite different natures and needs as models of how we are to act on them (the third). Toward inferior beings we can ask ourselves only to be sympathetically helpful, and then only so far as this does not conflict with our doing for ourselves what ought to be done, in view of our comparatively higher value.

The Golden Rule urges us to transform a foreign agent, thought of as operating on us as he ought, into a patient of our own act, and thus to use him as a means while we respect his status as an end in himself. Since it is impossible ever to treat anything as a mere means or as a mere end, since each being retains some modicum of privacy untouched by foreign determinations, since each is and must be used either directly or indirectly in the course of its existence, the Golden Rule is to be understood not as an expression of a new kind of fact but as an agency helping us to determine the proper degree and manner in which all beings, including ourselves, are to be used as instruments. It helps us to become aware of the kind of values others embody; it teaches us to impose a distinction between intrinsic and instrumental values on ourselves similar to that we impose on them. It is a principle of sympathetic service, having different applications and meanings in different contexts. He who follows it intelligently will be decent and reasonable, attending to what others are and require, and thus one who keeps losses in value at a minimum. Used woodenly, without regard for the need to vary direction and emphasis in different situations, it will produce more evil than good. Its value increases the more it is treated as a form, a structure which has a different import in each case. It is a rule governing the art of dealing with beings properly, analogous to a rule of prosody, or of lighting or perspective in painting; it offers a blueprint, an outline, not the substance of what is to be done. If we fill in that outline properly we will make possible the realization of an excellent community of cooperative, considerate men, whose positive laws will express, in a limited, local and rational form, what it is absolutely right to do.

X

NATURAL AND POSITIVE LAW

1. CIVIL AND CRIMINAL LAW

EACH community has its own structure, its own rhythm. None has an absolutely fixed nature, for in none do men grasp the same values and to the same degree all the time. There is, though, a minimal nature which each one has, as a consequence of the degree of communion achieved by its members in the past. We do not start afresh at every moment to grasp what things really are but begin with what we have already learned. Child labor is today not congenial, not because we are natively more sensitive than our predecessors but because we have already come to recognize the promise of children. Today our task is to move from this minimal apprehension, characteristic of our community, to more penetrating apprehensions. We must grasp the nature of the promise and make further positive provisions for its realization. It is up to us to grasp the special flavors of different individuals, the genius of each, now partly hidden by and partly hiding his common nature.

Each community has a future from which it is inseparable, a good expressed in the form of a rational set of interlocking demands whose realization would perfect the community. That future expresses in one of many ways a future pertinent to all communities, a *natural law*, prescribing how members of any community must act if they are to be rational and right. The natural law is the future of any community, so far as this can be discerned through reason, and serves as the final test of what justice requires. Neither legislated nor imposed, it is the future in terms of which the most sensitive, cooperative of modern men live, the standard to which one must refer to know how the codified and uncodified rules actually governing a community are to be changed.

Positive law comprises the formulations of legislatures as supported by the decisions of judges and the practices of enforcement officers. It expresses the meaning of natural law only partially and sometimes with considerable distortion. It is rarely framed in the light of the natural law, and too seldom changed because of it. Yet, until this is done, the positive law can be only the expression of legislative caprice.

Law, both natural and positive, formulates what is required of members of a community as having such and such positions in relation to one another. It prescribes what each ought to do, by stating first what his position requires and then what position and thus what tasks he is to have, should he fail to meet the first requirement. He who does not live up to the requirements of his position is defined by law to be a man who is to adopt the new position of one who pays the community with time, property, or privileges. By placing disagreeable alternatives before a man, it makes desirable the fulfillment of the initial assignment. It does not itself compel him who fails to take up a new position; it leaves this compulsion to others.

Civil positive law creates and defines new tasks for men, accomplishing this in part by changing their conditional freedom—transitory, local, and social—through the imposition of definite limits on what enforcement officers and institutions are permitted to do. Criminal law, the other great division of positive law, demands of all members acts of forbearance and performance with respect to the essentials of life, freedom, and property as appropriate to humans of different sexes, ages, health, maturity, and normality. The two together partly express, and then as pertinent primarily to some one limited community, the meaning of natural law—criminal law specifying tasks in the light of essential positions, civil law specifying positions by means of assigned tasks.

He who fails to live up to a criminal law is subject to fines, imprisonment, exile, and other restraints designed to compel offenders to do what natural law requires of man in the given community and as possessed of essential drives, needs, and rights. He who does not behave properly when under restraint, say while in a prison, is by criminal law faced with the alternative of having the restraints increased and increased until he reaches the extreme where he is nothing but an impoverished, famished, solitary, or trapped animal on whom we can rely—because capable only of weakened biological, physical, or economic activity—to behave in required ways. The law relies on all men to do or forbear doing certain central things, offering them only the alternative of doing them with more or less constraint.

The civil law refines the meaning of some actually assumed position by ascribing to it various tasks. He who fails to do what it prescribes is by it assigned new tasks, such as that of paying a penalty, altering the nature of an enterprise, submitting to new conditions. He who does not meet the new demands of the civil law is given another task, and so on, until we reach the point, defined by the law, where the failure is equated with a failure to respect the law itself. It is then treated as a basic threat, as criminally jeopardizing the essentials of life, health, freedom, and property, and is met by death, exile, or other extreme and effective impositions of the law.

If we could succeed in reaching the goal which many criminologists, sociologists, and psychiatrists have set before us, we would free law from every moral connotation. The only difference between criminal and civil law would then be that the criminal law would start from a consideration of the essential differences in the talents and abilities of men and the absolutely essential tasks which must be performed in a community, while the civil law would start from a consideration of the special tasks which a particular community requires to have done and would define positions and men in the light of their capacity to engage in these tasks successfully. But whether or not the differences between them are refined and overcome, they form a single body of positive law, a tissue of formalized expectations that men will occupy certain positions in the community and perform certain tasks or have new positions and tasks assigned to them under duress.

Newly assigned tasks need not be more onerous or more unpleasant than the old. Even now it is sometimes the case that the law accepts with equanimity the willingness of men to pay for the privilege of violating some legal injunction. We can, if we wish, refuse to pay our income tax this year, providing we are ready to pay a fine and the tax with interest next year. The fine and interest indicate where the community's predilection lies, but there is no necessary condemnation of one who takes the second rather than the first alternative. If a pure positive law is to be possible, all infractions must be capable of being viewed in this detached way. The most heinous crimes must be approached with the same objectivity and dispassionateness that now characterize a decision to refuse a man a license to fly a plane because he cannot see very well. He is not condemned for having bad eyes, but he is denied a right and this solely because he does not have the equipment which the law defines to be essential to the exercise of the right.

Positive law, so far as it is freed from moral connotations, lays down the qualifications which must be met if a man is to be allowed to take up a certain position, and then states what he must do should he fail to bring about what one in his position should. But there is now, and there will always be, an undertone of condemnation in every one of its formulations, reflecting the existence of that natural law which all positive law attempts to express in some fashion.

2. PUNISHMENT

It is not indifferent to a community which of a number of legally defined alternatives a man will take. Community life is predicated on the supposition that, even if various alternatives were all morally and productively equivalent, most men would take one rather than another. He who fails to take the commonly chosen alternative is communally at fault, whether or not he is also morally at fault, and is punished accordingly.

The law holds men accountable for some acts which no foresight could have prevented, which have nothing to do with intent, desire, decision. Disease carriers, epileptics, idiots, habitual drunkards, and the congenitally absent-minded injure others, often despite a genuine effort to benefit them instead. The law forces these men to take up new positions, sometimes of a most disadvantageous sort, though they may not be in any way responsible for the things they brought or tend to bring about. There is no regard paid for what they intend but only for what they tend to do. To be sure, there are in the law constant references to intentions. These are ways of referring to prepared or anticipatable, in contrast with unprepared or unanticipatable, acts. An "intended" or prepared act is more likely to be repeated than an unprepared one, for it rests on habit, on knowledge, or on an insistence that something is desirable. In similar circumstances it will probably be repeated. If its consequences are undesirable, greater penalties, more stringent demands, larger obstacles are put in the way of those who "intend," who prepare themselves to go counter to a legal rule, than of those who do not. They are made to feel the undesirability of alternatives to what the law requires, and thereby are prompted, it is hoped, to direct their energies in a different way than they tended to direct them.

The epileptic, as Mr. Justice Holmes pointed out, is accountable for being out in the street where his fit might seize him to the detriment of others. He is to be treated more severely than the one who acts negligently for one unaccounted moment, since he goes out on the street as an epileptic, as one to whom a fit can reasonably be expected to come. He "intends" since he prepares to go out in public where he can be a menace. He does not intend to have a fit of course, but he does intend to be where it would be harmful for a fit to occur, and he is penalized, if one likes, not for having a fit but for being at a place where the fit will injure others. He who is guilty of simple negligence could not have reasonably expected that he would fail to do what he legally ought; he should therefore be subject to less constraint than he who "intends." He is, if one likes, penalized for having a fit of carelessness, though it is one he could not have expected would occur. He is penalized because others also expected that it would not occur and were, to their loss, deceived.

When the consequences of a simple negligence are more serious than those of a prepared act, the negligent man is penalized proportionately more. In a world ruled by law, men are to be judged by what they do to others and not by what they would like to have done. But if the consequences be ignored, the penalties would have to be reversed; he who is unprepared to do harm is to be penalized less than he who is prepared, because he is more readily redirected, less likely to repeat. He who sets out to injure his neighbor slightly has less to account for than he who by accident injures his neighbor severely, but he is also less of a man, more guilty, more at fault.

No one of us can claim protection from our neighbors for all injuries; by coming into the public arena we say, as it were, to the rest of the community that the normal hazards of existence are accepted by us—for example the pushes and shoves which are of the essence of rush-hour travel, the indifferent cooking of most highway inns, the delays of trains, the oversights of maids and porters, the slighting remarks which are the common coinage of many routine conversations. It is when men subject us to more than the normal hazards that there is a case against them; it is then that they deserve to be punished, forced to take up other positions, less desirable than the ones they previously occupied.

Most students of the law seem to favor the idea that punishment is to be imposed only so far as it serves to prevent a repetition of the undesirable act, whether by the offender or by others. The fact and nature of punishments, they think, are announced publicly so that he who guides himself by knowledge will be able to alter his course; the malefactor is punished, they suppose, as a way of training, edifying, or transforming him, or in the case of capital punishment as a way of edifying and intimidating the rest by providing them *in concreto* with a public announcement of the nature of the punishment they themselves would suffer were they to do as he does. Punishment on this preventive theory is training, the transformation of a man who did wrong into one who will tend to do right thereafter, or it is education in the form of statements or in an example having the shape of a malefactor.

The theory is not adequate. If we sought only to prevent wrongdoing we would not punish those who, to the best of our knowledge, reform after committing a crime; we would not punish those who out of resentment to the punishment would most likely decide to do worse things in the future. We would punish only those who were amenable or who, though they had as yet done nothing wrong, would most probably do something wrong unless now punished. It might prove most educative at times to take an innocent man and subject him to radical punishments, since we might thereby be able to show the rest of the population how severely wrongdoing will be repaid. How effective it might sometimes prove to grab some innocent man and punish him severely with the remark to all the rest that much worse punishment would have been inflicted had he been guilty. Punishment on this theory has nothing necessarily to do with what men in fact have done but only with what they might do. But then why should we always be searching for evidence of what was done? What is to be made of the interest all of us have as to who is guilty and who innocent of past deeds, regardless of reform and likelihood of repetition? Which one of us would willingly give up such search and interest for an inquiry into tendencies and likelihoods that this or that might be done by this or that man? The inquiry would be most desirable; wrongdoing all would like to prevent. But its prevention, even when it works hardship, is not the same as punishment. And no matter how careful we were in our training and in the punishments we attached to wrongdoing, actual or prospective, we could not thereby prevent the ills that follow on the bad judgment which men of good will constantly make, often to the injury of their fellows. Such ills are past and regretted; if we are punished for them it cannot be because we or others are thereby helped to do better.

We do and should punish men for what they have done. The retributive theory sees this. That theory asserts that all punishment should look backward rather than forward, that it give a *quid* for a *quo*, a tit for a tat. It finds strong support in the fact that men have long thought this and still continue so to think. And if the distinction between deliberate and nondeliberate acts is replaced by a distinction between prepared and unprepared acts, this common view will be seen to have great power. Retribution keeps its eye on the injury and does not attend to the nature of the desire, choice, decision which brought the injury about. It rightly insists that an injury to the offender be appropriate to the injury he brought about, though it goes much too far when it suggests that until the offender is injured there will be a strain in the universe, revealing a corruption in the community in which it occurred, polluting its entire subsequent career. We should, the retributive theory affirms, strike out against evil and evildoers, deny their denial of what we cherish. It claims that by some miracle two wrongs can produce a right. But if good is to result, we must recompense for, balance wrong with right, not add to whatever wrong has already been done.

A law-enforcement agency is an instrument of justice; it should make evident and insist upon the claims of the right. This it cannot do by physically punishing guilty men, by matching wrongs with other wrongs, by ignoring what the outcome of the punishments will be. What is gained, by what right does one punish the awkward and the malformed? They have misfortunes enough; to match the ills they do by other ills is to multiply, not overcome evil. They are to be punished for the unnecessary evils which they produce, but not in order to prevent such production in the future or to balance the evil by another evil.

Legal punishment is reconstructive. It carries out a tacit social demand that men find niches in which they can be relied upon to do what the positive law demands. Statutes are primarily devices for acknowledging and taking account of men's multiple abilities; they are not agencies serving to help us judge virtues or to distribute rewards and punishments. The intent of the law is to require the negligent, the awkward, or irregular to act inside those confines where it is reasonable to expect that they will not promote unnecessary injury. It demands that they compensate for the injuries brought about, not primarily as a means for making them suffer or as a means of preventing a repetition but as a means for helping the injured to recover a forced loss of status and to be protected from similar injuries thereafter. Men are to be forced to take positions other than those they occupy, not primarily to prevent them from doing certain things but to help them to do socially desirable things in another way. The law is an instrument of good, not an agency for doing wrong or a machine which warns men not to make missteps. It demands that they be law abiding, fill socially needed positions in the best possible way, conform to a natural law to the best of their abilities. If they fail to do what one position demands, the law offers them another, equally legal, equally legitimate, equally social, but not necessarily equally pleasant or prestigious.

Reconstructive punishment is retributive to the degree that it is pertinent to and justified by some injury; it is preventive in as far as it refers to the future, assigning new positions to men, positions they are more likely to fill with benefit to the rest than those they occupied before. It offers a means for remaking men but only when and to the degree that they have made evident an inability to fill, in a socially satisfactory way, the positions which they now occupy.

3. The Limits of Law

A man, though relied upon to respond to a community's demands, might not be responsive to its needs. He would live in but not belong to his community. He would live in consonance with its positive laws as partially expressing a natural law. These positive laws, while illustrating natural law, may conflict with one another. Each after all fails to take account of some need of man, and if taken as absolute, will get in the way of the use of other laws. Each, while illustrating, may therefore defeat the intent of a truly absolute natural law and thus of the very community which formulates and even insists on the fulfillment of some particular positive law.

Natural law is law pertinent to any community. It is universal and rational, expressing the meaning of the good for beings who can take some account of one another's values. It is variable in meaning, a schema, a paradigm specified by legislators—not always accurately or consistently—as the positive law of the community. Positive law is natural law made relevant to an actual community through the agency of specifications and references to limited conditions. Unless these specifications and references go no further than to localize, to orient the natural law, the positive law which results will be of little more than a set of self-conflicting codes, a set of arbitrary and opposed injunctions and decisions.

When the legislation of a community has the character of genuinely good laws, formulating the nature of a worthy order in which men can live without loss of individuality, there will be no room for those positive laws now on the books which are little more than indications as to when animals in human form are to be coerced. Positive law, instead, will exemplify the justice expressed in natural law by means of rational, relevant sets of rules, enabling men to discover experimentally their proper places in their community.

Those who legislate can be confident that they have formulated laws and not codes only so far as they legislate for rational and just men. Only then can they confidently hope for that free acceptance of positive law without which it could be what men try to evade even while they obey it.

Though formulated in a community and in terms singularly appropriate to the members of that community, positive law ought to be more than a set of orders given, commands uttered, the expression of what a community of men would like. It must appeal to reason, must offer itself as transparent, as articulating the meaning of right and wrong for men now. Claiming to state what is just for all, it goes counter to its own intent if internally discrepant or opposed to the positive laws of other communities. It should ask for approval because of what it says, not because of its efficacy or because it is supported by threat or force. It cannot demand an exclusive loyalty but it can demand that all acts be subject to it, that they occur inside the area it embraces. It should not ask that some acts or interests be denied but rather that all be interpreted as falling within its range.

Some acts, though just as effective and communally significant as others, and equally subject to communal judgment, never come within the scope of law. Law hardly touches the field of manners, a conformity to which contains so much of the promise of most men's happiness. Nor does it require men to pledge themselves in its behalf. It does not ask them for loyalty; it allows them to devote themselves to other goods and other gods, merely relying on them in specified directions and offering them alternatives should its reliance be misplaced. It offers a kind of irrefutable hypothesis to the effect that men will be subject to it, if not in this role then in that, if not under threat then under duress. But it does nothing to see that men live up to it. In itself it contains no assurance that when men fail to live up to its initial demands, they will accept the alternative it offers.

Men offer their private testaments and contracts for public certification; they freely choose the legal order of their time because they see it as embodying a universally applicable principle of justice, a universal law which pertains to them even in those cases where it has not had a legislative formulation. When they see all legislation as an instance of this universal law, having an appeal to the reason of men and applicable everywhere, they can extend the province of legislation even to those cases which the positive law does not comprehend. The positive law relies on them in fact to extend its scope as far as they can. And if men fail to do this, it is the positive law and not they who are at fault, for positive law should state in unmistakable terms what is truly and objectively just for that time and place. If it fails of support it fails because it fails to appear as a universal principle of justice in a local, recognizable dress. Instead it becomes what law too often is, an outraged cry preceding the use of unreasonable force, alien to the spirit of the community and alienating men from a sense of legal accountability. It will be a set of edicts and commands opposed to the intent of natural law, a positive law in appearance because legislated and placed alongside others, but not a positive law in fact, if this is to be what illustrates natural law appropriately for the circumstance. The true positive law provides a standard of values for men who, while remaining in a limited part of the world, act as members of the whole of it; what is less than this may be a positive law for lawyers but is only an imitation of it for the rest of men.

By attending to a sound positive law, and beyond that to a natural law, a man focuses on a special form of a possibility which it is of his essence to point at and to endeavor to realize. He turns to law comparatively late, however, in his career as a cooperative individual or as a representative of the race, and then reaches only to part of what he by nature needs and persistently seeks. To see this somewhat better it is desirable to retrace our steps a little and ask again how and why men change from beings with unknown but unavoidable concerns for an all-comprehensive possibility into men who are concerned with that limited form of it which we know as law, natural or positive. We shall then be in a somewhat better position to see why cooperation will never be the final answer to his question as to just what he is to do, why he cannot be content with living up to even the best of positive laws or with conforming to natural law, why it is not enough for him to choose well, why it is that he must creatively exercise his will.

PART III

The Creative Will

XI

THE EVOLUTION OF ETHICAL MAN

1. SITUATIONS

ANIMALS act in terms of overly narrow and determinate possibilities. There is a wide world outside their interests, a mine of surprises, a host of neglected possibilities pertinent to the fields toward which they direct themselves. Man has conquered both the narrowness and determinateness, but he has thereby lost something of the animal's sense of the brute, substantial reality of external things. Not until he combines breadth with relevance to what is now going on can he reach the summit of natural existence. The evolutionary limit which he now represents is a limit which merely allows him to be prepared for all things vaguely and for no actual thing definitely. He needs the directness, the immersion in the steady grooves of nature characteristic of the animal, to supplement that flexible, omnivorous appetite for all existence which is one of the marks of his superiority over animals. Only then will he cease to be a creature of the world and become a master of himself living in nature as fully as before.

From the beginning a man has a self and a body. The former guarantees his identity. Though his body changes and his morals improve, though his mind grows and his memory flags in the course of his career, he remains selfsame from birth to death. He cannot be reduced to a mind or a body, a virtue or a habit. An adequate description of him must find room for these, but it must also take account of that self of his which quickens and sustains them all.

The self is a constant, undeviatingly concerned with and yet conditioned by an all-comprehensive possibility. Since the self does not in this life exist on its own, but is inseparable from and is biased toward a particular, limited body, it cannot make use of its all-comprehensive possibility except by infecting that possibility with its *bias*. A man, because he is a self with a body, specifies the all-comprehensive possibility in the form of a constant, highly general, vague, biased outlook, an individual accent which colors everything that he confronts.

Man's first category is the all-comprehensive possibility, distorted, determined a little, but still universally applicable and vague. It is the substance of him as nought but a self biased primarily toward this one body; and it is this which he expresses in every move, every look, every turn, whether these be bodily or mental, conscious or unconscious. It is this which provides him with a means for matching from within conditions imposed by his contemporaries from without. Everything that they might do to him is in general already anticipated by the possibility which he has made his own. But precisely because that possibility is a possibility for everything, it has no specific relevance to any one of the things which he happens to encounter. It is just as pertinent to what is near as to what is far, to what now presses on him insistently and to that which gives way quietly, to what he wants and to what he abhors.

From the first man fails to take inward account of the specific external conditions to which his contemporaries subject him. But could those contemporaries be made continuous with him, could they function as elements in his bodily infected bias, they would have a status for him somewhat like that which his body has. They would then no longer externally determine him—and he would therefore no longer be conditioned by alien beings—in ways he did not provide for from within. They would instead specify the possibility which characterizes him as a man, with a body here and now, possessed of these or those organs, engaged in these or those acts, in the same way that those bodily organs and acts specify the possibility which characterizes him as a self steadily biased toward the body. Such a result he achieves by adopting external things as his boundaries, thereby extending himself beyond the borders where his body is normally located and making what is now an alien condition into a condition he himself sustains.

From the start man realizes the all-comprehensive possibility in all others, functioning as limits of himself, and as a consequence becomes *spatialized*, a being who encompasses those others, no matter where they are. In focus here, he extends everywhere, his boundaries being constituted by whatever there is. The other beings have a force, a power, a logic of their own. They resist him, they change and vary without regard for what he is or does. An adoption of them must be protean. A man must adjust himself constantly to them, or what he is from without will not constantly accord with what he is from within. The adoption must be charged with spontaneity, with fresh, fluent spurts of energy, matching the unexpected turns in their various careers. A man thereby makes not only his presence but his power felt; he becomes one who not only possesses but helps forge his own boundaries.

The accident of geography makes some things more important because more obtrusive than others. They assert themselves more, they force a man to take account of them more directly, more effectively than he does of others. They form *situations* with him, limited groups of beings to which he, primarily and with some spontaneity, directs himself in the effort to make them bounding parts of himself. His future as a biased self is intertwined with theirs to constitute a single, limited future, expressing what he and the others in the situation can be and do.

Every situation has a situational possibility which its members help constitute and which encompasses whatever they could together bring about. That possibility comes to be and passes away when the situation does, expressing as it does only what the situation can become. Yet it has a being of its own. It could not be a mere dangling function of the situation without ceasing to be a true possibility expressing what is to be. Nor could it be indifferent to the situation without belying the truth that only what will occur can occur. Only that will be which the situational possibility allows. That possibility must therefore control the situation, delimit it, deny it certain outcomes and allow it others.

2. Expectation

A man must internalize the situational possibility and guide himself by it if he is to control himself. This he does whenever he engages in a creative, freely expressed *expectation*.

Expectation enables a man to lay hold of the situational possibility he and others constitute and make it inwardly effective, to guide and condition himself in the situation. It is because of his expectation that he sees things not only as they are here and now but as they may be there and then. He sees them here and now in fact only because he looks at them as having a future of a certain sort. He who saw only a round, ruddy, glossy thing at arm's reach would never, except by sheerest accident, pick it up and eat it. He would never know there is such a thing as an apple. Such knowledge requires a reference to what is not yet, to the future, as that which is implicated in what now is and which delimits what can now occur. No one can escape from such a reference, for even the acknowledgment of a shape as round, a color as ruddy, a texture as glossy is an acknowledgment which requires a reference to what will appear when the perspective changes and other things and circumstances are altered. A round shape is one which will appear elliptical from this angle or that; a ruddy color will change its look as the lighting is altered and the distance is varied.

We are never wholly immersed in the present; we are tensed, expectant beings having some grasp of what will be the outcome of what now is. That is why induction is an insoluble problem only for logicians, men without a future, and why only philosophers, who are lost within the mazes of their own mentality, bedevil themselves with a problem of "the knowledge of other selves and minds." Others live the solution of these problems; they are expectant beings who hold on to their own and others' futures while living in the present. No combination of shapes and colors will ever yield an apple, or indeed yield the theoretician who is vainly seeking to know how he knows that there are apples. No study of men's bodies or acts, as confined to here and now, will even ground a precarious argument of analogy which will hint that others have minds and selves similar to our own. We rarely see our bodies and acts in a perspective similar to that which we assume when looking at others, and where we do, we have too little knowledge of our own selves and minds to warrant an inference to "similar" ones. We know our fellows because we know the kind of future they are bringing about. When we say of them that they have selves we but assert that they now constitute and are constrained by possibilities we also help constitute and which also effectively constrain us.

A *disposition* is a bias delimited in reference to but a few contemporaries; it is a bias quickened not by the all-comprehensive possibility but by an expected situational version of it. It is the substance of us as involved with these things here and now rather than with those things then and there; it characterizes us as *located* men ready to act in any one of alternative, isolated ways with respect to the few things we now situationally face.

Because we are biased beings we make the future in which our expectations terminate relevant to us in a special way. We overspecify it; we personalize it, make it subject to our individual hopes and fears. As a consequence we often misconstrue and almost always think the future to be more determinate and peculiarly pertinent to us than it in fact is. Whether we grasp that future correctly or incorrectly, with or without distortion, we make its power felt in the form of dispositions to accept and reject the things about as more or less agreeable, more or less wanted. The disposition is a vector; by virtue of it we are more than spatialized beings or, while existing as cosmic beings to whom nothing is alien, are at home in some limited part, directing our energies, acts, and even our dreams on it alone.

The things in a situation with us are more than mere termini of the dispositions we have toward them; they have a reality of their own; they are active on their own account and in their own ways. In order to meet the challenge that they put to us we are forced to charge our dispositions with spontaneity, *interest* ourselves in them. Interest is disposition made flexible; it converts the object toward which we are favorably or unfavorably disposed, but of whose specific contours and actions we did not take account in our dispositions, into bounding parts of us, thereby qualifying and limiting our expectations. Men interest themselves in only some of the objects toward which they are disposed, and of those interested objects only a few ever come near the focus of their attention. Only a few are sufficiently insistent on themselves, compelling men to attend to them and to neglect the others; only a few benefit from that inertia of man's which occasionally comes to expression in the form of memory and which makes him stay with some things more than others.

We are inertial beings, holding on to what we often consciously neglect. We tend to turn to familiar objects, allowing new ones to impinge on us indifferently. So far as we can, we use new ones to form a background enabling some other occurrence to come to us in the guise of a familiar thing in which we are interested. No one of us ever simply expects the eating of an apple; rather, what we expect is the pleasure of eating an apple like other apples previously eaten or like other items of food or like some other ruddy things. The apple now is the counterweight of our memory; it is a familiar object which will, we believe, unfold itself in the way others did. We deal with it inertially, awaiting a future which interests us but which may not be the future which is of its essence in fact. We hear the clock ticking but do not attend to it until it stops; we see our nose all the time but do not note it until we are bothered by a persistent itch at the tip. We hold on to what we now undergo and make it dictate some difference to what new things are to mean and what it is we will expect from them.

Inertia helps us narrow our environment by leading us to ignore some things which otherwise would be important and to enhance others which otherwise would be of little interest. It turns a man from one whose boundaries are defined by the reach of his dispositions into one whose boundaries are limited by what is familiar. It makes him an experiencing being with a narrow world richer than the wider he lived in before, since the items in it more than make up in importance for what they lose in number and variety.

Inertia, conscious or unconscious, preserves the past in the present. It endows things with a kind of surplus value or disvalue. Because of it we are interested in the apple not only as an item in the environment but as an object which contains within it the meaning of the past and thus promises a future it otherwise would not. Because we remember, we inertially expect to be rewarded or punished more than things by and of themselves can promise we will be.

We may be disposed toward any number of unfamiliar fruits, but these are of no consequence in comparison with an apple if this lies within the field of our experience and thus is capable of producing results which none of those other fruits can bring about, even were they by accident encountered and eaten. The pleasure that the apple offers is a pleasure for one interested in apples. There are new tastes, new pleasures, new things all the time; we are constantly being offered new treats and are making new experiments with objects never before dealt with. Did we deal with them in isolation from what we remember, did we have no inertial expectation of the result they might produce, we could be thrilled, excited, soothed but never pleased, disappointed, disturbed, pained by them. Because we deal with them inertially, we face them as objects in which we are interested; we recognize that they promise us some joy similar to that previously granted by apples.

3. POSSIBLE EXPERIENCE

An interested man forms an *experiential whole* with others. He has a dignity, a status denied to one without interests. Occupied with a more limited circle of things, he helps constitute possibilities more determinate and more meaningful than, yet as realizable as, those he constituted and faced before. With each item of experience he constitutes a limited, pertinent possibility of experience, defining the nature of the future open to him as dealing with that item. That possibility has a being of its own. More indeterminate than the beings which constitute it and the situation in which they are, standing to the present situation as a universal to a particular, it is pertinent to other situations as well. In its more abstract aspects and thus as more and more remote, it is pertinent to more and more and eventually to all possible experienceable things. It is to such remote, quite indeterminate yet pertinent possibilities of experience that we turn when and as we concentrate in variable ways on bringing about limited futures in limited wholes. That is why what we bring about here has bearing on what we bring about there, and we as a consequence are not caught inside cubicles of experience filling up little unrelated blocks of time.

The most abstract but pertinent possibility to which we as experiencing beings can turn is the *ideal of a possible experience*. This is contained as an abstract part of every limited future pertinent to an experiential whole. Isolated, it forms the limit of our horizon as experiencing beings. It allows for all that can be experienced by us and denies to us what cannot be experienced. Determined by it from without, we must internalize it; otherwise we would be subject to a future, and balked by the objects it sustains, in ways for which we made no provision. To be within what we are without, the ideal of a possible experience must govern us internally as it now controls us actually. It is such internalization which lays the ground for the conversion of a man who merely experiences into one who is *social*.

The possibility of experience determines in part what an interested, inertial man will accomplish. The adoption of it as a *category* jeopardizes its purity. It individualizes it, delimits it, infects it with the individual's nature, so that a man looks out at the world with a biased *attitude,* expressing not only the meaning of the category but the nature of his stresses as well. Attitude is disposition as sustaining a category of possible experience. It is the agency by which we attend to items in experiential wholes.

Because attitudes express in individual ways the meaning that possible experience has for men, they are able to narrow the limits of the world in which men live to but a part of what can be experienced. Men are habitually directed to but a few of the things they might consider. Since those things act independently, men must, to maintain a hold on those things as true, bounding parts of themselves, respond to those things flexibly and spontaneously.

The *culture* of a man is that portion of the experiential environment toward which he has *responsive* attitudes and thus toward which he, as a biased bearer of the category of possible experience, is geared to make an appropriate response. No man, though, can concentrate on all the objects toward which he has the appropriate cultural attitudes. In the course of his life he is subjected to innumerable and unnoted institutional pressures, making him concentrate on but a few of the objects which constitute his culture. He and his fellows are given different *roles* to fill in limited places with respect to a limited number of cultural objects, each role marking out a limited *cultural* field, the totality of which makes up a society.

A *society* is a set of interconnected cultural fields. Each of these fields has its own possibility, controlling, and future, overarched by the single possibility characteristic of the society as a whole. As appropriate to a cultural field, each subordinate possibility is relevant only to the occurrences in that situation; it expresses what could be the outcome of the present interplay of the items of the culture. The overarching social possibility in contrast provides a standard in terms of which the different cultural fields can be judged.

Society offers men a limited objective. It is possible to reject it to advantage. Saints as well as criminals are often asocial. And asocial all of us to some degree must be. The supposed full-fledged member of a society lives in fact a divided life; he shows some love for his children and some interest in art or truth which ill accord with the well-defined patterns of his society. Social men are monks by day and profligates by night, keeping in narrow grooves only under the pressure of public light.

The hope of social planners is that they will be able to construct a *civilized* world broad enough to encompass all human activity, the arts and the sciences, the economics and the love of men; that they will be able to provide for needs more coherent and extensive than any other society can. There are, however, a number of coherent, extensive schemes—the Marxist and the democratic, those of Christianity, Islam, China, and India. They all seem to be quite comprehensive. No one appears to be all inclusive. Each leaves out as unimportant much that the others include as central. There is no way of adjudicating their claims except by standing outside them and invoking some standard common to them all. In the perspective of history that society or civilization is superior to others which outrides the vicissitudes of men, which allows them to live in different ways at different times and thus to act appropriately as conditions change. A theory which refuses to have recourse to a moral or ethical standard can do nothing less than judge societies and civilizations in this way. That is best, it must say, which best withstands the ravages of historic time. But then all it will be able to tell us is that such and such a society or civilization is historically viable, not that it is desirable or good or even that it has made an impress on man's mind, attitude, or act.

Socially imposed objectives, whether endorsed by history or not, are internalized in the form of *goals*. Goals specialize and individualize objectives and provide a test in terms of which all objects can be effectively utilized. Narrow in scope, goals can be made pertinent to every object. The narrowest of goals can be made to subtend the universe by treating it as the objective which everything else must promote or hinder. Narrow or wide, the goals dictate to us what things we will accept or reject as means; in short what we will *prefer*.

4. Preference, Choice, and Will

Preferences convert external things into the boundaries of men who have privately decided to bring about some goal. So far as things are possessed as such boundaries whatever is done to them is done for oneself as the bearer of a goal. A change in the goal or in the weight it has for us will make necessary a shift in our approach to things, making us prefer what before we did not.

To make provision for the careers and importance things actually have apart from our adopted goals, what lies beyond us must be made into bounding parts of ourselves. Our preferences must be charged with spontaneity to enable us to deal with things as independent objects in nature. By thus modifying our preferences we make ourselves into *reasonable* men, men who deal appropriately with what lies outside so as to realize adopted goals.

Education teaches men how to associate with other beings, how to *appreciate* them. To the degree men are educated they live under the aegis of a *social morality*, a common possibility pertinent to a world of appreciated things. Initially constituted by and immediately relevant to but a fragment of a society, that morality is capable of application beyond the society's borders. When so extended, social morality attains the status of an *absolute morality*. This is the future pertinent to whatever we *do* and thus to real objective values, whether or not these are known, endorsed, or rejected by society, civilization, or history.

Absolute morality is social morality idealized and freed from an exclusive reference to some one society or time. Made relevant by responsible man to actual values, absolute morality assumes the form of an *ultimate end*, a principle of value in terms of which all things can have their worthiness acknowledged, compared, and ordered. An ultimate end is pertinent to everything; it is the frame, the focus, the future for whatever we do and whatever has bearing on our acts and their objects. Nothing is outside its reach, not because, as in the case of a goal, whatever is can somehow be related to the goal as a means but because it is ultimate, a totality of value relevant to existent things as possessing some degree and kind of worth. It dictates the degree of *approval* or disapproval which should be accorded an act; it is inseparable from the determination of the objects we, as conscientious men, will *choose* to preserve or destroy.

An act of choice is a practically effective intent, dealing with appreciated objects in terms of an ultimate end. It enables men to use as boundaries things whose values are preserved in that end, to treat external, valuable things as involved in whatever is done. Those external things can by no thaumaturgy be deprived of their externality, their independence. Choices succeed only in making things into momentary boundaries. To make things into more permanent boundaries, to possess them as our own in steady ways, we must adopt them as they are and not merely as having bearing on our commitments and duties. We must approach them in flexible, spontaneous, effective ways, come to appreciate them as valuable, independent beings with their own careers. This result is most readily achieved by means of great works of art. Under their stimulus we come to appreciate what things independently are.

Works of art, the excellent products of techniques grasping what is essential and important in the real, are for responsible men what education is for reasonable ones. They subtilize and extend the range of natural appreciations. They help men focus on the essence of things, to become more alert to the objective values, the needs, careers, and rights things have.

The greatest works of art are the watersheds of history; they divide the past from the present, one historic epoch from another. Because of what men learned from Homer and Aeschylus, from the Bible and cathedrals, and from such living works of art as Buddha and St. Francis, Lincoln and Gandhi, they broke away from one historic epoch and began new ones. Great works of art represent crises in the history of mankind, leading us to appreciate what things substantially are, and as a consequence to live with those things in a way which answers to their natures and careers and not merely to our duties and commitments. Art must always be novel in nature and perspective, not only because it is creativity almost naked but because it is its task to push all toward new dimensions of value otherwise unnoticed.

To experience a work of art is to experience beauty. Such experience is not necessarily reported in any behavior. But the having experienced it must be so reported. The experience of beauty is a crucial experience; to have undergone it is to have begun to change one's ways. He who sees beauty is transformed; under its influence his behavior becomes subtler and more appropriate than it had been before. As an effect of it he acts with others more harmoniously than he did; he treats things as being more precious, as being of greater import, as deserving to be worked over more, to be cared for more than they had been. No one can be said to have had a vision of true beauty, to have a genuine grasp of a great work of art, to have the gift of tongues, to have seen a value beyond the reach of those immersed in a given epoch, unless he shows in his acts that he is sensitive and concerned with the rights and needs of others in and of themselves. He must form a community with the beings whose natures he appreciates and vary his activities in consonance with the Golden Rule. He must commune with them as beings having an interiorness of their own, cooperatively live with them as substantial, independent, interlocked, valuable beings, determining his roles and tasks by means of positive laws.

The common good of a community of sensitive beings, when freed from an exclusive reference to that community, is one with the idea of perfection, of excellence, with the idea of an *absolute good*, and thus with the final principle of a universal *ethics*, having application to this and other epochs, to the subhuman as well as man. This absolute good is that very same all-comprehensive possibility which, in more or less distorted and limited forms, men faced in the other stages of their careers and in terms of which they acted on the world about. A universal principle of harmony for whatever values there be, it is pertinent to whatever exists, taken as substantial, objective, and interrelated. Natural law gives it a rational, communicable form as germane to men in some community or other, and the creative *will* enables it to be made real without distortion by us.

Man contrasts with other beings as one who is permanently bound to and responsible for the absolute good. It is his task to realize it everywhere. Usually, though, he acts so as to realize much less than the absolute good demands; too often he gets no further than the consideration of ultimate ends which he is committed to realize by virtue of his past activities and promises. Since he then does not regard the values and careers, the rights things actually have, he then, even though reasonable and decent, does not necessarily do what he objectively should—promote a world in which he and all others are maximally perfected. To do all that should be done, to be a fully ethical man, he must make and remake himself and others to the limit of their capacities.

XII

NATURE AND VALUE

1. ETHICAL FACTS

IT is never enough to alter the circumstances in which men act, to vary the pressures put on them, to subject them to new conditions. Pigs can live in palaces and saints in sties, a little more uncomfortable than usual, perhaps, but still unaltered essentially. Men change only if they act on external beings, respond to them, reorganize themselves and the things while dealing with them—in a word, only if they create.

We speak sometimes as though we could by depriving men of food change them from fresh, independent thinkers into frightened ones. But if they did not somehow see and dislike the shape of hunger, they would not necessarily, even when debilitated and miserable, act in a manner much different from that in which they acted before. Men change, to be sure, without becoming aware of why or how, but their every change is the outcome of the kind of answer they freshly and freely make to the conditions which hem them in. A shrewd guess can be made as to how most men will respond to certain changes in the world about; we can plan to and can in fact change many men radically and by merely altering some of the more familiar features of their physical and social worlds. Yet all the time the men have the capacity and the energy, all the time they are free to cancel every such change by a decisive effort to remain in principle as they were before.

It is the unimaginative use men make of their freedom which endows external circumstance with such grave promise for good or ill in their lives. Better use can be made of freedom. There seems indeed to be no limit to the degree to which men can freely reduce the import of even the most insistent disturber of their minds and bodies. And where a man fails, as he so often does, to match from within the compulsions he suffers from without, he answers nevertheless and with his own stress. Man makes himself, let circumstances be as they may. And he makes himself in a nature permeated by values, a nature in which he acts and judges as a full-bodied, ethical, self-determining being.

Men make ethical judgments all the time. They decide that this kind of act would be wrong, that kind right to do, often without hesitation and with satisfaction to all. Even the theoretician who professionally opposes them tells them and us that not this but that should be believed, that a man *ought* to think thus and so and not otherwise. A man has no right to say that there are no values in nature but only that he is sometimes mistaken as to just what is good and what is bad, that his judgments, like ours, are hazardously forged and liable to error. And with this we can all agree.

Wanton murder, injustice, betrayal are absolutely wrong, all of us believe. The wrongness, all of us hold, does not depend on how we happen to judge such acts; it is not jeopardized by changes in customs or morality, by shifts in goals or in the nature of our chosen ultimate ends. These acts are essentially wrong, intrinsically wrong; they and wrongness together make an irreducible ethical fact which it would be folly to deny. He who does not know such facts, who does not know that peace is good, that the world is not the best possible and should be improved, that men can be guilty for crimes committed years ago, that love is better than hate, is insincere or mad. Or so we all believe, and many of us say.

These seem to be facts as obtrusive, as well grounded, as evident as anything can be. Since we seek to understand a world and not to deduce it, must we not accept without cavil all these as ultimate and unrejectable? Must we not cling to them and perhaps finally end with nothing less than the whole galaxy of facts that good men have recorded and have always insisted on as irreducible and brute?

A spirit of generosity, a refusal to prejudge anything or anyone, a submission to history may prompt us to try to answer these questions affirmatively. Every proffered ethical fact seems on its face to be just as respectable and ultimate as any other. If we were to take all of them without cavil, we would exhibit ourselves as free from provincialism, sectarianism, and the arbitrary pronouncements of absolutists. No longer would we be tempted to force others to be free the way we are; we would be impartial men, prejudging nothing.

Attractive though the prospect of accepting all ethical facts on their face value is, it must be resolutely put aside. No one of us does, no one of us can, and no one of us should try to make that prospect real.

No one has ever taken every supposed ethical fact as genuine. They are not all compatible. Some are to be justified by their consonance with impulse, some by their opposition to it. The philosopher who would try to referee is usually on one side or the other of these conflicting claimants. And if he tries to stand in between and say that each side is satisfactory in its own terms and within its own area, he is faced with the fact that some of the claims of each are thereby denied, for each takes itself to be absolute, denying all legitimacy to the other.

When it is said by one side that the production or possession of pleasure is absolute ethical fact, what is intended is not that it is such a fact for some men at certain times but that it is a fact for all everywhere, and that he who does not acknowledge it in practice or in theory is mistaken. To grant to each of the rival claimants to absolute truth a half of it is to satisfy neither. Each side dismisses its opponent and the referee as mistaken, denying that what the others offer to be ethical facts are facts at all. Since nobody accepts what both sides claim, nobody accepts all supposed ethical facts on their face value.

Nor is it possible to accept every supposed ethical fact without question. The history of ethics provides considerable evidence that some men have thought the pursuit of pleasure to be good, while others held that the possession of virtue is futile; some have thought that meekness is a greater good than power, others have held that might make right. These cannot all be true; some must be rejected if there is to be some semblance of order in our discourse. He who would accept them all would be in conflict with himself.

Nor should any man accept all so-called ethical facts as ultimate and unimpeachable. This would require him to be so flexible as to destroy himself, to abrogate his distinctive, definitive nature. What are offered as ethical facts form such a heterogeneity, constitute such a pattern of opposing and irreconcilable items, that to encompass them all a man would have to make himself infinitely passive and malleable, an amorphous receptacle where the most disparate items can be placed without any effect on him or he on them. Since to be a man is to exclude, to demarcate, to accept some things and to reject others, he who would accept all supposed ethical facts would want not to be a man at all. He would want what he ought not and finally cannot want, for it is man's inescapable task to be a man, not something else.

Not all supposed ethical facts are to be accepted without qualification. Indeed, he who accepts any at all seems to beg a question. Are not all so-called ethical facts so obviously derivative and conflicting as to preclude the acceptance of any? They all seem to be ungrounded, unjustified, so evidently constituted of nonethical components—of experiential content, emotional responses, and conventional attitudes —as to make it seem foolish for one to suppose they express anything more than the fact that men approve of some things and do not approve of others. Yet if we seek to reject all presumable ethical facts, we but seek to reject a warrant for inquiry, for criticism, and for the rejection itself. These have ethical importance and ethical consequences; they cannot be instituted without establishing the ultimacy of some ethical fact. All rejections involve the acceptance of at least the value of the rejection.

Every claimant to ultimacy and truth should be subjected to careful, rigorous examination. There is nothing which has a right to complacent acceptance. Everything deserves investigation, clarification, and certification. We must be cautious, reducing our suppositions to a minimum and thus putting aside much that seems attractive and ultimate. But if we are to make an open investigation, if we are to make a genuine attempt to clarify and certify, we cannot rightly begin except by accepting what we have available. Only then are we in a position to decide whether some or all of our initial material deserves to be retained or requires instead to be modified or abandoned.

Perhaps it would be best then to reserve our judgment as to the ultimacy and legitimacy of any given claimant to basic ethical status and content ourselves with the task of describing the items that men in the past have put forward as basic? In this way we would be able to prepare the way for a well-grounded, sober statement of what are genuine ethical facts. It is the mark of philosophic maturity to examine before deciding what to accept and what to reject; philosophy is a critical enterprise, content with forging the right questions if all it otherwise could have are dubious, uncertain answers. It would appear to be a good idea then to describe what we see and stop at that.

It seems the essence of moderation to request that all judgments be suspended, that nothing but description be attempted; actually, it is a form of dogmatism. Only those men whose ethical decisions favor the good of truth above all else honestly suspend their judgments and then with respect to but some limited object or class of objects. No man ever—and most surely at the beginning of inquiry—brackets all supposed ethical facts as equally suspect or tries to rest with mere description. An honest man can suspend his judgment only to further the ethical ideals of inquiry. Description involves selection; it can serve as an agent, as propaedeutic; never can it satisfy as something final. Description presupposes, as well as makes possible, classifications and explanations unifying its heterogeneity; it is a means for surveying, for organizing material which has, at least in part, already been accepted as ethically significant. There are millions of things to describe and millions of ways to do it. Were description ethically neutral, were there no choice of direction, means, objective, no standard of excellence or adequacy of description, there would be no reason why any two men, equally perceptive and acute, should ever agree on what they describe. This room in which I sit has enough angles and relations among them to occupy any man for the whole of his life; yet it is as quiet as a tomb, with only an occasional mumble of a voice heard in between the click of typewriter keys. How much more there is to describe in the richer, wider, noisier world outside.

He who tries to accept all, he who tries to accept none, and he who tries to avoid deciding which supposed ethical facts to accept equally presuppose that some and only some of these facts are to be accepted. As a consequence each stands in the way of his own thesis, opposing himself in principle and in fact and denying that he is a man with a definite nature, who is and always remains experienced and concerned. From the beginning to the end of inquiry a man can do no more and no less than acknowledge some supposed ethical facts and reject others.

We cannot start anywhere but at the place where we now are. That means that whatever now appears to be an ethical fact must be a datum with which the inquiry must begin. Later perhaps there may be reason for modifying the judgment, rejecting some of the initial data, or accepting a host of others. Intelligent skepticism follows, it does not precede the acknowledgment of data. The skeptic must have something to be skeptical about.

The expansion, contraction, the alteration of the field of inquiry is a consequence, not a precondition of inquiry, for we must have the field first in order to operate on it. Relativism is a weak-kneed view primarily because it is so dogmatic and naïve. It fails to recognize that its position must be won against the pull of a nonrelativistic position with which it, like every other, must begin.

The true question is: what ought to be accepted, what ought to be rejected as ultimate ethical fact? Not, are there ultimate ethical facts?

The most widely held point of view as to what we ought to take as root ethical fact is a variant of that entertained by Aristotle, the most influential of ethical thinkers. Ethics, in his view, is a science to be studied and understood by mature, civilized men, men who have already learned what the right values are. In Aristotle's system the men are well-born Greeks and the right values are those they endorse when they reach middle age. The view evidently trenches on provincialism, and in the guise of an absolute system offers only a relativistic account appropriate to a limited number of men at a limited time and place. The "best" men of a time have standards of value which differ from the "worst," but we beg a question when we suppose that what the former endorse ought to be endorsed by all. It will be true again, as it was so many times before, that the values of the downtrodden and the despised will encroach upon and replace the values of those who had been acknowledged to be more civilized, more reasonable, better educated.

The fat of success can surround men thin in spirit, men who have been strengthened by fortune but have little strength of their own. The most eminent and honored, the "best" men in a society may not be the most perceptive; the facts they reject may be the very ones that should have been stressed; the society in which they live and which they sustain and so excellently represent at its best may be defective and perverse. The Greek, or any other society, is not absolutely good, determining what ought to be done and what ought to be avoided everywhere.

The decision as to what to take as basic truth must be forged by each man in a living act of inquiry, even though he may then be doing nothing more than inquiring with others in terms they provide and for ends they endorse. And that inquiry, if it is not to be a private play of thought, must be directed to realities beyond the man.

2. The Value of Things

The process of inquiry presupposes the value of itself as a living pursuit of truth. And it presupposes values in nature, for there is where inquiry occurs. Because inquiry has value and because it is an activity analogous to that which all beings engage in, because the values it presupposes are interlocked with the natures of the things with which it is concerned, values must be recognized to be objective, grounding the reality of ethical facts.

No one refuses in fact or theory to acknowledge values in nature. But it has often been argued that these values are derivative and adjectival, mere adventitious products of emotions, minds, states, or gods. These emotions, minds, states, or gods alone are said to be ethically ultimate. They dictate just what values things are to have; there is no good or bad but the objects so designated by these somewhat capricious masters. We ought, we are told, to love our neighbor, not because he is intrinsically lovable but because he is a fellow creature, a fellow sufferer, a fellow citizen. Traditional Christianity urges us to love him, not for himself but for that spark of divinity in him which alone makes objects worthy of love. From another side we are told that we should acknowledge that alone to be lovable which is the object of our approvals or disapprovals. Freed from these, the world would be a neutral realm of things. Our fellow man and all about are said to be endowed with values and ethical import only because we look at them through an astigmatic mind, from an arbitrary standpoint, as satisfying some human need. These two views seem opposed; their defenders are passionately so. But they share a common supposition revealing that they present the same error in different ways. Both ask us first to separate value from the realities in which it seems so conspicuously to be an essential ingredient, then to locate it or its ground in domains whose existence and nature are far from evident, and finally to come back to the very point from which we began, to affirm exactly what should have been affirmed in the beginning.

Why deny the intrinsic lovability of a neighbor—and thus the rightness of the act of loving and the wrongness of the act of hating him—if we grant that lovability is integral to the very meaning of neighbor? What reason is there and what gain is there in saying that we are to love him only because, like us, he is a creature of a God from whom all goods flow? Grant that he is such a creature, that God endowed him with his existence and his value: in what way does this deny that he has the existence and the value? If God gave him value, he has it, and can be acknowledged to have it here and now; if he does not have the value, if to acknowledge him as worthy of respect and concern, of sacrifice and devotion, is but to point to a God beyond him, then it cannot be said that he is actually endowed with value, that he was created as a valuable being, but at best as a valueless one in which a divine value happens to be resident. To create is to make, to allow to stand apart; to endow is to make essential to, to make ingredient in. We do not glorify God by denying that His creatures have intrinsic values. Instead we minimize Him, denying that He produces anything valuable at all.

Similar observations are merited by the view that values are the emphatic, the epiphenomenal products of minds or societies, without substance, independence, or genuine presence in external beings. If to approve is to make things valuable for us, are they then not *made* valuable? And if so made, do they not stand apart from us the makers? We cannot claim they are unrealities, that nature is value free, encompassing only minds and neutral objects without claiming to go behind the empirical scene and there seeing what no empirical eye ever can.

Dogmatic religionists and skeptical empiricists are brothers in spirit; the one keeps eye focused on a world beyond the stars and therefore dismisses as unreal all that we ever know, while the other keeps ear tuned to what scientists seem to say and therefore dismisses as unreal all that even the scientists know. Neither takes the facts as they appear, laden with values, ethical and otherwise.

Were ethical facts not as hard and objective as other facts known by common sense, by the natural and social sciences, by the arts and philosophy, ethics would have to be acknowledged to be occupied with what men have mistakenly, though perhaps unavoidably and necessarily, taken to be real. It would be a branch of psychology or perhaps even of sociology or biology, reporting on the nature and import of what men do in nonethical ways. Yet were there ethical facts which existed apart from the needs of the discipline of ethics, the world would be other than other disciplines report it to be. A thing, apart from us, would not only have such and such a size, shape, and position but in the very place where these are would have a goodness or a badness as well.

These two alternatives—that ethical facts are the man-created, fictional subjects of ethics and that things are intrinsically good or bad—are both attractive and repugnant in turn. The one makes us view the most vital and central of our activities and judgments, the ethical, as having no genuine footing in what is real, while the other makes us suppose that a thing is a locus of a heterogeneity of such traits as weight, color, cost, beauty, and goodness, independent of yet interpenetrating one another and acknowledged for quite different reasons. Nothing less than both views will satisfy, and thus nothing less than both as qualified by one another. There is no necessity that what men do in nonethical ways should be devoid of ethical import; nor is there any necessity that the different traits of a being, though independent of one another, should turn it into a heterogeneity. It is possible for an ethical fact to be ultimate yet dependent for its being on other realities; it is possible for reality to be saturated with values without conflict with or separation from shapes, sizes, masses, colors, unity.

As Berkeley observed, such primary qualities of figure, motion, and extension are no more and no less objective and impersonal, no more exterior and ultimate than the so-called secondary characters of color, taste, smell. And what he said of the secondary applies to the tertiary as well, as he himself sometimes seemed to see. Where the primary and secondary are, there too are the rest. All these qualities are but phases of a richer reality in which men note and communicate, where they pursue inquiries, speak to one another, check one another's remarks, write books, and act publicly with reference to one another, thereby revealing themselves to be more than qualities, whether these be primary, secondary, or tertiary. Were there nothing but qualities, of whatever order, there would be no real reporting of them, no concrete living men who could mistakenly, as the hypothesis requires, take them to exhaust reality.

Knowing well that values are caught inside restricted frames, that what is a value from one viewpoint is not always so from another, and that a valued yet hallucinatory mermaid has no power or concern, we tend to suppose that values are without objectivity or that there can be no values transcending the imposed limitations. But relativity is not the same thing as subjectivity. Values can vary from context to context and still be objective, just as for a solipsist or God they might exist only in mind and yet be absolute. A being varies in its rate of motion as the density of the surrounding medium changes; this is an objective fact in no way requiring that motion be either absolute or subjective. Just so, a being can vary in other modes of activity, in its characteristics and value in different contexts, without substracting from its objectivity. Nor is this in conflict with the acknowledgment of an absolute valuational as well as nonvaluational nature for the being. It is the selfsame man who is father and husband, brother and son, carpenter and citizen, friend and foe. The traits of a being exhibit its nature in a context provided by others without derogating from the reality of the being or the reality of its traits, valuational or otherwise. If the object is hallucinatory, its being as well as its traits are sustained by real objects of perhaps quite different natures and values from it. The hallucinatory object is an epitomization, a concretion of the value which the man and some genuine object together constitute. It is wrong to suppose that it has a being of its own; it is no less wrong to suppose that it is nothing or that it is something subjective. The hallucinatory object is a relation solidified, given terminal status and apparently independent being. It *is* the value it is supposed to have; that value belongs to a nonhallucinatory object when that object is hallucinatorily acknowledged. Like every other value, it gives, with possible distortion, the public import of the value which a nonhallucinatory object has in itself.

3. The First Step of Ethical Inquiry

Because each of us can begin only at the point where he now is, he can unquestionably do nothing less than acknowledge real, objective values, and particularly as having an ethical import for men who responsibly do right or wrong. We must start with a heterogeneity of ethical facts, whatever else we do.

Our beginning could also be our end, and thus no beginning at all, were there not among our initial facts something which was disturbing, unsatisfactory, and were there not something beyond the initial material which promised greater satisfaction than the material now does, driving us to go beyond it. Were we satisfied now with what we have, we would have no reason to move from where we are. It does not follow, though, that if we are unsatisfied we will be prompted to move elsewhere. We can remain indefinitely in a state of confusion, even conflict, indeterminacy, dissatisfaction, or pain. It is possible to remain miserable over long spans both in theory and in practice. There might be no better state perhaps which we could achieve, there might be no better place than that at which we now are, bad though it be. The present, no matter what its quality, provides no ground, no impetus, no force for departing from it; we can be driven beyond it only if we discern some more attracting good beyond it.

To move away from where we are, in theory or in fact, we must be occupied with something outside, beyond, over against the data we have initially. There must be an objective which ought to be. Acknowledgment of it does not prompt a movement toward it; for giving up our present position more is necessary than the observation that the new position is an excellent one. The new position must lure; it must be vividly felt now to be an excellent place to occupy. Otherwise it will have the status only of a bare prospect, not necessarily pertinent, not necessarily attractive, not necessarily enabling us to progress from where we now are. We move to the good because it first moves us; it dislocates us, disturbs us, forces us to break away from the confines in which we now live.

The disturbing good is less powerful, less compulsive, less concrete than any God is supposed to be. This is why we are more than creatures of what is external to us, why we are not dragged out of our present positions, why we are able to deal with the good creatively and hazardously, examining, evaluating, accepting, and rejecting alternatives on our own initiative, in different ways, with different ethical outcomes.

Gifted with a twofold vision, we look at what is present from the standpoint of an attracting good and at that very good from the vantage ground of present data. The unsatisfactoriness we directly feel with our present position is due in part to our approaching it from the standpoint of our objective; the objective in turn is able to dislocate us because it is attractive, that which we want to make concrete, specific, and present.

A bifocal vision can be as astigmatic as a single one. Both the good and our present data may be seen exclusively from the vantage ground of a particular class or time in history. To avoid being trapped inside the dogmas of our time and station, we must use the good to help us look critically at our data, and conversely. The good must help us select, among all the acknowledged values with which we begin, those items which subtend all theories, men, times, and classes; the data must help us penetrate to the good as common to all men, no matter what their upbringing, their background, and their desires.

We are constantly tensed between the present and the future, holding to both and possessing neither adequately. We are constantly trying to close the gap between them, as a consequence of which we inevitably modify them both, sifting the data on the one hand and making the good more determinate on the other.

The closer we men get to the common good, the more certainly do we insist on some data as basic and unrejectable. The more we insist on ethical facts, the more surely do we direct ourselves to the good which all exemplify. In practical affairs attention is primarily riveted on data, since action concerns the concrete. There is little interest in making the good more evident, in freeing it from transient limitations, but great interest in grasping the facts and making the action right. In theoretical matters an opposite stress is evident. There, more interest is shown in what ought to be achieved than in what has been accepted as data. Little interest is shown in this or that fact, much interest in the nature of the result that should be reached.

Since ethics is a theory, the latter stress is unavoidable; but since it is a theory which originates with and serves to guide practice, the counterstress is also evident in it. Grounded in a set of absolutely reliable data, an ethical theory starts from and ends with the practical judgments that such and such are basic ethical facts. It takes for granted, it makes use of and helps us focus on an absolute standard for testing and ordering the values ingredient in things and enabling us to evaluate what we do as right or wrong.

XIII

THE RELATIVITY OF ABSOLUTES

1. Nihilism and Skepticism

IN every act the value of some thing is actually reduced. Unless no reduction is worse than another, there must be a standard of value which transcends all actual values and yet is pertinent enough to each to enable them all to be compared.

Theoretical nihilism denies that any standard, absolute or otherwise, is possible. It is a position at once dogmatic and inconsistent. At least implicitly it maintains that truth is a good it is right to support, so that in the very act of expressly denying the existence of standards it exhibits in intent and act, if not in words, its conformity to the principle that only truth ought to be affirmed.

Were nihilism both consistent and pertinent, it would itself grant that it had no position to defend, that it had nothing to urge against those who took a different stand. It would allow that it is neither right nor wrong to be a nihilist or not to be one and neither right nor wrong to reject this last assertion. The coherent nihilist must be indifferent to the fact that he is a nihilist and others are not. Since he denies himself the opportunity and right to judge the decisions of himself and others as being right or wrong, there is, for him, no way of justifying his adoption of what he thinks is a truth instead of some other view or instead of its denial. He has no warrant for objecting to one who takes a different stand, to one who adopts the nihilistic position and its denial at the same time, or to one who adopts neither. For the consistent nihilist neither his consistency nor his doctrine has any value. He must grant that it would be just as right to abandon it as to accept it, to state it badly as to state it well, to give it expression on alternate week ends as to insist on it all the time.

In the face of these embarrassments the nihilist is inclined to retreat a step and reappear in the guise of a skeptic. Instead of maintaining that there is nothing right or wrong, he would then maintain that one cannot be sure just what is right or wrong. Since the skeptic contents himself with asking questions and sedulously avoids giving answers, it is not possible to dislodge him—not because his position is impregnable but because he has no position from which to be dislodged. It is impossible to refute one who has nothing to say. The skeptic does not stand opposed to anyone; he stands only in the way, performing the valuable task of making one aware that every answer raises further questions.

Skeptics, like everyone else, are dogmatists in practice. Theoretically unsure perhaps about the right or wrong of lying or stealing, killing or helping, they make evident in their attitudes and friendships, their plans and sacrifices that they recognize some acts to be right and some wrong. And even on purely theoretical grounds the skeptic is forced to give up his skepticism once he asks himself whether or not there are acts which are wrong always and everywhere. He may doubt whether or not it is right to kill another man or even whether or not it is right to kill his friend. But like the rest of us he knows that it is wrong to kill his friend deliberately and wantonly. This is for him no less than it is for us bedrock fact; he differs from us only in his resolute refusal to face up to the consequences of this unavoidable admission.

Were the skeptic to shape his position to conform to the contours of his own actions and admissions, he would affirm that certain acts are really wrong, and thus would give up his skepticism for some such position as that of the relativist. This at least allows him to be skeptical about other men's views. The relativist admits that he condemns and approves just as roundly as anyone else, both in theory and in practice. He goes on to affirm that his condemnations and approvals are nothing more than the reflex of custom and habit. Were we trained differently, did we belong to a different society or epoch, our judgment, he thinks (and his, too, he sometimes admits), would have taken a different turn. But there never was a time or a group in which the wanton slaughter of friends was not condemned. And if this were not true, it would still be true that, in the very situation in which the relativist finds himself, in the light of the conditions which now prevail, the acts he condemns are in fact condemnable. There is no difference between the relativist and others on the question as to whether or not there are acts which are wrong, but only in their interpretation of what makes the act wrong and the universality of the standard in terms of which wrongs are defined.

The relativist maintains that the rightness or wrongness of an act is a function of the frame of reference in terms of which it is approached and that the frame can be changed in an endless number of ways. He is traditionally opposed by those who claim that acts are right or wrong in themselves. The history of ethical controversy is largely the story of man's shuttling back and forth between these extremes.

Extremes can be made to meet. Relativism and absolutism can be reconciled. Though there is an unmistakable shift in values as we go from society to society and though some of the things which one condemns are approved by the others, it is possible to discern a common component in all, justifying the theoretical absolutism which affirms that some acts are wrong everywhere and all the time.

The absolutist is on safe grounds when he rests his case on immediately apprehended wrongs. He knows what is wrong and his knowledge involves a reference to an absolute and universal standard of the right; but what that right is he does not fully or stably know. The relativist finds ample justification therefore when he attends to what men have signalized as right. Our grasp of the right is shifting and loose and gives little hope that there is an absolute standard to know. The relativist and the absolutist can be reconciled by recognizing that the standard may be known without being known in detail, and that general principles have diverse, and sometimes even conflicting illustrations.

2. The Religious Standard

It is widely and tenaciously maintained that a standard adequate to the needs of both absolutism and relativism, making possible the judgment of all acts and beings, must express the dictates of a God.

God, as man knows Him, however, is quite parochial, somewhat inconsistent, and often unreasonable. He changes His injunctions from prophet to prophet, from religion to religion capriciously, exhibiting a decided and rather arbitrary preference for limited groups and rituals, and every once in a while urges men to engage in outrageous acts. Even the most devout man recognizes that God's words must often be edited to avoid folly, vice, and immorality. To escape religious fanaticism, the passionate pursuit of error in the name of God, supposedly divine injunctions must be corrected until they are both wise and ethical. But once the need for such correction is admitted, the attempt to look to divinity to test what is right and wrong is evidently abandoned.

No religious determination of right and wrong is possible, for religion either invokes an arbitrary rule or expresses in another form the essence of nonreligious ethics, sanctioned perhaps by an endorsement or command attributed to God. Were there no nonreligious ethical standard, the statement that the more religious a man, the better he is would reduce to the tautology that the more religious a man, the more religious he is. A religion may claim to have made men more acutely aware of what apart from God is the true standard of the good—though this is questionable. Whether the claim be just or not to judge that a man has been improved by his religion we must refer not to the fact that he is religious but to a standard of right and wrong.

It is possible, of course, to insist that whatever God commands is right and that we know what is commanded by Him by consulting some such work as the Bible. A good man will then be one who obeys God's commands. But struggle and strain as we like, we cannot avoid the admission that if the Bible is His book, He is the prompter of much wrong. In both the Old and the New Testaments God encourages injustice, lies, and slaughter. We condemn these supposedly divinely sanctioned acts and in doing so recognize that God, so far as we know Him through His supposed words, does not always command what is right. This does not mean that God in Himself is bad or that a religion is antiethical, but only that the good is good because it is the good and not because (should that also be the case) it is endorsed by God, and that a religion is ethical because it is ethical, not because it is a religion.

Both God and religion are to be judged as commanding what is right or wrong, good or bad, by a standard they do not necessarily provide, endorse, conform to, or support. There may be other principles appropriate to God or religion alone; God may have His own reasons, His own goods, His own ends. But if so, they are outside ethics. They neither constitute the ethical good nor, on the hypothesis, are subject to it.

3. THE PLATONIC GOOD

The absolute standard which is appropriate to man's acts and with which he is concerned is, as Plato remarked, a good which is other than and beyond him. According to him it is the source of all being and all knowledge, and in the *Republic* describes it as most real and perfect, invisible, transcendental, and eternal, the ground of all power. He goes, I think, too far.

Plato's theory is interesting on its own account. It is interesting too for its effect on the history of thought. What he says about the good is, with incidental modifications and additions, substantially what classical theology, from the time of Origen to that of Calvin, says about God. Two serious difficulties confront both theories.

Firstly, they both put selfishness in the saddle. Since for them the good is already perfect and complete, it evidently cannot be benefited by man in the slightest. A self could be said to be concerned with it only for the benefits or glory which the self would thereby derive.

Secondly, according to these views, the more surely a man desires the good, the more surely must he be bad. "Everyone who desires, desires that which he has not already, and which is future and not present and which he has not, and is not, and of which he is in want; these," says Plato, "are the sort of things which love and desire seek." If a man desires the good then he must, on this view, so far be bad. The conclusion is intolerable.

Men want a good they have not. Their desire for that good does not testify to their badness; rather it provides excellent testimony of their goodness. Whatever is wanted is ennobled by being wanted; he who wants the good does good to it to some degree. He also does good to himself. Merely by desiring the good, just by making it the terminus of his desire, he infects himself with it, transforms himself, makes himself and perhaps others better, while making the good more determinate, more specific, more realized than it had been. Both he and the good are better for his having desired it—though of course not yet good enough, since successful action is still needed.

The satisfaction of a desire for the good is a good. This satisfaction is not the object of desire. It is desirable, not desired, being the outcome of a successful effort to get a different object. Desire for the good marks a man as one who is not as good as he can be; it does not define him to be somehow bad and inadequate. It does not require that he be of less value than the desired good itself; it requires only that the successful realization of the desired good be a good greater in value than the desired good or the desire for that good, because more concrete and complete than either.

The root of Plato's difficulty is his supposition that the good with which a man is concerned is a substantial reality, already finished and complete. If that reality alone is truly good, all else is bad. What is distinct from it, what is other than it, is to be condemned. But the good which men seek is not now, as unattained, better than they are. It is instead abstract, thin, far from perfect, lacking the vitality and substantiality of the concrete, and dependent on what now is for its power and direction. Man gives substance, vitality, concreteness to the good when and as the good gives order, universality to him. The good is wider than man but he is richer than it; he needs it and it needs him. Without the other each is not as good as it could be.

The good is not very good. Perfection is not perfect. Nor is humanity human, thoughtfulness thoughtful, honesty honest. Plato was misled by words when he held that the good was good, holiness holy, and the idea of dirt somehow dirty.

Perfection, absolute goodness, is an ideal which becomes perfected in being realized. The concern for perfection is a dynamic relation between two beings, one concrete and here, the other abstract and remote. The concern draws the two together, enriching the one by the other and promoting actions which draw them still closer together.

That concern is desire free from psychological overtones, a good constituting, with the beings it interrelates, a good greater than itself or the others. The more closely these beings are brought together, the greater is the good that is produced. We ought to be ethical, we should be more intimately concerned with the good, for we thereby more adequately perfect ourselves and it.

Aristotle was on the verge of saying this. He constantly affirmed that what was desired was a form, and that matter and form were correlates needing one another. His Platonic training proved, though, too much for him; again and again he spoke of such forms as the rational soul and God as though they could exist apart from all else, perfect, complete, and actual. Form needs matter as surely as matter needs form. The two are never and can never be completely asunder: form in general, indeterminate, unifying matter; matter is dispersive, local, activating form.

So far as a being is excellent it exemplifies the form of perfection, but that form must in turn be exemplified if it is to have more than that minimal degree of goodness characteristic of it as a form which should be embodied. The characteristic Platonic-Aristotelian refusal to distinguish between a form necessary to a perfect being and the perfect being exemplifying such a form leaves in its wake the insoluble problem as to why the form of perfection should ever be exhibited. Were the form of perfection perfect, there would be nothing which it could gain by being exhibited. Nor could other beings exemplify it except by ceasing to be what they are, for the exemplification would involve the replacement of their natures by alien ones. Just as humanity requires men to give it substantiality, to make it human as it were, so perfection requires beings here and now to give it substantiality, to perfect it in fact.

4. Nominalism and Conceptualism

Perfection is the common denominator of all the possible ends to which men can subscribe. A universal, having a constant meaning, exemplified in diverse ways in diverse places, it is related to different worlds of value as color is to red and green and as humanity is to you and me. It is at once outside all ends and differently and perhaps even oppositionally embodied in each.

Nominalism, however, claims that no universal is more than a word. Since it maintains something general, something that applies to all supposed cases of universals and to all kinds of words, it is a view which at once passes into conceptualism, the doctrine that universals are nothing more than concepts, ideas in the mind, meanings entertained, devices by which different things are bundled together. Yet were conceptualism true, a concept, idea, meaning would have nothing to which it could refer; it would not intend anything; what could be understood or meant by it would be precisely what was not so. Moreover, like nominalism, it presupposes what it ignores; it makes use of a universal, referring as it does to all supposed cases of universals. Were there no common character in all supposed cases of universals, conceptualism would say something about them which could not be true of them.

Conceptualism is grounded in realism. It requires different universals to have the universal character of being concepts and presupposes that the concepts men employ have universal components. But whatever reason one might have for acknowledging universal components in concepts gives reason enough for the acknowledgment of universals in the objects to which those concepts refer.

The view that there are genuine universals, though ostensibly opposed to the usual formulations of the doctrine of nominalism or conceptualism, is consonant with what many and apparently the original conceptualists intended. They wanted to avoid the Platonic view that universals were both more important than the beings which instance them, and had a substantial, separate existence of their own, independent of all existents, human or divine. They were opposed also to the Aristotelian view that universals were unaltered by whatever embodies them, that they had causal power, and that they exhausted the nature of the individual.

Philosophers of the individual, it is to them that we must turn for much of the inspiration of Protestantism, democracy, and romanticism. We can share their denials and endorse their objective and yet need not deny, as they do, that there are real universals. All that conceptualism needs is obtained by the admission that universals have a reference to existents and that they become determinate by being embodied diversely from case to case.

In ethics it is necessary to be at once realistic, conceptualistic, and nominalistic. It would be wrong to say that all universals are only abstractions, even if it were true (which does not seem to be the case) that the universals used in science and relevant to nature are of this nature. Universals in the field of ethics, in any case, obligate; they are binding; they must have a status of their own, outside and beyond the actual state of affairs that prevails. Universals define what it is toward which men should strive; but the universals exist only with reference to existents. Concern and realization determine them, complete them, perfect them, and thereby separate them from one another. Disoriented from the objects which distinguish them, universals merge into one another.

The universal standard of perfection is embodied in different ways and in different degrees by different entities. It has a different concrete meaning in each case. The nominalistic Occam was right to insist, therefore, that individuals are ultimate realities and that any so-called universal which could be common to them must fall short of full being. This truth does not oppose the admission that there are universals ingredient in different individuals; it denies only that universals have an unaltered meaning in different contexts. Universals are in individuals.

Universals can be abstracted from individuals, by reversing the original process of concretion through which the universal originally achieved embodiment and became an integral part of the individual being. The abstracted universal, as the conceptualist Abelard observed, has no being except in the form of a concept or idea. He rightly took it to be a concept which expressed what was intelligible in whatever exists. He did not note that concepts refer to universals exterior to them and integral to actual beings. The conceptualistic universal is in the mind, but it refers to itself as enjoying the status of an integral part of real, external things.

The universal good is concretely exemplified in every case somehow and to some degree. It can be abstracted from every occurrence, though it must be abstracted in different ways. The more adequate an exemplification, the better a being is and the more it fills out the standard properly. The less adequate the exemplification, the worse a being is and the more it distorts the standard in the concrete. In both ways the good is exemplified, but in the one it retains its integrity and in the other it does not.

The good is a standard of excellence for subhuman as well as human beings. It is wrong to torture an animal even though the act has not the slightest effect on men or their societies.

> ". . . the poor beetle that we tread upon,
> In corporal sufferance finds a pain as great
> As when a giant dies,"

if a Shakespearean exaggeration, is not yet sheer fiction. The standard is pertinent to plants and stones as well as to men. These have excellences and defects apart from their capacity to interest men or their promise to benefit or injure him.

Because we all do abstract the good somehow, we are all able to judge our objects and acts and compare them as better or worse. Were there no universal standard, did it not exist apart from things, were it not exemplified in them to some degree, we would not be able to do this. The standard is a universal, a meaning, an object of reason which, though related to actual values, transcends and tests them all, and can be obtained by abstracting the constant value which every one incorporates. It has application to all things and to all the situations in which they find themselves, being the meaning which all contain and ought to exhibit. It provides a basis for judging men, societies, subhuman beings, severally and together, and is invoked by every man and grasped to some degree by each at every moment.

5. The Kinds of Perfection

The standard in terms of which actualities and possibilities, objects and situations, individuals and groups, goals and ultimate ends are to be judged is the absolute good, perfection. Perfection, however, has many meanings, of which four are fundamental.

Something might be perfect in the sense of *fulfillment*, realizing its promise as completely as possible. It may be perfectly *pure*, be free of all defect. It may be perfect in *composition*, fully harmonize subordinate entities. Or, finally, it may be perfect in *scope* and provide a place for all pertinent objects.

Perfect *fulfillment* may occur inside narrow limits, characteristic of only some type of being. Were a rose, tiger, liar, or thief to possess in fact what other roses, tigers, liars, or thieves possess only latently, it would be more perfect as rose, tiger, liar, or thief than those others. It would realize a characteristic promise to the full, but it would not fulfill all the promise that it has. The most perfect rose does not necessarily realize all the promise resident in it as a plant, any more than a perfect tiger, liar, or thief realizes all the promise of animal or man. Perfect roses, tigers, liars, or thieves can be imperfect as plants, animals, or men.

A perfectly *pure* being contains no trace of evil, ugliness, folly, of the chaotic, the conflicting. It exhibits a certain nature simply and completely. The degree of its purity is not dependent on the degree of fulfillment it has achieved. It is possible to achieve one of these perfections and not the other. A consummate villain completely fulfills the promise of villainy latent in us all. Perfectly fulfilled as villain, he is not perfectly pure. We do tend to say of him that he is a pure villain. By that we mean he is all villain, that there is nothing in him which is irrelevant to his villainy, not that he is perfectly pure, for the villain, by virtue of the evil in him, is in conflict with himself. He stresses parts of himself not only so as to suppress, deny, oppose other parts but so as to reject the very whole on which they depend. He is a villain at the expense of being a man; he is a "pure" case of villainy in the same way that a cacophony is a pure case of noise or a chaos is a pure case of impurity.

We cannot reduce purity to fulfillment by treating innocence as an ideal which men should try to realize, for we begin in innocence and can remain so only by neglecting rather than by exercising powers. An empty canvas is perfectly pure, but that is all. An ideal innocent, similarly, is perfectly pure. He is not perfectly fulfilled, for he has his purity only because he neglects to exploit powers characteristic of him. The only innocence that can be striven for is that contained in wisdom; it is the innocence of unspoiled truth and is to be glimpsed through the mesh of sophisticated discourse and knowledge.

A saint is perfect both in purity and in fulfillment. He realizes human promise to the full, but in such a way that there is no defect in the result. He knows and yet lives as the innocents do; he exercises only some of the possible powers that he can, though in such a way as to make a man who has realized whatever good a man can.

In addition to perfection in the line of fulfillment and in the line of purity, a perfection of composition is possible. Such perfection involves the mastery and unification of subordinate parts while allowing each its full value. The colors of a picture may be poor, unsaturated, unfulfilled as colors; they may provide spots which are aesthetically unsatisfying. The picture as a whole may say little while giving the best possible unity to the elements provided. It may prove to be a composition which could not be surpassed, the best possible picture that could be had by making use of just such a set of unsatisfactory colors.

As the example of the picture reveals, there can be a perfection in composition without a perfection in fulfillment or purity, either on the part of the components or the whole. Unless it be the object of the picture merely to combine colors, unless it be the object of painting to say nothing, a splendid composition may be imperfect in the line of fulfillment; and since a composition may be excellent though its colors are dilute, it can also be impure. Conversely, there can be a perfection of fulfillment and purity in the absence of a perfection in composition. It is possible to bring together pure, saturated colors in such a way as to produce an inharmonious whole which may nevertheless be extraordinarily expressive.

All three modes of perfection may be combined. Each of us perhaps knows a Shakespearean sonnet or a musical composition by Bach which he would characterize as perfect in all three dimensions, as having a purity of quality, a maximum expressiveness, and a compositional excellence which cannot be surpassed.

Still another mode of perfection is possible. Whatever comprises all the elements pertinent to it has perfection of scope. A complete dictionary lacks the perfection of a book. Though it may have all the words of literature in it, it says even less than Pater ever did. But taken merely as dictionary, it, like a ruler of all mankind or a zoo with all kinds of animals, is perfect in scope because all embracing. This perfection is independent of, but compatible with, the other modes. A dictionary in which the words were not systematically arranged would fail to exhibit that perfection of fulfillment possible to a dictionary. If it contained errors as well, it would lack the perfection of purity. If its definitions clashed so that the words finally silenced one another, it would be imperfect in composition in addition. Yet all the while it might be perfect in scope. An ideal sonnet, on the other hand, would be perfect in fulfillment, purity, and composition. Since it has to leave out much that a sonnet could include and which is actually included in other sonnets—themselves not necessarily as good as it in fulfilling the promise of sonnets or as pure or well constructed—it is not perfect in scope.

The cosmos has a perfection of scope. It could not be otherwise, for the cosmos comprises all there is. Because its scope is greater than the scope of anything else it has an absolute perfection of scope. But it still is not *completely perfect*. It lacks perfection in composition, for it does not harmonize the elements within it to the greatest possible degree. It is streaked with incoherence, tragedy, evil. It would also, to be completely perfect, need to have a perfection of purity; there would have to be no ugliness, no vice, no folly in it. And it would also have to be perfectly fulfilled, having the maximum amount of value that a cosmos could have; it could not contain any unfulfilled beings or potencies.

A cosmos in which each part was perfectly pure and perfectly fulfilled in the richest possible harmony would be a cosmos which was perfect in all four ways. It would be the summum bonum, the greatest possible good. It would be a totality in which each being was at its best in perfect harmony with all the rest. Such a cosmos does not now exist. It is an ideal, an excellence applicable to all that is or can be, an absolute "ought to be," *the* good, enabling us to judge what is good and bad, right and wrong, virtuous and vicious. Every single "ought to be" specializes and is subordinate to it.

XIV

THE PRIMARY ETHICAL PRINCIPLE

1. Ought and Can

THE perfection possible to a being is what ought to be realized in it. For each being there is an appropriate excellence. Because it can be perfected as that kind of thing, it ought to be so perfected. "Can" implies "ought."

A being can become excellent only so far as and in the dimensions it ought to be excellent. It cannot be asked to be excellent if this excellence conflicts with the very possibility of its retaining its nature. We cannot rightly demand of a cat that it acquire the excellence characteristic of pigs or poets; the excellence appropriate to cats is that excellence which cats can conceivably realize. "Ought" implies "can."

Restricting attention only to those possibilities which portray the excellence of some type of being or other, "can" and "ought" are equivalent terms. The perfection which ought to be can be; the perfection which can be ought to be. Both of these are synthetic expressions, involving a genuine transition from one idea to another not contained in or implied by the other, though the two together constitute an interchangeable equivalence.

"Can be," mere possibility, might conceivably be devoid of all value; it acquires the status of an "ought to be" only when infected by the values of actual things. "Ought to be" might conceivably be an ideal of perfection having nothing to do with anything in this universe; it acquires the status of a "can be" only by being made pertinent to things. "Logical" possibilities, mere "can's," are possibilities of value because they are possibilities for valuable actualities; "ideal" values, mere "ought's," are relevant possibilities because values are supported by concerned actualities. The two are as ideas distinct; but supported by the only world in which they can occur they are interlocked as absolutely one. The world of actualities unites the two synthetically and inseparably.

"Ought to be excellent" and "can be excellent" are equivalent. "Ought to be a man who does what is right" (since this is an excellence for man) is, as a consequence, equivalent with "can be a man who does what is right." It is not equivalent with "he ought to do *this* right act," nor is it equivalent with "*he* can do this right act." What "ought to be" "can be," but it is not necessarily that which this man ought to or can bring about. Your debt should be paid, but not by him, for though he can pay he did not borrow from you. And your debt should be paid by the borrower even though he, by placing himself in a position where his powers of action cannot be exercised successfully, cannot pay it. All things ought to be perfected, and it is man's task to perfect them all to the limits of human ability, though this may far outstrip what this or that particular man could possibly do.

Each being concerns itself with a specialization of the all-encompassing "ought to be"—with ideal perfection as pertinent to itself as a limited being possessed of a limited nature. Each, because it has a limited nature, is occupied with a limited possibility which it endeavors to realize and thereby become as perfect as it is possible for it to be. Since all beings are part of a single cosmos and since all possibilities are part of a single future, the delimitation of that ideal by one of them may conflict with the delimitations required by the others. Were there then no being which could deal with the whole realm of possibility and thereby reorder the subordinate possibilities, a harmony of those subordinate possibilities might not be achieved and what exists might then not be able to be as good as it otherwise could. Some being must, through the use of a single all-inclusive possibility, convert the often opposing possibilities of the rest into a single, harmonious totality of interrelated possibilities. That being is man, and the agency by which he reaches to and uses the all-inclusive possibility to enhance and harmonize the possibilities pertinent to other beings is his soul or *self*.

The self is a flexible, perduring being, occupied with that universal good, that single all-comprehensive possibility which is fractionated by other beings into a multiplicity of prescribed and prescribing possibilities. It concerns itself with that good; the good is its permanent and unavoidable objective. It must, to complete itself, realize that good. To perfect the promise of the man of which the self is a part, the self must lay hold of that good, use it to convert the possibilities which confront his body and other beings into a single mosaic of enhanced possibilities. Only then will the man be in a position to complete himself in a world where things can be perfected together. Only then will he be able to promote the good to the greatest possible degree.

All selves are occupied with the selfsame future, the absolute good. Taken by itself, each has the same nature and objective as the others; so far, they are indistinguishable. But no selves are by themselves. Each is part of a man, a being with a body as well. Each is biased toward a particular body and therefore uses the absolute good primarily to enhance the possibility that is pertinent to that body and only secondarily to enhance the possibilities pertinent to other beings.

Did the self enhance no possibilities, things would promise less than they could; the self would make no difference to the world. Did it not stress the possibility pertinent to the body, a man would not tend to promote the greatest good of his body; he would treat his own body as no more precious than any other and would therefore not occupy himself with the promotion of its welfare. His self would make no human difference to him.

The self enhances all possibilities but with a stress on that possibility which is pertinent to its own body. It thereby inevitably distorts the good. Involved in the affairs of a body which is somewhat opposed in need and right to the rest of the world, it makes the good pertinent to that world from a special perspective. When a man acts he must rectify this distortion or fail to act wholly as he ought.

The absolute good is at once what can be and what ought to be, and this whether or not there be men. It can and ought to be just so far as things have values that are capable of being increased. Only man, though, through his self takes it upon himself to realize that good. Only he makes himself responsible for what ought to be. Only because he exists is an ethics possible.

Since the good is pertinent to every possibility and fact, ethics has a cosmic sweep, an unlimited scope of application. Its range is as wide as that of physics or chemistry, but unlike them it tells us of a world which exists only so long as there are men. Its penetration is as deep as that of psychology and religion, but unlike them it tells us of a world which is not centered in man or God. Ethics comes to be and passes away with man, the being who is at his best when he knows himself to be responsible for the universal realization of the absolute good. It recognizes him to have more value than other beings but denies that they exist only for his sake. They too have rights, though it is only man who knows that they do; only he, though too infrequently, tries to do them justice, to answer to the needs of their natures. Only he is and can be an ethical being.

2. The Foundations of Ethics

The absolute good is perfection as future and possible, common to all that exists. It is, as was remarked before, not of great value in itself. It has less value than any concrete object, no matter how trivial, vicious, or ugly, being dependent for its being on whatever is and lacking the power and virtues which pertain to any existent. Though in itself of little value, it is yet of tremendous importance for existent beings, since it provides the frame, the prospect which all realize in some way or other, to become better or worse than they had been.

Because man has an essential relation of concern to the absolute good he is perfectible to a degree not possible to any other being. He is superior to all others because the possibility that is pertinent to him is an absolute "ought to be" of which all other possibilities are fragments and specializations. That good loses none of its power or relevance if men fail to acknowledge it, fail to live in terms of it, or are unable to realize it adequately. The inescapable terminus of the self, it defines a man as perfectible to a degree not possible to anything else.

Ethical facts come into existence when men use the absolute good, which ought to be, as a test and guide for every thing and value. And they do this to the very degree that they are responsible beings—and conversely, to the degree that there are ethical facts, to that degree are men responsible. Men relate ideal possibility to existents and in that act transform themselves and those existents to bring about a new world in which the old is enriched by the humanly sustained and insistent operation of the "ought to be." The ethical facts the men constitute are as objective and as real as the men themselves. They add to things not a character but a meaning, an ethical dimension, changing their import. Their action is no more mysterious than is the conversion of an amble into a walk, reactions into responses, things clung to into things possessed. In these various cases nothing in the physical dimension is necessarily changed; the same results may, though they most likely will not, come about in any case. By bringing the ideal into the present, by controlling what is done by what may be, the entire meaning of the thing is changed. Acts, by being infected by the good they are to promote, become more than they were in import if not in accomplishment.

Ethical facts are constituted by man's being, not by his attitudes, interests, or knowledge. And they can be so constituted and yet be both external to him and pertinent to the objects which lie outside him because it is of his essence to sustain the absolute good as relevant to all that is. He introduces a new dimension into existence, the dimension of objective though relationally determined ethical values, by means of a power which marks one of the great differences between him and other beings. With his coming, things acquire new rights and importance because measured and ordered to greater goods than they had been before. Man enhances the possibility and thus the promise of each by harmonizing it with those of the rest, by means of the all-comprehensive good. He acts on and for others to realize the totality of possibilities which he, by means of the good, enhanced and harmonized.

The nature of the absolute good is initially but vaguely grasped. Nor need it be known clearly in full detail. It suffices for practice and for at least the start of theory to know some of the ethical facts which it guarantees to be irreducible and unrejectable.

The "ought to be" can be misconstrued. Practical judgments like theoretical ones may be mistaken. We may misuse the good; we may distort it in acknowledging it or in using it as a standard of right and wrong, and thereby mistake what we ought to approve and do. And having fallen into error we will with great difficulty avoid being mired in it. Indeed, it would appear that we are faced with an insoluble puzzle: how could one ever know or rectify such an error? If we have a sure way of finding out what errors we make, we have a sure way of knowing the truth; and if we know nothing with surety, we cannot know that we have surely made an error. Probabilism, fallibilism, universal hesitance are disguised dogmatisms, asserting too smugly that errors are everywhere. If the truth is now obscure, from where do the doubtful ones get the light by which to see the darkness, and so clearly?

There are two possible answers to the difficulty of how we can make errors regarding the basic truths of ethics and still be men who know absolute ethical truths. We can think of theorizing as a series of experiments in which each effort serves to rectify the limited results of the preceding one; we can imagine it taking its rise with dubious data, moving to the acknowledgment of an ideal serving to clarify, evaluate, and eliminate some part of it, and then using the residue to enable us to get a better grasp of the ideal in its true ideality and thereby a better grasp of what is the case.

Since this answer permits us to engage in an endless series of preliminary skirmishes or investigations devoted to the finding of a good starting point, it grants that we may never get to a single, fundamental fact. It allows us to be involved in preliminaries all our days. There are, to be sure, investigations where this offers no problem. Men have been studying populations and population trends for decades, without having come close to the point of deciding what to do about population; if there is such a thing as an integrated science which is a pure tissue of firm truth, then the science we have today is but a propaedeutic to it. This is only to say that an applied theory of populations or a purely theoretical science is not actual and may perhaps not be possible now or later. To say something like this in connection with ethics is fatal, for it is to try in another way to maintain the impossible position of a genuine suspension of ethical judgment.

We need not act about population trends; we can exist without a perfect science. But ethical beings we are all the time; any view which does not yield an ethics, rooted in unavoidable ethical fact, falls short of saying what an ethics should. Offering us no way by which we can progress from one stage to the other, this first answer allows us to revolve forever around the circle of our initial errors.

We seem to have but one alternative left. The data with which we start cannot be absolutely reliable, for we do make wrong judgments. We cannot avoid beginning, as the first answer realizes, with all the confusions, prejudices, and mistakes characteristic of our times, stations, and individualities, as well as with those we happen now to make; still it is not necessary for us to experiment with shaky ethical schemes, hoping somehow to improve them. It is possible to start on an absolutely sound basis, for the "ought to be," in the very act of being adopted even in a partial, inadequate, or misleading way, serves to force into focus those items which perfectly accord with its demands. Though no one begins with any other data than those he has in fact, though no one begins with any other principles or results of evaluation than those he now accepts, everyone, by his very attempt to reduce the tension by which he spans the distance between fact and ideal, isolates the "ought to be" and reorganizes his data—thereby allowing only those items to come to the fore which are at once local and universal, limited and ultimate.

No man ever started with an unsifted collection of ethical facts. The Aristotelian civilized man is an ethical fiction. Only when that man has selected out of the items he daily accepts some few which are sanctioned by the absolute good does he make a start in ethics.

Good habits and right opinion are desirable means by which we keep a grip on bedrock. They help us save considerable time in inquiry; they reduce for us the risk of error and help us avoid needless and dangerous experiment. But they are neither necessary nor sufficient for one who would know what ought to be. They do not necessarily point to the absolute good. Habit and opinion uncritically endorse whatever they happen to favor as that which ought to be. Nor are good habits and right opinion sufficient, since they do not alone provide for the separation of that which men accept or reject from what they ought to accept or reject. The separation is achieved only when the good is adopted and employed because of the excellence it expresses, an excellence which requires one not to accept but evaluate what habits and opinions recommend.

A bad, mischievous, or misleading objective expresses excellence as surely as does any other; it too enables us to focus on specific cases of right or wrong. Unfortunately, it also leads us to accept as data what only our limited objective endorses and others condemn, and thus what is excellent only from some limited perspective. Moreover, local and specialized objectives are often opposed to one another. They lead us to characterize situations in opposing ethical ways. We feel confident that we should not have lied, and yet know that it was right to relieve anxiety. We should have matched confidence with sincerity; but also we should have helped our friend prosper. Each position is sanctioned by a limited objective which presents itself as excellence; each makes some claim to be the absolute good. To adjudicate the question as to which should give way we must isolate their common "ought to be." Only this will enable us to distinguish what is absolutely right and wrong from what is so only locally, instrumentally, and relatively.

Every item of existence has an absolute status, an integrity, value, substantiality of its own. The "ought to be" is pertinent to all of them, defining as it does just what degree of excellence or completeness each thing has. Because objects are complex, many faceted, one side of them can well be excellent while another is defective. The "ought to be" separates the good and bad, divides each thing into phases, breaks it up into its components, some of which have high and some of which have low value. It forces a division of the objects into many parts and just to that degree abstracts from and falsifies the world in its concreteness. By requiring us to accept what is absolutely good and to repulse what is absolutely bad in a situation, the absolute good forces us to divide a thing against itself—not physically, to be sure, but no less significantly in attitude or thought.

We are able, despite the fact of error, to have an absolutely sound basis for an ethics because we have some grasp of the absolute "ought to be," which sifts out the good from the bad automatically and without error. But this very "ought to be" forces us to make a false division in every fact. Every thing is absolutely good in some respect and absolutely bad in others, with some excellencies and some defects; yet the absolute good requires us to hold on to one while repulsing what is inextricably tied up with it.

In order to get an object which answers perfectly to the demands of the absolute good, we must abstract a good component from some concrete thing. This is most easily accomplished by starting with one which is predominantly good or bad. Since anything which is predominantly good repeats in a restricted form the very nature of the good which calls it to the fore, we learn nothing much by isolating its excellence and using this as our initial object. The repugnant evil is better for the purpose. The repugnant stands over against us and, if genuinely evil, contrasts with the good that ought to be.

Men are clearer on what ought to be avoided than on what ought to be pursued. The ethical truths common to all are expressed largely in warnings, injunctions as to what is to be rejected and abhorred rather than as to what is to be accepted or approved. Pictures of hell are clear and frightening and of somewhat similar design; those of heaven are vague and anemic and differ from tribe to tribe. Ministers who castigate hit home; the others are driven to deal with political and social questions in order to give their exhortations substance and meaning. We seem to know what evil is but not the nature of the good. The evil we seem to know immediately and in the concrete, the good indirectly and in the abstract. We are weak when it comes to *theories* of evil, blind when it comes to *beings* that are good.

A repugnant object has attractive components from which we must abstract if we are to have a single, homogeneous, ethical, absolute, repugnantly evil fact. If an unnecessary lie be told to a friend, some pleasure is achieved. Perhaps also some disagreeable situation is incidentally avoided. The lie moreover gives evidence that we have some imagination and some knowledge of the truth we are endeavoring to keep from the other, and is so far good. But preponderantly it is bad, as is evident when we abstract from the pleasure and virtues which the telling of the lie entrains and get face to face with the lie itself. A lie which gave no joy, which was transparent and put forth thoughtlessly, without regard for a bitter truth which it might help protect from examination by another, would, taken by itself, have nothing to commend it. It would be absolutely wrong, wrong without qualification. It would not, however, be maximally wrong. It would be as wrong as lying can be, but it would not exhibit as much wrong as there could be. It would have no good in it, but a greater wrong than it could be conceived. Absolutely wrong, it would not be wrong to an absolute degree.

To find a case of absolute wrong to an absolute degree we must intensify the wrongness which the lie to our friend involves. The lie fails to affect all the values of the situation; it rides on the surface of our friendship, allowing us still to love, respect, aid, and consider one another in other situations; the injury it involves is less than might be. We must convert it from an act in which we merely unwarrantedly say to another what is false into an act which unwarrantedly robs him of some basic cherished good. Only an act such as one in which we wantonly kill a friend destroys maximally. It alone tears at the roots of his being; it alone provides a saturated case of wrong.

It is absolutely wrong wantonly to kill a friend. Men need no training, no code or set of rules to help them see this. They are usually shocked even by the prospect of the act. It runs counter to their dispositions; it conflicts with their bent. Should they kill a friend in anger or in jealousy, they would look for some excuse, some justification, some reason, making it something less than a wanton, an unjustified, indefensible act.

There are acts which need no justification. Were we to burst into song, were we to hazard a jump a little more reckless than is our wont, were we to cavort in an undisciplined way, with no injurious results, we would look no further. The acts themselves would be their own justification; they would be accepted as good in themselves, as moments of ebullience, of spontaneity, modes in which we exhibit ourselves to be living human beings. Should these acts result in the death of a friend, we would try to excuse ourselves by pointing up the good of ebullient expression, the innocence of spontaneity, the lack of intent, and perhaps also the limitations and vices of him who was our friend. Our justification would fall miserably short, but it would suffice to mark off these irresponsible acts, which incidentally resulted in the death of our friend, from a wanton, irresponsible act of killing him.

The wanton killing of a friend is absolutely wrong, wrong without qualification, a pure and maximal wrong. If it is to be justified it must be either by the nature it happens to have or the results it happens to produce. But though an act of killing has some value, allowing as it does for the exercise of muscles, ingenuity, intelligence, enabling us to get rid of pent-up emotions and irritations and to exercise some creativity, it is an act which is permeated by an antagonism to life and thus is at odds with itself, exhibiting the meaning of life while denying it. It is an act in which a part of life rejects the whole of life. To justify it we cannot refer to the nature it has. Shall we ask after the amount of good it produces? A wanton murder, though, is precisely that which is performed without reference to the kind of results that might ensue; the results, whether good or bad, are extrinsic to it. To refer to the results it brings about is to suppose that the act is not wanton, that we must look beyond its present confines for its explanation and part of its meaning. The wanton murder of a friend is a pointless, unjustifiable wrong.

The wanton murder of a friend stands apart from a wanton act which results in the death of a friend and also from a justified act of killing a friend. Unlike the former of these, the killing of the friend is of the essence of the wanton act of murdering him; unlike the latter, it is performed without reference to any consequences or to situations outside it. It is deliberate, purposed, and self-contained, an act in which we approvingly destroy a good we approve. We cannot justify it; we can carry it out in fact only by having the destruction exceed the limit of our vision.

The wanton murder of a friend stands opposed to what the "ought to be" demands. We do not know that "ought to be" with any clarity; we hardly look at it. We approach all things, though, in terms of it, approving what we can and disapproving what we must because of what it requires. Clinging to the absolute good, we are forced to reject the wanton murder of our friend as an act in which values are primarily and radically reduced and thus as an act in which a grave wrong is being done. Our impulses, our excitement may drive us past the point of self-control which the good would require us to exert; they may turn our acts over to the control of our bodies or circumstance. Our acts will then no longer be ours; nevertheless we will be responsible for them, since it was our task and since it was at least once within our power to prevent the destructive acts from escaping our control.

There is no such concrete ethical fact as a perfect wanton killing of a friend. Every injury, even to death, directed at a friend is grounded in some desire to reach something thought good. It always involves some such good activity as the concentration of the mind, the exercise of the muscles, and the expression of the self. The pure, maximal wrong of killing a friend wantonly can only be a predominant and abstractable moment of a partially good act in which our friend is in fact unnecessarily killed by us. We isolate the good part by means of the absolute good; it is due to the absolute good that we assume a bivalent attitude toward our friend's death, that we separate out and hold the absolutely wrong component in the situation apart from the component that is right and thus can come to know just wherein the act is wrong and why.

3. ETHICAL ABSURDITY

It is wrong to kill a friend wantonly—unqualifiedly, absolutely wrong. This is bedrock, a certainty on which we can rest the whole of ethics. We arrived at it by starting with the commonly accepted wrong of an unnecessary lie and intensifying this to its maximum, to reach a situation which is exhaustively what ought not to be done.

It is absolutely wrong to kill a friend wantonly. To deny this is absurd. No one, no matter what his background, his upbringing, his appetites, and his aims, can cancel or reduce the ultimacy of this fact. To reject it as error is impossible; to attempt to circumvent it foolish. This does not mean that he who says it is right to kill a friend wantonly has produced a logical clash between terms antecedently defined in opposite ways. "Friend" has a wide range of possible meaning; the idea of killing is neither contained in nor excluded from it. The combination of it with killing does not include or preclude the idea of wantonness, and the combination of these terms with wantonness is

similarly neutral with respect to right and wrong. It is good English
to say any of the following:

1. It is right to save a friend for good reason.
2. It is wrong to save a friend for good reason.
3. It is right to kill a friend for good reason.
4. It is wrong to kill a friend for good reason.
5. It is right to save an enemy for good reason.
6. It is wrong to save an enemy for good reason.
7. It is right to kill an enemy for good reason.
8. It is wrong to kill an enemy for good reason.
9. It is right to save a friend for no reason.
10. It is wrong to save a friend for no reason.
11. It is right to kill a friend for no reason.
12. It is wrong to kill a friend for no reason.
13. It is right to save an enemy for no reason.
14. It is wrong to save an enemy for no reason.
15. It is right to kill an enemy for no reason.
16. It is wrong to kill an enemy for no reason.

Some of these will be instantly termed true and some will be instantly termed false by most; about the others we may remain in
doubt for a time and perhaps even indefinitely. The first and twelfth
are indubitable. How is it then that the second and eleventh are intelligible, assertible? The necessary requires that its opposite be impossible, absurd. But the first and twelfth are necessary and their
opposites are the second and the eleventh. These opposites make good
sense, though what they assert is absurd in ethics.

The resolution of this difficulty requires that a distinction be made
between two not altogether unrelated types of absurdity. There is
logical absurdity, the absurdity of an intended denial of a formally
defined, necesary truth, of an attempt to hold together terms which
had been antecedently defined to be antagonistic; and there is *existential* absurdity, the absurdity of trying to maintain something to
be true though the affirmation requires the destruction of the possibility of making the affirmation. The one is the absurdity of trying to
reject what is supposed; the other is the absurdity of trying to reject
what is presupposed. Although it is possible to avoid the former while
trapped by the latter, the latter (since the presupposed can always
be supposed), can always be expressed as an instance of the former.
Hence the logician's supposition that all absurdities are logical absurdities. Whatever is absurd can be expressed as a logical absurdity,
but only because the presupposed has been made into something supposed. It is because there would *be* a clash, because it is impossible

to make a concrete, actual unity of the elements represented by such terms as "wanton killing," "friend," and "right" that the terms are to be defined so that their unity in thought or fact would constitute a formal, a logical contradiction—not conversely.

There is nothing absurd in the idea of right, a friend, and a wanton killing being conjoined to constitute a single proposition. If we affirm the proposition we will, though, take a position with respect to it which the proposition itself says it would be wrong to take. The proposition says it is right to do an injustice, yet to affirm this is to appreciate, to consider, to have regard for the nature of what is there, to do justice to it.

It is futile to attempt to assert that things are not to be appreciated for what they are, that they are not to be considered on their merits, to be dealt with as they deserve, that we are instead consciously and conscientiously to assert what is false and to deny what is true. To attempt these in discourse is to deny them in act. The asserting of them requires a denial of an assertion of them. He who says in any form that it is right not to take things for what they are, in that very act asks us to accept his claim as it is. In a minor way he does what is done by one who asserts that it is right to kill a friend wantonly, for the latter, too, tries to affirm in assertion what he denies in the asserting. To say "it is right to kill a friend wantonly" is to say that a friend, one who ought to be cherished, can rightly be killed without warrant. This is to say that he is not to be given the consideration he merits. Yet the assertion is offered as a truth demanding the consideration a truth deserves. It is impossible to honor this claim rationally without accepting the thesis that all things (including our friend), should be treated in consonance with their natures and the claims these entail. Except by destroying the integrity of the very act of maintaining it, it is impossible to maintain that "it is right to kill a friend wantonly."

What is true deserves to be affirmed because affirmation is appropriate to it. But then what is affirmed must not prescribe that something else is to be treated undeservedly; whatever warrant we have for affirming a truth is warrant enough for asserting as right only those acts which preserve or enhance a value. Only if we could find some characteristic of affirmations, some feature in truth which demands just treatment of the truth but precludes or is indifferent to the just demands of others, could we ask someone to accept as true some such proposition as "it is right to kill a friend wantonly." But this would require truth and affirmation to contain within them the very meaning of right treatment. This is not the case. There is no contradiction in the idea of a truth abused, of affirmations improperly made. Neither truth nor affirmation contains as essential to its meaning the idea of right treatment. The right to be affirmed is a right synthetically attached to truth in the process of making a true affirmation in a way similar to that in which the "right to be cherished" is synthetically united with "friend" *inside* the affirmation.

An absurd existential proposition is one which is inconsistent, not formally, not in relation to its terms, but concretely. What it supposes is intelligible, but what it presupposes conflicts with this. If what it presupposes were expressed as a supposition, the whole would be reduced to the form of a logical absurdity, since the proposition would deny at the end what it acknowledged in the beginning. It is logically absurd to say that "it can be truly asserted it is right to kill a friend wantonly," for the "it can be truly asserted" brings into the proposition a consideration which is in conflict with that allowed by the remainder of the proposition. It is conceivable that from the vantage point of a God or inside a scheme where all that counts is self-expression the wanton killing of a friend might be right. But it could not be right in any world in which men consciously and conscientiously affirm what is true. Were the wanton killing right, our affirmation that it was so would have to be guaranteed by a God or be but a form of self-expression; it could not be a means of relating us to an objective truth, since this requires consciousness and conscientiousness, the treating of a proposition as it deserves to be treated.

A proposition which explicitly denies the possibility or the fact of asserting it as a truth destroys its own ground. This it does in an evident and sharp way in the case of "it is right to kill a friend wantonly," since it there says that wanton killing is appropriate to a friend, though a friend is one who deserves to be cherished and wanton killing is unquestionably not a way of cherishing him. If we acknowledge such an act to be right, we lose the right to assert it is a truth.

He who says that the wanton killing of a friend is right produces an existential absurdity; he is the proper object of an ad hominem argument, an argument which belittles, discredits, abuses the man who puts it forth. As Frederic Fitch has observed, this argument is not a fallacy; it is instead sound and illuminating. It shows us that skepticism and nominalism, positivism and relativism cannot be offered for acceptance without the theories' wrongness being assured. The ad hominem argument is vicious and misleading when it serves to turn one from an assertion to the irrelevant nature of the man who asserts it; it is excellent when it serves to help one see the existential absurdity of an assertion by pointing up the nature of the world which the assertion requires in order to be asserted, and thus the kind of things the assertion cannot assert without denying itself a place in existence.

The proposition, "it is never right to kill a friend wantonly," is a *synthetic* proposition having its ground not wholly within itself. Its truth cannot be ascertained by examining the terms in which it is affirmed; account must be taken of a reality beyond it. But it is also *analytic* in that each of the terms, by virtue of its appropriateness to the others, helps clarify their meaning. We know, by virtue of it, a little better what "right," "killing," "friend," and "wantonly" mean. We know that, though exterior to one another, they form a single, necessary whole.

Since the proposition cannot be denied without absurdity, it is *necessarily true*. It cannot be rejected without destroying the ground and reason for the rejection. Still, its denial can be conceived. It is therefore only *contingently true*. Dislocated, abstracted out of the situation in which it is affirmed as true, it can be thought of as false.

It is a *material* proposition relating to what can occur in this universe. Nevertheless, it deals with an especially constructed case, a case antecedently acknowledged not to answer to anything really concrete, now or later. It is therefore a *formal* proposition.

The proposition is known by us to be true apart from any actual experience of the situation it portrays. It is *a priori* in nature. Yet we learned of it only by operating on items in experience and by taking full account of the existential situation in which the judgment of it occurred. It is therefore *a posteriori* also.

The proposition relates to a limited situation, incapable of duplication. It is *particular*. Still it holds for all men, regardless of place, time, or circumstance. It is therefore a *universal* truth as well.

"It is wrong to kill a friend wantonly" is an a priori, material, synthetic, necessarily true, particular proposition in ethics at the same time that it is an a posteriori, formal, analytic, contingently true, universal proposition when abstracted from the existential affirmation of it here and now as true. It offers a challenge to those who insist that what is a posteriori and contingent cannot be formal, analytic, or universal, or that what is a priori and necessary cannot be material, synthetic, or particular. For our purposes, what is more interesting, it allows for the extraction of much more far-reaching, though equally unrejectable, and perhaps less immediately evident, ethical truths.

4. THE PRIMARY ETHICAL PRINCIPLE

"It is absolutely wrong to kill a friend wantonly" correctly characterizes a maximal and pure ethical situation in which an act attempts to wipe out the very good it presupposes. The situation remains just as pure, but less intense, if the injury, while still in disaccord with the nature and deserts of the object, does not wipe out the good entirely. He who lies or steals from a friend injures him, but not as much as he might. Because injury in any form does violence to a friend, it is correct to say that "it is absolutely wrong to *injure* a friend wantonly," where "injury" is a term referring to any case in which a friend is abused. The proposition characterizes every case of pure wrong, saturated or unsaturated, maximal or not, directed at friends.

A friend is one whose merits and value have already been acknowledged in act if not in mind. He is a man, not necessarily better than others, whose nature has been appreciated more than theirs and with whom a bond has been formed. The wrong in injuring him lies not in our having acknowledged his merits or the bond; the acknowledgment of his merits and the bond are but means for helping us see the virtues he has and the reasons why an injury to him would be absolutely wrong. Even if we do not acknowledge his merits, even if we ignore the bond we formed, even if we injured him in areas which we thought irrelevant to our friendship, it would be true that, so far as he had value apart from us, there would be wrong in injuring him. It is wrong to injure a friend because of the qualities he has, because he is one who ought to be a friend. But then it must be wrong to injure him, not because he is a friend but because he could become one. When he is our friend in fact we note some of the qualities he intrinsically has, the values which enable him to become a friend. The friendship does not define or delimit these values. It is wrong to reduce these values, whether he is actually our friend or not. Accordingly, it is legitimate to move one step further and categorically assert, "it is absolutely wrong to injure a befriendable being wantonly."

Injury is correlative with good. Wherever there is good to be found, injury is significant. It is not necessary then to remain within the restrictions imposed by the idea of friendship in order to acknowledge and to take account of wrongs. It must be the case that "it is absolutely wrong to injure a good being wantonly," for the wrongness of the injury lies in the fact that the injury goes counter to the goodness of the thing.

The injury of a good being is absolutely wrong always, but the injury itself might have another side to it, might serve some larger end, and to that extent, without losing its status of a wrong, might sustain the character of being relatively right. The idea of wantonness does not add to the wrong which the injury involves; it serves but to bound it, to define it to be one for which there can be no wider setting in which it could be right. Wantonness thus expresses an extreme form of irresponsibility, of acting without warrant, of being unjustified; it is not essential to the idea of absolute wrong.

A man might injure another so as to make possible a greater good, to see more justice done, to enable him and others to prosper. His act would not be wanton; it would be right as subserving these desirable ends, yet it would also be a wrong act, as is evident from the consideration that it would be better to achieve the same outcomes by some other type of act not involving so much destruction of good. As subserving a good the act accrues to itself the externally determined character of being right. It would still though be absolutely wrong by virtue of its opposition to the demands of the absolute "ought to be." The latter fact is independent of the former; the wrongness does not depend for its quality on the wantonness. Because the wantonness of the act does not determine the degree of wrong that is involved in injury or even that the injury be wrong at all, we can justly reduce "it is absolutely wrong to injure a good being wantonly" to "it is absolutely wrong to injure a good being."

Injury carries a strong suggestion of physical ill-doing. In order to provide for cases in which men are injured through word and attitude, it is desirable to rewrite the last proposition to read, "it is absolutely wrong to reduce the value of a good being." "Reduce the value of a good being," is however redundant. If a being has value it is so far excellent, possessed of worth, good. To reduce the value of a good being is the same thing as to reduce the value of a being. Our proposition must therefore read, "it is absolutely wrong to reduce the value of a being." Since values are increased and decreased only so far as beings are acted on, "of a being" is also eliminable. We are now in possession of an absolutely universal but basic ethical truth: "it is absolutely wrong to reduce value." This truth is "it is absolutely wrong to kill a friend wantonly," lithe and free of ethical irrelevancies, able to measure the worth of any act.

"It is absolutely wrong to reduce value" lacks the concreteness, particularity, and vividness of "it is absolutely wrong to kill one's friend wantonly." In compensation it replaces constant by variable terms, the concretely individual by the indeterminately general, without losing the necessity and the materiality, the synthetic and a priori features of the initial proposition.

There may be considerable difficulty in knowing what particular value a situation embodies, just what would constitute a reduction of it, and what is to be done in the face of the necessity to engage in such a reduction if greater values are to be preserved or produced. These difficulties must be met. Whether they are or not, it would be absurd to try to void the truth at which we have arrived: *It is absolutely wrong to reduce values.* Broader in application, having reference to minor as well as to major wrongs and values, it is no less significant and stable than the truth from which it was derived. Its denial is existentially absurd, just as the other's is, since it cannot be carried out without illustrating its affirmation. Like all denials it claims to be pertinent to the facts, to deny only what should be denied, and this it absurdly fails to do.

Only when abstracted from the act of being denied by a responsible man does "it is absolutely wrong to reduce values" have a significant contradictory. Existentially viewed, it is necessarily true. Relating as it does to this existent universe, it is material in import. Since its truth is in no way jeopardized by the vicissitudes of history, it is a priori. Because it has an unrestricted range of application it is universal as well. Like the truth from which it was derived, it is at the same time contingent, formal, analytic, a posteriori, and particular, for it can be rejected without logical self-contradiction, is stated in terms of variables, is derived through a process of analysis, is discovered in the course of inquiry, and deals with only some of the objects in the universe. It makes little difference just which of these characters we use to express its significance. What is important is that it represents an ultimate truth for ethics, in breadth, in strength, and in finality.

XV

SOME BASIC DEFINITIONS

THE judgment, "it is absolutely wrong to reduce values," marks a necessary antagonism between an absolute "ought to be" and an injury to some existent. No act ever exactly and fully embodies the "ought to be," for none is absolutely perfect. That something is absolutely wrong here and now we can always confidently assert.

The "ought to be," the absolute good, the standard of absolute right is never perfectly exemplified. If we know it, it cannot be from experience. It cannot be found there. Still we have no innate knowledge of it. Children do not know its nature. Many adults are ignorant of it; some few deny its reality outright. Those who know that it is and have some inkling as to what it is must struggle long and hard to get it clear.

We have our first glimpse of the standard, the "ought to be," the absolute good, perfection, when we consciously turn toward the possible future as pertinent to whatever is of value. We become clearer regarding its nature by reflecting on the limits of other claimants to be absolute. But we know it best as a reflex of our awareness of some wrong. We are repelled by wrongs sharply and quickly, recognize things and acts to be defective because they clash with an incipient act of approval endeavoring to express the absolute good here and now. We invoke the good without thought or deliberation, immediately disapprove of the things it disallows, holding on to both only by relating them through the characterization of the disallowed act as "wrong."

We aim at perfection and thereby find ourselves unable to approve of some of the things we see and do. The more firmly we keep the idea of perfection before us, the more evident it becomes that everything is imperfect in some way and to some degree, and the less able therefore are we to approve completely anything we do or encounter.

Whether we understand the standard or not, we always aim at it. Though we rarely make explicit use of it, we grasp and use it often as is evident from the knowledge we have of the meaning and use of such central ethical terms as good and bad, right and wrong, virtue and vice, from our awareness that things have comparable values, and from our ethical unity and flexibility. If we had no grasp of the standard, if we did not make the universal "ought to be" into a responsibly acknowledged good to be realized, we could correctly approve or disapprove in each specific case but would not know what makes a thing worthy of approval or disapproval.

A being is *good* to the degree it possesses those traits which are common to the members of any universe of value. To exist is good, to have power is good, to act with others is good. All beings and acts, though imperfect, exemplify the good to some extent by virtue of their existence and the powers that existence entrains.

Every being and act, though good because it is, because it has power, and because it acts in accord with others, is also bad. It has defects and fails to exhibit some trait necessary to perfect members of perfect totalities. Whatever is is bad, for it has defects; whatever is is good, for it illustrates perfection in some dimension. Whatever exists is at once good and bad, valuable and imperfect, something to be cherished and something to be used.

> "The world in all doth but two nations bear,
> The good, the bad, and these mixed everywhere."

To preserve and promote what is good is *absolutely right;* to destroy or decrease what is good is *absolutely wrong.* It is wrong to kill a friend wantonly not because he is a friend, not because it is wrong to do something wantonly or because it is wrong to kill, but because it is wrong to decrease value. Killing involves a radical decrease, wantonness denies one an excuse; a friend is a being with a high and recognized value. Killing a friend is just an obtrusive illustration of a decrease in values for which no justification could be provided.

No one can do only the right. To help or enhance one being others must be ignored or curtailed, injured in some sense directly or indirectly. On the other hand no one can do only the wrong. To injure a being it is necessary to engage in the rightful act of exercising body or mind. Even the deliberate killing of a friend—an absolute wrong— is accompanied by the preservation and promotion of some good. It involves the expression of oneself, the exercise of one's body, and perhaps the manifestation of independence. The act is absolutely wrong as decreasing the value of the friend, but the performance of the act involves the incidental production of something right.

A man is *ethically sensitive* if he grasps the values things actually have. If he has little ethical sensitivity he will primarily promote the familiar, the vivid, the agreeable; the more sensitivity he has, the more he is able to penetrate beyond these temptations to the values actually possessed.

Two men may pursue the same course and yet not be equally sensitive. One may tend the common way because it seems to promise him an increase in value; another may tend toward it because some feature of little value happens to appeal to him. Patriotism and cowardice, fear of censure and foolhardiness are equally effective in helping a man stay his ground in the face of pressure to move elsewhere.

A man of ethical sensitivity finds no appeal in the prospect of hurting or killing men. But this could become a desirable prospect for him when thought of as a means to some desirable goal or if required by an accepted ultimate end. Since hurting and killing are acts which produce considerable loss in value, the goal or the end which are to justify their election must have great force or value. Helping another, on the other hand, is desirable in itself. It is preferable to hurting or killing even when these are viewed as means to goals of quite high value. Though a man might reasonably intend to kill some men in order to preserve or enhance the rest, society, or some greater good beyond, if he is sensitive he will be disinclined all the while to produce the wrong his decision requires. No matter how well sanctioned by goals and ultimate ends, these acts are absolutely wrong, and are known to be so by ethically sensitive men.

No man has perfect sensitivity and no man is devoid of all sensitivity. All have some grasp of what men are like, but none seems to know just what each suffers, wants, or can be. This, the moral-sense school of Shaftesbury, Hume, and Adam Smith underscored. They saw that all men have a sense of values, a grasp of where excellence lies, and an ability to see how things fall short of absolute excellence in different degrees, but they appear to have erred in taking only those things to be good which awaken a man's approbation. A man's sensitivity is unfocused, general, indeterminate; it fastens on this or that object at the risk of serious error. Nor should it be overlooked that man has this sensitivity not through the action of some new sense over and above those he is usually accredited with having but as the outcome of a concern with the absolute good and his consequent rejection of things so far as they fail to conform to the requirements of that good.

Men deserve *punishment* for not having or not exercising that minimal degree of sensitivity which marks a member of the civilization that prevails. They are not to be *condemned* except so far as it is within their own power to increase their degree of sensitivity. Some men through the accident of birth, education, or opportunity have a greater sensitivity than others, but all are insensitive in some dimension. And all are condemnable to some extent, for all can increase their ethical sensitivities to some degree, by extending the range of their interests, by taking advantage of available knowledge, and by readying themselves to appreciate whatever values a situation may contain.

A man is *directly* accountable for whatever acts he can, as man, then and there control and thus which, were other reasons offered, he would not repeat. He is *indirectly* or derivatively accountable for all acts and efforts which, though beyond control, are the reasonable outcome of others over which he had control. A man is directly accountable for taking a boat out in stormy weather, for leaning too far out of a window, for juggling knives without having first learned the art of juggling. He is derivatively accountable for the anticipatable outcome of these acts—for losing the boat, for breaking his neck or another's, for cutting himself or ruining the knives—though these results may be beyond his power to avoid once the previous acts have been performed.

The extent of *blameworthiness* or *praiseworthiness* is measured by the nature of the acts for which one is directly, as well as by those for which one is indirectly, accountable. It is a serious thing to shoot at a man deliberately; it is foolish but not necessarily serious to shoot off a gun idly in the market place. The one is rightly termed a grave crime, the other a misdemeanor. If a man is hit the blameworthiness is increased in both cases. One is then rightly charged with murder or manslaughter, depending on whether the gun was aimed or not. It is laudable to jump in after a man who is drowning, less laudable to stand on the dock and advise. If the man is not saved the degree of praiseworthiness is unchanged. If the man is saved as a consequence, it is increased, and the benefactor rightly rewarded as a hero or a wise man, depending on whether he saved the other by physical act or safe suggestion. Men are blameworthy and praiseworthy because they are capable of exercising control, but the degree of deserved praise or blame is increased, and that to a considerable extent, by consequences over which they have no control.

Direct accountability requires that control be then and there freely exercised. Derivative accountability presupposes that control could have been previously and elsewhere exercised. We are directly accountable for our decisions and derivatively accountable for whatever consequences it is reasonable to suppose will follow on those decisions.

A man is absolutely praiseworthy so far as he does what is absolutely right. He has a *good disposition* if he inclines toward acts which are absolutely right. A good disposition and a habit of doing what is right combine to make a *good character*. An absolutely blameworthy man does what is absolutely wrong; if he has a *bad disposition* he inclines toward such acts, while if he has a *bad character* he adds to a bad disposition a habit of doing what is wrong.

It is *relatively right* to do what is required by the totality of values one is committed to realize. It is relatively right to kill every living being that stands in the way of our attaining a perfect world of men. But the act of killing them, since it is an act of decreasing values, is an act which is preponderantly wrong from an absolute standpoint. What is relatively right may be absolutely wrong. Were we to save an animal to the discomfort of men we would do what was absolutely right but relatively wrong. What is absolutely right may be relatively wrong.

An absolute wrong is one which has no intrinsic warrant; a relative wrong is extrinsically unwarranted. What has the one warrant may lack the other, so that what is done may be relatively wrong but absolutely right, relatively right but absolutely wrong. We constantly commit absolute wrongs in the endeavor to do what is relatively right, and we constantly do what is relatively wrong in doing what is absolutely right. That conflict is inevitable; it is part of the tragedy of being a man.

A man is *committed* to fulfill the pledge he inevitably makes by reducing values in fact. He is *obligated* to realize the *"ought to be."* He has a *duty* to do that which will most promote the ultimate end to which he is committed or the good to which he is obligated.

A *conscientious* man lives up to his commitments. No man, however, is perfectly conscientious. All fail to do what they are committed to do. Yet none seems to be completely devoid of conscientiousness. All live up to their commitments to some extent.

An *ethically responsive* man lives up to his obligations, realizes the absolute good by bringing it into some actual situation. Since every man has an awareness of the absolute good and some power to express it, all can be ethically responsive.

A man has *vices* so far as he has the habit of doing what he ought not; he has *virtues* so far as he has the habit of doing what he ought.

Obligations demand actual fulfillment and thus apply only where such fulfillment is in principle achievable. We are obligated to see that the "ought to be" is realized, if not by us then by others. Our obligations are fixed though our abilities, powers, and opportunities vary. They vanish only when they are fulfilled by someone somehow. We are released from our debts when our debts are paid by others, even if we could have paid them ourselves. A bungler is bound and remains so as long as it is possible to have successful action performed by somebody. A man is free from debt once his debt has been paid, but he is obligated, regardless of capacity or opportunity, so long as it is not paid. And since he is obligated to perfect everything, he is always one who does less than he ought.

A man is *guilty* so far as he fails to do what the absolute good demands, regardless of whether he is sensitive or responsive, committed or not, for he is required to bring about the absolute good everywhere. It is this obligation which marks him off from all other beings, for it is by means of it that he holds on to and internally determines himself by the all-comprehensive "ought to be."

Ethics is grounded in an "ought to be," but it does not exist until men have adopted that "ought to be" as their responsibility, have obligated themselves to act so as to perfect all things to the limit of human capacity, even though they have not the opportunity to succeed. Man makes the "ought to be" into an *"ought to be realized by man"* by accepting it as the terminus of his concern and thereby marking himself off from all natural kind. But he cannot turn that "ought to be realized by man" into a "can be realized by *him*." He can only try to realize what "ought to be," try to make himself into one who can do what he ought to do. This requires him to make use of a creative will.

XVI

THE CREATIVE WILL

1. THE NEED TO WILL

PERFECTION is the future as pertinent to all ; it is the absolute good, that which ought to be. Offering a harmony of all possibilities, it is that in which human concern inevitably terminates and which all ultimate ends, goals, and occurrences specify in divergent ways. In the face of it, the goods of pleasure, happiness, order, and knowledge pale, as too limited or determinate to be appropriate to all that is. These demand, as no absolute good can, that some values be neglected or reduced so that the rest be enhanced.

As merely alive, a man brings the absolute good to realization, but in a biased way. He determines its nature so that it is pertinent to but a few things, and then exhibits that determined nature within established constraints. When he prefers he does more justice to the absolute good, allowing it to appear and operate in the form of a goal pertinent to many things and giving it expression in the form of intentions. Intentions, however, may not be in consonance with the nature that circumstance imposes on acts ; they may be quite different from acts in result and meaning. Knowledge of what a man is planning to do is to be gleaned not from his intentions but from the tendencies which those intentions help encourage. The intention to make a fortune, to do good, to invent and discover may prompt a man to be complacent. Blunderers and fanatics with good intentions hurry to bring about what ought not be. Ostentatious philanthropists may have bad intentions but help others more than the rest of us would or could.

Kant and Plato gave intentions much more power than intentions could possibly have. They thought them irresistible and therefore believed that a man always did what he intended. For them the body was a transparent, nondistortive medium, though again and again they themselves pointed up facts which indicated the opposite. Hobbes and Spinoza took the opposite extreme. They cut intentions off entirely from the realm of action, denying that they had any effect on the world of bodies. For them the mind was divorced from the body, the very opposite of what they often wished to say. Separately and together these different thinkers revealed a deeper truth : good intentions help but do not compel men to act in desired ways.

To intend the good is to work on its behalf on the inside and to be prepared to work on its behalf on the outside, not necessarily in consonant ways. To achieve such consonance a higher grade of freedom must be exercised. An interest must be taken in an objective as good apart from the appeal it may happen to have, and this objective must determine the kind of action that will occur. This is what happens when a man chooses. He then makes the absolute good determinate in the form of an ultimate end to which he commits himself while and in choosing some present alternative. His activities are then not confined by alien structures or restricted to adopting possible means for appealing goals; he is a responsible being who makes some determinate form of the good sanction an alternative here and now as the best possible, and thus make it the alternative a dutiful man will bring about.

It is not, however, left to a man to decide which ends he will confront. He imposes determinations on the absolute good, to be sure, but these determinations are largely dictated by the nature of the choices he made before, the education, imagination, and interests he has. His freedom of choice is exercised among ends he did not freely select for consideration; he is free to deal with only some ends.

Able to embrace any of the ends he in fact confronts—though not able to confront any of the ends there may be—a man in choosing determines what character he will have. His freedom is a true and basic dynamic freedom, a freedom to make himself good or bad in character. It is a freedom, however, whose outcome is a new restraint, the ethical restraint of being committed to choose the chosen end again.

The exercise of freedom of choice is thus a way of restricting freedom in a twofold way. It restricts the scope of freedom, cutting a man off from ends which might have been chosen; and it restricts the good man's exercise of freedom subsequently, since the end that he chooses is an end he is thereafter committed to and thus, if good, endeavors to choose. To be free to exercise a choice is to be actually and ethically compelled not to exercise the freedom of choice to a degree theoretically possible.

Choice does not merely influence action as preference does; it prescribes what action is to occur. Since it does not control the body through which, and the world in which, the action is expressed, it does not guarantee the nature of the action. It may make allowance for the nature and habits of body and world but it never masters them. He who chooses properly may be carried away by his appetites or may find that the course of the world is not in detail what he expected it would be. Only if he can reconstitute as well as utilize the channels of the body and the world, only if he can control his medium when and as he plans to use it, will he be able to express adequately in public just what it is he privately decides to do.

While intention only turns appealing things into useful means, choice drastically reconstitutes both ultimate end and its alternative, turning the former from a desirable into a sanctioning end, the latter from a valuable into the best possible alternative. Choice, though, fails to deal with an all-inclusive good as pertinent to the values, and thus to the rights, all beings actually have; it does not take account of things as deserving, apart from us and our needs, to be preserved and enhanced. Making some provision for the way in which the body and the world behave, it does not control their operation. Both it and preference confine the absolute good too narrowly and allow its realization to occur inside limits passively accepted from the body and the world. Neither makes provision for the unconditional adoption of that all-embracing perfection which a man must make real everywhere in order to be complete, a man as excellent as a man can be.

Perfection is pertinent to all that is, living or dead, the subhuman and the human, to those who intend and to those who choose. There is no force which guarantees its acknowledgment or fulfillment. That is why it must be grasped and utilized by men if it is to be realized in any other way than through the haphazard, unguided course of nature. We make it our own, in preference and choice, and thereby perfect ourselves by means of it and change the course of the world. But these modes of determining the good distort it; they make it take a shape which is singularly pertinent to ourselves and the limited things which interest us in a world over which we exercise no control. It has hope of being realized adequately only if it is accepted as appropriate to all things, and thus as a genuinely objective good, enhancing and harmonizing all objectives.

Because the good can look to no force to guarantee its acknowledgment or fulfillment, because it cannot back its demands with the promise of the exercise of disagreeable pressures, it can hope to be adopted and realized as it should be only if it is what men need and can know they need in order to be men at their best, truly and fully men. To the question, "Why should a man be ethical; why should he look to and live in terms of perfection, the good that ought to be?" an answer can then, despite Bradley, be given.

A man must accept the good no matter what he does. The good is the unavoidable object of his concern which he personalizes and specializes in the form of limited goals and ultimate ends until he reaches the point where he becomes a full-fledged ethical being and occupies himself with it in its all-encompassing form. When he is ethical he consciously and deliberately focuses on this inescapable objective and uses it more effectively than otherwise, thereby perfecting himself to a degree greater than he otherwise could. The ethical man does directly, clearly, and more satisfactorily what a man somehow always does and must—concern himself with, possess, exhibit, and thereby realize the absolute good. A man should be ethical in order to become perfected most effectively, to become an excellent man, to satisfy his need to be himself in himself, self-sufficient, complete, lacking nothing valuable.

The good, though unavoidable, is freely adopted as a value which is to be exhibited in every limited objective and occurrence. Were that good not capable of being freely adopted, there would be nothing for the ethicist to do but record the brute fact that men happen to have this or that position in relation to it. There would then be no meaning to absolute right and wrong, good and bad, guilt and innocence, duty and obligation; we would have to content ourselves with saying that men worked toward this or that result rather than toward some other, not because they so decided but because they had been so compelled by heredity and circumstance. What is would allow no room for genuine responsibility; there would be an "ought to be" but it would not be of concern to us.

To become perfected a man must adopt the absolute good without distorting or delimiting it. Not infinitely rich or flexible, he cannot concretely realize that good in his person. But he can make himself responsible for it; he can hold on to it, identify himself with it, fill it out with his own substance. Responsible for it, he then would be obligated to act so as to realize it outside himself as well. He can realize the good internally to the greatest possible extent only by also making himself subservient to it, by making himself an agency by which it is exhibited elsewhere too.

A man who does not make the good his responsibility but allows it to be personalized and specialized in possibly conflicting ways does not thereby escape it; instead he acts to realize it and in such a way as to face it in its absolutivity once again, but at a greater distance than it had been before. The absolute good is a kind of inescapable hypothesis to the effect that men have no other role to play but that of doing what is good everywhere, and that if they fail to do their work today that work is only postponed and then with penalty. The alternative of not living up to the good is having to deal with it again but in less favorable circumstances than before. A man ought to look to and live in terms of perfection because he cannot escape it, in the first place, and because in the second, the more he attends to it the more he makes himself a man.

The will is that power by which a man reaches beyond the focused objectives of mind or body to an objective which is appropriate to both. It is a *limited* will so far as the objective it adopts is an objective of the mind or the body used to elicit an appropriate action by the body or the mind. Were the will *unlimited,* the objective adopted would be the absolute good, lying beyond and outside both mind and body and appropriate to them and all other beings. The will is *effective* so far as the actions which it elicits actually serve to bring about the objective; *ineffective,* so far as, though capable, the body or mind fails to act to bring about the common objective. It is a *flexible* will if the elicited actions serve also to realize limited objectives while realizing the absolute good; *inflexible* if it is a limited will, or if, when unlimited, it does not elicit activity serving to realize the objectives appropriate to others. Finally, the will is *creative* if both effective and flexible and thus also unlimited. Such a will lays hold of the absolute good so as to elicit mental and bodily activity directed toward the realization of that good in and through the realization of the limited objectives of other beings. It is a dynamic agency by which man's native freedom is most effectively utilized and the conditional freedom which he allows them is most effectively altered.

The creative will is a concern utilizing the absolute good so as to determine action which is appropriate to specific things, and thus which has regard for their rights as realities with such and such natures. The good it lays hold of is at the limit of indeterminacy; that is why that good can be exemplified in every case. It is a good which is outside the subordinate possibilities as a common generic character; that is why things in their several ways can not only pursue their different possibilities independently of one another but can come into conflict with one another. The will makes the absolute good more determinate by imposing it on possibilities pertinent to others and then generates activity geared to those others so far as they are concerned with the possibilities as harmonized by the good. To the degree that the will is creative it varies the contours of acts to make them accord with the rights things have as independent beings which deserve to realize what has been harmonized by the absolute good.

By means of the creative will a man exhibits the absolute good in diverse acts and places as a harmony for them to illustrate severally and together. By means of that will he reconstitutes his body and the world, freeing them from the limitations characteristic of preference and choice. By means of that will he determines himself, forging a fresh, unpredictable course of action whose very essence is beyond the grasp, until produced, even of omniscience. Unlike preference and choice and the acts these promote, the will has no preassignable specific objective to vivify. What we creatively will to bring about achieves its specific nature in being brought about. The creative will produces it by making determinate that radically indeterminate good which is the future of all beings in such a way as to make it possible for them to be so many different versions of a single harmony.

2. THE POWER OF WILL

Beyond the control of either body or mind, the will is not bound by what has been chosen or by what the body tends to do. It enables a man to determine himself as a whole, to remake himself and others by bringing them into a harmony which they would otherwise violate. This, the highest kind of freedom he can exercise, is very difficult to carry out. The body and mind are constantly tempted to act in ways which preclude the realization of the fullest possible excellence of one another and other beings. The noise of battle prompts a man to run the other way; unless he wills to keep himself in the fight, to hold the end of fighting before him and crowd out incitements to other kinds of action, he will perhaps run away. Just so, unless he wills creatively to realize the good, to make all things embody it to that maximum which is consistent with their remaining themselves, and in the face of their efforts to realize their individual goods regardless of others, he will not do all he should.

At every moment a man must pit his willed objective against the objectives which his body, mind, and other things primarily favor. Each defeat marks him as a man of weak will, a man who is insufficiently *resolved* to focus on the good or who is insufficiently *resolute* to be able to overcome other enticements. The more resolved and resolute a man, the stronger is his will.

At each moment each man is challenged to put his will to the test. At each moment he comes out stronger or weaker than he had been before. He might say to himself he was strongly decided on doing something. But not until he actually put his will to the test of trying to realize the good without distortion could it be known just how decisive he was, and with respect to what.

A man's struggle with other provocations to action is a creative, unique process in which his decisiveness is then and there given nature and degree. Since it is impossible to determine a decision until it is determined in fact, it is impossible for anyone to ascertain in advance which way the struggle will go. Lifelong habits and preliminary pledges will help promote steadfastness, but both habit and pledge are general and vague and do not suffice to determine the specific, actual, definite form which a decision assumes when made. It is not until opposition is overcome that it can be known whether it can be overcome by this man as having such and such a will exercised in such and such a way with such and such strength.

A man of iron resolution determines his acts by the willed good alone; he alone has a pure creative will. A man of no internal strength allows present circumstances to determine entirely which way he will behave. But men of iron and men of water are fictions. No actual man is absolutely firm or perfectly fluid. None is perfectly creative. And no one can tell in advance just how creative he will be. At most he can only prepare himself to be more than he was before.

A man never knows fully in advance what he will do. He surely does not know what he will do when confronted with the sudden death of his son, the loss of his fortune, the legal or medical verdict that he must die. These are but striking illustrations of what faces him at every moment—situations which can be dealt with in advance and in the abstract in one way, but which in the concrete and present are often dealt with in another. Each is forced to test his will at every moment. At every moment he must decide to mold himself along old or new lines. Each decision is fresh, beyond the reach of past decisions, something he cannot avoid engaging in, if only to do as he had done before.

Should a man fail to will effectively at any given time, his failure will not force him to will ineffectively the next. He can indulge himself for a moment without it making much difference to his nature, character, or strength of will. Reform is in principle always within his reach, no matter what he has done; he can theoretically even indulge himself for a lifetime and then reform. Still, to have constantly erred or to have remained steady is to have strengthened bad or good habits and thus to have made more and more probable the continuation of the kind of results previously produced.

Each decision is freshly made and is to be judged as an individual occurrence, regardless of the nature of him who forges it. Each is a crucial occurrence, a turning point in a man's life, even though it may actually serve to repeat what had previously been done. A wrong decision is no more or less wrong if it be the first or the hundredth. Nor does the number of times a wrong decision is made affect the degree of condemnation which it each time deserves. But the *man* who makes the wrong decision for the first time has a nature which is better than that possessed by him who errs for the hundredth. Not all who do wrong are equally bad; yet there may be no difference in their acts or the wrongs these involve.

Human nature is made by decisions and in turn makes decisions of a certain kind probable. Neither the nature of the most hardened wrongdoer nor that of the man with the most untarnished virtue is ever completely formed. At every moment both decide and thereby help form their natures further. Each type of man will tend in a different way from that characteristic of the others; but tendency is not compulsion. Each can decide at every moment to go counter to the way he had decided before. No man is so old or so set in his habits that he is unable to redetermine himself through his will to start in a new direction—though he may be too old or too set for the decision to have a significant effect on what he does after he has started. A hardened wrongdoer will most likely decide wrongly, not because he cannot will differently but because he has great difficulty in making a new kind of decision effective in his body and his world, indurated as they are with the structure of his past decisions, all going a different way. He finds it difficult to make his fresh decision effective in practice; he finds that he has, over the years, built up a set of habits which cancel the force of the decision and so infect his body as to preclude the effectiveness of his will, if this be exercised in no stronger way than it had been exercised in the past. Despite his freedom to will, the hardened wrongdoer is so habituated to act as a wrongdoer that he cannot be expected to act otherwise. His habits defy his changes in resolution. He must constantly exert more than his usual force of will to overcome the tensions which were set up by his past habits. He can do this, but it is not reasonable to expect that he will, for it is reasonable only to expect men, in the ordinary course of events, to exercise their wills to the degree they have exercised them before.

A man of strong will, steadily expressed through the years, is no less free to will weakly than one who previously and persistently exhibited a weak will. Both constantly face new occasions in which they must will anew and freely, regardless of how they willed before. Both, because they normally will with the strength they exhibited frequently in the past, can be expected to will as they had before. Yet neither can avoid the demand that he freely test how strongly resolved and resolute he is with respect to the case now before him.

No man is so fixed and solid in nature that he can be sure just how much strength of will he will exhibit later. No one controls the future and can dictate now what in detail it will be; all we have the power to do is to decide what the immediate present shall be. As the years go on he who has held to a single resolve will have weakened his interest in other objectives. He will find it easier to keep to his resolution thereafter. And if the world is stable he will not have to struggle so much in order to achieve a new victory.

Neither the man of strong nor the man of weak will can avoid struggling, and each can win or lose in any particular struggle in which he engages. The former can lose in an easy conflict by exerting himself considerably less than he usually does; the latter can gain a difficult victory by making an unusual effort. The noblest saint on occasion may yield to a slight or to a great temptation; the worst of sinners may on occasion keep steadily to a new resolve and resolution. We know what would be the outcome if they willed with the strength they did before, but we can never tell—nor can they or any god—how much strength they will use in this case or that. Future victories can never be taken for granted, just as no defeat of will is ever final. All that can be expected and all that can be hoped is that each man will take advantage of his successes and exert at least the same strength of will on subsequent occasions that he did in the past, so as to make sure a subsequent and easier victory.

The habitual drunkard is no longer in a position to meet the challenge of a drink before him. Yet he can will not to drink when he eats or at the moment when he wakens, provided that the drink is kept out of sight. He can thereby learn to overcome the prospect of drinking at those times, learn to crowd out these lesser provocations to action, and gradually build up the power to resist the enticement of a drink right before him. There are more radical methods of cure than this, but these are primarily ways of reconstituting the body so that the drink does not incite the tendency to drink to the same degree it did before. They are not means by which a man reconstitutes himself; rather they are means by which his body is reconstituted for him. All of them evidently could be set at defiance should the man decide to will in defiance of his body.

When we will we are perfected, because thereby infected by the good on whose behalf we are obligated to act. Since that good is the possibility of the existence and essence of other beings, those others are in a sense possessed to the very degree that the possibility is. By making the absolute good our own, we in a way master the things which lie outside us, make them become our boundaries, the limits of ourselves. The world becomes more intimately a part of us the more adequately we possess and realize the good and thus the more surely we will creatively. The world beyond, through our adoption of the good, becomes part of us, functions as the terminus of ourselves as obligated, responsible beings. When we will the good we not only adopt it but identify it with ourselves. We vitalize it and thereby make it alter the nature of our acts. Other things then become the willed termini of our acts as good or bad, and we as a consequence live in the center of a universe of man-made good and evil.

Because of our will the good is no mere unitary future outside the several subordinate futures that specify it; it is instead a future integral to those subordinate futures. It is a future which through our efforts qualifies and orders subordinate possibilities, which harmonizes them to constitute a more determinate future common to us and others.

Man makes a difference to the world in many ways, not the least of which is that he, by willing the absolute good, alters the import of the goods pertinent to other beings and thereby changes their promise. His actions and theirs may belie and defy this change. Should his his actions, though, express adequately the absolute good he imposed on the possibilities which concern others, should he exercise a strong, good, flexible will, he will improve the rest in a way they themselves cannot. By his will a man alters the promise of others and sometimes helps them to attain something of the excellence appropriate to them as independent beings which, to be improved most, must be improved in harmony with one another.

3. Could, Would, and Should

A man *should* exert his will with sufficient strength to do what is right. He *would* do this were he subject to different conditions. And he *could* do this, for he is radically free to will at every moment.

"Should, "would," and "could" are independent ideas. We criticize men for not doing what they should, even when we think it true that they neither would nor could do otherwise. We know they are flexible enough to be able to change the course of their activities, even if there is nothing they should do and even if they were not free to do it. And it is possible for them to be free to decide, even in those cases where all conditions are as they had been and though there were nothing right or wrong for them to do. Man's freedom does not depend for its being or knowledge on ethics—just the contrary, and contrary to Kant.

Because "could," "would," and "should" are independent and compatible, there are eight possible ways of dealing with decisions. Whatever decision has been willed, it is possible to assert that a man

1. could, would, and should have willed otherwise;
2. could not, would, and should have willed otherwise;
3. could and would, yet should not have willed otherwise;
4. could not and should not, yet would have willed otherwise;
5. could and should, yet would not have willed otherwise;
6. could not and would not, yet should have willed otherwise;
7. could but would not and should not have willed otherwise;
8. could not, would not, and should not have willed otherwise.

1. A man is always free to make decisions, though not always free to realize them in act. Swayed though he may be by what for him seem to be inescapable compulsions, he is always able to decide in a different way. Having decided in one way, he can become aware of the implica-

tions of his decision as he had not been before and thus see that a different decision would have been better. He knows that had he the opportunity to make the decision over again he would have decided otherwise. If his decision was wrong, he should have made it take a different direction.

Because a man knows he could, would, and should have decided otherwise, it is possible for him to know that, were he given the opportunity to will again, he would freely avoid doing what he now sees should not have been done. Such knowledge lies behind the feeling of regret which tinges our awareness of our responsibility for acts we recognize as wrong.

2. A man can decide otherwise than he does. But he cannot, with the same ease, always act otherwise than he does. His will might be weak. There may be obstacles in his way, preventing him from realizing some possible, desirable course of action. So far as decision relates to activities which can be performed with no more ease or blameworthiness than others, there are limits to what a man can decide. There are things he could not do. Following Spinoza, one might go further and contend that he has no power at all to make a free decision; that there are definite and determinate grounds dictating what he will decide to do. Were one to take this extreme position, it would still be possible to affirm that, though he could not have willed otherwise, he would and should have willed otherwise. He would have decided otherwise were his decisions compelled by circumstance or rational considerations and were these different at different times. And because there is an absolute standard of right and wrong, it is possible to say of such a man that, despite the fact that he could not help, on the hypothesis, deciding as he does, he should have decided otherwise than he did. The denial that a man is free to decide means that he is not responsible for the course he adopts; it does not necessitate the supposition that he would always decide as he had or that he decides as a man ought.

Because "could not," "would," and "should have willed otherwise" are compatible expressions, it is possible for men to blame themselves for what they do, not because they are free but because they have the natures they have, and lack information which they might have had and which would have led them to do something else. We define as mad those who, having done what is wrong, would not have done otherwise than they did, despite the knowledge now available to them. We excuse those who, freed from a passion possible to any man, would have decided otherwise than they do when in the grip of the passion. We blame only those who would have done otherwise had available knowledge been utilized.

3. Not every decision a man could and would have forged is one he should have. I know that under circumstances I could commit a serious crime. And I know that it would be something I ought not to have done. I know that, as I look at a criminal, it might be I.

Because "could," "would," and "should have decided otherwise" are compatible expressions, it is possible for a good man to know that he could have decided in another way, and can be swayed to do so. An excellent man arises through decisions, not by accident. He knows that he wills as he should and that the decisions are his own. His saintliness is not a gift but the result of a continued effort; it is always on the verge of being lost. And there are circumstances where he would most likely have chosen as the rest do, knowing all the while that he was freely choosing what was wrong.

4. A man who should not have decided otherwise than he did is one who decided correctly. If he could not have decided otherwise, he would be an automatic good man, one from whom good acts flow by necessity. Of such a man it is possible to say that he would have decided otherwise were circumstances other than they had been. An accident, a chemical change, a thousand and one things would have forced his decision into a different channel, and he as a consequence, though he should not, would nevertheless have made a different decision than he did.

Because "would," "could not," and "should not have willed otherwise" are compatible expressions, it is possible to view men who do good as temporary and changeable vessels of what ought to be. Some such concept lies behind the modified Calvinism which characterizes much of the Protestantism of today. For Calvin a man did not have power enough to elect that life which was really good and worthy of salvation. What he should will he could not. Calvin seemed also to hold that the nature of a man is fairly fixed from the beginning, so that it is impossible to say of a given man that he would have chosen in a different way than he did, since his decision was the inevitable outcome of the fixed nature that he had. Those who came after Calvin agreed with him that there was an absolute standard of what a man should do but that it was impossible for a man freely to elect to live up to it. Man, they thought, was made in such a fashion that he lived in one way or another and nothing he could do would make a difference to his fate. The followers diverged from Calvin in holding that the nature of man was modifiable and that therefore he would be able to decide in other ways than he had. They saw that "should not," "could not," and "would" were compatible. It was this change which made it possible for later Protestantism to make a serious effort to alleviate the lot of those who were held down by circumstance, thereby enabling them to make a different decision were the opportunity to appear again. Calvin denied to man the power to make a decision; his followers held on to this denial but recognized that there were conditions which affected the kind of things man wills to do.

5. A free man could make a different decision. And he can will as he should not. He can be one who not only could have but should have decided otherwise. Nevertheless he may not be one who would have decided otherwise. There may not be strong enough reasons which would make him want to revise his decisions had he the opportunity to decide again. A man has a tendency to keep on deciding as he has been accustomed to decide. Reform, though always possible, is difficult to carry through. We are in the grip of habits which we can break only by a resolution we are too indolent to carry out. Because this is so, it is possible for a bad man to know he would be bad again, freely and responsibly, were the opportunity repeated.

"Could," "should," and "would not have decided otherwise" are compatible expressions. It is possible for a man to know what he should do, be able to do it, and yet not do it. An old reprobate finds it hard to reform because he is too inflexible and weak to match changed circumstance with changed response.

6. If a man could be damned from the start he could not and would not will otherwise than he does. Yet he could be punished for not being and therefore not deciding as he should, if the punishment and criticism were impersonal, comparable to the incarceration and seclusion which accompany the judgment on carriers of infectious diseases. Because "could not," "would not," and "should have decided otherwise" are compatible expressions, it is possible to punish men who happen to fall short of the ideals of an absolute standard, even though they are not blamed for doing what they do.

7. Some decisions are as they should be. A man can will as he should. Convinced of the rightness of his cause he can know that were he to decide again he would decide as he had before. So far as he is free he is then one who could have but neither would nor should have decided otherwise than he did. It is because "could," "would not," and "should not have decided otherwise" are compatible expressions that it is possible for a good man to know that he can continue to do what is right. The fact that he could do wrong at any moment defines him as one who does what is right not automatically but freely.

8. Finally, it is possible to be one who could not, would not and should not have decided otherwise than he does. It is possible to conceive of a saint who has neither freedom nor flexibility but who automatically and forever conforms to eternal principles of right. He would be a permanent and automatic good man. When Spinoza de-

fines God as being without free will, from which all things necessarily flow, he speaks of Him in terms somewhat equivalent to these.

Because a man can be said not to have decided as he should, it can be said that there is evil traceable to him. Because he can be said to be one who would have decided otherwise, it can be said that some of the evils are avoidable. And because a man can be said to be able to decide otherwise than he does, he can, having done good, bring about evil, and having done evil, bring about good. But the problem of evil is much larger than this; what evils he does are but part of a world of evils, in no way traceable to him, beyond the power of his will to master. If he could will continuously and in such a way as to remake other things so that they do nothing else but realize perfectly the harmonized possibilities appropriate to them, they would be excellent parts of an excellent whole. But since he cannot will continuously, and since when he wills he alters only a part of them, he is left at every moment facing a world in which there is genuine, objective evil.

XVII

EVIL

1. The Will and Evil

THE creative will is universally relevant, endlessly malleable, internally grounded, and externally manifest. It enables a man to meet external challenges with inwardly instituted replies and thus to make things into, not merely adopt them as bounding parts. By means of it he can take full account of both the careers and values of others and thus avoid being frustrated or controlled by them.

When he creatively wills a man faces his mind and body with the absolute good, an objective which is appropriate to both and all else there is. By focusing on that objective, insisting on it, he forces everything in his mind and body to be subject to it. So far as he is able to subjugate himself and others to the good by reorganizing and reconstructing his mind and body, his will is *strong;* so far as his reorganization results in the perfecting of things, his will is *good.*

A man may have a good strong and a good weak will, the former bringing about the maximum embodiment of the good, the latter some minor embodiment of it. He may have a bad strong or a bad weak will, the former reconstituting things so as to leave them worse than they were, the latter embodying the good in only a partially bad way. Those who have strong bad wills often have multiple virtues; they are continent, competent, disciplined, but in their strength a greater weakness is contained, for they use their powers to reduce rather than to enhance things and thereby themselves as well.

The most effective and desirable use of the will is that by which things are so reorganized that they, as well as ourselves, are made to embody all the good they can. In the case of inanimate objects and subhuman beings, the most we can do is transform them, make them objects of our art so that they will embody, point toward, and act to realize the absolute good again. In the case of men we must try to awaken in them, as was awakened in us, an interest in realizing the good as a good of all.

The will is met by the insistencies of things; their claim to have a nature and future of their own, a right to be enhanced and perfected in accord with their needs and natures. So far as they insist on themselves, they oppose the reassessment we make of them and are so far in conflict with us, evil.

In speaking this way we seem to slide, without question, into what is, to be sure, the dominant view of our civilization, but which is still not beyond all evident cavil and doubt—the view that evil exists only over against men, opposing their wills. It would be but a short step from this doctrine to the older and perhaps once equally favored view that all evil is a product of human wills. In either case we seem to do less than justice to the existence of natural evils, that which ought not to be, whether there are men in the universe or not.

2. INTRINSIC EVIL

There are evils. Only one cut off from this world could deny the fact and regrettability of death, injury, disease, sorrow, suffering, and pain. And only one who was callous could deny that these were evils, what ought not to be.

All of us at some time or other have had to swallow the tragic truth that there is much in this cosmos that ought not to be. The fact demands an explanation. That explanation is beyond the reach of any empirical inquiry but still within the grasp of one who has no theological concerns. The most complete empirical account of why evils occur will still leave open the question of whether or not there should be evils; without turning to God we can ask what relation evil has to good and seem able to answer the question without having to leave the cosmos in which the question was framed.

The problem of evil can be ignored. It cannot be made to vanish by turning toward either science or God. Evil is that which ought not to be. Its occurrence anywhere is sufficient to raise the whole problem of evil and thereby make pertinent the question of what ought to be, why what ought to be does not exist, and what we, with our wills, can do about it.

Disease, injury, and the rest are evils. Are they all eliminable? Could we by changing our ways or our wills, by doing something to ourselves or others, get rid of these evils? And if we could, should we? Are evils an essential part of existence? Are they needed in order to make possible some greater good?

If evils are required in the nature of things, if their absence would compromise the existence of the universe, they are *ontologically* necessary. If evils are required in order that good should be, if their absence would mean that there would be less good than otherwise, they are *valuationally* necessary, indispensable instruments for the production of good. Only if man created the universe would all ontologically necessary evils have some relevance to man. As it now is, only valuationally necessary evils need have any relation to him.

It seems quite clear that pain, suffering, sorrow, death, disease, or injury are not ontologically necessary. Each and every one of them might conceivably disappear without jeopardizing the existence of all else. With the disappearance of sentient creatures, pain, suffering, and sorrow would have to go. With the passing of the organic, disease and death would disappear. In a state of thermal equilibrium, injury would no longer be possible, since bodies then would be able neither to move nor to act. These evils are not ontologically necessary. The universe could be, though they did not occur. This state of affairs, where such evils no longer exist, may never occur; these evils may never in fact vanish. But they nevertheless are not ontologically necessary, since the universe could continue even though they were absent.

Sometimes such evils are valuationally necessary. Sometimes they stimulate, provoke, induce, sustain the search for and the attainment of goods not possible otherwise. They prompt men to appreciate, invent, reform, and reaffirm. Just as discords are necessary if there are to be complex, beautiful harmonies, so these evils are sometimes preconditions for the existence of real goods. Without the goad of experienced, encountered, or anticipated evil, man would have failed to reach many of the heights he has so brilliantly scaled, and he surely would sip untasting and unaware many of the goods that evil now brings into focus. Death points up the value of life, disease the value of health. The most solid of joys has a bitter, brackish center; its being depends on the knowledge and perhaps experience of a deep and abiding sorrow. The joy of a child is a world to itself, but the joy of a man is an island momentarily thrown up from the depths and now held out over against force already beginning to pull it down again.

Pain, suffering, disease, death, sorrow, injury are *intrinsically* evil, evil of and in themselves in the very way in which an innocent pleasure, a refreshing sight, the glow of health, the feel of life, a childish joy, a surge of strength are good, in and of themselves. These various evils ought not to be. No matter how effective they might be in preventing the existence of greater evils or in promoting the attainment of goods, they are and continue to be intrinsically evil, evils which remain evils whether needed or not. Useless, they have no values as means; useful, they do. But in either case they are undesirable, what ought not to be. So far as they are not valuationally necessary, so far as goods could be as effectively promoted by other means, no one would hesitate to affirm that these other means be employed.

3. Explanations of Evil

What promotes the good may be intrinsically good or intrinsically evil. If it is intrinsically evil, and if it promotes the good because men react against the evil, the evil thing is good as playing a useful role. It is good in the way in which it might be interesting, distant, owned, noticed—as serving to terminate a relation from the outside. It might in this respect be no better or no worse than an object which was less or more evil.

The knowledge that something promotes the good and is thus valuationally good provides no clue as to whether it is intrinsically good or evil, or to the degree of good or evil it might possess. Conversely, it is not sufficient, in order to know whether something will promote the good, to know whether it is good or evil. The intrinsic worth and the valuational goodness of an object are distinct and may be quite different, though the latter always depends in part on the presence and the nature of the former.

Intrinsic evil is brutal and ultimate; its nature is not altered by its having other functions, good or bad. This does not mean that it is unintelligible, inexplicable, a surd which defies all explanation. There are, in fact, at least three different ways of accounting for it—*scientifically*, in terms of its antecedents and the course of nature by which it is brought about; *analytically*, by isolating its constituents and making evident the ways in which those constituents interplay; and *speculatively*, in terms of universal principles which the evils illustrate in a limited guise. In all three ways we abstract from the valuational necessity of evil to concentrate on its intrinsic nature, preliminary to an examination of the question as to whether or not evil is ontologically necessary.

We need a scientific account of evils, for this helps show how the evils are to be controlled and perhaps eliminated. To know that a certain disease is brought about by such and such a plant is to have the data in terms of which the disease may be conquered. A scientific account, however, not only takes for granted that the disease is evil but ignores the question as to just what in it is evil. At best it explains the occurrence, not the nature, of evil. It tells us what makes the evil be, not what makes the evil evil.

We must engage in an analytic study of evils if we are to grasp why they are evil. By analyzing out the components of an evil, we come to see just what in it is responsible for its evil. We are then in a position to alter it and thereby obtain what is good. To know that a particular evil is the outcome of two particular goods in conflict, for example, is to be in a position to eliminate the evil, not by controlling or eliminating its occasions but by changing its structure. It is to be able not only to be scientific but to use science for the mastery of the evil itself. But neither separately nor together are the scientific and the analytic explanations of evil satisfactory. They know evils in detail and never in general and thus never face the problem of evil as such.

The scientific approach to evil is the work of specialists. He who knows how to eliminate the pain of childbirth does not necessarily know how to control or eliminate elephantiasis, or conversely. The analytic approach is primarily the work of literary men. It is not our scientific psychologists but our novelists who have made evident just what the components of our sorrow and suffering are. They alone have mastered the art of analyzing concrete values. They have made it possible to direct a pointed scientific attack on evil. The speculative approach is the concern of the philosopher. It is his task to provide an account of those principles which are explanatory of all evil—principles illustrated in special cases, deserving analysis and scientific understanding, and to whose comprehension in turn both analysis and science contribute.

The speculative thinker tries to understand whether or not evil is ontologically necessary, required by the nature of beings, and if so, why this should be. His answer, couched as it is in universal terms, makes it possible to avoid the special conclusions one might be tempted to draw from a consideration of only familiar evils or from evils which are only valuationally necessary because indispensable instruments for bringing about more good. It makes it possible too to evaluate a scientific program designed to control or eliminate evil. In addition it should help us to understand a little better who we are, what the universe is in which we must live, and what therefore we ought to do.

4. The Necessity of Evil

Evils such as pain are sometimes valuationally necessary. They are not ontologically necessary. The universe could exist even if they did not occur, unless perchance the universe requires for its very existence living sensitive beings subject to disagreeable experiences. Since the universe can, without jeopardizing its existence, contain only inanimate beings, some evils can evidently be eliminated without ruining the universe. It is perhaps true that there is not one single evil which has to be, whose elimination would involve the destruction of all else. This does not mean that *all* evil is eliminable. Some evil might be necessary to the very existence of the universe, but it might not be necessary that the evil have this form or that. It is possible that there must always be some evil somewhere. We must ask ourselves whether or not there could be a universe if there were no evil of some kind.

The temper of modern theology is to answer this last question in the negative; classical theology answers it in the affirmative. Both are too hardheaded to deny that there is some evil in the universe, and both insist that God is the good creator of all there is. They are both faced with the alternatives of limiting God's power or accounting for the evil as the product of created goods. The moderns take the first of these alternatives. In the last resort they are forced to view evil as inexplicable, a taint in the divine being for which there can be no explanation. The second, classical, view is better, for it at least tries to offer an explanation for evil. According to it evil is a derivative fact, the outcome of the desirable exercise of good powers on the part of angels or men. It does not deny that there are evils. In fact this is insisted on. The existence of evil is treated as basic, undeniable truth. But it is affirmed that evils did not have to be, and even that there actually was a time when no evils were. Had angels or men not abused their absolutely good will, nothing, classical theologians think, but good would be. Their position, however, cannot be maintained.

Firstly, not only do they not explain but they presuppose—just as surely though not as suddenly as do modern theologians—the existence of an inexplicable evil. The classical theologians cannot avoid affirming that there is something wrong in angels or men—ambition, pride, ignorance, conceit—from which all the other evils flow. In the last resort they thus suppose at least one inexplicable evil in terms of which all others are to be understood. They have evidently simplified the problem, not resolved it. Secondly, they are forced to assert that were men innocent or good there would be no earthquakes and tidal waves, no toothaches or heartaches, or that such things would not be evil. But surely these exist whether men be good or bad. And they surely are evil. An earthquake is a destructive force, ruining animals and plants and defining the most protected Garden of Eden as either too calm to be part of a vital world or marked by regrettable violence and confusion.

There is no evident correlation between the dates of the occurrence or the intensity of natural evils and the incidence and magnitude of man's virtues. Natural evils—marked by ugliness, defects, imperfections, violence, chaos—do not depend for their being on the goodness or badness of men. Indeed, they exist and are evil even where and when men do not exist.

A better answer can be found by turning from the writers of theologies to the writers of theodicies, from an Augustine to a Leibniz, from an Aquinas to a Hegel. They at least have a place for evils which are independent of vice. Whereas theologies try to explain evil by referring to wickedness in men or angels, theodicies try to explain it as the inevitable consequence of finitude. They remark that the totality of reality is absolutely good and that what is less than that totality is so far not good. Evil for them is the imperfect, the defective, the finite, and exists only so far as there is something individual, separate, less than the whole. Their position, however, also is not tenable.

Firstly, they give evil more than its due. Taking evil to be but another term for finitude, they suppose that a being is evil so far as it has a distinct place or nature of its own. But then it must be maintained that no individual thing ought to be, no matter what its individual virtues or excellences. A good man, we would have to say, is a bad one, precisely to the degree that he is an individual man. But if he is not an individual, who then is it who is good? Secondly, the view fails to account for pain and sorrow which, if anything, refer to rather than turn away from being. We are pained at losses suffered by our own beings. We sorrow for other beings who are with us no longer or who are about to pass away. Thirdly, it fails to find a place for limited goods. Individuals have pleasures as well as pains. They have joys as well as sorrows. If evil is one with finitude, separateness, individuality, there cannot be anything like an individual pleasure— or if there is, it cannot be good.

Theologies tend to confuse the fact of evil with an origin; theodicies tend to confuse the fact of evil with its locus. The one reduces evil to the status of a sin or a derivate from it; the other reduces evil to the status of an imperfection. According to the one there would be no evils were there no wickedness; according to the other there is evil wherever there is finitude. The first has difficulty with cataclysms, the second with joy. But the first is surely right in maintaining that evil can be the outcome of the good activity of good beings, just as the second is right in remarking that the occurrence of evil is not solely dependent on spiritual failures. We must hold to both views but must avoid their common supposition that evil is somehow eliminated when it is freed from the taint of sin or a reference to individuals.

Evils exist because goods oppose one another in such a way as to constrain or reduce one another's values. Evil, in other words, is a product. We can account for it, with the classical theologians, as the outcome of the desirable exercise of desirable powers by good beings. But, with the writers of theodicies, we will have to affirm that the good beings and the evil they produce are not necessarily sin infected. Evils are, as the latter observe, wherever there is finitude; but, as the former know, evil and finitude are not necessarily one.

Evils, familiar and otherwise, are constituted by entities which, in relation to one another, function as undesirable restraints or as means of reducing values. The entities into which the evils are analyzable may themselves be intrinsically evil. If they are, they will—since evil involves a plurality in conflict—presuppose other entities, and so on, until we come to ultimate entities, be they protons, positrons, atoms, molecules, cells, or organisms, out of which all else is built. These ultimate elements, because not constituted by something more ultimate, cannot be evil. They are and must be actually good, since each is a single unity which cannot but exemplify harmony in a restricted way.

Evil, in the last resort, presupposes the existence of good elements in conflict. It marks a discordant situation constituted by restraining goods, each making others less than they might and ought to be. It depends on goods functioning as instrumental evils. Those goods might instead have supplemented one another to constitute larger, intrinsically good wholes, and these in turn might have constituted still larger good unities, and so on. The cosmos would then contain no evil.

There are evils in the cosmos, constituted by entities in conflict. The conflict is conceivably avoidable; these evils are not required by the very nature of the cosmos. But they will never be entirely eliminated. The very goodness of a thing is inseparable from an urgency on the part of the thing to spread itself, insist on itself, impose itself on others without limit. It is the restlessness of each good, the overflowing character of its goodness that makes each interfere with others and almost always do them some harm. Only one who knew exactly how far and how insistently each good ought to spread itself, and who could control all action in terms of this knowledge, could eliminate the evils which arise because good existents make conflicting demands. Not until all things were firmly in the grip of an omniscient, omnipotent good being would there be a prospect that existent evils, though both ontologically and valuationally unnecessary, could be eliminated. But this would require the annihilation of time, the end of this particular cosmos.

There will always be evils in existence, for it is the essence of things to urge their goodness beyond their proper bounds. Even if there were no existent evils, even if all evils built on the conflict of opposing existents were overcome, there would still be evil in existence. Understanding by the cosmos the totality of particulars, the universe minus the future that lies beyond and toward which all things point, we can say that a cosmos need not have evil in it, though ours always had and always will. A universe must always contain some evil, reflecting an opposition between whatever cosmos there be and its future.

The universe embraces a cosmos of conflicting though harmonizable existents. It embraces also an abstract, absolute good which is realized in diverse, sometimes conflicting, sometimes harmonizing ways. These two stand forever apart, needing and yet opposing one another.

No matter whether all existents are in harmony or in conflict, whether they constitute good or evil situations, they are inseparable from the future. That future is the good as general, abstract, and absolute. It is the good, since it is a harmony of all possibilities; it is general, allowing for an indefinite number of different realizations; it is abstract in that it lacks the concreteness and specificity characteristic of present things; and it is absolute, for it is the ultimate unity which encompasses the possibility of everything whatsoever.

The absolute good has some characteristics all things ought to but none does possess. Not only is it universal, excluding nothing, but it has an indefinite duration. These are desirable traits. Things, therefore, because but parts of the universe, and because existing for but part of time, could not be perfectly good. On the other hand, the absolute good lacks the richness of things, their concreteness, their inward substantiality, vitality, and power. It ought to give way to something more concrete than itself, though no less universal and absolute. It is now less than it ought to be.

The cosmos and the good make one another possible, for there is no future without a present and no present without a future. At the same time they perpetually oppose one another in the very act of trying to maintain their own identities and locus. Each is a means for preventing the other from being an absolute concrete universal good. Each is less than the whole good and is therefore so far not as it ought to be.

The universe thus is constituted of two kinds of entities—concrete existents and an abstract future. In themselves each is good and each does the good service of sustaining the other. Each is also defective, pointing to the other as embodying what ought to be. And each stands in the way of the enhancement of the other and is therefore instrumentally evil.

The universe is built on the reality of opposing defective beings. Is it therefore evil? Evil is what ought not to be; it stands over and thus presupposes what ought to be. Were the universe necessarily evil it would therefore presuppose an "ought to be" beyond it. This argument, a kind of design argument in reverse, shows that evil cannot characterize the universe, or that what we call the universe leaves out at least one being who, as other than and as related to the universe, is necessarily defective. A God who was a correlate, sponsor, sustainer, or source of an evil universe would be faced with what ought not to be, and would be, together with it, a defective part of a wider whole.

Evil, precisely because it makes reference to a further reality, a good that ought to be, can never characterize the totality of all there is, the universe. The universe, though there must be evil in it, we must say, cannot itself be evil, since there is nothing beyond to which the evil can be referred.

If the universe cannot be evil, it either must have no character or must be good. The former alternative is impossible. Even the barest aggregate of things has a character expressive of the fact that the things coexist. And it is always appropriate to ask whether the aggregate ought to be or ought not to be, whether it should be enhanced, reduced, or sustained. Even Aristotle, who tried to suppose that there were no all-pervasive characters, found himself forced to acknowledge that the diverse species in existence were caught in a single spatio-temporal scheme which had the desirable character of being ordered to and oriented toward divinity. The universe has a value of some kind.

We are left with the alternative that the totality of things and futures has the character of being good. Unlike the evil, that good requires no reference beyond itself. We do, of course, sometimes say that something ought to be, and mean thereby that something else exists which is not as good as it should be. We seem then, in speaking of the good, to be presupposing the existence of something evil. Actually we are only remarking that what ought to be stands in contrast with some existent which ought not to be; we are not showing that the good presupposes this or any other contrasting being, that it needs it, requires it, that it must have a prop. The universe, as a whole, is as it ought to be, and contrasts with nothing.

The *knowledge* of the good may perhaps require a reference to a contrasting evil, though this is questionable. In any case the nature of the good requires no such reference. The good could be, though nothing else was. Nothing, however, could be evil unless there was something else with which it was in fact opposed. The evil is what ought not to be, standing over against and opposing what ought to be.

Because what is in the present needs and yet stands opposed to, is needed and is yet opposed by the abstract absolute good, there is and must always be evil inside the universe. Nevertheless the universe as a whole is good, since it is a unity whose character involves no reference beyond itself.

The goodness of the universe, in one sense, cannot be increased, since it is the character which pertains to the universe no matter what it contains in detail or how things interplay. The universe—not the cosmos of existing things—is thus the best possible, not in the sense that there are many possible universes of which this is the best but in the sense that no better is possible. A universe which replaced ours would have the very same character of goodness that ours has, since that character would depend for its nature only on the fact that the existent things in the universe needed the abstract good they made possible, and conversely.

The concrete things in the cosmos, however, are not as good as they can be in themselves or for one another. There are evils now in the cosmos that need not have been. They make the present state of the cosmos less than it might and ought to be. The cosmos, viewed as a distributive totality of concrete beings, is then far from being the best possible. A similar observation is in order with respect to the future. That future embraces all that is possible for the beings now in the present. It is a future pertinent to the present, a future which while standing outside and even opposing the present is inseparable from it. When things in the present change in character the nature of the future they then face is proportionately altered. No child has the possibility of being a father, but only the possibility of being a man, who when he appears will then be faced with the possibility of being a father. The future that is faced today is thus not the same future that was faced in earlier days. When then the present is altered so that it is good where it was bad before, it is inevitably faced with a richer future than was possible before. The very fact then that there are evils now in the cosmos which need not have been makes the future one that can be enhanced, and makes the universe containing it less good than it might be.

Because the universe contains two improvable goods—the present and the future—it is far from being the best possible. Though the structure of it is constant, as good as can be, the coloring of it, the character it achieves by virtue of the coexistence of an enhanceable present and an enhanceable good, is capable of being changed for the better.

The goodness of the universe, both as a constant structure and as the unity of enhanceable existents and futures, is a harmony which exists only so far as there are items which it harmonizes—items which need one another and are to that extent not as good as they ought to be. The goodness of the universe depends for its possibility on limited defective goods inside it. The universe is good only because there are evils in it. Evil is ontologically necessary, necessary to make a universe be. Evil is also cosmologically unavoidable in this particular cosmos; it is not a cosmological necessity for every possible cosmos.

A creative omnipotent God might have made a better cosmos than this. He could have eliminated and muted some of the forms of evil that now prevail. He could conceivably have made all calm and pleasantness, an Eden everywhere, without apples. But He could not have made the universe contain no evil, no defect at all. No matter how good and concerned He might be, and no matter how few of the possible evils might exist, there is always an ontological evil to mark the fact that the universe is not internally perfect. The drive of beings toward perfection is resisted by the very perfection they would realize.

5. The Need for Virtue

Natural evils are not ontologically necessary; they are not even cosmically necessary. In our cosmos they seem, though, to be permanent guests. Cataclysms, earthquakes, tidal waves, and hurricanes, the "leviathan and behemoth," which "esteemeth iron as straw and brass as rotten wood," arise not because men are bad but because insistencies happen to conflict with insistencies. The wind does not need to blow violently, the earth does not need to rumble and rock. When they do, though, it is not because men sin but because force is confronted by force, with victory going to the stronger and more destructive.

Beyond these evils are those which naturally arise but which have man as their focus. These are but special cases of natural evil and express the conflict between man's appetite and other beings. Sickness and injury, the distresses of the body, physical suffering are but special cases of natural evil. In society and organizations of men they are supplemented by a psychological and a social suffering. These evils are real. Philosophers who assure us that such sufferings are like ugly spots in paintings which disappear, or are even ennobled when seen as part of the beautiful whole they make possible, overlook a point: it is a living man who suffers. The suffering may seem like nothing from the perspective of the world. It is not, as we saw, essential to the being of the universe or even of a cosmos. But it is all the world to him who suffers. It is real, it is vital, it is ultimate. It must be reckoned with. It is not dependent on wickedness, for the good also suffer. It is to be conquered, not by improving our morals but by improving our bodies, our minds, and our societies. Since it is not necessary that men suffer, that they be sick, at odds with themselves or others, it is at least possible for all of us to make such evil vanish for each. But whether we do or not, the evil is sometimes the outcome of a conflict of will with nature or will with will.

From the vantage point of will there are two kinds of evils—those which illustrate a defied insistence, an insistence which does not come the length of mastery, and those which represent a defying insistence, an insistence which does wrong. In the former class we have indolence and ineptitude; in the latter we have sin, evil spirit, and wickedness.

Sin is a term cherished by theologians. But it can, without sacrifice to its fundamental meaning, be made applicable both to those who, like the followers of Confucius and Marx, are without a God and to those who, like Job, firmly believe in one. He sins who is disloyal to a primary value accepted on faith. Blasphemy is one form of sin and treason another—or equally, treason is blasphemy practiced toward a state, sin is blasphemy practiced toward some primary good. These and other forms of evil-doing but begin a process of alienation from the land of consistent living and almost always end in a spiritual and sometimes in a physical death.

It is not necessary that a man sin, though it is a fundamental tenet of most theologians' beliefs that all mortals since the days of Adam are sinners. The only thing "original" or unavoidable about sin is that each man sins in his own way and that though no one of us must sin all of us do. We are faithless again and again to the things we most cherish and which give our lives meaning and unity. It is foolish to hope that a perfect world could be achieved if only men were true to God, the state, or science.

Evil spirit is an apparent hairbreadth from sin, but is actually a world away. It is setting oneself to break an ethical command. Like sin, it is privately achieved; it does not involve the exercise of the will except so far as the will is thought of as stopping with something in the mind. It is a matter of the inward parts, of private decisions, of preferences and choices rather than of reconstitution by action. Unlike sin, it has a this-worldly reference always, and is concerned with the good open to reason. The man of evil spirit fails internally to live up to what reason commends.

He who wants to cheat the orphan and the widow, who steals, lies, or kills, is one who violates what reason endorses as right. He who is not religious does not necessarily find these prospects more congenial than does he who is. A religious man may indeed at times be more unethical than a nonreligious one, for a religion may demand that on behalf of it its adherents defy their reason and destroy the lives, property, and prospects of others. The history of religion is in good part a story of our progress in civilizing our concept of God. Throughout the ages we have edited supposed divine words to make them conform to what we know to be ethically correct. He who would avoid all ethical evil must not cling too close to the practices and faith of his fathers.

It is conceivable that a man might not be without evil spirit, though it is hard to believe that there ever was a man so insensitive that he never was tempted by the smell of novelty, a challenge to his daring, or the promptings of his conceit and flesh to think pleasantly of what his reason tells him is wrong. Evil spirit and suffering do not necessarily go together. There are those who intend to do good to others and those who intend to do good only to themselves. Often it is the former who get the grit while the latter enjoy the grain. And if there be no afterlife, the balance may never be righted.

Every man has an evil spirit, if only for passing moments. Fortunately for our society and civilization most of us do not allow our evil intentions to pass the threshold of the mind and to be expressed in practice. Most of us are not wicked. Occasionally unethical in intent, we publicly and regularly do much that is good. Though we may not be able to avoid sinning and intending to do evil, most of us avoid wickedness, the evil of carrying out an evil spirit, the willing of what is wrong.

Wickedness is self-defeating. It destroys value and thereby injures him who was finally to benefit. A man ought to avoid wickedness because otherwise he stands in his own light. Others are needful to him and he needs them to benefit himself—but they must then be perfected to be most serviceable. And he needs them basically in order to be complete. He who is wicked opposes himself, since he does what the very completeness of his nature requires that he should not do; he destroys what is inseparable from his very being, what despite its distance and independence has the status of a genuine bounding part of him. He may gain the whole world, but since he thereby loses himself it cannot be himself whom he profits. It is not true then that the wicked prosper. They may be at their ease, they may have pleasure, property, admiration, honor, security. They may be unconscious of any wrong. Everyone may account them happy. Yet it would be wrong to say that they really prosper, since they defeat themselves, forcing themselves further and further away from the status of beings who are perfect, complete men.

A man should want to do the good and should avoid injuring others. But he also ought not neglect the plight of any. Every single being deserves to be cherished and helped. Yet he who concentrates on one here must slight others there. Each has only finite energy, finite funds, finite interests; none can be everywhere. Each thus fails to fulfill an obligation to realize the good completely. Even if one gave up all he owned, he would still be guilty of failing to fulfill an infinite obligation to do good everywhere. Even he who gave away all possessions would still be guilty of neglecting the needs of most of mankind, though he would be better than most since he would not neglect as many as the rest do. Not necessarily wicked, each man is necessarily guilty, humanly evil, one who fails to will all that ought to be willed.

The price of guilt is chastisement. This dark, somber truth means that anything less than perpetual chastisement is an undeserved bounty, warranting paeans of thanks to a beneficent nature or a merciful God. Every reward is an unwarranted gift, for men are guilty beings always failing to do all they ought, all they are under obligation to do.

We have heard much in recent years to the effect that doctrines of this stripe paralyze and frighten men, that they overwhelm and discourage them. Were this the consequence it would not follow that the view was untrue but merely that he who was interested in preserving the mental health of men and could take no risks in subjecting them to the winds of doctrine would have to protect them by censorship or other device. Actually the view need not have a debilitating effect. If we stress one side of it, an opposite effect is actually to be expected. If we force into focus the fact that the cosmos is a source of undeserved rewards we will be tempted to become Jack Horners faced with undeserved plums. A cosmos in which one is constantly rewarded beyond one's deserts is a cosmos in which to delight. It may conceivably dampen the ardor for the absolute right, since it may tempt a man to concentrate on his undeserved goods and thereby forget his obligations and guilt. A knowledge of our guilt should serve the excellent purpose of preventing us from becoming too satisfied with the cosmos as it is, too complacent, too ready to believe in luck, too prone to the use of magical devices designed to bring about undeserved goods at desired times.

Avoidable evils usually arise because beings insist on themselves excessively, denying thereby the rightful claims of others and preventing the fullest realization of the absolute good. When men will wrongly, they but insist excessively, in a peculiarly human way, on themselves, and sometimes on behalf of other beings, denying thereby some rightful claims and precluding the greatest possible embodiment of what ought to be. They reconstitute things in ways which do not harmonize them fully with what others seek, are able, or ought to be and do. To have the will operate as it should, they must become virtuous. Lacking virtue they may do much that is good, though this is not likely. Possessing virtue they will still fail to do much that they ought, though they usually will do more good than most. In any case, the evil which they produce they can make less or more, as they will.

XVIII

ADVENTUROUS HUMILITY

1. VIRTUE

A MAN may have the habit of responsibly doing what is right. If so, he will have one or more virtues. A *virtue* is a habit of doing what is right, of so acting as to preserve or enhance values.

A man may willingly produce the greatest possible good. If so, he will be *virtuous*, for virtuousness is the state of one who does what he should.

A man may have virtues and yet not be virtuous; if he is virtuous he must have virtues. Should he habitually live up to the demands of duty he will have the virtue of courage. Should he go beyond the call of duty, should he incidentally exhibit the virtue of courage when and as he transcends it in the act of reconstituting himself and others so that the maximum good is achieved, he will be virtuous.

Virtues are good habits of dealing with beings as having rights in themselves. The virtuous man, through the aid of his virtues, willingly completes himself and others by embodying in them and in himself as much of the good as they can then sustain. He interests himself in making the absolute good concrete and real here and now. He does to and for others what ought to be done for them, even though they do not ask for help. He cooperates with, works for them, not in order to buy their cooperation or even because he has accepted an end which demands that he cooperate but solely because this is a good thing to do. He treats others as both means and end at every moment, living not alongside of but with them, helping them because this is a good which it is right to promote.

As many as are the habitual ways of doing justice to the rights of beings, so many are the virtues which are possible. Whatever their number, though, they can be conveniently collected into four kinds. There are the virtues which stress restraint and those which stress adventure; there are those which promote the good of the agent and those which promote the good of others. Temperance is a virtue of restraint, promoting the good of oneself; gentleness is a virtue stressing restraint so as to make possible the promotion of good for others; ambition is a virtue of adventure primarily promoting the good of oneself; generosity is a virtue of adventure promoting the good of others.

Virtues are beyond the reach of the subhuman and beneath the dignity of the divine, presupposing a combination of tasks and powers not compatible with either. There can be neither virtue nor vice in stones, animals, or gods; only men have the obligation to embody the good everywhere, to enhance all things according to their rights. Only they are capable of habits of responsibly doing what is absolutely right or wrong. Only men can have virtues; only they can be virtuous.

That man has a minimum of virtue who is insensitive to all types of value but one. He avoids doing wrong because he is unaware of temptation. A better man risks doing wrong in the attempt to conquer temptation, and thereby attains or uses new virtues. Such a man would still be inferior to a virtuous man, a man who, though sensitive to the full value of the tempting, found it no temptation. The less virtuous a man, the more insensitive he is; the more virtuous, the wider and deeper his interests. To be completely virtuous is to be absorbed in the realization of the good everywhere.

2. Virtue's Fourfold Form

It is possible to have one virtue without having others. But he who has only one mimics the state of those below him. If he had all the virtues he would, reciprocally, reflect the state of whatever beings there might be above him.

Each virtue illustrates the nature of virtue in limited contexts. Each exhibits all four components with an emphasis all its own. No one of them exclusively stresses adventure or restraint, egoism or altruism. To be exclusively restrained is not to be geared to doing good; to be exclusively adventurous is to be prepared to do much that is wrong. If the virtue benefited the agent alone it would involve a destruction or at least a neglect of others; if it concerned only others it would involve a loss or neglect of himself.

Nothing is so foolish and futile as the effort to be an egoist. To be egoistic without also being altruistic is not only to play at the game of ruining the lives of others by neglecting what they need and deserve, but is to do injustice to oneself. A man's being and prosperity are endangered if others suffer because of what he is or does. His happiness fades in the presence of the misery of friends and relatives; if it did not it would still require for its presence the support of or at least a nonopposition by others. These others must be allowed and perhaps helped to prosper in their own way if we are to be able to profit either from their happiness and aid or from their lack of need of us.

The more anxious we are about ourselves, the further and further

afield we must go to support and preserve the goods of others, for
these make it possible to possess and retain our own. We can seek our
own good only so far as we seek for others the good at least of being
able to stand over against us, with some independence, power, and
dignity. Effective egoism, as Plato saw long ago and reported in the
tale of the shepherd who is best a shepherd when he takes account of
what sheep need, requires us to treat others as having values of their
own, worthy of consideration even if only because such an approach
provides an indispensable means for the achievement by us of a
private, selfish, and unworthy result.

Sheer altruism is no more sensible than sheer egoism. It is a mark of
arrogance, the attempt to give to others what is not held to be sufficiently precious to obtain for oneself, the refusal to provide others
with an object toward which they can be equally altruistic. No man
can rightly seek for others that which he does not hold to be good for
himself. And what is good for himself he can and should make his own.
Altruistic beings are not fully altruistic if they do not desire that
private benefit which accrues to those who devote themselves to the
interests of others. This private glow ought to be something he wants
them also to have. He must allow them to benefit him if he is not to
cheat them of the pleasure of being altruistic too.

If we are to act virtuously with respect to all things, a virtue having
regard for one type of object must be supplemented by virtues having
regard for the remaining types. The more the set is completed, the
more surely is its possessor a virtuous man. Virtuousness requires adventure and restraint, egoism and altruism to be in equipoise. This
result is greatly helped by making use of the Golden Rule. Equating
actor and recipient, outgoingness and passivity, all four tendencies
at once, the Golden Rule points the way by which adventure is to be
balanced by humility and egoism by altruism, enabling men to work
together for the promotion of a good for all.

The virtuous man balances an egoistic effort to treat himself as
ultimately valuable and others as less so by an altruistic effort to
treat himself as having less value than others. He thereby avoids the
egoistic error of supposing that the kingdom of ultimate goods has
only one member, himself, and also the altruistic error of supposing
that one man, himself, has no part of the kingdom. He avoids taking
everything to be a means to the good of the agent or to the good of
everything else but the agent, and thereby doing wrong either to
others or to himself.

All four stresses are balanced in courage, which unites adventurous
egoism with restrained altruism. They are balanced also in liberality
which is restrainedly egoistic and adventurously altruistic. To have

both courage and liberality in one undivided habit is to have the all-inclusive virtue of adventurous humility, from which the others can be obtained by stressing one component more than others and applying the whole in limited domains.

He who is adventurous approaches the universe from his own perspective, seeking to master other things for his own good. The virtue, of course, becomes the madness of unrestraint when there is no consideration of how men are limited in power and capacity; it takes the shape of cruel ambition when it overlooks what other things need and deserve. It does teach a man, however, that there is nothing which he cannot and should not utilize to make himself as perfect as possible, judging things in terms of what he requires and desires. It enables each to see that he has some value and ought to preserve and enhance it by making use of other things. We express its meaning in part when we say that the world is here for us to use to the best of our abilities— important and precious in its own right, yet something to be conquered, controlled, and used.

At the opposite extreme from adventurousness is humility. Man is an insignificant creature in the immensity of nature and should see himself as having slight value when compared with the totality of things. If it is forgotten that a man always has some value, humility becomes the vice of cynicism which treats man as though he were worth nothing, or the folly of cravenness which exaggerates the value and the power of other things.

A man ought to recognize that he is a part of nature, possessing but a fragment of the value of the whole. He should not deny, though, that he has value of his own. Perhaps the remark is unnecessary: the most modest of men knows that modesty is a virtue. He who wished to believe in the ineradicable sinfulness of man could perhaps find no better evidence for it than this ironic truth. Each ought to look at himself from the standpoint of what lies beyond, see himself as others see him, appreciate the value he actually has, know that he is valuable but not essential, important but not all-important, with limited rights and usefulness. If he does, he reaches a true humility, showing regard for the natures and values of other beings, and restricting his conquests so as to do full justice to their value.

Virtue enables a man to determine the nature of his relevant future more precisely than he otherwise could. By means of his virtue he prescribes the range of possible acts in which he will engage. Without it he would be more amorphous, unpredictable, irregular than any mature, habituated, and adjusted being in fact is. The virtues are, if one likes, freedom used in advance to make likely a more decided, favorable result.

A virtuous man decides and acts in terms of a perfection to be obtained and retained. But he acts here and now. As the situation changes, a different way of expressing adventurous humility is required. Responsiveness, not temperance, is wanted on a day of jubilation. Sympathy, not prudence, is called for at a time of grief. Purity is a virtue but it stands in the way of the acquisition of wisdom. Justice sometimes obscures the need to be gentle and friendly. All these are illustrations of the one virtue of adventurous humility in limited contexts, opposing or supplementing the illustration of the same virtue in other contexts at the same time.

In one sense then there is only one virtue—that of adventurous humility—which assumes different forms in different situations. In another sense there are as many virtues as there are distinct contexts in which restraint and adventure can be brought together to promote one's own good and the good of others. In the one case virtue is a generic habit, in the other it is a particular habit. Every instance of genuine virtue has both a general and a particular side, allowing us to take it both as illustrated by and one among the others.

As attention is shifted from things which need improvement most to those which need it least, one component of adventurous humility must be emphasized more than the other. There are times when we ought to be more adventurous; other times when we ought to be more humble. A maintenance of the balance between the two requires that as much weight be given to the one as to the other only in those cases where the objects on which a man works are as valuable as he is himself.

The traditional lists of virtues reflect interest in limited contexts. A practice of looking only to such special contexts hardens the tendency to exaggerate the value of some one virtue, with the result that the individual, though acting then as he ought, acquires an attitude which prevents him from acting appropriately in other cases. "Every man has his fault, and honesty is his." It is the wise and courageous soldier who becomes the timid and foolish statesman or the arrogant and ruthless dictator. Virtues appropriate to one context are mistakenly carried over into inappropriate ones.

It is possible to master the virtue of adventurous humility in one context and not in another. It is possible therefore to have virtue even when one is doing wrong. In fact it is essential to have virtue if wrongs are to be produced deliberately. A wicked man must be prudent, temperate, and courageous. Otherwise he is a hopeless blunderer. His villainy consists in his willful commission of a wrong, to realize which he utilizes habits of virtue which should have been directed to the doing of something right. What he does is at once absolutely right in a limited domain and absolutely and relatively wrong taken as a whole.

There is much good in a villain, more than is sometimes found in those who vehemently oppose him. He is a man of strong will who excellently exercises a limited form of the virtue of adventurous humility under the dominating guidance of a desire to injure. Most men, like the villain, have only limited virtues. But they either are not guided by a desire to injure or are guided by a desire to help. In behalf of his country and his fellow soldiers a man might scheme to get rid of a bombastic and naïve general such as Othello was. His act would be just as wrong as Iago's but it would not be villainous, because performed with the objective not of destroying but of enhancing values.

Tradition has more or less, though not entirely, hardened the use of the terms "virtue" and "vice" to describe excellent habits which have to do only with the good of man. But traditional ethics is too anthropomorphic to be adequate to the comprehension of man's responsibilities. It is wrong for a man to kick a dog, mutilate an insect, step on a sea shell wantonly, irrespective of whether those actions affect his attitude or behavior toward his fellows, or whether or not his fellows are in any way concerned with what he has done. These are wrong acts even if the man is too insensitive to be affected by the outcome, or even if what he does is unknown to others. A brute of a man kicking a dog in the privacy of his cellar may not give the matter another thought, and his act will be unknown to others. Yet, for all that, it is a vicious act, an unwarranted one, absolutely and irreducibly wrong.

Ethics cannot stop short of a consideration of all kinds of things so far as they are possible objects or conditions for voluntary action. Every being whatsoever is within its purview; every being limits man and may become the object of his act, through some intermediary. Let us stop then following the traditional ethicists in their shameful neglect of the truths all men know. There is something amiss when one animal kills another, even though the killer is thereby pleased or even when the act promotes the good of the species or the good of man. It is not indifferent that there are things which are ugly, plants which do not flourish, and animals in pain, whether these facts be known by man or affect him in any significant way. Hunting is no mere game, even though it is not men who are hunted. A daffodil improves the world, just by being itself, and it is wrong to destroy it out of hand. Even a disease germ, playing havoc on all about, has value in itself. To exterminate it is relatively right, but inseparable from an absolute wrong.

There are multiple defects in all things. Their removal does not necessarily contribute to man's well-being. To ignore the things and their values is to suggest to man activities which do not increase and which may result in a decrease in the total good there is or will be.

Because men *must* use and destroy other beings does not mean that the use and the destruction are not wrong. Eating is no mere indifferent activity; it is ethical through and through, not only in the sense that it affects the well-being of the eater but also because the eaten is thereby forced to contribute to another's good. It is justifiable if the good to which the eaten contributes is greater than its own, and if that good needs the latter in order to be. Eating, however, can never be an act unqualifiedly right, for it always involves a loss of the value of the eaten. Vegetarians avoid one evil in order to concentrate on another. They are appreciative of the value of animals but overlook the value which vegetables embody, and which the vegetarians together with the animals cheerfully and somewhat excessively destroy. We can mitigate and relatively justify, we cannot avoid, all the wrong which the act of eating necessarily involves.

The use of another, even if it thereby participates in or contributes to a greater glory, can be justified only if there otherwise would be a loss of that higher value altogether. Gluttony sins against the right of lower beings to remain unmolested so long as they are not needed for the preservation of that which is superior to them. Political radicalism is gluttony in the affairs of state. Unless there is an intolerable state of affairs, unless this is the only means for preserving a state otherwise on the verge of extinction, a revolution is not desirable; anything less than a desperate revolution abandons unique and irreplaceable values before they have to be abandoned. Needs ought to be anticipated, but they should not be satisfied before they have arisen.

3. ABSOLUTE RIGHTS AND OBLIGATIONS

An ethics is unethical if it does not take account of the rights and values things have in themselves. It must have a cosmic sweep, comprehending all that is good and bad and its possible perfection.

Each existent has a right to the value it has, a claim to exist as it is and promises best to be. To deny it this right is absolutely wrong. Each being contributes to the constitution of a collective good proportionately to the value it has, and each has a right therefore to be enhanced in value proportionately to its contribution. The more its value is enhanced, the more it contributes to the constitution of the good and the more it therefore deserves to get in return. Each being precisely because it has a right to have its value enhanced, therefore, has a right to have its rights increased. All beings together make possible a collective good whose realization involves an increase in the value of them severally and together; this result in turn makes possible a richer good, and so on endlessly.

A man's obligations extend beyond his rights, for they extend to the good. He owes it to the good to realize it. That good realized is existence enhanced. He ought to perfect others and himself because he owes it to the good to realize it, and this requires that he perfect them and himself.

A man must not only respect the rights of others to retain the values that they have but must try to fulfill their demands to have their rights increased. He is under direct obligation to them to respect their rights and under an indirect obligation to increase their rights, the latter being a consequence of his obligation toward the good which is to be realized.

No one is so powerful and so well organized that he alone is able to bring the good into existence in such a way that each being is perfect and in perfect harmony with others. All that an individual can do is acknowledge this as his absolute obligation and prepare himself to fulfill it at every moment to the maximum possible degree. So far as he succeeds in effectively willing the good, he remakes the world by increasing the values of other beings. He also thereby remakes, perfects himself, enhancing his own value and thereby increasing his own rights.

To fulfill one's obligation is to be at once selfish and altruistic, adventurous and restrained. Because no man can do all he should, none can ever be as selfish or as altruistic, as adventurous or as restrained as he ought to be. There is though no preassigned limit to what he can do. Every man fails and must fail to be perfectly ethical, to do all that he is obligated to do. But just where he will fail and to what degree, he can discover only after he together with others, has made a concerted effort to live up to his obligation to the full.

Man is the guilty creature, a being who can never entirely live up to his obligations, and knows it. He never succeeds in being as perfect as it is possible for a man to be because he never succeeds in perfecting others to the degree they deserve. But there is no particular wrong he must commit, no particular form his failure must assume. He cannot limit his responsibility in the hope of thereby living up to it more successfully, for any portion of the world he might exclude as outside his interest is no more alien to his nature than any other portion, and is, in principle, just as realizable as the rest. What is necessarily unrealizable by a man is the whole good in its entire reach, but this he might be able to bring about with the help of others. Men are obligated to realize a good beyond their individual, not necessarily beyond their collective, capacities to realize.

A man ought to do all he can, but what he ought to do is not defined by what he happens to be able to do. Even if a man were as powerful as a man could possibly be, he would have obligations he could not fulfill. Men are inescapably guilty, because to be human they must take upon themselves the realization of the absolute good. They must realize that good if they are to be complete men.

Unlike the relative responsibility of fulfilling a commitment to realize an end, the obligation to realize the good goes beyond the need to justify a choice; it requires one to do more than make up for losses in value. A man obligates himself to bring the good about in whatever way is possible to a man—therefore not through an endless life, or by erupting as a volcano does, or by living without food or shelter. He is obligated to realize the good through a creative, dynamically free use of all his powers and what they make possible.

Obligated to do whatever he can to realize his obligation, yet unable to realize the whole good now, a man should either a) use instruments which conquer the limitations of circumstance; b) cooperate with others; c) obtain the help of some other power; or d) alter his nature.

a) If he is to act with respect to beings at a distance, having powers and requirements which transcend his reach, a man must turn to science or technology. These will provide him with agencies which will help him do what he ought. He may by their aid get himself to the position where he can do what he as an individual ought; he will not necessarily get the things done or succeed in doing all he should. This sometimes needs the work of a group of beings, an organization.

b) Even such a quiet, apparently self-maintained activity as the pursuit of knowledge presupposes work on the part of others which might have been done by oneself. It is conducted by men who eat, drink, move, and act on objects, disturbing, modifying, and destroying some, if for no other reason than that these activities are necessary if such men are to exist. These men, no less than others, are able to free themselves from some tasks only because they make themselves part of a wider community which takes over some of their obligations. An organization allocates and distributes the work of men in such a way as to enable each to engage in projects outside his interests and to bring about results beyond their several capacities. It is man's hope that cooperative enterprises will suffice to bring about whatever good the individual cannot. The hope cannot be realized. No man can transfer his obligation to an organization without thereby pledging himself to sustain that organization, and without that organization therefore adding to his burdens. And should the organization fail to do what should be done, he has no other recourse but to reassume the obligation and fulfill it as best he can.

c) Should it be the case that men cannot do what they ought, severally or together, even when using knowledge, organizations, art, and other devices at their disposal, they have two recourses. They can look to a God for help, or they can change themselves. But men ought not to look to a God until they have reached the limit of human capacity. God is an ethical vanishing point, necessary only to the degree that obligations are beyond the hope of fulfillment. Ethically viewed, He is the unprobed residue in the state or man, to which men give exterior status and to which they refer in times of tragedy and incompetence. He may prove to be, for ethics, an unnecessary hypothesis, since we have no need of Him except at the point where all human power, present and future, fails. But then we cannot rightly invoke Him, in an ethics, until all other forces have been fully expended.

"God" is for the ethical man not the name of a being who does work; He is the name of that reserve, that residue which might be left over after all other agencies have been employed. The orthodox religions have work for God to do because, having antecedently limited man's powers and agencies, there is nothing left to them but the denial of man's obligations or the insistence that God actually does help man fulfill those obligations. Unfortunately for their position, man's limits are not evident and God's existence, nature, and operation not clearly known. We have no right to say that God functions as an ethical agent, that he perfects anything. The religious man has faith that God does exist and will do what ought to be done. His God, though, he at times admits, will not come into the open again until history is done, at the Day of Last Judgment, and thus cannot be a vital factor in any ethics having to do with what exists now in this world of ours. He is really where the rest of us are, incapable of invoking a God to make possible the realization of the good which we are all obligated to realize.

d) Man's task is to alter himself if what he now is and does does not suffice to bring about the good. He has an infinite task and is guilty if he does not complete it, whether this be because there are no instruments available or because he does not get all the help he needs. He would be free from his infinite task if he did not have to realize perfection—but then of course he would be less valuable than he actually is. He cannot withdraw from the state of having an infinite obligation without denying that he is a man, for to be a man is to want perfection realized.

Man is perpetually guilty because he has an infinite obligation and a finite power. He has a future which belongs to others as well; he can properly make it his own only by giving them their appropriate share —and this he never fully does. To deny that he is guilty is to deny that he owes himself and others a perfection which he cannot entirely bring about. It is to deny that he ought to do or has failed to do what is absolutely right. He reduces his guilt to the degree that he perfects others and himself. Since he inevitably leaves something still to be perfected, he must continue indefinitely in the task of enhancing the values of all.

Man alone is able to recognize his obligation and fulfill it to some extent. A lack of knowledge on his part, though, of what good and evil are does not remove his guilt. Nor could any God wash that guilt away. His guilt is not a consequence of sin but of the fact that he owes it to himself and others to be perfect, and this obligation he can never entirely fulfill. The mother laments and blames herself because she cannot make her child as happy and as perfect as possible, though this is beyond her power. She knows the guilt of being human in a poignant way. The rest of us do not differ from her except in the locus of our distress and the degree of anguish we feel at various times.

Absolute guilt, the guilt of being unable to fulfill one's obligations, differs from the guilt of having made a wrong choice. The latter is a consequence of doing what is relatively wrong, whereas the former is a consequence of not having done all that is absolutely right. The great tragedies, particularly those of the Greeks, are rooted in the acknowledgment that men are guilty because the fates are against them, which is but a special way of remarking the truth that there are things beyond their power but which they are obligated to do and for whose failure they are responsible. Men would be without guilt if they were able to realize perfection, but then they would not be finite and thus not human.

A man of good will resolves to focus on the absolute good and is resolute in holding to that good in the face of other intriguing prospects. If he is virtuous as well he enhances the values of existents in harmony with one another, actually realizes the good which he wills. He balances adventure and humility with respect to himself and others. No man, however, is completely virtuous to begin with; seldom is he virtuous to a high degree for long periods. Every act of his is an experiment in being virtuous, and never yields a perfect or final answer. Since to benefit one thing some must be ignored, others used as instruments, and still others destroyed, the most a man can promise himself is to do as much good as possible, to set himself to enhance the values of all beings at every moment and to minimize the wrongs he must necessarily commit.

Just as he who wishes to choose a realizable end must keep his absolute wrongs to a minimum, so he who wishes to be ethical must do as little wrong as he can. The difference between them is that while the former avoids wrongs because of what they commit him to do, the latter avoids wrongs because he is obligated to do the good. Both are creative. But only if they creatively *will* do they express their human freedom outside as well as inside the limits imposed by the body, the past, neighbors, and the world. Only the creative will enables them to bring to realization that ultimate good all beings need and which man alone obligates himself to realize.

The highest form of activity is creative willing, the virtuous balancing of adventure and humility, altruism and egoism, in theory and in practice. Theory and practice must evidently be reconciled. Until they are we cannot take proper account of the needs of minds as well as bodies.

4. Practical and Theoretical Men

Because both practical and theoretical men are men they are interested both in the concretely real and in not yet realized ideals. Neither of these interests can be completely inhibited without disaster. To be immersed in the concrete, without concern for what ought to be, is to live without plan, without hope, and without responsibility. To lose oneself in the ideal, conversely, is to live without roots, inert, idly dreaming of what may never be. To attempt the former is to attempt to live the life of a brute; to attempt the latter is to attempt to live a life possible only to a God. We do live and ought to try to live as men, enriching the real by means of the ideal and illuminating the ideal by means of the real.

There are two ways, however, of being concerned with the real. One can concentrate on it in its particularity, on it as occurring here and now, standing in contrast with whatever else there may be. Or one can acknowledge it as exemplifying universal principles which are embodied in all existents, everywhere. The former stress is intensive, exclusive, relative, that of the practical man; the latter is extensive, inclusive, absolute, that of the theoretical man.

Neither type of man is entirely devoid of the spirit that animates the other. The practical man grasps something of what is common to many things; otherwise he would not learn from experience, and would have to encounter each fact directly in order to know anything about it at all. The theoretical man grasps something of the unique flavor of what he now confronts; otherwise he would be unable to distinguish things and would not know that existents agree, not only in having common traits but in having divergent flavors. The two types of men nevertheless differ in interest, the one primarily adjusting himself to a limited environment and a limited group of men, the other working more directly to bring about a harmonious cosmic whole.

This difference in stress toward the real leads practical and theoretical men to assume different attitudes toward the ideal, and eventually to act in radically different ways. The practical man is concerned only with those ideals that can function as plans or programs, showing how to make the future better. He finds no joy in the contemplation of ideals as such. Those that are not pertinent to what is going on here and now, or that cannot function as instruments for the achievement of particular goods, he puts aside as fantasies which hover over moments of idleness or even folly. The theoretical man, on the other hand, enjoys the contemplation of ideals and concentrates on those which have a more universal and constant meaning. He does not look at these ideals as agencies for improving what is real here and now. The reverse rather is the case. He makes use of the real as a means for getting a better grip on the ideal.

The objective of both is a unity of real and ideal. But they desire unities of different kinds and achieve them in different ways. The practical man desires to unite distinct items of reality with limited ideals, whereas the contemplative man desires to unite universal ideals with the single substantial whole of all existence. The one attempts to transform reality so that it acquires a desired form; the other attempts to provide ideals with their proper correlate.

The two ways of approaching the real and the ideal and of integrating them abut on one another. Each results in the achievement of goods one ought to have. It is tempting then to shuttle back and forth between them in order to have both of them together. The temptation must be resisted for in that way one loses the full value of each and blurs the meaning of both. It is desirable that the child and the student be so prepared that they can go either way; but by the time a man is mature he ought to decide to go one way or the other, or some third way combining the merits of both.

A general might write philosophy on the side, a poet might chop wood for exercise. They do not then follow two modes of life, but only one, using the other as means to fill in interstices. Each as a mode of life demands a full measure of concentration and devotion. It is irresponsible to pledge oneself to be practical and to make the world better today, and yet refuse to make it better tomorrow or to preserve the gains one has achieved. It is equally irresponsible to pledge oneself to be theoretical and to cherish the absolute good today, and yet refuse to cherish them tomorrow or to hold on to what has already been mastered. Neither end is once and for all attained. The world ought always to be improved; the good ought always to be better mastered. No gain is permanent; each must be constantly renewed.

The practical and theoretical man should be one. Since the very nature of existence requires that some detailed work be done here now, every man must be practical. It is desirable that he be theoretical; but it is not essential to his very existence. The end result that is to be achieved is therefore one which requires that account be taken of necessary practicality. The so-called practical man does not do this; he exaggerates the necessity that some practice be engaged in into an unwarranted demand that nothing be recognized but the realm of practice, thereby leaving practice dull, undirected, and less good than it should be. To be full men, doing what we ought, we must be as theoretical as possible and practical only as much as we must. Only then will we succeed in encompassing all that can be encompassed by man.

Here and now while stretching the mind to the limits of its capacities we must and we should engage in necessary practical affairs, thereby remaking ourselves into men who unite the two in fresh and more satisfactory ways than we had. Only so far as we do this can we actually perfect ourselves.

If we properly weld adventure and humility we will function as men whose minds and bodies have been stretched to their limits in harmony. But if we do not also make room for sacrifice (and for love) we will not succeed in balancing egoism and altruism. Indeed we can view theorizing as the outcome of a necessary sacrifice which body makes to mind, in the effort to have the two of them work in harmony for benefit to both and the objects with which they are occupied. This can perhaps be seen more clearly after we have achieved a better understanding first of the nature of sacrifice, and then of the nature of love.

XIX

SACRIFICE

1. The Problem

SACRIFICE is an idea charged with paradox—which is only to say it is an idea but partly grasped.

a) The most extreme form of sacrifice is that in which a man gives up the meaning of his life for the sake of another. It is perhaps the most praiseworthy of all the acts of which he is capable. But how can an act be praiseworthy if it involves the loss of something as precious as a human life? Can an act be praiseworthy which precludes the making of further efforts to bring about what is good? Can that act be good which makes impossible further goods?

b) We sacrifice ourselves for others. Do those others have a claim on us? Do we in sacrifice but pay back what we owe? If so, ours is an act by which we fulfill an obligation and deserve nothing but the praise which accrues to one who does his duty. But if others have no claim on us, we give up what we have a right to, so as to benefit one who does not and cannot have a right to it. If a good act requires that altruism be balanced by egoism, can sacrifice be good?

c) He who sacrifices is to be praised for his virtue. He acquires in the act the distinction of being one who has so far been ennobled. Yet if his sacrifice ennobles him, wherein is his sacrifice? If what he loses, gives up, forfeits, but provides the occasion for his attaining that most desirable state of being a really good man, what can his sacrifice be but a strategy for getting what he ought and perhaps wants to have?

d) There is sacrifice only if what is given up is thought to have some value. It is something appreciated, wanted, clung to, given up only under the compulsion of circumstance. Yet there is no sacrifice unless there is a volition, a free, outgoing, generous act. But can an act be at once free and compelled?

e) So far as a self is active, it is not sacrificed; so far as it is sacrificed, it cannot be sacrificing. The self which sacrifices cannot be the self which is sacrificed; yet there is no true self-sacrifice unless the two be one.

Sacrifice would seem to be both praiseworthy and not praiseworthy, appropriate yet excessive, a self-denial which is self-rewarding, a free act which is compelled, demanding an actor who is wholly passive.

There is something amiss here, or self-sacrifice is so absurd as to be below the possibility of existence or beyond the grasp of reason. Since sacrifices do occur, and since nothing should be antecedently placed beyond the grasp of reason, we must begin with the supposition that there is something amiss. And we must not rest until we find what it is, and use our discovery so as to make evident what it is we all somehow already vaguely but surely know.

2. The Inescapability of Sacrifice

Sometimes men give up their time, money, energy, reputations, and in the last resort their lives to promote the good of others. Their acts may or may not be required. Whether they are or not, though, they are not different in principle from those in which they engage all the time.

All of us constantly cut into our substances; we are forced to deny ourselves at every moment in order to do anything at all. Each of our activities demands the exercise of some restraint. Even when we concentrate on ourselves, when we are most egocentric, we sacrifice some tendency and satisfaction we could have furthered had we done something else instead.

We sacrifice regretfully. We would rather that a sacrifice were not required of us or of others. Still, it always is, as part of a present act of doing something definite. We do not inhibit a tendency to drink, run, and play in order to make eating easier, better, more desirable—though these may be consequences—but as an element in the organic process of making eating a definite, specific act. Eating requires the neglect and suppression of other activities; like every other in which we engage it has definiteness, structure, direction only so far as other possible activities are then and there kept in the background. Sacrifice, even when serving as a means for the production of goods, is inseparable from another, more egocentric, supplementary, affirmative, positive, self-assertive activity constituting with it a single organic act.

Sacrifice is unavoidable. It is also valuable. Firstly, what is good deserves concentration and devotion. Not to give it our attention, not to devote ourselves to it, not to put aside possible competitors is to slight it, to do injustice to it. We ought to be loyal to the values we discern, denying, sacrificing an interest in other things in order better to concentrate on these. We show our appreciation and love by what we deny, by the degree of concentration we devote to an object. He who loved all things to the same degree would love few adequately— if his relation to them could be called love at all.

Secondly, our lives have limited patterns and structures, partly dictated by ourselves and partly by circumstance, each demanding the slighting and even forfeit of a host of things. If we tried to avoid determining what pattern we should have, we would deny ourselves the right to decide what ought to be given up and when, and nevertheless would have to neglect as much as or more than we had before. To allow circumstances rather than oneself to determine what is to be given up and when is to deny oneself the benefit of guiding action by knowledge; it is to risk losing direction, control, and unity for no gain. It is good to sacrifice, for in this way we, not circumstances, determine what limited pattern is to be ours.

3. Grades of Sacrifice

Sacrifices occur all the time. They are required if anything definite is to be done. We shall hereafter, however, follow common usage and call only those acts sacrifices which regard the needs of others more than is usual, and which generously express and try to produce a good for others, which stress altruism at the expense of egoism.

The more valuable the object sacrificed, the greater the degree of the sacrifice. The more valuable the sacrificed object is thought to be, the greater the nobility of him who sacrifices it. There might be little nobility involved in a sacrifice of a valuable object; much in the sacrifice of an inconsequential one. A miser who gives up his gold, a glutton who gives up his food, a child who gives up a toy, a saint who gives up his life may all, so far as nobility is concerned, be on a level. But the degree of their sacrifices would nevertheless differ radically.

Were there no objective values, were every value only the function of an interest, a private judgment, or arbitrary decision, these different sacrifices might be equal in worth. But he who gives up a life which he held to be of little value does not perform a lesser sacrifice than he who gives up a little time, though this was thought to be very precious. He has less nobility but his sacrifice is greater in degree. It surely is not true that the more arrogant and conceited a man the greater is his self-sacrifice, or that a self-sacrifice on the part of one with real humility is without value. The former's sacrifice may be more noble than the latter's but it is not greater in degree.

When we honor heroes we rightly refuse to ask what value they put on their lives. We ask only whether they risked their lives more than we have a right to expect of men. It is of course a reasonable assumption that all men value their lives to about the same extent. Yet it is not because we make such an assumption that we are ready to honor equally all those who sacrifice themselves in the same way and for the same reasons. Even if we knew that a hero had put little value on his life, we would not honor him less than we would another who had put a great value on his. Starting with the acknowledgment that his life is no more and no less precious than any other, we honor him for engaging in a higher degree of sacrifice than that which is normally practiced.

It is true, of course, that in our society and most surely in aristocratic societies, those on top assign little value to the lives of those below, and often conclude that when those lives are sacrificed the act is less significant than a similar one performed by a member of the upper class would be. Aristocrats do not think of themselves as arbitrarily assigning a low value to the lives of those in the lower classes; on the contrary they think of themselves as making a correct judgment of the true value which those lives have in and by themselves. They are mistaken, I think. In any case they are not willful. They do not hold that the value of a life depends on the point of view one has regarding it. They know that the value of a life is not determined by feeling, by judgment, by the attitude one takes with respect to it. Their mistake is more serious; it is ontological rather than epistemological. They erroneously suppose that some men can be of human kind and yet be devoid of a common human nature.

Though all aristocrats believe there is an intrinsic difference between men, some aristocrats approach all men as though they had the same value. Balancing them are democrats who, while believing that all men have the same human nature, disapprove, dislike, hate, and even enslave others. The attitudes of these men are not appropriate to the facts as they themselves interpret them. They allow some incidental, accidental quality or occurrence to lead them astray, and as a consequence they fail to answer objective values with an attitude proportioned to those values.

Empiricism in ethics and elsewhere proves to be unsatisfactory largely because it is so prone to substitute a priori theories for obtrusive facts. Surely it is unrealistic to say that the aristocrat, even when he acts as though all men were equal, supposes that they are. No less than the democrat he firmly believes self-sacrifice is to be evaluated in terms of a value which the life sacrificed has intrinsically. Agreeing with the democrat on this score, he may or may not agree with him in attitude and act, and in any case, disagrees with him as to the value men intrinsically have.

The aristocrat and democrat have different opinions about the nature of men. They both acknowledge that there are objective human natures, shot through with value. The aristocrat is justified so far as he looks at man in social contexts, for there men differ in function and in achieved public value; the democrat is justified so far as he looks at man in himself, for in himself a man has the same degree of value as every other. A democrat who would not acknowledge that some men had proved themselves to be of greater benefit to society than others, that some had achieved more and perhaps even had promise for doing more social good than others, would ignore quite commonplace truths, and would somewhat simple-mindedly suppose that what a man was on the outside was nothing but the reflex of what he was on the inside. Similarly, an aristocrat who denied that some men of lower station could and sometimes did contribute to society as much and sometimes even more than many men of higher station would deny a truth of history and make the unwarranted supposition that men had no other value but what they or their ancestors had already manifested. The aristocrat's error is graver, for it translates a public, a superficial difference into an essential one, whereas the democrat merely ignores a public difference, skips a fact instead of contradicting one.

4. STRATEGY AND SACRIFICE

The highest form of sacrifice is self-sacrifice, the deliberate acceptance of a most undesirable alternative, usually entailing the loss of one's life, or at least making such a loss most likely. At first glance such sacrifice seems to be indistinguishable from suicide. Yet the two are poles apart. Suicide is the expression of weakness, self-sacrifice of strength. The one is selfish, the other not. One can be excused perhaps, but never praised; the other can be lamented perhaps, but never blamed.

Both the suicide and the self-sacrificing man can act as remote or immediate causes. They both can place themselves in the path of something which will take their lives, and both can go the length of wielding the instruments by which their lives are taken. The one, though despised, may prove the cause of great goods to come; the other, though praised, may be the occasion for the production of little good. The death of the suicide may be the occasion for the distribution of his wealth to more worthy men and for more worthy causes; the act of self-sacrifice may turn out to have been unnecessary. The two, suicide and self-sacrifice differ not in act or result but in aim, in what they seek to accomplish.

In suicide death is not submitted to. Rather it is chosen, and then as a means for avoiding something else. In self-sacrifice death is not chosen. Rather it is accepted, submitted to as a consequence of an effort to reach something else. The self-sacrificing man dies incidentally while reaching out, while giving something to someone; the suicide dies purposely at the end of an act of retreat, while holding on to himself as much as possible. The one is altruistic, the other is egocentric. What the one gives up is just as precious as what the other does, but the one does it in order to bring about a good, primarily for others, while the other does it to escape an evil and then for himself. Their acts are quite different though they may have a common appearance and a similar outcome.

A sacrifice, no matter how much virtue it reveals and how much good it brings about, is always to be regretted. It involves the loss of value. To make it reasonable, it must be shown to be valuationally necessary, the cause or occasion for bringing about equal or greater values elsewhere. But if this be the case, we must abandon, even reverse the usual accounts of sacrifice which suppose that it is possible and perhaps desirable to sacrifice to God or state.

Theologians commonly speak of sacrifice as primarily and essentially consisting of the destruction or forfeit of something valuable for the sake of attaining a community with God. Their position has both philological and historical justification. "To sacrifice" is in any dictionary to make something sacred, holy, to dedicate it, to consecrate it; for any history, sacrifice begins and perhaps ends with the loss of the valuable for the sake of divinity. But common speech and common sense have outrun the dictionaries and the histories. The term is now well secularized. It makes good sense to speak of the sacrifice of one's time, and of a sacrifice for an ideal or for a child.

What theologians term a sacrifice on behalf of a God is in principle similar to that which the Greeks endorsed on behalf of the state. Both assert that there are times when men ought to give up their most precious possessions, and perhaps even their lives, to the power that produced or sustains them. Both are faced with the difficulty that, if God or the state were perfect, the sacrifice could not benefit them. There is point to a sacrifice of a great and perhaps irreplaceable value to a perfect being if a) this is a means of increasing the value of the sacrificed, or b) the sacrifice can be warranted regardless of any benefits or losses it might involve.

a) Just as a seed gains in value in being conveyed from package to ground, so it might be said our possessions and perhaps even our lives gain in value in being transferred to an altar, a common fund, or the control of a state. A higher power might therefore ask us for sacrifices so as to benefit those possessions or selves. It is not evident, however, that we ought to give up everything to another which that other could benefit more than we could. It is hard to believe that a parent should give up his child to anyone who could care for and perhaps even love it more than he can. And in any case, when a man gives up his life to a God or to a state, he does not evidently thereby increase the value of that life. It is not certain that he who dies both lives on under the aegis of a state or God and is actually ennobled by them. It may be that many of us will in fact, when this life is over, suffer a sad decline in status.

If it be said that a man ought to die for a state or God because he is thereby ennobled by them, we but commend self-sacrifice as a kind of strategy, as a kind of prudence in which one takes what seems to be the worse but actually is the better part. And then one does not really sacrifice *to* a state or God but uses them, turns them into instruments so that something else can be enriched.

b) It is possible to maintain that whatever value we have is borrowed from some superior good. Being borrowed, it might be argued, it must be returned on demand. This, roughly, is the patriot's view. He supposes that he owes his state all the value which his life embodies and that he, as a conscientious, responsible man, must be ready, when the circumstances demand, to return what he had been loaned for a while. Socrates held a similar view in the *Phaedo*.

He who acts in this way acts out of a sense of justice. He pays a debt. He gives up his life to that to which he owed it, recognizing that if he refused it would be taken from him anyway, or would be defined to be without value since it would thereupon be cut off from the source of all value. He is a dutiful, perhaps a calculating man; he is not a sacrificing one. Misconstruing what he owes, moreover, he does little more than make a grand gesture and an unreasonable response. Starting with the supposition that a life owes its value to state or God, he goes on to commit the error of giving up something truly valuable without allowing any possibility for the loss being compensated. Destroying an irreplaceable value he impoverishes the world, and therefore does not what is right but what is wrong.

The category of justice is inadequate to encompass the meaning of sacrifice. Justice demands of us that we return what we owe; that we give another its due. In sacrifice, though, we return more than we ever borrowed, and surely, so far as other men are concerned, give them more than is their due from us. Sacrifice is not the consequence of an effort to pay a debt. It is the outcome of a desire to give others what they should have, regardless of whether or not we first borrowed from them. However, he who sacrifices in order to pay a debt comes closer to imitating a true act of sacrifice than does he who destroys something in order to establish a community with a God. The latter engages in an act of surgery. He gets rid of obstacles in the way of the possession of a desired good. His act is a strategy in which he gives up something he ought not have for the sake of what he ought. He should perhaps be congratulated on his shrewdness, on his confidence, on his faith, but not for his generosity, for a sacrifice.

We might well praise those who were willing to return to God what belongs to Him. We might even praise those who were willing to give up what was their own in order that they might thereby come closer to Him. We might praise them for their foresight, for their ability to detach themselves from what they had viewed as their very own. But we could not rightly praise them for having sacrificed. Their acts, because done on behest but not on behalf of a God, would not be acts *for* Him. And, because designed to benefit themselves, they would lack the graces which would make them generous, praiseworthy acts—and thus sacrifices.

5. The Process of Equalization

We are unable to sacrifice ourselves, or anything else for that matter, on behalf of something superior. He who gives something to a superior subtracts from his own and adds to the other's value or power; he thereby increases the distance between himself and it. Should that superior be another man, the giver would increase a distance that should be shortened; should that superior be a perfect being, the giver would vainly try to improve what could not be improved, and would unnecessarily reduce the power or value of what should be enhanced. At best, we can give up precious things in order to allow those things or ourselves to be enhanced, or in order to fulfill an obligation—reasons which reveal that such acts are not generous enough, are too calculating, to be acts of sacrifice.

If sacrifice is to be possible, it must be an act on behalf either of an equal or of an inferior. It cannot be the former. What point would there be in one man dying so another might live, if there be no difference in value between them, in fact or in promise? If one life is as precious as the next, there can be no reason for preferring one to another. If there is to be a warrant for sacrifice, that on whose behalf the sacrifice is made must be inferior.

We admire a Father Damien who lived with the lepers, or a man who gives up his life to save an unknown beggar or a crippled child. We praise those who sacrifice themselves for the sake of the sick and the miserable, the unformed and the malformed, the bad and the confused. A sacrifice must be for an inferior. But we ought to sacrifice ourselves for no one less than men, for otherwise we reduce the values in the world beyond the possibility of recovery. Since men as men are all equal, self-sacrifice must be a means for helping others exhibit and enjoy a common humanity to the degree the rest of us do. It must enable equals to free themselves from, to conquer or to transcend an undesirable but unessential inequality.

Even when a man dies for the sake of another who, from all appearances is no worse than he, the sacrifice is made on behalf of an inferior. He who sees another about to drown enjoys the momentary advantage of not having his life then in danger. He who is in a boat capable of holding only one has, over against one who tries desperately to get in, the advantage of being able to decide whose life is to be saved. He has the opportunity of exercising that unique privilege of man, the opportunity to make a free choice or to will creatively. He is his brother's keeper because he has the power to decide his fate. If he decided in his own favor, he would give to himself and deny to the other the opportunity to decide freely in the future. He would take advantage of his momentary superiority in status to deprive another of the opportunity to attain that state himself. Only through a decision in favor of another is it made evident that he really believes the other is a man as well, deserving as a man does the right to make decisions. He who decides in his own favor turns an opportunity into a privilege. He denies his basic equality with another and, in an important sense, transcending political distinctions, he is antidemocratic. In the very act in which he uses a power characteristic of all men, he defines himself not to be as human as the other.

6. The Rights of Man

Men are members of the same species, or in current biological terminology they are members of the same "family." This fact, supported by the investigations of biologists, physiologists, anthropologists, and psychologists, is confirmed by philosophic inquiries into the nature of speech and mind. All men, despite countless diversities in background, disposition, and achievement, belong to one natural group. This compels one to reject theories of racism and nationalism so far as these involve the supposition that some men have a natural destiny, right, or obligation not characteristic of the others.

All are equally entitled to that which enables them to exercise the functions of beings of their kind. Each man must be recognized to be deserving of human shelter and food, of an opportunity to grow, feel, think, and know, and of protection against injury, disease, and unnecessary pain. Some of these rights, such as that to food or to protection against disease, enable men to be living members of their species; others, such as the right to adequate human shelter or to protection against unnecessary pain, enable them to act in ways most beneficial to themselves and the rest. Together these guarantee what might be termed the *principle of human equality*, the right of every man to live and act in ways characteristic of humans.

Occasionally a denial of some of these rights seems justified. This cannot be because the individuals made to suffer are beings whose color, physiognomy, or rhythm differs from the rest. To justify the abridgment of human rights one must show that that provides the most satisfactory or just remedy against those who deprive others of their right to live as men; it must be seen as a kind of sacrifice by which these very rights can be more successfully and universally affirmed.

The acknowledgment of the principle of human equality does not presuppose the existence of any particular form of government. Dictatorships have at times explicitly accepted it; democracies have at times implicitly rejected it. It is compatible with monarchy and communism, with nationalism and internationalism. If by democracy though one means a way of life open to all the people, then this principle is an essential part of a democratic creed. A true democracy will not only affirm but assure it, while a true antidemocracy will not only deny it but prevent its realization. Such democracies and antidemocracies are in complete and irreconcilable opposition. To embrace the former but not to oppose the latter, to oppose the latter but not to defend the former, in theory or in practice, is to be but partially good, opponents of the false and evil or defenders of the true and good, but not yet both together. Until we are both we do not preserve while we enhance, conquer evil while we do good, wholeheartedly support the principle of human equality.

Each man is unique, with a value all his own. He is not merely one of a kind, a unit in a multitude, one who occupies a position in space not occupied by another, or who contains matter which another does not. He is also a person, a responsible, conscious being, possessing a nature no other has. He has a dignity and worth intrinsically as important and as deserving of respect as any other. To affirm this is to affirm the *principle of personal equality*. It is to recognize that each man is no more and no less a person than any other, that each is an ultimate and final source of decision and responsibility, the last court of appeal as to what is to be believed and cherished.

A person has the power and right to worship, enjoy, judge, and believe, by himself and on his own responsibility. Each has a right to a free trial and a right to have his needs, desires, and individual predilections given equal consideration with those of any other. He is a being to be judged in terms of what he is as well as by what he does. These rights are denied when men are forced to submit, without possibility of adequate reply, to the decisions of others as to what is right or wrong. They are endorsed when whatever makes men aware of what they are and what they ought to decide is publicly encouraged.

The principle of personal equality sets a limit to what an organization ought to demand of men. It should not compel anyone to view the person or the individual decisions of another as more precious than his own, or to delegate to another his privilege to decide where truth and goodness lie. The principle also indicates what a just and adequate state should do. It is required to encourage those enterprises and institutions—educational, communal, literary, and religious—which help men become more aware of what it is to be a person and what it is a person ought to do.

The principle of personal equality has been affirmed by lords of the manor, by capitalists, by slaveholders, and by anarchists. But one must not only affirm but promote its realization, and firmly oppose all attempts to deny, blur, or oppose it. Only then can one claim to have a vital faith in the native dignity of every man.

No man can realize all his potentialities alone, unaided. None can alone dynamically exhibit his native freedom to the full. To be fully human each needs the encouragement and support, the sympathy and help of others. A man must be recognized to have the right to come in contact with and to form lasting and intimate associations with others. He must, in particular, be granted the opportunity to make friends with any man.

Friends penetrate beneath the outward forms of one another. To deny to any man the right to make a friend of some other, no matter what his color, tradition, or faith, is to limit the range and direction of his growth. To be free to make friends as the spirit inclines is a privilege no one can rightfully proscribe. To admit this is to accept what may be termed the *principle of free kinship*, the right to cut across all established barriers of custom and convention to the person of another, no matter what his role or function, and to care for him for his own sake.

The principle of free kinship is perhaps the most novel and intermittent item in the modern democratic creed. Men have, in the past, occasionally been willing and ready to subscribe to the thesis that all were equal as humans and as persons, but have hesitated to admit that they all had an equal right to form intimate and lasting associations with others, irrespective of their differences in position, background, or religion. But if the principle of free kinship is not actively and effectively supported, men will not be able fully to enjoy and profit from contact with the endless variety which is man, and will, to that degree, be so much less rich and developed.

The promotion of free kinship is most effectively achieved through games, sports, festivals, assemblies, and work in which a multitude freely participates and which it can use as occasions for acting together, for discerning and appreciating individual flavors, and for the formation of lasting friendships. So far as this is true, the promotion of these must be one of the aims of those who are concerned with providing all men with the opportunity to be fully men.

He who would know men intimately and well must live with them. The knowledge of what individual men are like is a knowledge most readily obtained through continual association. It is this which the family provides. It is the family where men come most readily to know what others are and need. There men usually obtain that ready and honest sympathy and reproof, that direct experience and education in human affairs which is so essential to their growth and welfare.

The responsibility and position men have in their families limit the demands which larger social wholes have a right to impose—a fact sometimes recognized in economic and social exemptions allowed to heads of families. There is as yet, unfortunately, no clear policy as to whether and how punishment for crimes and reward for work should be adjusted to the fact that a man is a member of a family as well as a member of society.

The effect of penalties of any sort on the individual should be weighed against their effects on the dependent and innocent members of his family. Account should be taken of the degree to which the incarceration of a malefactor works hardship on those he leaves behind. If he has a bad effect on them as well as on others, his incarceration may prove eminently desirable. Where the family begins to suffer undeservedly, the penalties or their results ought to be minimized. Similarly, reward for work and services should vary in accordance with the extent to which others depend on it; the publicly functioning individual should be seen as a center out of which effects radiate not only when he does ill but also when he does well. If his ill-doing, because of the effect it is supposed to have on others, is to be socially viewed, so should his good-doing. The responsible members of a family have accepted as their own, tasks of the greatest benefit to others, and so far as they carry these out, their penalties should be minimized and their rewards increased.

Like the person, the family must be granted independence and internal freedom, so far as that is consistent with the growth and well-being of its members and others. To recognize this is to affirm the *principle of familial autonomy*, to acknowledge that each family is an ultimate division in which men perform indispensable functions valuable to all. Willingness to embrace this principle involves a readiness to oppose attempts to prevent the family from functioning as a source of experience and value, or to make its continuance difficult or impossible. It is to encourage familial solidarity, independence, and continuation, so far as these are consistent with each member of the family living as a person who may become the independent and responsible head of a new family eventually.

The personality of a man is his person made manifest, his private nature exhibited in a public matter. We say of a man that he has a pleasant personality, that he is someone we want to have live or work with us, because he at once reveals that he is an individual and that he respects the individuality of others. He restructures and yet submits to the demands of a shared common world. He who has a bad personality either under- or over-expresses his individual person, and thus either gives others too little or prevents them from having full personalities themselves. Each man comes into the open with a stress and meaning all his own, tinging a common and public content in an individual way which may or may not conflict with similar expressions by other individuals. Taken as a single being, he has a right to do this; taken in context, as a man among men, he has a right only to that personality which allows others to have personalities as well.

The personality is most effectively expressed when a man pursues an activity in which he is most interested. It is then that he exhibits and restructures his nature most completely and to the best advantage. Some of these activities are minor—hobbies and amusements of various kinds; some of them are of fundamental importance for the continuation and improvement of man—useful and public work, science, art, philosophy. The first is to be permitted and within limits to be encouraged. The second is to be encouraged and within limits publicly supported. Leisure is a time of preparation for good and needed work; work is a time of preparation for desired and necessary leisure. A man is most a man when he is able to express his abilities and individuality in both, and it is important to all that he should. All lose when some are deprived of the opportunity of exploiting their talents in the best and most congenial possible ways.

The principle of equal opportunity assures men the right to pursue any vocation open to the others. The place of each is to be determined not on the basis of race, creed, color, or wealth but on merit. No one must be antecedently prevented from occupying a position or role, and none must be antecedently proscribed from exhibiting his personality in and through his work, so far as that is consistent with his duties.

All have a right to an equality of opportunity to exhibit their abilities and individuality. None can, of course, in the face of competition and public need, be guaranteed the privilege either of continuing in his chosen work or of attaining the position he seeks. But an effective and satisfactory social organization will minimize and resolutely withstand all attempts to harden or increase the difficulties that now prevent certain groups of men from occupying the positions or expressing personalities as others can and do.

The members of one social group may fail to treat others outside as human, to respect their possessions, or to evaluate their lives, feelings, thoughts, activities, or environment properly. Still, to the degree that men have similar needs and must satisfy them in similar ways in the same world, they are all potentially members of the same worldwide community of men. So long as he fails to make use of those agencies which enable him to live in harmony with his fellow man, a man is, however, not actually a member of that community.

Most groups of men, even the best, deny on extraneous grounds privileges, opportunities, and rights to various of their members and exclude certain men from membership. These groups can be tolerated and even encouraged in somewhat the same way as the family is, provided that, like the family, they function to produce better members for the larger society and for the eventual harmonious universe which is the ultimate place of all.

The best society accords all the opportunity to function excellently. Any antecedent stratification or limitation ignores the fact that men require and deserve the benefit to be derived from an active, creative participation in the activities of which they are capable and which society allows, promotes, and sometimes makes possible. These activities are encouraged by free discussions and by education, since these enable men to know and appreciate diversities in temperament, opinion, need, and desire, and to learn the nature of the values which are the concern of all, the techniques of adjustment, and the existence and importance of majority and minority claims. These are all corollaries from what might be termed the *principle of social freedom*, the right of each man to make his presence and meaning count in the whole, so far as that is consistent with the exercise of a similar right by others as well.

The acceptance of these rights prohibits the attempt to deny them to others. There must be limits to the freedom accorded speech and the press, to what is urged or dogmatically affirmed. Otherwise the society will succeed in nothing so much as in nourishing and making possible the success of those concerned with destroying it. Men have no absolute right to affirm or criticize, nor a right to decide what can be listened to without injury by the rest. Affirmation and criticism are neither absolute goods nor perfect means; native wisdom is neither infallible nor a perfect protection against the false or insidious. More than education or reasoned discourse is needed to counteract the influence of propaganda, caricature, and willful distortion. No one can reasonably expect to promote tolerance by granting immunity to intolerance. Tolerance demands respect for all forms in which the good appears; it does not demand indifference to evil. But we must be very sure that what we extirpate is truly evil, and not a good we are insensitive to.

To acknowledge a right is to acknowledge a claim; to acknowledge a claim is to acknowledge an ingredient, essential power expressing the unitary nature of some substantial being. The acknowledgment of the right entrains a duty to extend and preserve it. He who is free to exercise the right should acknowledge its existence and oppose its denial in others. Freedom of speech and freedom of press need not be more important than other forms of public freedom. So far as they are employed, not as a means for investigating and educating but for making life brutish or unbearable, they demand restraint. A faith in man or democracy does not mean a blind extension of the principle of tolerance, to cover no matter what abuse, or a faith in the ability of men to withstand any attack, no matter what the device. It means only the acknowledgment of common rights and the obligation of men to help them flourish.

The foregoing principles—of human equality, personal equality, free kinship, familial autonomy, equality of opportunity, and social freedom—and the rights they assure—the right to food and shelter, growth, health, and reason, to conscience and responsibility, to private worship and moral decision, to social intercourse and leisure, to familial life and freedom, to justice and sympathy, to education, inquiry, religious activity, and work, and to the means to become members of a single all-inclusive community of ethical men—together define the good life. A democratic state is one in which the persistent attempt is made to attain these ends through universal suffrage, open political discussion, frequent elections, secret ballots, and a representative and parliamentary government. Like every state it has as its primary function the assurance, extension, and protection of the principles and rights which are necessary for the full growth and prosperity of all; unlike others it rests on the supposition that there is no better judge of the meaning and importance of concrete proposals and their relation to principles and rights than common mankind, deciding freely and without fear.

A democratic state should endorse, protect, and extend the principles and rights which define the good life. If it does only one of these it is a democracy at its minimum. If it does all three it is a democracy at its maximum, the only kind that can claim and hope for whole-hearted allegiance. Only such a state can serve as an efficient instrument for the achievement of that ultimate all-embracing community where men can be free, happy, and complete individuals living and working in harmony with their fellows. In such a democratic state advantages enjoyed by one must serve only to mark a need to sacrifice on behalf of others.

Our native freedom should be used to make it possible for others to express their freedom with equal effect and benefit. Until they are able to do this we, while substantially and in principle one with them and on a level, are publicly superior to and so far not one of them. To be a man with others we must, whenever we have the opportunity to decide for us both, favor them rather than ourselves. Even if on all points we were otherwise equal with them, we would, just by having the privilege to decide for both, be superior to them. Decisions should reduce the advantage that deciding gives the decider, if he is to remain one of a number of equal beings.

No one can rightly demand sacrifice of another. It can be demanded only of oneself. A man should sacrifice when a decision in his own favor or a refusal to decide at all makes him the other's superior. One's life is of course irreplaceable; a man has no right to lay it down for another. All he has a right to give up is a decision to favor himself to the other's detriment. Should he die as a consequence of having made such a decision, because he tried to be one man among others, in the face of circumstances which were forcing him into a privileged position, he would die not because he had decided to do so but because the circumstances required his death. He would die as a man who had exercised the highest human privilege—the privilege of freely acknowledging a common humanity in himself and others—in a world whose activities often preclude the realization of what had been planned by man.

He who refuses to decide in another's favor denies the humanity in him. His decision as a consequence puts him in opposition to all men, thereby defining himself to be a man for whom there are no other men, a man who tries to live at such a time and in such a way that there is no one with whom he can live.

A man can sacrifice himself only for inferiors, who may of course be equal with or superior to him in other ways. But why should he? Why should he not decide in his own favor? What can he lose if he does? Perhaps the good opinion of others? Suppose he did. Is that much of a loss? And as a matter of fact, many men, perhaps most, say that it is foolish to sacrifice oneself for inferiors; one would lose their good opinion by sacrificing, not by refusing to sacrifice. Perhaps, as we have suggested, he who refuses to sacrifice destroys his metaphysical unity with all other men? Perhaps he cuts himself off from the rest of mankind? But, it might be justly replied, such a unity does not seem to be known to most men, and in any case seems not capable of being destroyed by a man so long as he lives and thus is a man like and in that sense one with the rest. We must, quite evidently, look more closely and carefully at the nature of sacrifice than we have so far.

7. THE AVOIDANCE OF SACRIFICE

A genuine act of sacrifice is a generous act, fulfilling at least five conditions. 1) Something valuable must be given up. To sacrifice nothing of value is to sacrifice nothing at all. 2) The sacrifice must be made on behalf of another. To give up something for nobody is to abandon it, not to sacrifice it. 3) The other must be inferior in the dimension of the sacrifice. Otherwise the other would not need the sacrifice and the sacrifice would be irrelevant to it. 4) The sacrificed, or some cause or consequence of it, must satisfy the other. Otherwise the other would not receive anything of value, and the act, since it does involve a loss of value to the sacrificer, would so far be bad. 5) The sacrifice must bring about more good than is sacrificed. If not, it would be futile or wanton, the one if the same degree of good is recovered as lost, the other if a greater good is forfeited than that received.

He who enjoys an advantage over others has the ethical task of increasing the values of those others by sacrificing to them. He should sacrifice his time and energy if what others need from him is his mediation. He should bring them together for mutual benefit, so far as his time and energy are less valuable than the good that ensues from their use of one another. He must sacrifice his possessions if those possessions or their recipients are thereby increased in value to a degree more than balancing the loss to him. And in the extreme case, he must put his life in jeopardy if he thereby helps increase value to a degree not otherwise possible. Disagreeable, unwanted, regretted though a sacrifice may be, it is not only necessary but better than anything else he, the advantaged, can do. A man should sacrifice to become a man among men.

He who refuses to sacrifice defines himself to be one who is now not superior to others. He is a man who usually deserves less but requires more from others than he ought. He tacitly admits that he lacks the goods others have, that he cannot do what they can. He grants that he is defective in comparison with them, and that he therefore so far deserves to be criticized, admonished, punished, blamed. A man should sacrifice or confess himself to be, when he makes decisions, inferior to another.

A man may with justice refuse to sacrifice. He can correctly defend a nonsacrificial act on the ground that it enables him to attain a state where a much greater sacrifice or no sacrifice at all will be necessary, for every act, unless pointless or wrong, is a sacrifice, a means for attaining a state of superiority where a sacrifice is unavoidable, or a means for attaining that state of excellence in harmony with others, where sacrifices are no longer needed.

A refusal to sacrifice oneself on behalf of others is to be defended on the grounds that something better could now be done instead. This something better must in the last resort be a means for getting ready to act on behalf of inferiors, if there be any, or to interplay with others for mutual benefit. I can justify my refusal to sacrifice now on the grounds that I am trying to attain that stage of excellence where I will engage in better acts. I am to be blamed for not being in that state now. But my acts can be excused and this for at least seven reasons. I may be trying to get better intentions (see 1 and 2 below), to realize better objectives (3 and 4), to make better use of others (5 and 6), or to give up some things so as to improve them (7).

1) I may now be too limited in my interests; there may be broader goods in whose service I should enlist, better ideals in terms of which I ought to live. Now intending some good of my body or my family, I see that it is desirable to intend something more comprehensive, that it is better to intend, instead, to become educated, civilized, a man of vision, a man fulfilling an obligation to the absolute good. I rightly refuse to engage in a sacrifice today since I am now occupied in the more important task of making myself one who is to live on better terms hereafter. I am to be condemned because I am not yet in the state I should be, but I am to be excused for not now engaging in what would be only the inadequate sacrifice of an imperfect being. Instead of just giving something to others, I decide instead to first intend what ought to be.

2) Instead of trying to intend some ideal greater than the one I now pursue and thereby incidentally being able to act more satisfactorily on behalf of others, I might set myself instead to intend some goal *in order to* act satisfactorily on behalf of others. I might recognize that I have selfish impulses, that I incline toward self-love, that I often do what I know I ought not to do. In order to stop myself from going in the wrong way, I might try to intend to be of service, to become an other-regarding man. Condemnable because I am one who needs to steel himself against temptation and passion, I am not condemnable for refusing to sacrifice something now, if I am one who is preparing to act more satisfactorily later.

3) I can attend to as well as intend an ideal. I can occupy myself

not merely with acting in the light of an ideal but with acting to make it real. There are possible goods expressed in the laws, traditions, and languages of a nation or pointed to in such vague expressions as the "common good" or the "happiness of all" with which I might concern myself. I can do this even while intending something different. I can intend to be a philanthropist while actually saving money for myself. Condemnable for not being ready to act for others, I am not to be condemned for refusing to sacrifice now, for I am engaged in the laudable task of preparing myself to live in terms of an end whose realization would allow me to act in more significant ways later.

4) Instead of trying to attend to an ideal, and thereby being enabled to utilize some other beings more effectively, I might set myself instead to attend to an ideal *for the sake of* using those others. My act would seem to be quite selfish. Not only does it serve to make me attend to a future objective rather than to some contemporary, but it does it solely to enable me to use, master, take from others. The act can nevertheless be justified as a means of uniting myself with others and thereby attaining the position where better acts are possible. I am to be condemned only for not yet having attained this latter state, because I, instead of exemplifying an ideal already, must realize it as a means for mastering others.

5) A more extreme form of selfishness would seem to be exhibited when I try to make use of others, subordinate them to myself. I seem then to be turned in the very opposite direction from that which a sacrificing being should take. Instead of giving I receive, instead of submitting I master, instead of serving I use. Yet my act can be justified. I might need others in order that I might best act as a man. I might have to use them so that I can satisfy my needs and thus get into the position of becoming a perfected being who is ready and willing to sacrifice more than I now could, or for getting us all finally to the stage where no sacrifice is needed.

6) I might use others *in order* to enable me to realize an end shared by others. They might support me, add to my substance, my power, my ability to bring about the common good. I would be condemnable for not being at the stage I ought to be. But my acts would nevertheless be justifiable. I rightly refuse to sacrifice if I thereby am able to get to the stage of excellence in which a sacrifice more significant than what now is possible could take place, or even better, if I am thereby enabled to bring all men to the stage where no one need sacrifice to another.

7) Sacrifice is directed to the promotion of the good, but not all such promotion, even when it involves a loss to me, is sacrifice. Sacrifice requires a disregard of my advantage, even though it is to be justi-

fied in part because of the good it brings to me. I can, though, give up even precious things without sacrificing them. I can give them up so as to improve them, perhaps for my own or mankind's eventual use or benefit, but in any case not as part of a sacrifice.

We can rightly refuse to sacrifice because we must occupy ourselves with achieving a better position (see 1, 2, and 7 above), with realizing some objective (see 3 and 6), or with making ourselves more substantial or powerful (see 4 and 5), all for eventual common benefit. So far as it is desirable for us to engage in these tasks it is evident that we have not yet acted sufficiently on behalf of some common good, and that we need others more than they need us. Only one who is imperfect can avoid making a sacrifice, and then only because he is preparing himself to make a better sacrifice eventually, or because he is bringing all to that level of excellence where no sacrifices are necessary.

Might not then every man rationally and rightly refuse to give to or do anything for another on the ground that he must devote himself to preliminary tasks? He might—providing that he actually does make himself ready for this later work and provided that he is understood to be one who is now condemnable for not being at the better stage he is planning to reach. He who has the power of decision should sacrifice because in that act he makes himself the equal of others. To refuse to sacrifice is to confess one is less than such a man should be.

8. To Sacrifice or Not to Sacrifice

No man has an advantage over all others in every respect; none ought to act solely on behalf of others. Superior in some ways and inferior in others, each ought to work for others and for himself. Which, though, should he now favor—his superior or his inferior side? The slave who knows more than the king, the foolish man of wealth, the strong man without political power, the artist who has not yet been recognized—what are they to do? Should they give up their advantages or should they try to overcome their inferiority? If they do the former they put themselves below the rest and not only have to trust to the virtue of their fellows but actually obligate those fellows to improve them; if the latter they but increase the distance they are from the rest, making their sacrifice on behalf of the rest more and more imperative.

To these questions two answers might be given:

1) Men are related to one another in multiple ways and in terms of many different traits, powers, and promises. They form multiple systems, each having its own characteristics in terms of which the men are ordered as superior, inferior, or equal to one another. A man may belong to a world of rational beings and to a world of property owners.

In the former he may be superior to others, in the latter inferior. So far as he does not act to enable others to know as much as he, he does less than he ought as a member of the former system. So far as he must be helped by richer men he is to be criticized for not yet being a perfect member of the latter system. It is up to him to decide which of these failings is the more serious, which one reveals him to be the lesser man. If he supposes one is more serious, he will, at least for a time, have to ignore the criticisms which he, in terms of the other system, deserves.

His decision as to which system he ought to satisfy need not be arbitrary. A man ought to form a system with more men in a more enduring way. It is better to know than to own, the latter being after all only a means to something, such as knowledge, which is more satisfactory, more useful, and more comprehensive. Property is but one of a number of partial links between some men; it could conceivably be dispensed with without affecting their essence. The knowing slave then ought to teach; he ought to sacrifice his time on behalf of the king, while the foolish rich man ought to learn, ought to be made the object of the concern of others, poorer and thus inferior though they may be to him in the dimension of wealth.

Men form multiple systems with others. Each system provides standards in terms of which inferiors are to be criticized for their imperfections and superiors are to be criticized for their failures to act. That system which embraces all men is obviously the one in terms of which our ethical judgments, since these apply to all men, are to be framed. What is not embraced by that system is minor. He who can whistle better than others has only a minor obligation to teach whistling to others; he who whittles poorly has but a minor need to whittle well. The reluctance of the good whistler, the defects of the poor whittler are not serious. The one might otherwise be the most generous of men, the other might be excellent in all other regards, a man most excellently civilized.

The reply leaves us facing three great difficulties:

a) It invokes a standard for which it has made no provision. It merely says that the best of systems is one in which all men are united in the most enduring ways; it does not show this to be true and it cannot do so, so long as nothing more is affirmed than that a man is superior to others in some respects and inferior in others. A judgment of the merits of these different respects presupposes the acknowledgment of a system to which all men belong. It is in terms of this that men should decide whether it is better for them to sacrifice because superior or not to sacrifice because inferior. It is only as advantaged members of an enduring comprehensive community then that we ought to sacrifice; only as momentarily or superficially inferior members of such a system have we a right to defer a sacrifice.

b) Even if we granted that the best of all systems is one in which all men are brought together on an equal footing in an enduring way—as in fact we must, once we see that all men are equally human and should be on a level publicly as well as privately—our difficulties would still not be at an end. There can be multiple ways in which all men might be enduringly united, and some men might be superior in terms of some of these ways but inferior in terms of others. Let it be supposed, for example, that knowledge is a common denominator for men. Since there are many kinds of knowledge and since a man might be a master of some and not of others, he has still to face the question as to whether or not to sacrifice in the light of the former or not to sacrifice in the light of the latter. How is he to decide whether he who stands above the rest in historical knowledge but is quite deficient in scientific knowledge ought to help others become historians or ought to devote his energies to becoming better informed regarding science? How are we to decide between a system in which all men are equally secure and one where they are equally free? How are we to decide between two systems which are equally comprehensive and enduring?

c) Might there not be some system of men which is intrinsically better than all alternative systems? Perhaps there is a single system which, in addition to being comprehensive and enduring, is richer, more intense, more flexible than any other? Ought we not to say then that he who was superior to the rest in terms of such a rich system should sacrifice for them, while he who was inferior might rightly defer his sacrifice? If we do say this, we affirm that a comparatively advantaged member of the richest kind of system should sacrifice on behalf of comparatively inferior members. But it is absurd to argue that those who are better off ought always to sacrifice and those who are worse off should always defer a sacrifice. All men are, with equal justification, called on to make sacrifices. They do not now exist in a perfect system, ordered as superior and inferior to one another. Indeed, no system in which they are so ordered could be perfect, for it falsifies the relation men ought to have to one another.

9. ORGANIC ACTION

2) A second, more satisfactory answer to the question as to whether we are to sacrifice now or not is possible. It admits that a man who is comparatively superior to others ought to sacrifice on their behalf. But it recognizes that others are now superior to him in other respects. Other men have at least powers, virtues, goods, and excellencies he should possess if he is to be perfect. Every man has advantages over

others in some respects and is at a disadvantage in other respects. He ought both to sacrifice for them and be sacrificed to. He ought to give and take, adventure with humility, improve himself and others.

Acts should be at once self-regarding and other-regarding, expansive and contractive, the expressions of virtuous men exhibiting their native freedom freely to the greatest advantage of themselves and others. All of us should be perfected in harmony, receiving what we need to overcome our inferiority and giving up what defines us as superior, and this without reducing the values of either, or coming to a flat monotone of a world in which men are equal not as unique individuals but as mirrors of one another. There are three possible ways in which this can be done.

a) Sometimes it is possible to act on behalf of others so as to gain whatever one needs for oneself. A man may be willing to sacrifice the exercise of his freedom of speech in order to become more secure. He might take office so as to be better able to make others more at ease with themselves and therefore less dangerous to himself. But unless the act were geared to bring about such a result there is little hope that the result will be achieved, or that where it is, it will be proportionate to the loss which the sacrifice involves. To make sure that there will be at least as much gain as loss he must give up his freedom in such a way as to become more secure. But then his act would seem no longer to have that wholehearted, noncalculating, generous character which a sacrifice must have. An embodiment of enlightened self-interest might do much to benefit others and himself, but he will never deserve the palm reserved for sacrificing men. If we are to see that as much is gained as is lost and yet are to avoid destroying the possibility of sacrifice we must look to some external agent to proportion gains to losses, balance sacrifices with appropriate rewards, compensate for a man's disadvantages to the degree that he sacrifices his advantages.

b) There might be agencies which see to it that he who gives is rewarded proportionately, which makes sure that all gifts are balanced by gains. The markets, the laws, the government, the customs and traditions of society seem to be such agencies. They provide recompense for those who give up their advantages; they reward men for giving to others what those others need. Theoretically, a man in the open market gives to others what they want and he does not, and they in turn give him what he wants but they do not. Each, in the ideal case, sacrifices little and gains much. Taxation has a similar rationale. The rich are presumably taxed so that the poor can make the roads, cart off the garbage, deliver the mail, thereby profiting both.

None of these agencies works so perfectly that it exactly or more than balances every gift with a proper reward. Only in the remote future, or if and while human affairs are in the grip of a beneficent, omnipotent God, could there be an assurance that losses suffered on behalf of others would always be balanced or overbalanced with appropriate gains.

Such agencies must also look to some force which makes men give up to others what those others need. Without the force, these agencies would have no or little work to do. A market presupposes that hunger is a force, making men give up their possessions. It depends on that and similar drives to make men give up even things which they do not need. Behind every tax law there is a sheriff compelling men to do what frequently is best not only for others but for themselves. Men who would rather live in quiet privacy sometimes run for office because they fear the kind of government others would provide. Men give up what they have, even when this is of little value and would do great good, not freely or gladly but under pressure, immediate or expected. They must be prevented from forming monopolies, holding on to things for prestige, for sentimental reasons, out of habit—and often it is to their advantage to be so prevented. Pressure, compulsion, force of all kinds must support the agencies which are designed to balance sacrifices with rewards if men are to be made to give to others, and if what they give is to be properly recompensed. Force often provides the only way in which desirable, imperatively needed results can be achieved.

Men should be forced up to at least that *absolute minimum* level where they can exercise their characteristic human powers. The young ought to be educated, the sick healed, the helpless protected. To make sure that these results are achieved we force men to engage in activities which directly or indirectly bring about these results. Men ought also to raise others to that *civilized minimum* in which they can exercise their human powers in the best possible way. They must be forced to give up what they possess in order to bring about the increase in the leisure, the extension of the imagination, the improvement of the skills of others. They must be compelled to contribute to the support of institutions which enable mankind to reach new levels of human achievement in the arts, the sciences, and social living. These two minima are so important that we dare not risk leaving their fulfillment to individual decision and will. To make sure we will reach these levels we compel men to give up advantages and put into operation effective agencies to compensate them.

It is desirable, however, for men to attain a *maximum possible* level of achievement. All should become virtuous, wise, self-sufficient, humanly perfect. This is a result we cannot compel them to bring about. We must leave its achievement to human volition. And in any case, since only where there is volition is there sacrifice, no agency forcing men to give up their advantages can do justice to the needs of sacrifice and the rights of sacrificing men. What must be taken away by an exterior power is not something which a man possesses, controls, and really sacrifices.

An external agency forcing a man to sacrifice denies the very nature of sacrifice, since this must be voluntary. But might there not be an agency which did not depend on force and which, on the occasion of each act of giving, made some provision for overcoming the giver's disadvantages? If so, it would be possible for sacrifices to be compensated. Such an agency, however, will be unknown or known. It will be like an unknown grace-infusing God who takes account of generous acts at once and then and there improves the actor proportionately, or it will be a known and thus a temporal agency, like those which provide for the canonization of saints, bestow medals, and otherwise honor men.

Of what is unknown we obviously know nothing. And of what is known too much would be known and too late. Knowing that the agency would compensate us we would know too much to be able to sacrifice. It is almost inevitable that if we knew our gifts would be balanced by rewards we would soon gear our acts in terms of the actual, predicted or suspected behavior of the agency, and thereby destroy our ability to sacrifice. And, in any case, the agency would have to wait for the sacrifice to take place and would be able to determine what loss was to be compensated only after the sacrifice was over. Such an agency might begin to work very much after the date of sacrifice, and after the sacrificer was no longer capable of anything but posthumous glory. Presumably too the agency might never have time to function, and might never take account of this or that particular case.

No knowable outside agency, by its very nature, can, except by accident, provide adequately for what is lost in sacrifice. It must stand outside the area where volition takes place, and get to work only after a sacrifice has been made. If a man is not, while giving up his advantages, to be saddled at the same time with all his disadvantages, and thus reduce himself below the others, he must, when and as he sacrifices, be able to overcome his inferiority and thus end on a level with the others.

c) It is characteristic of the two preceding accounts of how losses involved in sacrifice might be compensated, to treat a man's superiority as though it were distinct from and independent of his inferiority. As a consequence, both accounts are faced with the insoluble problem of providing a means by which one who acts generously is to have his consequent loss erased. But if it be recognized that superiority and inferiority are aspects of an organic whole, the impasse will be by-passed. After all we are single beings, substantial, unitary, concrete. We are not made up of a power to will, a state of being secure, a fear, an opportunity to think, and so on. These are abstractions, in terms of which we can be significantly compared with others. They are important, they are revelatory; each has its own requirements, each implicates us in tasks which we, as single beings, must carry out. But none is to be thought of as something to be satisfied in isolation, independently of all other aspects.

It is not desirable to try merely to sacrifice or merely to defer a sacrifice. In that way we make the whole of ourselves serve a part, instead of conversely. Our every act ought to be both sacrificial and nonsacrificial, because it ought to improve both ourselves and others. Instead of acting as one who is superior or inferior, we ought to act as one who is to be reconstituted together with others, so that we are all on a level but better than we were before. We cannot be sure, of course, that we will receive as much as we freely give. Sometimes we will lose precious goods and gain little. Sometimes we will give little and yet get something of great value. We will always get and give something, but cannot say in advance just how they will compare.

We cannot rightly act merely as advantaged or as disadvantaged beings, as though we had nothing to do but to give up that which makes us superior to others or to obtain whatever enables us to overcome our inferiority. We are single organic beings who are required to do justice to every part and aspect of ourselves and others No one of us though knows just what exactly is the best way to act in a given situation. We ought to lean toward giving rather than receiving so long as we are on the whole more self-sufficient, more perfect than others, and lean toward receiving rather than giving so long as we are on the whole less self-sufficient, less perfect. Guided from behind by the wisdom of the race and the lessons of experience, from ahead by the goal of equality in perfection, and alongside by a recognition of the defects and achievements of others, ours ought to be a creative act in which we attempt to make ourselves and others into self-sufficient beings living in harmony.

10. The Art of Living

He who is confronted with a drowning man must make an immediate, important decision. He must choose to take one of a number of mutually exclusive courses. He need not, however, restrict his decision to the alternatives, saving or not saving, getting the man out of the water or leaving him in it. In the act of deciding he can forge a new alternative. He can help the other *and* himself, care for the other while and after he is being saved, at the same time that he takes account of his own limitations and needs. Just how much emphasis is to be put on helping the other and how much on helping himself is a matter to be worked out in the act. Sometimes one emphasis is required, sometimes another. All that matters is that each man recognize others to be as human as himself, that he view them and himself as having individual needs which he must satisfy or cease to be a man with them.

The drowning man is in serious danger. He is now decidedly the inferior. But he is not inferior in every respect. While we are trying to save him, his status and ours might quickly be reversed. The situation should be faced as a whole, not merely as requiring that he be saved regardless of all else. The drowning man himself needs more than safety, and we have a right to it ourselves. It would be wrong to view him as a being in jeopardy, who happens to be human; he deserves always to be treated as a man, though now of course as one who is in extreme danger. But we who are in less danger are men also; we ought not to act so as to deny ourselves human rights and privileges.

We ought to lean toward the drowning man because he is now so decidedly at a disadvantage; we must strain every nerve, risk our lives even, but never in such a way as to ignore our own needs and rights, our own inferiority. Those who disregard such admonitions, who jump into the water without regard for themselves, are often honored. But should we discover that they acted uselessly and perhaps injured themselves and others, we would condemn them. We honored them because they went so sharply against the usual tendency of men to look after themselves more then they should, because it *seemed* as if they were doing what was right. Our subsequent condemnation shows that we were too hasty. The practiced lifesaver who saves others and himself should be our model, not he who seeks to save others but not himself, or himself and not others.

The rich man with power, the slave who knows more than the king, the foolish man of wealth, the strong man without political influence, the unrecognized artist have somewhat similar problems. It would be a mistake for any one of them to sacrifice what advantages he enjoys without reaping any benefit for himself, just as surely as it would be a mistake for him to look after himself, to overcome his limitations without taking any account of the needs of others. At one and the same time there should be a generous giving of what is had in comparative excess and a willing acceptance of what will help one get to the stage where others are. The answer all must find is to be achieved through the exercise of a creative will which enables opposing tendencies to be restructured, redirected, reconstituted to become coordinate though divergent tensions.

All of us have a similar problem in connection with children and with the state. These are our inferiors. The child is an adult in prospect. I ought to teach it. But if I give up all my time to it, more or at least as much value will be lost as is gained. When teaching it I ought to learn from it—perhaps what innocence is—or experience the joys which its joy makes possible. My gains ought to be incidental, not planned-for results, if I am to act generously, if I am to do more than treat the act as a means to my good. Yet if all I did was to act as though the child were someone to teach and I were someone who is to benefit incidentally from it, I would be caricaturing us both. I am more than a teacher, more than a learner, more than both together; the child is more than someone to be taught, more than someone who has already learned something, more than both together. We are both concrete beings who must be constantly reorganized. Instead of trying to teach the child and incidentally gaining something thereby, I ought to remake it and myself through an act in which it and I both teach and learn.

Since the child needs teaching more than I do, my act should be one in which teaching is a dominant feature. That teaching does not and cannot occur in isolation. It takes place in a context of attitudes, expressions, habits, preparations, movements of all sorts, directed only in part toward the child and its environment. As and while all genuine teaching occurs, learning occurs as well, the greater need of the child though requiring that learning should not now be a dominant feature of my activity with respect to it.

Men ought no more to try to be merely generous than they ought to try to be merely selfish. These are both features of more inclusive activities which cannot be properly described in terms appropriate to either, or even to both together. Our acts are generous or selfish on the whole, not exclusively one or the other. Generosity and selfishness are coordinate, inseparable components of an encompassing effort at the reconstitution of ourselves and others. Neither need be treated as the condition or outcome of the other. The ultimate objective is a harmony of perfected men. That result is now best achieved by stressing giving rather than taking. We ought to help the poor, care for the sick, work on behalf of society because we are better off than these for the time being. Just how much stress we ought to put on these other-regarding activities cannot however be determined in advance. We must decide that question in an adventurously humble act in which we try to improve ourselves and others.

Should we fail to achieve the end we set ourselves, we but reveal ourselves to be imperfect beings who fail to do what we ought. Should we fail to achieve the end but yet improve ourselves, we make ourselves men who ought to sacrifice to others. Should we attain our end and thus become perfected in harmony, we have no other work to do but interplay with our fellows so as to increase the value of all of us together.

An act which stresses generosity is not necessarily better than others. If it is better, it is better because it is better adapted to making the various sides of a human transaction equally excellent. Whatever happens is concrete, within which a sacrifice can be but a moment and whose value is to be judged in terms of the contribution it makes to the perfection of men in harmony.

11. The Paradoxes Once Again

We are, I think, now in a position to free ourselves from the paradoxes with which we began.

a) It was asked how self-sacrifice can be the praiseworthy act that it is, when it involves the deliberate risking of something as precious as a human life. The question has a paradoxical ring only if it be supposed that one was being asked to evaluate an act in the light of the way it balances the worth of our lives against other goods. But our acts are to be evaluated on other grounds. They are to be praised or condemned depending on whether or not they provide the best way of helping ourselves and others to be perfected, it being understood that a refusal to risk oneself at certain times is but a way of losing the most precious values possible to a man.

b) We asked ourselves what claims others have on us, why we should give up things for them though they had no claim on us. The question supposed that what we did was to be judged in terms of claims and counterclaims. We must sacrifice to them not because they have a claim on us but because, in the endeavor to preserve and enhance values even for ourselves, we must act on their behalf.

c) We asked ourselves whether or not we gained anything when we sacrificed, and thus whether sacrifice was an act of strategy or of folly. We thereby supposed that if there were a gain it had to be the object of the sacrifice. There ought to be a gain when we sacrifice, but we ought not sacrifice in order to gain. At one and the same time we ought to give and to obtain what is needed. Both should be supplementary parts of a single act designed to perfect men; neither should function as a cause, explanation, or justification of the other.

d) We asked ourselves how we could recognize the value of something and yet give it up gladly. The question seemed paradoxical because we supposed that an act which is free or gladly engaged in, in one respect, cannot also be compelled or reluctantly engaged in, in another. We do not want to sacrifice. Because of the circumstances in which we are, we find that we must sacrifice if we are to do good. Whether we sacrifice or not our decision and our act are free. It is always up to us to decide whether to sacrifice, or to reduce ourselves in value by refusing to help others when we should.

e) We asked ourselves how a single being could actively sacrifice and be passively sacrificed. The paradox was rooted in a pun. "Self" refers to a private innermost core, the locus of responsibility and ultimate decision, and also to a full-bodied being in a real world. The self as an innermost core sacrifices, jeopardizes its status as part of a public world. It actively puts one in positions to be affected in various ways, the core all the while remaining active and single, the outside passive and complex.

All men have an excellence of some kind setting them over all others; all are deficient in some respects, the inferior of others. Because men are both, they must sacrifice but can never merely sacrifice. They must give as well as receive, receive as well as give, be adventurously humble, altruistic and selfish at once. There is no question then as to whether one ought to sacrifice or not; there is only the question of how much one should sacrifice, and when and how. Man is a relatively excellent but absolutely deficient being. Since he seeks to become perfected with others, and since in that state he but prepares himself to interplay with them, his great question is what is best for him to do in order to become a good man who need never sacrifice. The answer has long been known: he ought to love. Love has its moment of sacrifice, but it intends in its outcome and drive to make all sacrifice unnecessary. It is more creative and yet conserving, more generous and yet satisfying, more voluntary and yet spontaneous, more perfecting and yet exhausting than anything else we can do.

XX

LOVE

1. Four Views of Love

FOR Plato, love is a metaphysical category, characterizing the nature of the relation which connects needing, imperfect beings with the perfection they need. For Luther, it is a theological category, characterizing the relation of God, the highest and best of realities, to man, an undeserving lower being. For Augustine, love is a religious category, characterizing the relation of man, an impotent creature, to God, the source of all that is real and good. For Freud, it is a psychopathological category, characterizing the nature of an irresistible human drive, which finds some satisfaction somehow all the time.

Each of these views has great strength. Each emphasizes an important phase of love. The Platonist stresses the value of the beloved, and the good that entrains on its acknowledgment. The beloved, he knows, is for the true lover the embodiment of great and precious value which enriches and empowers. For the Lutheran, love is essentially generous; it is open and uncalculating. He knows that love is creative, never to be confined within pre-established frames. The Augustinian emphasizes the humility of the lover, his submissiveness, his readiness to abandon himself completely to the mercies of his beloved. He knows that love involves the taking of a risk, the placing of oneself in danger, hopefully and yet with abandon. The Freudian in contrast points out that love is appetitive, insistent, urgent, demanding, at once a mode of expression and a way of possessing. He knows that it is a force for good or for evil, omnivorous and insistent.

No one of these four phases (conveniently, and more or less in consonance with historical usage, designatable as *eros*, *agape*, *caritas*, and *cupidas*) can be neglected without disaster. But love is more than any or all of them together allow. The four views in fact share a common mistaken belief that love is always operative. In different ways they deny that love can ever be commanded, commended, demanded, or denied. They treat love as though it were beyond all control, as though it occurred independently of all virtue and intent. They make none or little provision for the obtrusive truth that love marries a kind of expressiveness with an avidity to master, a creativity with a constraint. As a consequence they obscure its passion and hide its ethical meaning. The idea of love, like the ideas of freedom and sacrifice, must, without detriment to its multiple nuances, be freed from unnecessary limitations.

2. The Lover

With Freud and Luther it is perhaps best to start with the lover, the source of all love and its ground. Without him there would be no love, that goes without question, even for those who insist that love requires a beloved as well. Indeed, should it be true that the beloved is essential, even central, that truth is not so evident and not so clear as the truth that love requires a lover.

The lover, Plato and Augustine remind us, gives himself, places himself at the mercy of the beloved as a being better than himself— and this in a double way. The lover at once *exposes* and *sacrifices* himself, the one for a selfish, the other for an unselfish reason.

He who loves opens himself, exposes himself, places himself in jeopardy. He allows himself to be wounded, shocked, destroyed, to be used, debased, enslaved. He is engaged in that most important of efforts, the purging of himself, the freeing of himself from the encumbrances, the habits, the limitations that had been accreted over the course of his life. He abandons not so much himself as that which prevents that self from standing out and being itself, clearly, naked and pure. Violently, convulsively, dramatically, the lover tries by one sudden wrench to rid himself of his follies and conceits, of irrelevancies accumulated and imposed. He tries to get down to that core of innocence which is his natively, to allow himself to be in fact and for another what he is essentially. Love for him is an occasion to be himself. He gets rid of what served to insulate and protect him in the past, for this hides and distorts, hinders the growth and free activity of what is himself most truly.

The lover tears off and through the disguises which he and his fellow men erected over the years. He breaks through those barriers which he and they put up between themselves, in part because they wanted to move in routine, untroubled ways through routine tasks. His fellow men and he have lived and will for the most part continue to live largely as beings who sustain functions, tasks, assignments, who fill positions, who carry out prescribed and externally imposed duties, requiring them often to repress their individualities, their unique flavors, to keep in the background those rich, private centers of value which alone make them be, and be worthy of respect.

Love, we say with startling accuracy, puts a man beside himself. It produces a set of actions which can no longer be centered in that core he calls his very self. Their center can only be in another; the other alone provides unity and excuse for what the lover does. The lover thus in exposing himself and freeing himself from all but what is essential bestows upon the other what is left over and thereupon endows that self with the virtue of being the meaning and unity of what, till then, all took to be essential to the lover.

The lover frees himself of what is strictly irrelevant, exposes himself, gets down to the essential, at the same time that he presents to the beloved material enough to define that other as the proper center for it. His act is selfish, freeing himself of encumbrances and orienting them in another. But love also includes its element of sacrifice as well as of exposure. It is generous, presenting to the other that very core of self left after all purging. The lover offers not merely dross and expression but that most precious self, that most recondite and private self of his, without reserve. Love is self-abandonment, sacrificial, excessive to a fault.

No one can of course really give up his self, annihilate his very substance. What the lover gives up is the self-centeredness of the self, its tendency to refer all things to it. The lover is filled with himself to overflowing, to superabundance. He has expanded to the limits of his being, has taken up the slack, filled out the emptiness which environed him when he purged himself. His self is no longer a center for the stable and routine, for the alien made familiar. He is through and through only self, and thus more than others who have hedged their selves in with protective and obscuring tissue. He has a self to comparative excess; he is richer, more energetic, more empowered than others. He can consider another's good, having already reached his own. If he did not thereafter consider another's good, he would wrongly try to perpetuate or increase the distance that now separates them.

The lover gives the beloved his attention, his interest, his consideration; he is occupied with the other's welfare; he looks out on the world no longer with his own eyes but with the eyes of his beloved. He sacrifices the self-centeredness of his self to make the self of another a center for him, thereby endowing that other with a new status. He becomes one whose dimensions have been reduced, directly facing another whose dignity he has enhanced.

The poor in body or spirit cannot fully love. They can long, give to others a naked self which those others may perhaps clothe, fill out for them. Not having expanded their purged selves to their full dimensions, they have no selves which can be centered by others.

A dispirited man cannot love. A Don Juan does not love. To be sure, he is robust, he risks and enjoys; his acts are marked by excess and abandon. But he never gives anything, never gives himself. He expands to the utmost limits of his being, but does not offer that self or any part of it to anyone. He keeps his self hidden, taking no risk of having it abused or misused; he allows himself no freedom from the shackles he and others have gradually molded to the very semblance and shape of his self. Instead he accepts himself and his situation as they are and contents himself merely with expressing his self in the material which hems them in. He expresses himself without purgation; he gives out without giving to; he enjoys without satisfaction.

Were there a God and did He create, His act could be an act of love only if, on the one hand, there were something from which He could purge Himself, and on the other He could really abandon Himself to the mercies of an alien and perhaps antagonistic being. The first of these considerations has found no place in our traditions. God is, to be sure, acknowledged by both Neoplatonists and the main body of subsequent theologians to act through the agency of an overflowing love, but it is not affirmed by them that God is Himself perfected through the act of overflowing, by giving up something of Himself. There is such a stress on God's intrinsic completeness and perfection, on His absolutivity and ultimacy, that there is a tendency in these thinkers to deny that what lies beyond their God is truly real, truly created beings with powers, careers, and existence of their own. Yet, if there be genuine overflow and genuine creation, there must be something now outside God, to wit, ourselves and all that coexists with us, which has being and value apart from Him. But then a creating God, to make such things, must somehow diminish Himself—which seems a foolishness—unless His creation is a pure act of love involving the purgation, the exteriorization of extraneous factors.

A God, no less than you and I, must purge Himself if He would love. But also, like all of us—as it is one of the meanings of the Crucifixion to emphasize—He must at the same time give something of Himself, offer Himself to whatever He had separated from Himself. He must allow Himself to be wounded most cruelly by the beings He loves. He must give to the ideas He exteriorized an existence which they can possess for a while and which they can use perversely if they so would. Not unless He does this does God create; otherwise He can at most be said to fulgurate, to flash out in momentary lightning strokes having no effect and no consequence but that of allowing Him to be Himself simply.

The lover, be he ordinary man, Don Juan, or creating God, must give up something and give to others what remains. He must at once expose himself and express himself, stand out naked and present himself in his nakedness to the other as a gift, generous and uncalculating.

But this is far from enough. For love to be, there must also be a beloved.

3. THE BELOVED

The lover needs the beloved, and this in three ways. He needs him to provide an *opportunity*, to function as a *provocation*, and to permit of a *self-completion*.

A beloved is necessary if only to provide an *opportunity* for the lover to purge himself. Without someone loved, the lover could and would undoubtedly continue to remain as he was. If he purged himself merely to free himself from encumbrances, his would be an act not of love but of reform. To love, a beloved is needed.

A loving self-purgation has a double focus; it is performed for oneself but under the eye of an actual or expected beloved. Normally men purge themselves on encountering others for whom alone they wish to appear as naked selves. The others provide opportunities for loving; they are felt to have a dignity, a worth, justifying the signal act performed in their presence. In the absence of such an occasion men try to imagine one, try to purge themselves in terms of a possible spectator, viewed as worthy of being the center of that which has been cast aside and also of the naked selves that remain. Where there is no one really worthy or where such a one cannot be imagined, the lover has no recourse but to accept as beloved whatever he can. Failing human beings, men love instead things, animals, ideals, utopias, and Gods, projected or imagined, supposed to stand apart from and perhaps even to be made real by the very act of love itself. Failing these, men sometimes love instead such derivative things as money, honor, property, fame, institutions. The beloved offers an opportunity quite often because it has first been solicited. The lover will love, stand what brute realities there be in the way. He needs a beloved, and if there be none worthy or available some beloved he will soon self-formulate.

There is no one worthy of being loved by a creating God. And before He creates there is no actual beloved, of any kind, to which He could reveal Himself. Creation as an act of love presupposes the imagination by a God of a beloved far His inferior. He must project Himself outward, exteriorize Himself in the form of a prospective beholder which, precisely because it is His creature, must be infinitely inferior to Him in being, worth, and dignity. When men not merely love realities which are unworthy of them but direct their love toward ideas of these, they turn themselves into images of a supposed creative God. They love more fully when they love actual things, no matter how low in the scale, and love most of all when they love what is no less real than themselves in value.

The beloved provides the lover with an opportunity for self-purgation. He also provides him with an opportunity to give himself freely. Love is a gift, and a gift requires not only someone to give but someone to receive. The gift may not be wanted; it may be rejected or ignored. If so, the gift will nevertheless in some sense have already reached its destination, for rejection and ignoring presuppose something to be put aside. To have loved is therefore not to have lost; it is to have reached one's mark, though not necessarily exactly nor with the consequences one would like to have entrain.

The lover gives himself, not substantially but as something to be seen and perhaps used. He gets down to his very center and then refuses to allow it to be central. He turns himself into pure subject, but only so as to give his beloved an opportunity to look upon and deal with a purified object, an object which is concrete and precious, and secret to all others.

The lover is active for selfish and unselfish reasons. But rarely does he activate himself; rarely does he look about for occasions to love. Men are for the most part content to live inside stable and public frames. Purgation is painful, and giving is dangerous. Protection, security, is a good not lightly put aside, and advantage, abundance, is not readily given up. Men must be *provoked* to love. The beloved must intrude on them, awaken them, force them out of their complacency. The beloved provokes for good reasons. He is the locus of precious, needed goods, and to become aware of them is to want, to strive for, to insist upon having them. It is the beautiful we love, not because beauty as such is lovable but because it is revelatory of the essence of that self which it insistently calls to our attention. We love the self which is beautiful, not the beauty which is in the self. Just so, we do not love goodness as such but the good which is of the very essence of the self and which, if we are fortunate, makes itself manifest and intrusive, revealing the depths of value characteristic of the self.

When we love what we think to be unworthy, when we imaginatively anticipate or project the existence of a beloved, we perhaps are not as self-motivating as it would appear. We are being provoked to love even then, but by what and where we do not clearly know. We feel that we lack something valuable that is outside us. We are stimulated by some unnoted reality and are therefore, almost without knowing it, already probing, inquiring, restlessly searching, forgetting ourselves in order to find that, in the world beyond, which we need for our very good. Only a God who was all-creating would be able to initiate an act of love without any provocation, but then there would be a mystery as to why He began when and as He did.

All realities seem to have some provocative power. There is nothing to which one can point which must, by its very nature, fail to arouse someone to the act of love. Let it be ugly, destructive, let it be self-devouring, embittered and embittering. Still it has a power of its own, a center all the more significant because it has dared to come so far into the open. Each of us is sensitive only in some areas; we are aroused only by certain types of objects and in rather special circumstances. We could be aroused by any of the others were we only willing to attend to them, to concentrate on them, to look below their surface, did we not blur their natures in the search for more worthy, more readily acknowledgeable, more lovable objects.

Every object in the universe has some merit, some grace or virtue which at least as a representative, or as a part, is capable of provoking us to love, if not it, then that for which it stands and which it helps constitute. And men in particular are all lovable, taken in their root and promise, putting aside their public dress and their public achievements or failures. Most of them do not know how to intrude on us so as to enable us to see how valuable they intrinsically are and how necessary they are to us. They are men in hiding, who force us to look for them, to cut through an underbrush of irrelevancies to get to the precious heart; they make us break through a host of foolish restraints and reserves, to put up with much that offends. They tire us, wear us down, make us give up well before we reach the selves which alone made the effort worth while. All men are lovable, but there are some who make it difficult for others to love them readily. They hedge themselves in, they do not love us sufficiently, and thus do not purge themselves sufficiently; they give too little of themselves to enable us to love them easily. To be loved, it is best first to love.

We hate primarily because we love the very beings at which we seem to direct our anger and our spite. We hate what caricatures, distorts, what threatens to destroy and debase man, whatever stands in the way of our reaching what is worthy of love. We hate not men but that in them which we feel or think, perhaps mistakenly, prevents us from readily loving them. We hate what does not let us love, for to fail to love is to fail to be a full self; it is to confess that we are not superabundant selves capable of sweeping aside and through all that stands in the way of our getting to other selves. The object of hatred irritates because it frustrates while and as it reveals a lovable being, a man who may win our respect and even admiration for being so surely a man behind all that disturbs us.

Contempt is less violent but more searching and sometimes more dangerous than hatred; it knows full well the priceless worth of the other's self and scorns therefore the tawdry, inadequate expressions and semblances which that self puts forth. Hatred attends too much to what obscures, but contempt too often acidly bites away the very good it wants most to preserve.

The hated and the contemptible can provoke our love. Unlike others, though, they frustrate while they lure, forcing us to use most of our energies in breaking down and destroying barriers instead of reaching toward what lies beyond them.

The beloved offers us an opportunity and a provocation for love. In addition he offers us something we ought to have. Unpurged, we are men divided against ourselves, needing a proper locus for the irrelevancies that now encumber and obscure us; purged, we are bifocal men, with centers elsewhere which we must recover if we are to be ourselves in ourselves. Intruded upon, spurred to give to others, we are at the same time stimulated to intrude upon them, to reach to and to possess them to become more *self-complete*.

Each of us is incomplete. We lack what would make us full men. There is something human which we need and do not now possess. We want not merely to be but to be cherished, esteemed, sustained by being made the focus of some self. We reach to the other to make him attend to us, and then we cling to him, as one who possesses what we most dearly need. The lover seeks, attaches himself to the beloved as one who is over against him, possessing a needed power and virtue. Without the beloved, the lover is an Aristophanic half who can never see himself as he is; to know himself he must await the clear eye of another and then make the perception his own. By clinging to the beloved, he retains a hold on him before whom alone he stands naked, who has with him also treated as irrelevant all the barriers behind which he had previously hidden, and who has served as the object of his gift.

The lover must possess his beloved or remain conditioned by what is outside and independent of him; if he does not possess his beloved, the lover, even when most exuberant and generous, is but an adjective, a fief to one on whose very presence, word, and move his meaning precariously depends. He must own this which owns him, or be a man who has lost himself, not in love but in longing.

4. LOVER AND BELOVED

In the ideal situation lover is also loved. He who gives receives, he who receives gives. There is a meeting of lovers, each of whom makes the other his concern. Each clings to the other as having a self superior to his own, because able to attend to him. Is love then anything more than a way of interchanging positions, much ado about nothing, a fair, bare exchange of surplus goods, a time for making a great effort and taking a great risk merely to get back to where one had been in the beginning? Or is it instead a paradox involving the union of two beings, each of which is or becomes the superior of the other, and for the same reasons?

The semblance of nonsense and paradox vanishes, perhaps, with the recognition of the way in which lover, beloved, and the relation between them are altered by the very act of love. As a consequence of loving, the lover is purged of irrelevancies, conceits, and self-centeredness and is stripped down to essentials. If he is loved in return two purged beings face one another. Each has freed himself from what was irrelevant by assigning it to the other as that which is to give it unity and thereby a greater dignity and worth than it had before. The assignment does not involve a transportation; nothing is carried from self to self. Instead the purging begins and ends in the lover, consisting as it does only in a change of attitude toward what the lover had accreted to himself, a remaking of it and himself through the agency of an evaluation. Nor is it added to the being of the beloved, thereby getting in his way. Through purgation the direction and import of the lover's acts are altered, thereby permitting another to view him as having an existence and worth not confined to or by what is publicly evident.

As a consequence of loving, the lover is not only purged but pivoted about the beloved. Having made the beloved the object of his attention, the center of his concern, having occupied himself with the beloved's welfare, he has so far sacrificed himself for him. If he is loved in return, two sacrificing beings face one another, each occupied with the other's good. As a consequence each is dealt with more conscientiously and adequately than otherwise. We fear too much, we hope too much, we are too clearly beneficiaries to be able to act in the best way for our own good. We are most satisfactorily served if others lovingly look out for us. The lover and the beloved form a unity in which each by giving himself gets more than he gave. Each is served by the other as one who seeks to treat him as deserving only the good, which is more than he can do steadily for himself. Each is made more complete by his possession of the other, and thus is made more worthy to be possessed than he was before. Mutual lovers are not one another's superiors, but they are superior to what they themselves had been. Mutual lovers increase one another's value; they both give and receive more than they had. By mutually loving they provide each other with better objects to love.

In love new values are created, but only for a moment; they exist only during the act of loving. The burning act of love lives for only a moment. To keep love alive it must be constantly rekindled. This is best done by focusing on some common fruit of past love, some product of the loving union, allowing it to recall for one the precious power of the beloved. Such a product is however but an occasion, a guide, a focal point, sustaining one in weakness. Love must be initiated directly in relation to the beloved; the common child, the common future, common goods are only instruments for reminding men of the creative strength of themselves and those they love. Ideally, love is a continuous activity, taking account of new sides, new dimensions at every moment. It is a creative force which must be creatively expressed all the time, welding lover and beloved into a union which has a value and a power surpassing either alone, because including the being and force of both.

5. LOVE OF GOD AND NEIGHBOR

Theologians urge us to love God. This we can do, if love be an act of purging and an act of possessing. In prayer the religious man purges himself in the presence of his God, puts aside, as properly belonging to God, all that he has accreted in the course of life. He stands empty and powerless before his Maker. By faith he clings to that Maker, treats Him as a pivot, as an eternal priceless good he must somehow possess in order to be himself most fully. But if that God be perfect, lacking nothing whatsoever, it is impossible to give Him anything. Yet what is love without a giving? If God can be loved, He is not completely perfect. He must be able to benefit from our occupation with Him. And this is possible—unless our lives have no meaning and no content of their own. We have goods which God does not have, we are free in ways He is not. There is much good which He could profitably receive from us. Each of us lives through time, has specific experiences, flavored with pain and pleasure, qualitied with colors, tastes, odors, beyond the reach of any being unpossessed of flesh. These are precious experiences; he who lacks them is so far deficient, needs some goods. By loving God, we make Him a gift of these experiences, enable Him to take and benefit from what we have, through our flesh, had an opportunity to obtain.

Conversely, a perfect God can love us, if love requires only that the lover give to and possess the beloved. A perfect God has much to give, and if all-powerful can hold on to the very substance of the beloved. But He has nothing from which to free Himself. If love involves purgation, then either God cannot love or He is not perfect. A loving God is one who has accreted to Himself a mass of obscuring and hindering details, which He distinguishes from Himself in the act of love. The details can be identified with his ideas of things, with essences contemplated, and the distinguishing of Himself from them can, in fairly good accord with established usage, be taken to represent what is normally meant by His creating, in the first place, and His providential concern thereafter.

He who would take the doctrine of creation seriously as an act of genuine love ought to affirm perhaps that God first environed Himself with ideas or essences in the attempt to understand Himself, and then freed Himself from these so as to achieve the state of being Himself in full simplicity. The essences of things, for a creating being, have the status of alienated essences; they are the ideas He once entertained and no longer wishes to possess. Satan for such a being is an angel who fell only because he was first pushed. All other angels presumably were pushed as well, but some apparently came back, at proper distances.

Love your neighbor, men are told, because they also are creatures, because they too owe their origin to God, the source of all value. Such reasons are based on the belief that nothing in this world has value of its own. Were the belief carried out we would have to say that nothing at all is worthy of our love but God, in Himself, and as manifest in others. But each thing has a nature of its own and is so far a locus of a limited, self-sealed value. If we ought to love our neighbor it is because he is himself lovable. And so he is. Not only has he a self whose support we need, before whom we can open our selves and to whom we could and should give of our superabundance, but he deserves a love which transcends flesh and situation. But we should love more completely than this. A love which also involves flesh is a fuller love than one which does not. Indeed it is so complete, so demanding, requiring nothing less than the full, exhaustive devotion of a man, that we cannot fully extend it to more than one living human being. The love we rightly extend to this neighbor is a love we could extend to that neighbor; it is a fleshless love and therefore less than love might be.

In consequence of love, a new dimension is achieved for the lover and for his beloved. Though concentrating on a single being, and in this sense losing all the world, the lover by his love extends the boundaries of his being, to make himself a man who thereafter looks out at the world in new terms, a world enriched by his love. Love is a cataclysmic experience transmuting all values; it adds another hue to the world, making it both more valuable and more appreciated than before.

The lover is a man reorganized, facing a new world in which he henceforth lives with opened eyes, able to see for the first time clearly what the dispassionate, analytic intellect never sees at all and what the emotions but faintly discern. The world is well lost for love because it is thus more completely gained. Yet the host of realities outside the lover and his beloved must be made the object of a genuine love. Otherwise the world of the lovers will prove but a momentary island in an alien sea. Neighbors must be loved, and finally all men, and all that is.

Love of neighbor stands to love of individual in the flesh as love of mankind stands to love of neighbor. It is a love we can share; it has bearing on more than one. We are not to love our neighbor's wife as we love our own, for she is but our neighbor; we are to love her as we love the wives of all our neighbors. This is obviously an attenuated love, though it does involve some degree of concentration, some degree of involvement. The love we can have for an individual is a concentrated form of the love we can have for neighbor, and this is a concentrated form of the love we can have for mankind, which in turn is a concentrated form of the love we can have for whatever there be. This last requires us to work on behalf of others, primarily so that they can have the analogue of what lovers gladly get for each other.

Love of self is evidently not possible, if love requires purging, giving, and possessing—unless these terms be used in a strained and a strange sense. It is foolish to speak of distinguishing our selves from accretions by giving those accretions to our selves, to speak of giving up something to our selves, or to speak of reaching out and possessing our selves. We can cherish our selves; we can act so as to promote our own good; we can love those who love us; we can have an inordinate regard for what enhances our joys or improves our prospects. But we cannot love our selves.

No man can be commanded to love if by command we mean that he can exteriorly and rightly be asked to direct his love to this being or that. Since, though, it is right that men should love, each can rightly be commanded to love. Each can be rightly asked to make an effort to approach others lovingly. And each can be rightly judged to have fallen short of what a man should be if he fails to love all beings somehow.

No one of us has the strength or interest to love many—or even a few or for long. We are all deficient in ethical worth and should be admonished and encouraged to improve. We owe it to ourselves to try to appear in full simplicity in the presence of all, to try to give of our selves, and to try, without loss to others, to make our own the goods which those others embody. Only thus will we and they become as perfect as humans can be. Only thus will we become men who no longer love as we did before but who love in new ways in a new world we through love helped to make.

XXI

AN ABSOLUTE INJUNCTION

THE truly good man is a lover who not only tries to avoid doing what is wrong but attempts to bring about the maximum good. He goes beyond the call of duty, beyond the need of sacrifice, to maximize values wherever he can. His one object is to make perfection concrete in a creative, willing, loving act. He shifts his means, his goals and ultimate ends, whenever this makes possible the result he seeks. For him everything, including the absolute good itself, is but one factor in constantly changing activity whose sole object is to make the good concrete, without limit. He works for and together with other men in a society which changes its codes in a stable way for ethical reasons. He treats the rules and laws of his own group as instruments for the attainment of the absolute good in that quarter, and works in and through society so far as it is possible to obtain in that way the desired result.

He creatively wills, lovingly acts on behalf of good. He is the creative man, par excellence, an artist who uses all his powers to make the good pertinent to and realized in all existents. He remolds himself, alters his pace, modifies his habits, varies his direction, shifts his emphases so as to be at once selfish and nonselfish, outgoing and restrained, to the greatest gain for all.

There is but one injunction he need follow: create. This requires him to reduce wrongdoing to an absolute minimum. He is required to enhance whatever he can, to perfect things by changing them so that they are more receptive to their own objectives as enhanced by the absolute good than they were before. Virtuous, he is a man of humility who adventures with success over the cosmos for his own sake and (since this comes to the same thing) for the sake of others. Unable to realize fully and everywhere the absolute good to which he, to be a man, freely obligates himself, he is, in the end, free only to be guilty for the occurrence of wrongs it was beyond his power to gainsay, for failure to realize goods outside his reach and capacity. Possessed of inalienable rights, deserving aid and improvement from his fellows, he is, because ineradicably guilty, one who should be perpetually grateful for whatever goods he can acquire and the world allows him to retain.

RECAPITULATION

1. *Men are predictable:*
    Otherwise what they did would have no bearing on what they or others had done, needed, or could do.   3

2. *Men are unpredictable:*
    Otherwise they would not be individuals, concrete, substantial, more than formulae and what these contain.   4 ff.

3. *Men have nonbehavioral aspects:*
    Otherwise behavior could not be explained.   11 f.

4. *Human nature is normative:*
    Otherwise there would be no difference between good and bad acts.   12

5. *The real has secondary and tertiary characters:*
    Otherwise it would be without primary characters too, and what is common and public would not be real.   13 ff.

6. *The future is external to the present:*
    Otherwise things would have no steady natures, no promise, no careers in time.   17 f.

7. *Men internalize the future:*
    Otherwise they would have no self-control, no ability to direct themselves, to live by plan and purpose.   19

8. *Men have privacies expressed in action:*
    Otherwise there would be no difference between expressive and unexpressive behavior.   19 f.

9. *There are external objects:*
    Otherwise there would be nothing to encounter, no truth, no knowledge, no interaction.   20

10. *Men are imperfect:*
    Otherwise there would be nothing real, external to them.   23

11. *Men are concerned with an all-comprehensive possibility:*
    Otherwise they would not have persistent selves, to which nothing was alien.   24

12. *Men specialize the all-comprehensive possibility:*
    Otherwise they would not be able to prepare themselves to act appropriately in limited situations.   24

13. *Men are creative:*
    Otherwise they would not be able to change other things and themselves.   25 f.

14. *Men have a characteristic native freedom:*
    Otherwise there would be nothing which men could do or be precluded from doing.   29 f.

15. *Men are conditionally free:*
    Otherwise they would have no occasion to exercise native freedom within externally imposed limits.　　　　　　　　　　32 ff.

16. *Men are not social in essence:*
    Otherwise embryos and infants would not be human.　　　　　　37

17. *Men are interested in nonsocial goods:*
    Otherwise they would not be able to defy their society or promote its good in an alien world.　　　　　　　　　　49 ff.

18. *Men freely determine goals:*
    Otherwise they could not prefer one means to another.　　　　60 ff.

19. *Men create when they prefer:*
    Otherwise they would not determine goals and turn possible into accepted means.　　　　　　　　　　62 f.

20. *Any alternative can be freely preferred:*
    Otherwise the repugnant could not be freely selected.　　　　63 ff.

21. *The inclinations ought sometimes to be followed, sometimes defied:*
    Otherwise the same desired goal could not be realized in differing circumstances.　　　　　　　　　　71 ff.

22. *Education is desirable:*
    Otherwise men's appreciations would not need extension　　　86 f.

23. *Pleasure is not the good:*
    Otherwise there would be no bad pleasures.　　　　　　　94 f.

24. *Happiness is not the good:*
    Otherwise an interest in it would not be a way of losing it.　　95 f.

25. *Order is not the good:*
    Otherwise creativity would not be good.　　　　　　　　97

26. *Men must be given different opportunities:*
    Otherwise they would not have equal opportunity to flourish.　　99 f.

27. *There is an absolute morality:*
    Otherwise no society would be better or worse than any other.　　102 f.

28. *There is an ideal, transcending morality:*
    Otherwise disconformity to established ways would never be good.　103 f.

29. *All beings have some value:*
    Otherwise they could never be wrongly injured or rightly improved.　110

30. *Men are committed to ultimate ends:*
    Otherwise they would not have to make good losses in value inevitably produced in every act.　　　　　　　　　　111 f.

31. *Men have duties:*
    Otherwise there would be nothing which their committing end requires of them.　　　　　　　　　　111 f.

32. *A compensation for a wrong must be promised in the act:*
    Otherwise the act would be unjustified.　　　　　　　112 ff.

33. *Duties should be fulfilled:*
Otherwise what had been done in the past would be wanton. 113

34. *Men are free to choose:*
Otherwise they would not be responsible for choosing what they do. 116 ff.

35. *There are multiple choosable ends, all equally good:*
Otherwise a free choice would be impossible. 116

36. *There are multiple equally choiceworthy alternatives:*
Otherwise some possible loss in value would not be justifiable. 117

37. *Good men commit themselves to different ends:*
Otherwise they would not elect different alternatives. 117

38. *Preference presupposes choice:*
Otherwise goals would be unavoidable or not involve a loss in value. 118 f.

39. *Men can freely choose not to prefer:*
Otherwise they could not directly choose an alternative. 119

40. *Men can freely choose to prefer:*
Otherwise they could not choose a goal. 119

41. *Freedom of choice involves the production of a reason:*
Otherwise choice would be either compelled or capricious. 120

42. *Thoughtless choices are free choices:*
Otherwise they would not be responsible for them. 122 f.

43. *Men should be conscientious:*
Otherwise it would be better for them to cut themselves off from their commitments and make what had been best, best no longer. 123 f.

44. *Some alternatives ought not to be chosen:*
Otherwise no end would be beyond a man's capacities to realize. 125 ff.

45. *Values should be maximized:*
Otherwise men would be infinite in power or be more guilty than they need be. 129

46. *Techniques should be mastered:*
Otherwise men would not be guilty for failing to be prepared to do what they should. 129

47. *Alternatives can and should be altered at times:*
Otherwise violations of duty could not and should not be minimized. 132 f.

48. *Reform or re-form are always necessary:*
Otherwise the world and men would be in harmony. 134

49. *Men must cooperate:*
Otherwise they would never need the support of others. 135

50. *Cooperation involves some wrong:*
Otherwise it would not involve a neglect of one's own end. 135

51. *Men have some self-knowledge:*
Otherwise they would not know they were men, needing understanding and mercy, possessed of minds and bodies. 140

69. *Men have some grasp of the absolute "ought to be":*
Otherwise they would not know some ethical facts with certainty. 206 ff.

70. *Ethical truths are at once necessary and contingent:*
Otherwise it would not be at once absurd and possible to deny them. 210 f.

71. *Ethical truths are at once synthetic and analytic:*
Otherwise they would not be significant and what was presupposed could not be supposed. 212 f.

72. *Ethical truths are at once material and formal:*
Otherwise they would not relate to existence, and the absolute wrong would not be an abstraction. 213

73. *Ethical truths are at once a priori and a posteriori:*
Otherwise they would not be known to be true apart from a particular case, and the absolute wrong would not be learned by operating on experience. 213

74. *Ethical truths are at once particular and universal:*
Otherwise they would not refer to unduplicable situations and hold for all men. 213

75. *It is absolutely wrong to reduce values:*
Otherwise it would be right to kill a friend wantonly. 215

76. *Absolute wrong and relative right are compatible:*
Otherwise one thing could not be benefited at the expense of another. 218 f.

77. *No one can do only the right:*
Otherwise action would not require the ignoring and use of others. 218

78. *No one can do only wrong:*
Otherwise action would not involve the desirable use of body, mind, and instrument. 218

79. *Men should be ethical:*
Otherwise they would be perfect. 226

80. *The will is free:*
Otherwise men could not reconstitute themselves and others to realize the good. 227

81. *Men are most free when they will creatively:*
Otherwise there would be a freedom greater than that which makes abstract perfection realized everywhere. 227

82. *Men ought to will creatively:*
Otherwise they would not be required to realize the maximum good everywhere, and thus would not be infinitely perfectible. 228

83. *To will the good is to become perfected:*
Otherwise he who realizes the most good would not be good. 231

84. *There are evils:*
Otherwise everything would be indifferent, or as it ought to be. 238

85. *Some evils are not necessary:*
Otherwise there could be no universe unless there were pain or sorrow in it. 239

INDEX

Date Due